The Interpretation of
The Acts of the Apostles
1–14

R. C. H. LENSKI

Augsburg Fortress
Minneapolis

THE INTERPRETATION OF THE ACTS OF THE APOSTLES 1–14
Commentary on the New Testament series

First paperback edition 2008

Copyright ©1944, 2008 Augsburg Fortress. All rights reserved. Except for brief quotations in critical articles or reviews, no part of this book may be reproduced in any manner without prior written permission from the publisher. Visit http://www.augsburgfortress.org/copyrights/contact.asp or write to Permissions, Augsburg Fortress, Box 1209, Minneapolis, MN 55440.

Richard C. H. Lenski's commentaries on the New Testament were published in the 1940s after the author's death. This volume was copyrighted in 1934 by the Lutheran Book Concern, published in 1944 by the Wartburg Press, and assigned in 1961 to the Augsburg Publishing House.

ISBN 978-0-8066-8075-0

The paper used in this publication meets the minimum requirements of American National Standard for Information Sciences—Permanence of Paper for Printed Library Materials, ANSI Z329.48-1984.

Manufactured in the U.S.A.

TO
AUGUST H. DORNBIRER

NOTE: The translation of the text is an effort in some measure to indicate the Greek wording and the Greek constructions for readers to whom this may be helpful. The following abbreviations are used:

R. = A. T. Robertson, A Grammar of the Greek New Testament in the Light of Historical Research. 4th edition.

B.-D. = Friedrich Blass' Grammatik des neutestamentlichen Griechisch, vierte, voellig neugearbeitete Auflage, besorgt von Albert Debrunner.

B.-P. = Griechisch-Deutsches Woerterbuch zu den Schriften des Neuen Testaments, etc., von D. Walter Bauer, zweite, voellig neugearbeitete Auflage zu Erwin Preuschens Vollstaendigem Griechisch-Deutschen Handwoerterbuch, etc.

M.-M. = The Vocabulary of the Greek Testament Illustrated from the Papyri and other non-Literary Sources, by James Hope Moulton and George Milligan.

R., W P = Word Pictures in the New Testament by Archibald Thomas Robertson, Volume III, The Acts of the Apostles.

C. Tr.=*Concordia Triglotta, Libri symbolici Ecclesiae Lutheranae.* German-Latin-English. St. Louis, Mo. Concordia Publishing House.

INTRODUCTION

Luther regarded Acts as a beautiful mirror in which one beholds the truth: *Sola fides justificat*. The fathers likewise admired the contents of the book, noting the great variety of subjects and the immense value of each: the great testimony in regard to the apostolic doctrine and the church; the fundamental outline of church government, church discipline, and church organization; an arsenal full of artillery against the antichrist; a laboratory full of remedies against all soul-destroying errors of faith and offenses in conduct; a larder stocked with all kinds of food for faith, patience, and hope; an inspiration for love and all its works; a very treasury of learning and right doctrine. By adding what students at present see in this great record we should become superficial if we lost or ignored this fundamental viewpoint of an earlier age.

One may say that the skies are now clearing after the critical storms that have raged around Luke and especially around Acts. These storms had very little to do with the things that made Acts so valuable to Luther and to the older students. They hurled their thunderbolts into the isagogical questions, those that concern themselves with authorship, sources, aims and tendencies, historical accuracy, method of composition, agreement with the data in Paul's epistles, and similar matters. A calmer, brighter day has come for Acts. When we consider that in this book Luke mentions one hundred and ten names of persons and many groups of persons besides; gives a long list of places and of provinces in the empire; furnishes all manner of geographical and of historical data that transfer us into an ancient age in which he moved with the greatest freedom and assurance, we see how readily the author made possible many questions for all critics who cared to challenge him on any of these points on the basis of their secular knowledge of the era in which Acts must be placed. No other New Testament book presented so wide and so inviting a field for investigation and for criticism.

But when we now survey the scene, although attacks have not entirely ceased, we must register the fact that the vindication of Luke is complete. Those have gone down in defeat who thought they had made breaches in Luke's citadel. Not even one pinnacle of his fortress did their critical artillery dislodge. The result of all this criticism has been tremendously valuable especially for our age. The sounder the learning, the more extensive the research, the truer the critical tests, the more complete is the assurance that Acts is trustworthy on every point, and that any further investigations will end as the many intensive ones in the past have ended. Acts is today better known as to its external side than it has been at any time since the book was written.

The additions thus made to our appreciation of Acts by the later scholars is of a more secondary nature. Luke himself has been placed into a clearer light. In fact, when we read the words of praise that are now being bestowed upon him we fear that the man, if he heard, would blush. Ramsay, for instance, after a lifetime of research ranks Luke as the greatest of all historians, ancient or modern. His book is called the most beautiful in the world. And so the praise goes on. Acts 27 is regarded as the most perfect account of an ancient sea-voyage ever penned. Luke's character sketches are found to be masterpieces.

We see from this praise that our scholars are captivated by the lesser things: by the writer, his accurate knowledge of externals, his insight into persons and events, his educated mind, his diction, his skill in composition, his personal characteristics, character, etc. Bring all these new treasures — we are grateful, indeed! This, too, is work that must be done. But when all this is said and done, we can only add this new knowledge to the essential contents of the book that was so supremely prized by the fathers. In so much of this scholarship, however, we miss the grand ancient acknowledgment without which all praise of Luke is after all hollow: the acknowledgment that Acts, like Luke's Gospel, was verbally inspired of God.

When we see how Acts emerges from all the critical tests to which the book has been subjected even by hostile eyes with not a single error in the entire complex record, we on our part do not marvel at "the infallible Luke" but recognize the hand of the infallible Spirit who guided Luke's faculties and who thought of us when, through this willing, human instrument, he gave us this piece of inerrant Scripture. Unwittingly these critics have proved a thesis that is more valuable to the believer than the historical accuracy of this beloved companion of Paul's. They merely verify what the church knew and believed from the time when it placed Acts into its sacred canon, namely, that Acts is inspired even as to its words, so that we can trust them also in all minor things as being errorless. What critical work remains to be done, when its final and true results are booked, will be only the adding of the last items in this elaborate proof. And this assurance makes it a joy to offer an interpretation of Acts. Such an interpretation cannot, of course, lose itself in exhaustive discussions of the critical work that has been done on Acts. A large volume would be required for that task, and, when written, would not be an interpretation of Acts and would not be what Luke himself intended Acts to be. His book is all that friendly critics now say it is, and yet it is more.

As a companion of Paul's, Luke, like the other assistants of the apostle, was a preacher. The supreme interest of his life was not medicine, nor the writing of history, nor his friendship for Paul, but the promulgation of the gospel. He wrote his Gospel in order to convert Theophilus and his Acts in order to enlighten this convert in regard to the course of the gospel from Jerusalem to Rome, from Judaism to the Gentiles. The purpose of his two writings is spiritual. To overlook that fact is serious and an injustice to Luke and to his books. So we propose to look well at the beautiful binding, the lovely printing, and the skilful workmanship of this volume from Luke's hands, but only in order to absorb the more delightfully the real things this volume offers.

It is rather interesting to observe how a critic like Harnack of Berlin has shifted from an advocacy (in 1897) of A. D. 78 as the earliest possible date for the writing of Acts to an advocacy of a much earlier date, probably the sixties of the first century. Robertson, in his *Luke, the Historian, in the Light of Research*, 34, writes, "So astonishing a surrender on the part of Harnack created consternation among many critics." For much more is involved than a mere date. The late date, 90-100 A. D., was required in order to make Luke dependent on Josephus in the matter of Acts 5:36, etc. A date after the destruction of Jerusalem in 70 A. D. was required in order to date also Luke's Gospel after that year; for the critics contended that Luke 21:20 with its plain statement about army camps closing in Jerusalem could be only a *vaticinium post eventum*, if not in substance then at least in the form in which this Gospel passage records that prophecy. And now Harnack himself advocates an earlier date.

Ramsay is another scholar who has gone even farther than Harnack. He started with the view that the Acts were of little value historically because, like

John's Gospel, they had been written with an ulterior purpose. But in his *Bearing of Recent Discovery*, p. 89, he confesses: "The more I have studied the narrative of Acts, and the more I have learned year after year about Græco-Roman society and thoughts and fashions and organizations in those provinces, the more I admire and the better I understand. I set out to look for truth on the borderland where Greece and Asia meet and found it here."

This commendable return to a proper estimate of Luke and the Acts has, however, produced some critical romancing which, although largely harmless, calls for a word of caution. Who was Theophilus to whom Acts, too, was sent by Luke? Where did Luke meet him, and what was their relation to each other? The data are extremely meager, and many go too far even when they themselves acknowledge that they are presenting only probabilities or possibilities. It is claiming too much to make Luke a slave of Theophilus in Antioch, to have his master set the young man free and even send him to the great university in Tarsus for a medical education, where he met Saul of Tarsus and formed a friendship that lasted for life. A beautiful romance which a novelist might work into a story or even a film but one that is without substance. Such by-products of criticism, however well intended, must be laid aside.

The fact that Luke is the author of Acts as well as of the third Gospel is so well established that we need not review the evidence. The date of Acts cannot be much later than the date of Luke's Gospel. It is more difficult to assume a long interval between the two compositions than a short one. This dating goes back to Luke's first contact with Theophilus. If this contact reaches gack to Antioch and the early years of Luke, it becomes difficult to explain how Theophilus could for so many years have remained without the certainty which Luke sought to convey to him by means of his Gospel, and why Luke should have waited so many years before finally making the attempt to produce that certainty in his prominent friend. We may say with some assurance that Theophilus came into contact with Luke only a short time before Luke sent him the third Gospel. The prefatory statement of the Gospel shows that its mission was missionary, namely to win Luke's friend for the faith of which he had obtained some knowledge, perhaps through Luke himself. Luke's object was attained. For in the Gospel he addresses Theophilus as κράτιστος, "Your Excellency," a title that was never known to have been bestowed upon one Christian brother by another. Luke follows his first book with a second but now omits this title. How could he do this unless something had intervened? That something must have been the advance of Theophilus from interest to actual faith.

This explains why Luke wrote a second time and continued his Gospel by means of the Acts. It is only natural to suppose that he did not wait long. Thus the date of the Acts and that of the Gospel are not far apart. Both dates come before A. D. 70; the only question is, how far before 70 can we safely go? Tradition says, not far. It tells us that Luke's Gospel was the third in point of time, and that Mark wrote the second after Peter's death in A. D. 64. This is the safest dating apart from the numerous hypotheses regarding this problem.

The dating has something to do with the place of writing. Of the three places suggested for Luke's contact with Theophilus — Antioch years before; Philippi where Luke was for a time left by Paul; Rome, where Luke was at Paul's side — Rome seems most probable. Paul was beheaded in Rome in A. D. 66. We take it that Luke left Rome following this sad event and shortly after that wrote the Gospel to Theophilus and on hearing of his conversion followed this by the Acts. To what place did Luke go? We cannot be certain, and tradition itself has nothing credible to offer.

Another way of dating begins with a consideration of the conclusion of Acts which ends with Paul's being in Rome, a prisoner for two years. It is assumed that Acts was written at that very time in Rome before Paul's trial came to an issue, and that this explains why Luke did not carry the story of the Acts farther and recount the death of Peter in Rome A. D. 64, and that of Paul in A. D. 66. So the Acts would be written before A. D. 62 and the Gospel before that date, perhaps already in Cæsarea. As for Theophilus, he would be located in Antioch or possibly in Philippi. The strength as well as the weakness of this combination rests on the explanation that is given of the way in which the Acts close. Since, however, the dates of the martyrdom of Peter and of Paul are certain, and tradition has Mark write after their death and Luke after Mark (which is certain), an insuperable conflict results between the dating of Mark's Gospel and that of Luke. So we again look at the closing verses of Acts and hesitate to make an explanation of this ending the determining factor in deciding about these interlocking dates. But whatever we decide, let us acknowledge that full certainty cannot be obtained.

This brings us to the interesting problem regarding Luke's original plan of writing. When he began to write the Gospel, did he already then plan to write a second book, namely, the Acts? And did he either at that time or when he began Acts plan to add a third book that would carry the story still farther and include the death of Peter and of Paul, his two heroes in the Acts, and sketches of the work of the other apostles?

A solution of this problem has been based on the word πρῶτος in Acts 1:1. We are told that this means "first" (R. V. margin) and not "former" (A. V.), and that "first" implies both a "second" and a "third" treatise, so that Luke intended to write three books when he began to write the first one. To this is added the further deduction that by ending the second treatise as he does Luke leaves us expecting a third treatise, one that would carry his series of books to a decisive end. The prolog of the Gospel is thus regarded as the prolog for all three books which reveals to us the method Luke pursued in gathering and testing all the material used in them. We are told that for this reason Acts has no prolog that is comparable to the one found in the Gospel but simply a statement that connects this new book with the one that was already in Theophilus' hands.

This view breaks down at what is regarded as its strongest point, the meaning of πρῶτος in Acts 1:1. In the Koine this superlative is freely used for the comparative πρότερον; in fact, Luke never uses the latter but only the former. He uses "first" when only two are involved, and his "first" crowds out "former" which he never uses. See M.-M. 554; R. 280; 663. The contention that at the very beginning Luke intended to write a second treatise cannot be established from the way in which he begins his two books. Other matters ought to be taken into consideration besides the wording of the opening sentences. Luke set out to give Theophilus the certainty concerning the gospel facts, what Jesus began to do and to teach until he ascended to heaven (Acts 1:1, 2), in order to bring his illustrious friend to faith. In his Gospel Luke certainly finished that task and also attained his object in the case of Theophilus. A second, or even a third, book was not needed to give Theophilus the certainty that constitutes faith in Jesus as the Christ. In other words, Luke's prolog to the Gospel is *not* at the same time the prolog for a second and even for a third book. Luke could not have known that he would write even a second book; for he could not tell in advance whether his Gospel would have the desired effect upon Theophilus or not. Even if it should have, the object of a second book would differ from the object of his first book, which had been attained. The moment one considers the books which Luke wrote and thinks of the need of the man to whom they were addressed, the view of a comprehensive preliminary plan of writing on Luke's part becomes unacceptable.

When Luke found that Theophilus had become a believer he wrote him a second treatise with the purpose of giving him further information and of confirming him in the faith. That is the primary and personal object of Luke. Luke performs this second task in just as masterly a way as he had performed the first. He sends Theophilus no mere chronicle of the events that followed Christ's ascension. First, he connects his second book with the first in a simple and natural way. Then he tells the story of the ascension of Jesus, with a brief form of which he had closed his first book, with greater fulness and records how the place of Judas was filled. Then comes the account of Pentecost as introducing the victorious progress of the gospel in its course from Jerusalem to Rome, from Judaism into the great Gentile world to which Luke as well as Theophilus belonged. When tracing this mighty progress for his friend Luke centers especially on two outstanding apostles, the ones that loom up largest in this brief period, Peter and Paul. Here is history, indeed, and a wealth of detail, but entrancing history and more than history, namely, the men who stood at the head of the entire historical progress. The story reaches its climax in Rome just a short time before judgment wiped out the Jewish nation. Here was a record on which the soul of Theophilus could feast, which could deepen his faith with every chapter and rejoice him with the knowledge that he, a former

Gentile, was in this mighty current of Christ which was sweeping out into and through the world.

The idea of publication is stressed by some interpreters. We are told in detail how the ancients went about publishing their books. Our beloved Luke becomes a writer of books for publication, and his rich friend Theophilus the patron through whom he hopes to have publication made. The fact that this idea contravenes the purpose of Luke's writing as expressed by himself seems to be overlooked by these learned students whose ambition it is to have their own books published far and wide. Writers of books themselves, they regard Luke as another. Theophilus becomes incidental. Luke's aim is a far wider circle of readers. But this view needs to be revised. Praise Luke's writing as much as we may, raise its value to the utmost, the fact remains that one man, Theophilus, gave occasion for the composition of Luke's books. Gospel and Acts are intended for him. Both might have gone no farther and have been passed on only to his friends. Let it be noted that Luke nowhere hints at publication. Did he think of publication? The matter took care of itself. Even if Theophilus, after he became a Christian, did not think of giving Luke's writings to the church, those whom Theophilus allowed to read these writings at once clamored for copies, and reproduction of the writings began. But this matter of publication should not unduly influence our view of these books as being originally composed for Theophilus. One man's need of certainty called forth the Gospel of Luke; the success in meeting that need called forth the Acts of Luke. The second builds up the faith wrought by the first. The original purpose of both writings still continues and ought to be recognized.

Where did Luke get his material for Acts? The "we" sections (16:10-17, etc.) speak for themselves — Luke was an eyewitness of the matter recorded in these. The prolog to the Gospel accounts for the rest of the book. Luke obtained his material for the Acts in the same way in which he obtained the material for the Gospel. Inventories have been made of all the contacts Luke had with original witnesses. These witnesses were certainly numerous. Did he have documents? Why not? He surely had a copy of the apostolic letter recorded in Acts 15:23-29; a copy of the letter of Lysias reproduced in 23:25-30; very likely also a transcript of Stephen's defense introduced in chapter seven, which many heard, among them being Paul. Why this question about Luke's sources, especially for the first chapters of Acts, should be as acute as it has been made is hard to understand when we know that Luke secured so much for the earlier period covered by his Gospel. Luke had a wealth of material, much more than he used.

The same is true with regard to the addresses which he recorded. They are exactly like those introduced into the four Gospels. They are for the most part greatly condensed but genuinely true in their condensed form. The critical students make comparisons with the speeches introduced into their books by secular writers. But the addresses recorded in the four Gospels are far superior to any found in secular authors.

Luke's division of Acts has probably always been recognized. Chapter one is introductory. Chapters two to twelve describe the progress of the gospel among the Jews with Peter being the dominant personage. This first half of Acts can be divided into two sections: 1) the progress in Jerusalem (chapters 2-7); 2) the progress in Palestine in general (chapters 8-12). The second half of Acts depicts the progress of the gospel among the Gentiles with Paul as the dominant personage. And again we have two subsections: 1) the progress while Paul was at liberty (13:1-21:16); 2) the progress while Paul was in captivity

(21:17-28:31). The whole depicts the progress of the gospel from Judaism into the great Gentile world or, more tersely stated, from Jerusalem to Rome.

Luke concludes his account with Paul's experiences in Rome. This apostle arrives, remains two years and, though under guard, preaches and teaches in his own house without restraint. This conclusion has puzzled many and has led to many precipitated discussions and hypotheses. The simple fact seems to be that Luke considered his goal attained when his account reached Rome: Paul being the first apostle to work in Rome, the capital of the world. Luke does not seem to share the view of so many that an account of the martyrdom of Peter and of Paul would have made a better ending. Perhaps we ought to revise our opinion in regard to Luke's account of these two apostles. However much he records about them, at the end he lets us see that his interest lies in their work or, more exactly, in the gospel and its success. Yes, we see Paul in the last verses, but the final note is: "Preaching the kingdom of God, and teaching those things which concern the Lord Jesus Christ." This was Luke's supreme interest when writing the Acts; it was to be that of Theophilus. Let it also be ours.

Did Luke issue the Acts in two editions, the first being briefer than the second which is now in our hands? Blass advocated this idea and extended it to the Gospel, supposing that, too, to have been issued in two editions. Zahn took up this idea but confined it to Acts. He has tried to reconstruct the shorter edition from Latin translations and from two Greek texts, notably from D. *Forschungen, etc., IX Teil*. But he is uncertain save for the hypothesis itself that Luke issued two editions of this book.

CHAPTER I

THE OPENING EVENTS, CHAPTER 1

Πράξεις τῶν Ἀποστόλων, "Acts of the Apostles," is the title of Luke's second composition, and this superscription is found as far back as scholars are able to carry their research. This title has remained constant even in the versions. The four Gospels have no titles, for the phrases "According to Matthew," "According to Mark," etc., were added at a later time, chiefly in order to distinguish these writings from each other. Their subject was the same, the εὐαγγέλιον, "the good news" ("gospel" in Old English) concerning Jesus Christ. The question whether Luke himself gave his second account the title it has always borne is affirmed by some although all admit that he left his first account without a title, and those who think that he intended to write a third account are naturally unable to say whether he had a title in mind and what that title might be. Since, however, Luke gave no title to his first account, it is hazardous to assume that he gave a title to the second.

We purposely avoid using the term "books." Luke did not call his first writing a "book" but a λόγος, an account. Both of his writings are of a personal nature and are addressed to one man for reasons that are personal to that man. We are not to think of Theophilus as a patron to whom Luke dedicated books in order that this patron might have them published. That idea has been advanced by men who themselves write books and seek to have them published. So they think that Luke wrote a title for what they call his second book but overlook the fact that he left what they call his first book without a title. When Luke thought of his writings as λόγοι or accounts he needed no titles and used none. The idea of a book is of later origin, hence also we have the captions, including the one that was affixed to his second account and that is still used everywhere.

1) The first account I made concerning all things, O Theophilus, which Jesus began both doing and teaching until what day he was received up after having given behests through the Holy Spirit to the apostles whom he chose for himself; to whom he also, after he suffered, presented himself alive in connection with many proofs, letting himself be seen by them during forty days and declaring the things concerning the kingdom of God; and while partaking together of salt he ordered them not to be withdrawing from Jerusalem, on the contrary, to be awaiting the promise of the Father, which you heard from me; seeing that John baptized with water, that you, however, shall be baptized in connection with the Holy Spirit not many days after these.

The periodic sentence with which Luke begins his Gospel is greatly admired as a wonderful example of the literary Koine, and in this admiration one feels a note of disappointment because of Luke's failure to score as highly a second time in the opening sentence of his Acts. But Luke did score just as highly; this time, however, he wrote a complex sentence which in a most concise and certainly masterful way connects Acts not merely with the Gospel in general but with all the salient points of the Gospel, so that these combine into one focus for the great new narrative that now begins. Instead of registering the fact that this is not another *Periode* (B.-D. 464) or remarking that here, too, Luke attains the literary Koine (R. 121), more attention might be paid to the aim and the contents of this complex sentence in summarizing the vital features of the entire Gospel so as to take up the thread of the new narrative.

Luke reaches back to John and his baptism and to the promise of the Father, the baptism with the Holy Spirit, which is now so close at hand; he brings to mind all that he had written about the deeds and the teachings of Jesus up to the time of the ascension; he lets his reader again meet the apostles whom Jesus elected for himself; he recalls the forty days in which Jesus gave all those proofs of his resurrection and spoke of the things of the kingdom in the light of his resurrection; and he repeats the command that the apostles must not leave Jerusalem, for in a few days the promise will be fulfilled. All this is arranged in one grand sentence. With it Luke places his reader just where he ought to be placed in order to go on with the new account. A study of the details of these five verses should not cause us to lose sight of their great sweep through the Gospel which brings us to the front portal of Acts.

We are unable to translate solitary μέν which merely lends a delicate stress to the clause in which it appears; "indeed" is too strong although it tends in the right direction. The older view that δέ should follow, that a contrast is implied, that this must appear at least in the thought, or that, with δέ absent, the construction is broken and results in a kind of anacoluthon, is untenable. See R. 1150. Solitary μέν does not require even a contrasting thought, to say nothing of a δέ. The fact that Luke had already written his second account the reader would see by having that account in his hands as he began to read. "The first account" is all that Luke needs to say in order to place the two side by side. The word λόγος does not mean "book"; the term never means "book," and even when there is a reference to a book, not the book as a book is referred to but only its contents. When Luke refers to a "book," the ancient manuscript roll, he writes βίβλος (Luke 3:4; 20:42; Acts 1:20; 7:42; 19:19) or βιβλίον (Luke 4:17, 20). "Treatise" in our versions is better. Luke wrote an "account" of certain things to Theophilus, a full account, indeed, but only an account, and is now penning another. He is not thinking of publication nor suggesting such a thing to Theophilus.

We have discussed πρῶτος in the Introduction. Luke uses it in the sense of "first" as well as in the sense of "former"; in fact, he never employs πρότερος, even as it is fast disappearing in the Koine, M.-M. 557; R. 280. Zahn supports his view by an appeal to Luke's education as a *grammatikos*; but the appeal must be made to the grammars and the lexicons which register the facts of language. But this implies that the word cannot be referred to as a support for the theory that Luke intended to write also a third book. When Luke writes that he prepared the first account "concerning all things which Jesus began doing," etc., we understand that "all things" is a popular hyperbole; for this statement has the preposition περί, "concerning." One can write "concerning" all things without actually recounting all of them. It is a correct summary of the Gospel when Luke calls it the account "concerning all things which Jesus began both doing and teaching until what day he was received up." The relative ὧν is attracted from ἅ to the case of its antecedent, and the antecedent of ἧς is itself drawn into the relative clause: "what day" for "the day in which."

As far as the use of "began" is concerned, the discussion about the force of this word overlooks two things, that the tense of the two infinitives is present and thus durative, and that the terminus of this doing and this teaching is named to the very day, the day when Jesus ascended to heaven. Jesus "began" (aorist, the start); he engaged in working as well as in teaching (present, the whole course of his work, both activities continuing together); "until what day he was received up" (aorist) records the end. So we dismiss the emphasis on "began" as though this beginning might be of special importance; and also the deduction that Luke implies that what Jesus began the apostles were to continue and to conclude. No; what Jesus began and also continued reached its end the day he ascended.

Nor should one overlook the fact that Luke gives a decided emphasis to the phrase "concerning all things" plus its relative clause by inserting the vocative between them, "O Theophilus." The name Theophilus and all these things regarding Jesus about which Luke wrote to him are thus brought together in what appears to be a significant way.

Does his omission of the title κράτιστε, "Your Excellency," which appears in the Gospel, mean anything? It will not do to say "no," for such high titles (Acts 23:26; 24:3; 26:25) cannot be bestowed upon a person at the beginning of one document and then withheld from that same person at the beginning of another document that is altogether similar. In early Christian literature we are told that no Christian addressed a fellow Christian with such a title. We, therefore, conclude that in the Gospel the title was in place because Theophilus was then not as yet a Christian, but that it is no longer in place in Acts because Theophilus had now become a Christian, for which reason Luke sends him this second account. The gracious and mighty miracles of Jesus (ποιεῖν) and the gracious and true teaching of Jesus (διδάσκειν) had won this man, who was either a Roman knight or a Roman official or a man of very great prominence, to faith. Luke's Gospel had scored a great missionary success.

2) The terminus of the Gospel is the ascension. In Luke 24:51 one verb is used, here, in v. 11 and 22, and

in I Tim. 3:16, another verb occurs, but all five verbs are passive: "he was received up," the agent in the passive being God. Yet in John 3:13; 6:62; Eph. 4:10; Heb. 4:14 we have the active: Jesus himself ascended. Both statements are true, for the *opera ad extra sunt indivisa aut communa*; they are ascribed equally to the different Persons. But before Jesus ascended, as the aorist participle ἐντειλάμενος shows, he gave behests to the apostles, ἐντολαί, as the participle suggests, *Auftraege*. Ἐντέλλω is not the common verb "to command" or "to order" which applies to slaves, servants, soldiers, and the like, but the verb that indicates a more personal relation. Beza has the idea: *Ut facere solent qui ab amicis, vel etiam ex hoc mundo, discedunt* — injunctions such as those leave who part from friends or who leave this world. We need not be told what these behests were. They were given during the forty days and are recorded in Luke 24:47; Matt. 28:19, 20; Mark 16:15-18; John 20:21-23. If anything were yet to be said, this last passage shows that the behests were given "through the Holy Spirit," and that this phrase should not be construed with the relative clause: "whom he did elect through the Holy Spirit." All the acts of Jesus were done in connection with the Spirit who had been bestowed upon the human nature of Jesus. We do not read that the election of the apostles was connected with the Spirit, but John 20:22 specifically informs us that, when Jesus sent forth the eleven, he breathed on them and bade them receive the Holy Spirit.

The relative clause "whom he did elect for himself" is added to "the apostles" in order once more to bring to mind the elective act which constituted these men "the apostles," the specially commissioned messengers (ἀποστέλλω, to send with a commission) of Jesus, we may say, his ambassadors. The middle voice is important: "he did elect for himself"; we may place a good deal into this middle; to represent him, to continue his work, etc. All this, too, lies in the title, "the apostles." Although it is sometimes used in a wider sense to include also the immediate assistants of the apostles (Luke was one), here it refers to the eleven only who received the final behests of Jesus.

Note the position of the phrase "through the Holy Spirit" before the relative clause "whom he elected." In the Greek the phrase might belong within the relative clause, but if that were the case, it would receive the strongest kind of emphasis, an emphasis for which no one could account in the present connection. Since it modifies the participle, "having given behests," no emphasis rests on the phrase. The Greek is content to mark only the past fact that lies in the aorist, "he did elect," whereas the English marks also the relation to other past facts: "he had elected."

3) In another relative clause (οἷς καί) Luke adds that these behests were given after the resurrection of Jesus, during the forty days. Jesus "presented himself alive or as living after he suffered." The aorist παθεῖν is constative and speaks of the suffering as something complete, thus including also the death. To present himself as alive or living (durative present participle) after this fatal suffering implies his resurrection from the dead. This presentation of himself was not a bare presentation but was "in connection with many proofs," sure tokens which made the apostles certain of the fact that their dead Lord was, indeed, alive.

Ἐν does not mean "by," for the proofs were not the means of the presentation but were "in connection with" it. In Luke 24:36 we see just what is meant: Jesus appeared in the midst of the disciples, then, however, he made them feel his flesh and his bones and also ate a piece of fish before them. These proofs were multiplied until they actually became many. This prodigality was intended to remove all doubt so completely as never to permit it to arise again. Luke makes the matter still clearer and adds more data: "letting himself be seen by them during forty days," etc. In this way Jesus presented himself alive. The temporal phrase is placed before the participle for the sake of emphasis. No less than forty days were used for these appearances. Again and again Jesus let himself be seen. The apostles (and others) had time to think, to consider, to talk the matter over, to make any new test they might desire. The present participle fits the repetition of the appearances to their proofs; the agent for the passive, as so often, is expressed by the dative "by them." Thayer calls ὀπτάνομαι a Biblical word, but it has been found elsewhere (Deissmann, *Light, etc.*, 79 and 252: "I am seen," "I let myself be seen"). It expresses exactly what Jesus did when he would suddenly stand in the midst of the apostles.

Valuable is the addition: "and declaring the things concerning the kingdom of God," as recorded in Matt. 28:18, etc.; Mark 16:14, etc.; Luke 24:25, etc., and 44, etc., John 20:21, etc. These were the same things Jesus had been teaching throughout his ministry, but now they appeared in a new light. Romanists insert the thought that Jesus instructed the apostles about the hierarchy, the seven sacraments, etc.

One of the greatest concepts of the New Testament is "the kingdom of God" (Matthew, "of the heavens"). It is misunderstood when earthly kingdoms are used as a pattern for this spiritual concept. An earthly kingdom is a land and a nation on which the king depends. Take his people away, and the king ceases to be king; they, too, are what they are without him as a king. But God (Christ) makes his kingdom, it depends wholly on him and could not exist without him. God's kingdom is found wherever God is and rules by his power, grace, and glory. He makes his own domain and his own people, and never they him. It is the kingdom of the heavens because heavenly powers make it and also give it heavenly character; the kingdom of God (Christ) because he is over and in it everywhere, at once its source and its control. This rule or kingdom goes back to the beginning and extends to eternity. When we look at the power and the omnipotence, it rules the whole universe; when we look at grace, it embraces the whole church; when we contemplate the glory we see heaven and all its inhabitants. The kingdom and rule of grace fills the whole Testament from Adam onward; it is the rule of grace through the Messianic promise. A new era began when the promise was fulfilled in Christ, the era of the New Testament which extends to the end of time.

It is of the kingdom in this sense that Jesus spoke during the forty days. About to ascend on high, he would rule with grace and through the apostles reach out to the ends of the earth. So he rules through their written Word to this day. But since this is a rule of grace, it makes all who are won by grace partakers of the kingdom. It makes them kings unto God (Rev. 1:6) so that they, too, rule with him by means of his Word and have kingly crowns awaiting them (II Tim. 4:8, and all the passages that speak of a crown). See the author's *Kings and Priests* where the entire subject is treated.

4) This verse does not begin a new sentence, for καί only carries the great introductory statement to its conclusion by adding the command to stay in Jerusalem for the coming of the Holy Spirit who had been promised already by the Baptist. Thus in one grand sweep everything from the time of the Baptist until Pentecost is combined with reference to the kingdom.

In συναλιζόμενος we have a *crux interpretum*. If the root is ἁλής, the adjective meaning "crowded," "in a mass," we have the translation of our versions: "being assembled together"; but if the root is ἅλς, "salt," we have the marginal translation of our versions: "eating together," or more precisely: "while partaking together of salt." Rather decisive against the former meaning is the fact that the singular fits only a collective noun, like a multitude, and never only a single person. Then, too, the tense should be the aorist, for the assembling must precede the commanding. Sense and tense are correct if we accept the other derivation, "eating with them," and we have in our favor all the ancient versions and the fathers plus also Luke 24:41-43, where Jesus did eat. Still we lack classical examples for this meaning. See B.-P. 1257.

One is surprised at M.-M. 601 who advocate a difference in spelling so that we have a verb that means "to spend the night with." We may take it that Luke refers to his own Gospel, 24:41-43, 49, where he reports both that Jesus ate broiled (and thus salted) fish and ordered the disciples to remain in the city until they received the promise of the Father. Luke recalls this order because he is now about to report the descent of the Spirit. He even uses the same expression: "the promise of the Father" (Luke 24:49), and adds that they had heard this from him before (the aorist where we prefer the perfect).

5) Ὅτι does not state the reason for awaiting the promise of the Father although it is quite generally so translated: "for" (meaning "because"), German *denn*. How could John's baptizing with water be a part of such a reason? This is the so-called consecutive ὅτι (R. 1001), "seeing that." In view of the fact that John began with water in order to have a greater than he finish by pouring out the Holy Spirit the eleven must stay in Jerusalem. Read Luke 3:16, also John 1:33. We repeat only in brief the exegesis of these passages. John's baptism was the baptism

of repentance unto remission of sins, hence had the Holy Spirit even as this Spirit alone wrought faith throughout the Old Testament era. To reduce John's baptism to a mere water ceremony that was devoid of the Spirit is to contradict Luke 3:3. John began the work with his baptism, Jesus was to finish at Pentecost. We know of none of the apostles who received any other baptism than John's; by receiving it they confessed themselves as repentant and believing.

This ἐν does not imply that the Spirit became the counterpart of "water," a sort of fluid that sprinkled, washed, or even immersed a person. We note fire at Pentecost and not a fluid. 'Ἐν is here used exactly as it was in v. 3: "in connection with the Holy Spirit"; βαπτισθήσεσθε, like our expression that the Spirit "was poured out," cannot be stressed to get the idea of a fluid. When Jesus was baptized with the Spirit, when the Spirit was poured out upon him, Luke 3:22 describes this as the coming down of the Spirit in a bodily form like a dove. There were different phenomena at Pentecost (sound of wind, tongues of fire), but the act was the same: the Spirit filled the disciples in a miraculous way and gave them great power. This is called "being baptized." And the verb is evidently used in a figurative and unusual way. The apostles had heard this before, but now they are told that the event will occur "not many days after these," a litotes for "after only a few days" (R. 1205). We must note that οὐ is always placed before the preposition (B.-D. 433, 3), that ταύτας is predicative (R. 656): *nicht viele Tage nach den jetzigen* (B.-D. 226), an idiom we cannot duplicate.

Luke has made his masterly connection with his great Gospel account; he is now ready to proceed with the new narration.

6) Now they, having come together, began to inquire of him, saying, Lord, art thou at this time

restoring the kingdom to Israel? He, however, said to them: It is not yours to know times or seasons which the Father did place in his own authority. On the contrary, you shall receive power, the Holy Spirit having come upon you; and you shall be my witnesses both in Jerusalem and in all Judea and in Samaria and to the last part of the earth.

Luke uses μὲν οὖν once in the Gospel but twenty-seven times in Acts; there are only a few other instances elsewhere in the New Testament; the favorite combination in Acts is οἱ μὲν οὖν as here, often with a participle. A δέ need not follow although one does follow (v. 7). The particles do little more than to express an accord of the new statement with the one that precedes and may be rendered "accordingly"; no deduction is intended; "therefore" in our versions is too weigthy. There is an ambiguity with regard to the participles as to whether these are to be substantivized: "those come together," or regarded as modifiers: "they having come together." We prefer the latter because it can be carried through while the other at times causes difficulty.

Luke is speaking of the apostles (v. 2); they came together on the Mount of Olives (v. 12) whither Jesus himself led them (Luke 24:50). Some think that the apostles were still in the house where v. 4 and the participle, "partaking together of salt," placed them, so that now the scene of v. 4, 5 merely continues through v. 6-8. Much labor is then expended on v. 9 to show that, without saying so, Luke transfers us to the Mount of Olives. But if Jesus is eating with the apostles in v. 4, why must Luke in v. 6 remind us that they had come together? There is no reason why the apostles should not have asked as they did when Jesus had led them out to the Mount of Olives. Luke is retelling with important additions what he told in the Gospel, 24:50-53. The descriptive imperfect reads as though more was said than Luke records, as though there was some hesitation, and the impression seems to be made that the apostles had talked the matter over and took courage now at last to ask.

In the Gospels κύριος is often only a form of address that indicates respect, but beginning with Luke 7:13 we find the title used as it has ever since been employed in the church in the sense of divine Lord which includes the deity of Jesus and the grace and the redemption which made him our Lord. We shall thus continue to meet "the Lord," "the Lord Jesus," "our Lord Jesus Christ," etc. Direct questions, like indirect ones beginning with εἰ, are called Hebraistic or elliptical: we should like to know "whether." Consider whether this εἰ is not merely an interrogative particle (B.-D. 440, 3) that adds a note of hesitancy to the question.

The point of the question is the time, whether "at this time" Jesus is restoring the kingdom to Israel. In his answer Jesus distinguishes "times" (longer stretches) from "seasons" (shorter ones, each marked in a certain way). So the apostles do not mean "right away" but "before so very long." The fact that the kingdom is, indeed, to be restored to Israel is taken for granted. The scepter had, indeed, sadly departed from Judah — would it now be restored in Shiloh, in Jesus? Luke 24:21: "But we trusted that it had been he which should have redeemed Israel."

There is a difficulty to determine exactly what the apostles had in mind when they asked this question. We venture to say that they thought of a glorious earthly rule for Israel, the Jewish people, through Jesus, the Messiah, who would soon return in his Parousia. Jesus answers only regarding the times and the seasons and does not explain about the kingdom (see v. 3) and how Israel (the remnant, Rom.

9:27; 11:5) shall have the kingdom restored. The fact that the apostles still expressed strong earthly conceptions by their question can scarcely be denied.

7) The relative clause contains the reason why it is not for the apostles to know even the times to say nothing of the seasons. The word χρόνος denotes a stretch of time but καιρός a definite period that is marked by what transpires in it. The genitive with εἶναι = it does not belong to you, is not your business or concern. The aorist infinitive means "actually to know" and does not exclude the idea that the apostles may know something about times and seasons. Jesus uses the plural to convey the thought that everything regarding time and season is in the Father's province. He placed times and seasons where alone they belong, "in his own authority," for him alone to determine their course and their length. This certainly ought to dissuade all timesetters (Mark 13:32). The fine old exegete Bengel made this very mistake of trying to determine the time of the return of Christ in a calculation that was most miserably wrong. Once for all, as the aorist ἔθετο shows, the Father has put these things beyond our reach.

By saying that they are placed in the Father's authority Jesus does not imply that the Father has not yet determined times and seasons and thus also the date of the end. In Matt. 24:22, and in Mark 13:20 Jesus informs us that the days of the final tribulation shall be shortened for the sake of the elect, and that the Father alone knows that day and the hour. The conclusion is, therefore, that God had, indeed, determined all times and seasons, but had done so by taking all things into account, especially those pertaining to his elect, and that he thus knows these times and seasons even as his omniscience is without bounds. As far as the Son is concerned, only during the days of his humiliation did he restrict himself in the use of this as of the other divine attributes to what was needed in his mediatorial work.

8) After a negative, ἀλλά brings the positive; so decidedly are the apostles not to know that, "on the contrary," their only concern is to be the promise of receiving power for their world-wide testimony. This is spiritual power which is communicated directly by the Holy Spirit in the Pentecostal miracle, a complete and an adequate equipment of mind and of spirit for the great future task. A genitive absolute explains how the apostles are to receive this power: "the Holy Spirit having come upon you." This describes the Pentecost miracle in advance and defines in Jesus' own way what "being baptized in connection with the Holy Spirit" actually means. "To come upon" is certainly far removed from anything like immersion. In a moment Jesus will leave these men, but he leaves them with this great promise; in fact, his leaving is to make good that promise, for the ascension of Jesus was necessary in order to send us the Holy Spirit.

Although the connective is only "and," the thought presented is the result of thus receiving power, and the future tense reads as though being witnesses is a continuation of the promise. This is not an admonition, but only a glorious future fact: "you shall be my witnesses" even as Jesus designated them already in Luke 24:48. They are to be more than heralds (preachers) who proclaim only what they are ordered to proclaim; they are to be herald "witnesses" in the sense of I John 1:1, men who have themselves seen, heard, touched, experienced, and are qualified, even called, to testify accordingly.

We must not pass too lightly over this word "witnesses." In the sense in which the apostles were Christ's witnesses no others were or could be. All the great things they saw could never be repeated; yet all these things had to be made known and made known properly, not only to the men of that age, but to the men of all ages. For this reason the descent of the Spirit bestowed a special equipment upon the apostles. They received the gift of inspiration in the sense of John 14:26, and 15:26, 27. Thus, besides filling the world of their own day with the gospel, by their inspired writings they are witnessing to the end of time. Individual names are, indeed, attached to the four Gospels and also to the other New Testament writings, but what these Gospels report is the testimony of all the apostles. In Acts Luke is only the scribe, the apostles here continue their testimony by deed and word. The same is true with regard to the Epistles. In the whole New Testament we have "my witnesses" speaking to the end of time in a great apostolic chorus. In their testimony speaks "the Faithful Witness'" himself (Rev. 1:5). "My" witnesses = called to witness by me, for me, about me, yea, all about me.

The course of the work of the apostles is outlined in one grand sweep: "both in Jerusalem," etc. The τε . . . καί, "both . . . and," is extended by the addition of a second "and." Note that Judea and Samaria are regarded as a unit since only one article is used (R. 787); also that to reach the utmost or last part of the earth involves passing through all the parts that intervene. The city is named first and made prominent because the apostles were to do much work right in Jerusalem, founding and extending there the mother congregation of all Christendom, radiating from which all the sister congregations were to be established elsewhere. Jesus here announces the program which we see carried out in Acts. We know, too, that Paul reached Spain and Thomas reached India.

9) And having said these things, while they were looking, he was taken up, and a cloud took him from their eyes. And as they were earnestly gazing

into heaven, while he was going, lo, two men were standing beside them in white apparel, who also said, Galilean men, why are you standing looking into heaven? This Jesus, received up from you into heaven, shall so come in what manner you viewed him going into heaven.

Except for the brief statement in Mark 16:19, we have only Luke's descriptions of the ascension, which are thus invaluable, especially this one in Acts which so graphically describes just what the witnesses saw and thus just what we are so glad to know. The Lord had concluded his address (hence the aorist participle). The eyes of the apostles were resting upon him (note the present tense of the genitive absolute and its emphatic forward position). The verb means to see, to look, to direct the eyes and the attention upon an object. Jesus was not suddenly snatched away out of their sight; this time he did not vanish as he had done when leaving them during the forty days. Now his leaving had a different meaning. Before this, when he would vanish, they knew that he would appear again; now his presence was slowly and visibly taken away, upward, in a heavenly way. They see it all with their very eyes as the witnesses they were to be.

An awed silence comes over them. Jesus spreads his hands over them in blessing (Luke 24:50) and slowly, majestically, mightily rises heavenward from the earth, higher and higher. Their eyes are wide with astonishment and follow him and strain in looking (ἀτενίζοντες, v. 10). Far aloft they see the holy body of Jesus until at last a flimsy cloud folds him in. They still gaze after him — but he is gone. They know whither — he has ascended into heaven.

The verb used is ἐπαίρω, "to lift up." It is passive like the two other verbs that were used with reference to the ascension in the Gospel and in Acts; see v. 2

regarding both the passive and the active. The ascension was visible solely for the sake of the apostles. The moment the cloud hid Jesus from their sight, he was transferred timelessly into the heavenly glory, the abode of God and of the saints and of angels. This is the great article of our faith: "he ascended into heaven." Chrysostom says: "Of Christ's resurrection the disciples saw the final part, not the first part, but of his ascension they saw the first part, not the final part." In ὑπέλαβεν the preposition conveys the idea that the cloud received Jesus by appearing under him. When it is said that the cloud carried Jesus up into heaven, motion is put into the cloud; it served only to hide Jesus. The ascension, like the resurrection, pertains only to the body of Jesus and thus to his human nature in union with the divine. The greatest part of the miracle was that which occurred after the cloud hid Jesus when he was instantly in the glory of heaven, seated at the right hand of majesty and of power in order to exercise these forever also according to his human nature.

Yes, he is visible in heaven as is Elijah. He has the same body that died on the cross and lay in the grave. But he is not confined in heaven like Elijah. He is at the same time wherever he has promised to be, and that according to both natures. It is incomprehensible to finite minds, and all who philosophize about it may know in advance that they are childishly wrong. The recorded facts are true, beyond them no man can go.

The cloud was only the divinely chosen earthly means in a final and appropriate way to remove the visible body of Jesus from the eyes of the apostles. They were to cease looking. Jesus was not rising on and on in the regions of distant space — he was gone — gone where there is no space, no time, or ony other mundane restriction. It is allegory to say that the cloud served "to make visible the gracious, saving presence of God," or to think of the cloud as "the visible revelation of the presence of God who receives the Son unto himself into the glory of heaven." Let no such allegory becloud the stupendous fact that all in an instant the body of Jesus was in the glory of heaven.

10) Ἀτενίζω refers to strained and earnest looking; the periphrastic imperfect, more than the simple form would do, pictures the continuousness of the act. The added genitive absolute with its present tense, "he going" ("while he was going") pictures once more what the earnest gaze of the apostles saw. In new words Luke describes what the witnesses beheld but now in order to add a second astonishing fact with the interjection "lo " Sometimes καί is added to introduce the main clause. This may be due to Hebrew influence although it is found also in Homer and strongly resembles ἐγένετο καί plus a finite verb (B.-D. 442, 7). This explains the untranslatable καί before the interjection.

Not after the ascension but while it was in progress the two angels appeared. When the apostles looked, there "they were standing beside them in white apparel"; the past perfect of this verb is always used in the sense of the imperfect and is here used descriptively. The presence of these angels marks the ascension as one of Christ's great saving acts. Luke calls the angels in the tomb ἄνδρες, "men" (24:4) and here he again writes "men"; Mark 16:5 has νεανίσκος, "young man." They appear in this form in order to draw as near to those to whom they appear as heavenly spirits can. They are, of course, without sex (Luke 20:35, etc.) but they come visibly as men, young men, images of strength and of beauty combined, never as women or maidens — a point which only the best artists have noted. On the rare word ἐσθησις see R. 267. The whiteness of their apparel is noted, which we may take as **signifying purity, holiness, heavenliness.**

11) No second look was needed to tell the apostles who stood before them in greatness, power, and glory. These angels had come to complete what was necessary in regard to this act of Jesus. They are his spokesmen who at once confirm the ascension and then also connect it with the future return of the Lord. We may say that here we have another part of the answer of Jesus to the apostles concerning the restoration of the kingdom to Israel (v. 6). These apostles are to fill the world with their witness; then at last Jesus will return for the consummation of his kingdom. We cannot entertain the idea that these two men were Moses and Elijah; but were they the same two mentioned in Luke 24:4? If we are asked in what garments Jesus appeared during the forty days and here at his ascension, the answer must be that no man knows, for the witnesses have left no word in regard to this.

The address, "Galilean men," is used less because these apostles were native Galileans (Judas alone was from Judea) than because it would bring back to them in a flash their long and blessed association with Jesus, especially in Galilee. "Why are you standing looking into heaven?" is not a rebuke. It was only natural to gaze after Jesus in this manner. The question intends to turn their minds from mere astonishment to more important thought. The ascension of Christ and his return at the Parousia go together. And these heavenly messengers bring a glorious promise to the apostles at this great moment. For now when Jesus is received up they are once more to hear that he will come again in the same visible way.

For a third time the ascension is described but now by the angel spokesman: "this Jesus, received up from you into heaven," this very one who is known by this his personal name and described by the act just witnessed, he shall return. On the passive participle of the verb see v. 2; compare the verbs in v. 9 and in Luke 24:51. A moment ago the apostles spoke with this Jesus, now his glorious reception into the heavenly world is already accomplished. What this implied Jesus had himself told them: not mere rest while they struggled here below, but a mighty, all-transcending exercise of power and authority. The angels have nothing to add to all that Jesus had told them on this subject; they restate another assurance which the Lord had left his apostles, restate it in the most emphatic and direct form: this Jesus "shall so come in what manner you viewed him going into heaven."

Note the emphatic words: οὗτος —οὕτως — ὃν τρόπον (a set phrase in which the antecedent is drawn to the relative, R. 718), *"this"* Jesus — *"thus"* — *"in the (same) way in which"* you viewed, etc. He departed visibly, he shall return visibly; he went to heaven, he shall come from heaven; he went away bodily, he shall come back bodily. It is not added that he will return in all his glory with all the angels of God about him for the final judgment, although Jesus had given these additions. It is not added that every eye shall see him when he returns, also those who pierced him, Rev. 1:7. But one may ask how this can be possible when the earth is a globe, and when he who appears on one side of the globe cannot be seen on the opposite side. All such questions assume that space, time, and earthly conditions as we know them shall continue and govern at the last day. But time shall be no more, space shall no longer exist, heaven shall come down to earth (Rev. 21:1, 2), and a few other tremendous changes that our science never dreamed of will so arrange it that even the most skeptical doubter shall not have the least trouble in getting the fullest view of "this Jesus coming out of heaven" for the judgment also of all skeptics and unbelievers.

12) **Then they returned to Jerusalem from the mount called Olive grove, which is near Jerusalem, a**

38 Interpretation of the Acts of the Apostles

Sabbath journey away. They returned "with great joy," Luke 24:52. It is important to know that the apostles returned to Jerusalem even as Jesus commanded (v. 4), and that the following events took place there. It is likewise of interest to know that the ascension occurred on the mount called "Olive grove." Sometimes a name is retained in the nominative, here it appears in the genitive in agreement with the genitive participle, and the nominative must be Ἐλαιών (not circumflexed). On the forms used in the passages in the Gospel see R. 267. The distance from Jerusalem to Olivet was as far as Jews were allowed to walk on the Sabbath, namely 2,000 paces. Luke might have given the distance in terms of stadia; the expression which he uses shows that he is following a Jewish source. "Having a Sabbath's journey" is the Greek idiom. Yet this does not state the entire distance to the place on Olivet from which Jesus ascended, but only the distance to the base of Olivet. Luke 24:50 indicates how far up the mount Jesus took the apostles, namely, to the place where the road branches, one branch going toward Bethany, which lies about 4,000 paces from the city beyond the ridge.

The spot now pointed out to travellers as the one from which Jesus ascended cannot be taken seriously. Because the ascension is so important Luke records the place of it for Theophilus in both the Gospel and the Acts. The view that the ascension occurred on Sunday is refuted by both the forty days mentioned in v. 3, which fix the day as a Thursday, and the distance indicated, for a Sabbath's journey would extend only to the base of Olivet and not to the place on Olivet from which the ascent was made.

13) **And when they came in they went to the upper room where they were abiding, both Peter and John and James and Andrew, Philip and Thomas, Bartholomew and Matthew, James of Alpheus and**

Simon the Zealot and Judas of James. These all were continuing steadfastly with one accord in prayer together with women, also Mary, the mother of Jesus, and together with his brothers.

"They came in" means from Olivet into the city. They did not scatter but at once went up "to the upper room where they were abiding." The relative clause cannot be separated from its antecedent so that it does not define which upper room is referred to, namely *the* one *where* they were abiding. But some make this separation in order to make room for the conjecture that this upper room is the same as the one mentioned in Luke 22:12, where Jesus celebrated the Passover, and for the added supposition that it belonged to Mark's father. But the article in the phrase "to *the* upper room" cannot refer to a passage in the Gospel. "They were abiding" means that the apostles and other disciples were making this room their headquarters while they were in Jerusalem. Nor can it be assumed that all of them, so many men and women, lived in this room. The best guess as to its identity is that it was the room where the apostles gathered after they heard the news of the resurrection, John 20:19, 26.

Such upper rooms were quite common. Sometimes they were merely booths that were erected on the flat roof of the stone building. The author saw many of them in the Holy Land. We shall note them in the Acts; the body of Dorcas was laid out in one of them. Sometimes they were roomy and even ornate like the one with its tiled floor that is mentioned in Luke 22:12. They were used as places for retirement and quiet and, for the company here described, as a place that was free from interruption and disturbance. The fact that the house belonged to a friend of Jesus need scarcely be added. The effort to locate this upper room in the Temple is futile. Nor does abiding in this room contradict Luke 24:53, the constant stay in the Temple; the disciples divided their time between the two places.

Luke introduces the apostles in verse 2. He intends to write about them in this account, presently also to tell how the vacant place of Judas Iscariot was filled. Very properly he lists their names at this point so that Theophilus may also know just who had witnessed the ascension of Jesus. The chief feature of this list is the order of the first four names which constitute the first group. Here Peter and John are grouped together, and James is third, for these three were distinguished by Jesus in Jairus' house, at the transfiguration, and in Gethsemane. Peter is always first but only as *primus inter pares,* for Matt. 18:18 gives to all the apostles the powers bestowed on Peter in Matt. 16:19. The only reason commonly assigned for pairing John with Peter is Luke's further narrative in which the two appear as companions; but the conclusion of John's Gospel shows that the two were also close friends and constant companions. Luke 6:14, etc., just lists the names, but if we make three groups we shall in all four lists find the identical names in each group although in varied order. The present list has four groups that are marked by asyndeton; but if we count three groups we shall find the same name heading each group as in the other lists, Peter, Philip, and James of Alpheus. Andrew and Philip have Greek names.

Philip is from the home of the two pairs of brothers and must be distinguished from the deacon and evangelist Philip. The other name of Thomas is Didymus, "Double" or "Twin." Bartholomew is a patronymic for Son of Tolmai; his personal name was Nathanael, John 1:46; 21:2. Matthew is the former publican, the writer of the first Gospel. The second James is distinguished by the genitive of his father's name: son of Alpheus. The second Simon is distinguished by the apposition "the Zealot," for he had at one time belonged to the militant Jewish party which contended for the honor of the law and the theocracy of Israel. Judas is distinguished from the traitor by the genitive of his father's name. We do not take "of James" in the sense of "brother of James," for we have just had a genitive of the father ("of Alpheus") and also a patronymic. If the last genitive is to be different and to indicate "brother," ἀδελφός would have to be added. If Jesus conquered the world through the testimony of these men, the victory was certainly not due to the men but to their Lord as whose witnesses they appeared.

14) These eleven, Luke states, not only had their headquarters in this upper room, but "were continuing steadfastly in prayer," τῇ προσευχῇ, a *res sacra* that was always directed to God. And they did this "with one accord," ὁμοθυμαδόν. This word occurs ten times in Acts and is a significant adverb to express oneness of heart and mind. Abstract nouns such as "prayer" may or may not have the article in the Greek. The next verses show that Luke does not have in mind a continuous ten-day prayer meeting with audible praying going on constantly. The word προσευχή is at times used in the wider sense of worship. Prayer marked these ten-day gatherings. This word has thus far been found only once in paganism in the sense of "prayer or supplication," in a lone letter, M.-M. 547, and is thus distinctively Jewish and Christian, that is, Biblical.

And now with two σύν Luke expands the group that was thus together in Jerusalem by adding women as one class and the brothers of Jesus as another. He does not say "together with the women" but only "women," an indefinite number and not a fixed group. Who they were we gather in part from the Gospel: those mentioned in Luke 8:2, 3, at the crucifixion, and at the tomb; but in these places a number of them is left unnamed. From Luke 24:49 we conclude that they were from Galilee. Luke names only the mother of Jesus (καί = "also") who was in John's care. With two exceptions in Luke's Gospel he calls her "Mariam," and a few texts have this form here. One cannot say apodictically that some of these prayers were directed to Jesus; if they were, Mary would have prayed to her son as did all the rest that were in the upper room.

A separate preposition adds "his brothers" and does this after mentioning the women. This makes it certain that none of these brothers of Jesus were apostles. In John 7:3-5 they are not even believers. It is generally thought that the resurrection of Jesus brought them to faith so that we now find them here. Who were they? As far as the writer is able to see, the problem is not solved. The answers given are: sons of Joseph by a former marriage; cousins of Jesus, sons of a half-sister of Mary; and the modern answer, sons born to Joseph and Mary after Jesus. Strong objections may be lodged against each one of these views. When the latter is stressed on the strength of the word ἀδελφοί, "brothers," the passage before us raises gravest doubts. Right after "Mary, the mother of Jesus," we read not "*her* other sons" but "*his* brothers." Why is their relation to Jesus instead of their relation to their own mother mentioned if she was their natural mother? Nobody has as yet been able to answer. Mary is under John's care; yet here are her own natural sons, even more than one, and why is she not in their care? We are still waiting for a satisfactory answer. We, therefore, leave the problem where it is and note only that the objections to making them sons of Joseph and Mary are very strong.

15) **And in these days Peter, having arisen in the midst of the brethren, said (now there was together a multitude of persons, about a hundred and twenty): Men and brethren, it was necessary that the Scripture be fulfilled which the Holy Spirit spoke**

in advance through David's mouth concerning Judas who became guide to those who seized Jesus, seeing that he had been numbered among us and obtained the lot of this ministry.

"These days" are those between Ascension and Pentecost. Here for the first time in Acts "brethren" is used as a designation for the disciples of Jesus; hereafter it is the standard term. The present meeting could not have been held in an upper room of a house; a place in the Temple courts also seems unlikely. So we are left without this information. The matter of filling the place of Judas must have been discussed, at least by the eleven, prior to the action that was finally taken. Jesus had appointed no substitute for Judas during the forty days. The fact that the number of apostles must be twelve according to the choice Jesus had originally made which matched the twelve patriarchs and the twelve tribes of Israel and the twelve thrones awaiting them to judge these twelve tribes, was taken for granted. But the eleven do not act by themselves; they wait until as large a number as possible could be brought together and then the eleven act only as brethren who are on a par with all these others. It is the first vivid illustration of what we shall see throughout the Acts and the early church. There is nothing hierarchical in their procedure. The apostles do not constitute a superior order. All are brethren, each having his place and his task; by Jesus' own appointment the apostles have the most important task.

Luke is not certain that exactly 120 were present; in general, he is not so precise in regard to numbers. Therefore his 120 is not symbolical, 12 times 10. In v. 14 he mentions no number. It seems that number was recorded for two reasons: first, because it was the church that acted, and secondly to show the ratio in which the disciples increased, adding 3,000, then growing to 5,000 men, finally increasing to so many that count is lost and many priests are won until the first persecution causes a great scattering. Ὀνόματα "names," is used in the sense of "persons," all of them being true believers. This, however, does not include the women. The phrase ἐπὶ τὸ αὐτό, "at the same place," is used in the sense of "together." It was natural that Peter should take the lead in the matter at hand just as he had done among the Twelve in past days. Nowhere do we note the least indication that he acted with any special right or authority. Today we should say that he served as chairman of the meeting by general consent.

Ἄνδρες ἀδελφοί is the formal address to a body of men and is quite commonly used thus; it is less familiar than ἀδελφοί, so that the translation of the A. V. is preferable to that of the R. V. The assembly consisted of men, otherwise ἄνδρες could not have been used; ἀδελφοί might include ἀδελφαί, just as today "brethren" may include "sisters," but ἄνδρες could not include γυναῖκες, just as to this day the address "men" omits "women." Throughout the Acts, in all the highly important transactions of the apostolic church, the men and the women abide in their divinely designed places.

Δεῖ may express any type of necessity; the imperfect refers to the necessity of a certain fulfillment of Scripture which was necessary all along and was now recently fulfilled. Some things God foreordains; when these are recorded in Scripture prophecy, the fulfillment is certain because of God's will and foreordination. But in all contingent matters such as the betrayal of Judas prophecy is fulfilled because of the infallibility of the divine foreknowledge. God did not decree the betrayal; Judas determined that himself; God foreknew that ungodly determination, foretold it, however only in a general way, and so Judas fulfilled the prophecy.

Here is Peter's clear definition of Inspiration: in the Scriptures the Holy Spirit is the speaker, and (in this case) the mouth of David is the medium for his speaking. This definition is oft repeated. The Spirit = the *causa efficiens;* the human mouth (pen) = *causa instrumentalis*. The significant preposition is διά "through" a medium or an instrument. And this was done not merely "through David" but through his "mouth," his very utterance. This is Verbal Inspiration, than which none other ever occurred according to the Scriptures themselves. The prophecies involved are quoted by Peter in v. 20, 21, now, however, saying that they refer to "Judas who became guide to those who seized Jesus," which graphically describes the act of betrayal.

17) Ὅτι cannot be causal "for" or "because"; it is what R. 1001 calls the consecutive ὅτι, here naming the point on which the prophecy rested: Judas was an apostle. If he had not been that, the Scripture could not have dealt thus with him. Peter puts this vital point, consecutive to which was the necessity of the Scripture fulfillment, into a double statement. First "he had been numbered among us," the periphrastic past perfect expressing his ordination as one of the Twelve prior to his act of betrayal. He had received from Jesus this highest station which was graciously bestowed upon so few. Such high honor, such glorious prospects were granted to Judas by the Lord's grace. Secondly, and helping to define the first statement: "he obtained the lot of this ministry." The highest of all offices came to him. Λαγχάνω, "to obtain by lot," is used in the general sense of "to obtain," hence κλῆρος, "lot," can be used with it and is here also used in the broad sense of "portion," the entire expression being a choice one for appointment to an office. "The lot of this ministry" is a portion or share in the voluntary service to which the apostles were called. Διακονία is also

choice, denoting a service freely rendered for service sake in order to help others. At the wedding in Cana not *douloi*, but *diakonoi* assist; in Matt. 22, *douloi*, slaves, invite, but *diakonoi* cast out the guest, and these latter are angels. "The lot of this ministry" is the one the eleven still have; the genitive is partitive and thus shows the great apostolic ministry to be a unit in which each apostle had his share. Back of the Scripture statements is this high position of Judas; this brought him into those prophecies.

18) **This man, accordingly, acquired a field out of the iniquity wage and, on going headlong, burst in the middle, and all his bowels gushed out. And it became a thing known to all that inhabit Jerusalem, so that field is called in their language Akeldama, that is, Field of Blood.**

The R. V. makes these verses a parenthesis, an insertion into Peter's speech. Yet when those who regard these words as a parenthesis admit that Luke wove them into Peter's address, we dismiss this idea and read them as the A. V. does. No parenthesis is indicated save the small insertion for the sake of the Greek readers: "in their language," and "that is, Field of Blood," which every reader at once notes as having been written by Luke and not spoken by Peter who spoke Aramaic. How Judas acquired a field "out of the iniquity wage," the silver paid him by the high priest for his iniquitous betrayal, might be doubtful if we did not have Matt. 27:3-8. Judas did not acquire that piece of ground by himself going and buying it but by throwing that money into the Temple, hanging himself, and confronting the high priests with the problem of what to do with this "blood money." They solved the difficulty by buying the piece of ground to make a potter's field of it. Peter is brief because all his hearers know the facts.

Acts 1:18-20

Matthew reports only that Judas hanged himself, but Peter adds the detail that, on falling headlong, his body burst open, and all his bowels gushed out. The two statements are not contradictory. We need only supply the thought that Judas must have hanged himself in a place where his body could fall down far enough to burst open the abdomen with such horrible results. Ahitophel, the Old Testament type of Judas, also hanged himself. The end of the traitor is most terrible.

19) It is not this end alone that Peter recalls to the brethren but also the fact that the whole city came to know of it with the result that that piece of ground was named by the people: Akeldama (*Akeldamach*), which Luke, like Matthew, translates, "Field of Blood." Here again something must be supplied from Matthew's account, namely, the fact that the high priests refused to put the money into the Temple treasury because it was "blood money" just as Judas said he had betrayed the innocent blood. All this became known together with the horrible death of Judas, and this name, "Field of Blood," was the result. The name primarily refers to the blood of Jesus and secondarily to the death of Judas who betrayed Jesus' blood. There is no evidence that Judas hanged himself on this very piece of ground. The later stories of Papias and others are fiction and are in part due to a misunderstanding of Peter's words.

20) **For it has been written in the Book of Psalms:**
   Let his habitation become desolate,
   And let not one be dwelling in it!
and,
   His overseership let another take!

Peter uses the common formula for introducing Old Testament quotations: γέγραπται, the perfect, "it has been written" and thus now stands as so written.

We see that David's "mouth" mentioned in v. 16 and his writing are regarded as being identical, something that is constantly done in the New Testament with reference to Old Testament writers. The γάρ is explanatory. When v. 18, 19 are made parenthetical, this "for" is connected with v. 17, but we see that it connects even better with v. 19. For all that is said of the terrible end of Judas accords with the two passages of the Psalms (69:25; 109:8) which are now introduced; in fact, γάρ may be translated, "for instance." Peter certainly knew the Scriptures well to be able to adduce these two striking statements. He does not cite them as by any means being the only ones that refer to the case of Judas. A glance at Ps. 69, for instance, shows its typical character. The Jews themselves refer many of its statements to the sufferings of the Messiah and thus to the enemies who inflict these sufferings upon him. When he exposed the traitor, Jesus, too, used Ps. 41:9, David's word regarding the traitor Ahitophel (II Sam. 15:31; 17:1, 23), Luke 22:21; John 13:21-27.

Peter cites two passages, one regarding the removal of Judas from his place and position, the other regarding the filling of his vacant place by another. Both passages deal with the enemies of the theocracy during David's time; it is thus that they apply to Judas who by his traitorous act stands forth among these enemies as their chief representative. All those enemies of David's time are the type of whom Judas became the great antitype. It is thus that the Holy Spirit spoke about Judas in advance. When he spoke through David, Judas was fully foreknown. When he quotes Ps. 69:25, Peter renders the LXX quite exactly and makes only verbal changes that retain the full meaning. David's plural is, however, made a singular because the passage is used specifically with reference to Judas.

The two lines are synonymous Hebrew poetry. The second line repeats and thus emphasizes the first with different words. "Let his habitation become desolate," his ἔπαυλις or dwelling, with Judas being forever removed from it; "and let not one be dwelling in it" in the sense of continuing what he was. So the damnable career of Judas ended, and no one was there to continue it.

Palm 109:8 already had the singular and called for no verbal change: "His overseership, his ἐπισκοπή, let another take." This means his high, responsible office, which is not the same as his habitation and dwelling. The abused office must continue. Since the unworthy incumbent is gone, the Lord will provide one that is worthy. This is true even with regard to the lesser positions of ordinary believers. When the Jews scorned to take their places, the apostles turned to the Gentiles, Acts 13:46. It is this second passage which both warrants and leads to the action now proposed, namely the filling of the office of Judas.

21) **It is necessary, therefore, that of the men who went together with us at every time the Lord Jesus went in and went out on us, beginning from the baptism of John until the day he was received up from us, one of these become a witness of his resurrection together with us.**

Οὖν draws the conclusion which forms a necessity (δεῖ) that was brought on by the act of Judas which entailed that another be put into his office. The entire sentence, packed full of a variety of statements, is neatly and compactly constructed. Peter names the qualifications which the man who is to replace Judas must have. He must be one of those who went together with the eleven every time Jesus came to them, walked with them, and then parted from them for awhile during the whole period that extended from the days of the Baptist until the ascension. Only one who had these requirements would be qualified to be the twelfth in the chosen band who were to act as witnesses of Jesus' resurrection.

We at once see from the modifiers that τῶν συνελθόντων refers to going together with the eleven during the whole ministry of Jesus and not as the same participle in v. 6 to only one, namely, this present meeting with the eleven. Peter also says ἐν παντὶ χρόνῳ, "at every time," and not, "in all the time," (ἐν παντὶ τῷ χρόνῳ), and describes these as the times when Jesus "went in and went out on us." The Gospels, too, show that especially during the first part of his ministry Jesus at times left the apostles and then returned to them. Note the designation "Lord Jesus" and compare 1:6 on "Lord." The grammars regard ἐφ' ἡμᾶς as applying only to the first verb: "went in on us," and let us supply for the second: went out "from us" (B.-D. 479, 2); but "on us" would have to fit the second verb if this were a case of zeugma and not the first. "On us" fits both verbs quite well.

22) The period thus covered begins with "the baptism of John," which simply denotes the time when John was baptizing and not merely when John had finished his baptizing. A point to be noted is that Peter connects the Baptist with the ministry of Jesus as the activity of these two is always linked together. This period ends with the ascension, for which Peter uses the same verb he used in v. 2 (which see) and in v. 11. The genitive ἧς need not be an attraction from the dative as R. 717 and B.-D. 294, 2, assert by pointing to one other example found in one other text (D in Luke 1:20); it is the genitive of time within which something occurs. "Until he was received up from us" (the eleven) does not imply that the qualification includes presence at the ascension; for we know of none but the eleven who were present at that time. It seems to be a hasty conclusion that quite a number

Acts 1:22, 23 51

possessed the qualifications here laid down by Peter; we venture to conclude the contrary. When investigation was made, only two were found.

The construction is δεῖ γενέσθαι ἵνα, "it is necessary that one become," and "these" at the end takes up and emphasizes the fact that only such men are to be considered. While the predicate (become a "witness of his resurrection together with us") is unemphatic in the Greek it describes the apostolic office according to its chief task, that of testifying to the resurrection of Jesus. This implies that every apostle must himself have seen the risen Lord and be able to testify accordingly. All else that he saw and heard about Jesus must reach a climax in this final sight. For it is the resurrection of Jesus that is the supreme and ultimate proof of his Messiahship, at once the seal and the crown of all his words and his deeds, especially of his Redeemership. Take away the resurrection, and all else crumbles; but when the resurrection is a fact, all else is established (I Cor. 15:13-22). The fact that those who had followed Jesus from the time of John's baptism would also have seen the risen Lord, Peter does not need to state. What he had to say was that one who had followed thus could join the eleven in their official witness-bearing regarding the resurrection.

23) **And they stood up two, Joseph called Barsabbas, who was called besides Justus, and Matthias.** Why only these two? Because only these two met the requirement laid down by Peter. This is so obvious that one is surprised to find the claim that quite a number of men met the requirement, and that only two of these were selected. And on the strength of two texts Zahn claims that Peter did this selecting. By what right were these two singled out and the rest discarded if the Lord was to make the choice. If the assembly eliminated many, and the Lord only one, he

did very little of the choosing. One out of many could just as well be selected by lot as one out of two. It cannot be said that the assembly or that Peter had reasons for eliminating all but two, for that would only be saying that Peter had not stated all the requirements. Only two met the requirements stated by Peter. The entire choice was left to the Lord.

We really know nothing beyond the names of the two here recorded. All that is worth noting is the statement of Eusebius that both belonged to the Seventy. The name Joseph was so common that it became necessary to state also his other names. The first, Barsabbas (Barsabas), is a patronymic, "son of Saba" or "son of the aged." On the significance of the spelling see Zahn, *Forschungen,* IX, 334, etc. Nor is it surprising that a Latin name was added, "Justus," even as Saul became Paul. In the case of Matthias nothing further than the name was needed because no other man with this name was connected with Jesus. From later sources it is concluded that he was also called Thulmai (Ptolomy).

24) And praying they said: Thou, Lord, heartknower of all, show forth whom thou didst elect out of these two as the one to take the place of this ministry and apostleship from which Judas passed away to go to his own place. And they gave lots for them, and the lot fell upon Matthias, and he was counted as voted in together with the eleven apostles.

The choice between the two was entrusted to Jesus by means of prayer. When the aorist participle expresses the same act as the aorist finite verb it indicates simultaneous action: when they prayed they spoke. Peter no doubt spoke the prayer in which all joined silently. The emphatic σύ is more than an address; Jesus is asked in contrast to any selection the assembly might make. And the reason for the appeal to him is that he is the "heart-knower" and thus able to choose with unerring insight. If anything is needed to show that Κύριε is here the Lord Jesus (v. 21) and that these believers are directing a prayer to him, the petition itself shows this, the very verb ἐξελέξω being repeated from v. 2 and from Luke 6:13. As their very name shows, the apostles are elected as his own ambassadors by Jesus in person. So Jesus is here asked to show "whom he did elect of these two as the one," etc.; ἵνα is predicative to the relative ὅν. The aorist "did choose" places the act into the past; all that is needed is that Jesus make this known.

25) The office is fully designated; διακονία recalls v. 17. The second genitive, "of this apostleship," helps to lend weight to the entire designation; at the same time it brings out the thought that the chosen one is to be an apostle. The relative clause adds the idea that this place is now vacant. Judas passed out of it to go to what is significantly called "his own place." The two words "place" are in contrast; but this means that, since the first does not denote a locality but, as the genitives show, an office, no stress should be laid on the second as being a locality although in Luke 16:28 we have "place of torment." The fact that Gehenna or hell is referred to is beyond question. Somehow even those who otherwise speak about an intermediate place, a *Totenreich*, "a realm of the dead," unanimously state that Judas went to hell. "His own" place means, of course, the one and only one befitting him. The view that this refers to the burial place his money bought is scarcely worth noticing. "To go" to his own place, an aorist, means that he arrived there, and this verb conveys the idea that he went of his own volition. He, too, made a choice: the high and holy place of his office he passed up and elected to go to this other place in spite of all the efforts on the part of Jesus to stop him.

26) The lots were not given "to them" but "for them." Somebody attended to this. Probably two markers, each with one name upon it, were placed into a vessel which was shaken so hard that one flew out. This one indicated the choice. The custom of casting lots in this way was very ancient; it dates back to Homer; compare Lev. 16:8. The lot fell upon Matthias; the marker that had his name upon it flew out. The verb συγκαταψηφίζομαι, from ψῆφος, the pebble, black or white, which was used in voting, is found only in one other place in Greek literature and is here used, not with reference to voting, but with reference to counting one as having been voted in, as belonging "together with the eleven apostles." The idea that he was in any way discounted as an apostle because he was elected so late is wholly foreign to Acts.

No further example of this Old Tesament method of turning a decision over to God appears in the New Testament. In the Old Testament it was justified since God often intervened in the affairs of Israel in an outward and a direct way; He himself appointed the casting of lots in Lev. 16:8 and in apportioning Canaan. Prov. 16:13. The Moravians wanted to continue this practice in the Christian Church in cases where the Word of God does not decide: in the reception of members, in allotting offices, in sending out missionaries (see, however, Acts 6:2, etc.; 14:23; I Tim. 3:1, etc.; Tit. 1: 5), in entering marriage (where, however, obedience was not compulsory). Even Zinzendorf finally warned, "Those having no call may burn themselves with the lot." Recourse to drawing or casting lots was abandoned already by the apostolic church; we must follow the enlightenment the Spirit affords and the indications of Providence in both church matters and our personal affairs.

CHAPTER II

THE FIRST HALF

The Gospel Among the Jews in Palestine.
Chapters 2 to 12

The time: 31-44 A. D.; Pentecost to the persecution of Herod Agrippa.

The center of activity: Jerusalem.

This missionary range: Palestine, Jerusalem, Judea, and Samaria.

The chief personage: Peter, besides whom appear in a secondary capacity: John, James, Stephen, Philip. Barnabas and Paul begin their activity.

Peter is prominent in six marked instances: 1) At Pentecost in his sermon, chapter 2. 2) In the miracles, that follow, chapters 3 to 5, and 9:31-40. 3) In discipline and in the appointment of deacons, 5:1-11; 6:1, etc. 4) In superintending the work in Samaria together with John, 8:4-25. 5) In bringing the gospel to the first Gentiles, chapters 10 and 11; 6) As a steadfast confessor during the first great persecution, chapter 12.

The First Quarter

The Gospel in Jerusalem, Chapters 2 to 7

THE COMING OF THE HOLY SPIRIT

1) And when the day of Pentecost was being fulfilled, they were all together at one place. Luke alone, here and in Luke 9:51, uses this verb, both times it is the present infinitive passive with ἐν τῷ to designate the arriving of a period or of a point of time. In Luke 9:51 it is not the day of the ascension that is referred to but the final period of Christ's life that culminated in the ascension. Here in Acts the Jewish day of Pentecost is referred to. The difficulty does not lie in the neat Greek phrase but in its translation as far as both sense and tense are concerned. The idea is that, by coming, this day is filling up completely a measure of time that was hitherto beginning to be filled more and more. Yet no mere dating is intended, namely the arrival of the fiftieth day after the Jewish Passover. The phrase is too weighty for that. Luke is thinking of the Lord's promise and of how it is now coming to fulfillment, the arrival of this day making full the measure of time the Lord contemplated when he made the promise. Hence also the present tense is employed. As the hours of this day began, the measure of this time was being filled up, and the thing promised was now due to occur, and Luke states that it did occur. Compare C.-K. 929 for the main thought.

The feminine ἡ Πεντηκοστή without ἡμέρα came to be the name of the festival; hence Luke writes: "the day of the Fiftieth," i. e., of Pentecost. It came on the fiftieth day after the Passover. Coming seven weeks after the Passover, it was also called "the Festival of Weeks." In this year the fifteenth of Nisan, the day of the Passover, occurred on a Friday (which, of course, began at sundown on Thursday). The count of fifty starts with the next day which was a Sabbath and thus brings us to another Sabbath as the day of the Pentecost of this year.

The Christian celebration of the descent of the Spirit did not begin until years later. The name Pentecost was retained, but the count was made from the Christian Easter, which was always celebrated on a

Sunday and disregarded the fact that the Jewish Passover always came on the fifteenth of Nisan, no matter what the day of the week. Thus our Pentecost is also always observed on a Sunday. Passover, Pentecost, and Tabernacles were the great Jewish festivals that were attended by Jews from everywhere. Pentecost, however, lasted only one day. It was the Jewish harvest festival that celebrated the completion of the harvest, Exod. 23:14, etc., and the description in Lev. 23:17, etc. Long after the time of the apostles a second day was added, and the entire festival became what it is for the Jews today, a celebration of the giving of the law on Sinai.

"All" refers to the persons mentioned in 1:12-15 and certainly includes the women; but the estimate that there were 200 seems high. Here ἐπὶ τὸ αὐτό, following ὁμοῦ, must mean more than "together" (1:16), namely "in the same or in one place." What Luke says is that this day found all the disciples in one place, and that none of the entire number was absent. They were ready when the Spirit came.

2) **And there came suddenly out of heaven a noise as of a violent wind borne along, and it filled the whole house where they where sitting. And there appeared to them, as distributing themselves, tongues of fire, and it sat on each single one of them. And they were all filled with the Holy Spirit and began to make utterance with different tongues even as the Spirit kept giving to them to utter exaltedly.**

The Jews stood when praying; sitting implies that the assembly of disciples was listening to some discourse that was being uttered, let us say, by one of the apostles. About nine o'clock (v. 15) a violent noise sounded out of heaven, descended, and filled the entire building where the assembly was sitting on the floor in Oriental, cross-legged fashion. Luke compares the sound to that of a violent wind borne along, i. e., moving forward. It was sound alone and not a wind. The roar started in the sky but soon filled only the house. This mighty sound was surely the symbol of power, and we may recall that both the Hebrew and the Greek words for the Spirit, *Ruach* and Πνεῦμα, denote wind or breath, and that Jesus himself compared the coming of the Spirit to the blowing of the wind, John 3:8. The volume of the sound denotes vast, supernatural power. The Spirit of God thus indicated his coming upon the disciples in an audible manner. But this roar also had the purpose of attracting the mass of people to the spot where all the disciples were gathered. And while the aorist "there came" registers only the fact of the coming, we take it that the roar lasted long enough to effect this necessary purpose.

Much effort is often spent in trying to prove that this οἶκος or "house" could be only one of the thirty halls in the Temple that were called οἶκοι. It is stated that this is the festival, the ninth hour, when all would be in the Temple, the great mass of people that quickly gathered and gathered so that Peter could preach to them. But why would all these disciples be sitting in one of these halls of the Temple at this hour of prayer? And would this roar not cause everybody on the entire Temple grounds to rush to this hall, all the Temple police, all the Sanhedrists likewise? Proving the house to be one of the halls of the Temple proves too much. Note the article: "*the* whole house," evidently the one already referred to in 1:13, 15, where 120 persons had plenty of room. But this was not a "house" in the modern sense of the term, a building with ordinary rooms. We, of course, lack details, but if Luke had a hall in the Temple in mind he surely would have written ἱερόν.

3) The second phenomenon was that of tongues resembling fire and distributing themselves to each

person present. There was no actual fire but only a resemblance to fire. This aorist again registers only the fact and not the duration of the appearance. The crowd speaks only of what it hears and not of what it sees. We may conclude that the flamelike tongues had disappeared by the time the crowd had gathered. Luke writes, "distributing themselves," and then adds, "it sat upon each single one of them." Luke does not intend to write a subject just as we have none when we say, "it rains," "it is lightning," etc. Perhaps we may say that the flamelike tongues appeared in a great cluster and then divided until a tongue settled on the head of each one of the disciples. Compare the phrase ἐφ' ἕνα ἕκαστον, with εἷς ἕκαστος in v. 6, and with the simple ἕκαστος in v. 8. Luke means "on each *single* one," not a single one being excepted, men, women, old, young. These firelike tongues are plainly the fulfillment of Luke 3:16: "He shall baptize you with the Holy Spirit and with fire." Pentecost corrects all other interpretations of Luke 3:16, and of Matt. 3:11. The sound roared indiscriminately in the house, but these tongues sat individually upon each person. The Spirit fills every single believer in the church, uses every one in his mighty and blessed work. Pentecost raises all to the same level.

Why tongues, and why like fire? May we say that these tongues point to the speaking with tongues? When the heart overflows with grace and power, the tongue is kindled into utterance. So all are to have the Spirit, to confess, to pray, and to praise. Firelike tongues may well recall the altar with its holy fire which send the offering up to God. Fire is also a symbol of purity and purification. Each disciple is to make his confession, prayer, praise, testimony a pure offering coming from a holy altar that is burning with sacred fire. Like the noise, the tongues were a supernatural, heavenly manifestation.

4) Once more Luke writes "all," namely "all were filled with the Holy Spirit." This is the miracle itself, the signs are only accompaniments. The emphasis is on the passive verb "they were filled," for it was Jesus who filled the disciples with the Spirit; the aorist simply states the great fact. This is the realization of the promise, "he shall baptize you with the Holy Spirit." At one time the Spirit descended upon Jesus in a wondrous manner; in an analogous way the Spirit came upon and filled all these disciples of Jesus. Through the Spirit he became the Christ (the Anointed), through the same Spirit his disciples become Christians (people anointed).

Yet we must remember that they all had the Spirit even before Pentecost just as did all the saints of the Old Testament. No saving faith was ever possible without the Spirit. In the case of the eleven we must also recall John 20:22. Here, at Pentecost, Jesus sent the Spirit in a new fulfillment of the promises stated in 1:5; John 14:16, 17; 15:26; 16:7. At Pentecost the Spirit himself came to dwell permanently, throughout all the ages, in the hearts of those who constitute the *Una Sancta*, the Christian Church. Hitherto he had, indeed, wrought upon men with his saving power and bestowed also this or that gift; since Pentecost he actually fills the church with his powers and his gifts, and that by way of his own blessed presence. Hence these miraculous manifestations on this day of Pentecost; hence the new influx of power into the disciples, especially into the apostles for this witness-bearing in all the world (1:8); hence also the array of spiritual and charismatic gifts which Paul lists in I Cor. 12:4-11. The effect was the spread of the church throughout the world and the radiation of power from the church in all the world. Once redemption was accomplished, all this could follow and did follow because of the presence of the Spirit. The great channels through which the Spirit dwelling in the church operates are the Word and the sacraments.

Luke properly records that all were filled with the Spirit before he adds that they all began to speak in new languages. The sound and the visible tongues were external, but this miraculous speaking was a personal act due to the inward presence of the Spirit. In Mark 16:17, Jesus promised this gift: "they shall speak with new tongues." These καιναί tongues are the ones Luke here calls ἕτεραι, "other or different" tongues. "Began to make utterance" is scarcely an Aramaic pleonasm but a circumstantial way of stating so important an action. Hence also the following imperfect as the Spirit "kept giving" to them. Every word of these strange languages was an immediate gift of the Spirit. The rare verb ἀποφθέγγεσθαι describes the utterance as being made in an exalted manner.

What this speaking "with different tongues" means is stated in v. 6: "everyone heard them speaking in his own language"; and in v. 11: "we are hearing them telling with our own tongue the great things of God." The disciples spoke in foreign languages that were hitherto unknown to them, in the very languages of the natives of the foreign lands who were presently assembled before them. This is what Luke writes, and the church has never doubted the fact and Luke's veracity and accuracy in reporting that fact.

But serious objection is raised by some commentators who say that Luke's words mean something else, or that he has reported the facts in a wrong way. The miraculous speaking mentioned in 10:46, in 19:6, in I Cor. 12:10, and in 14:2, etc., is referred to. Nearly every objector has his own peculiar view. Some even say that "tongues" means "the language of heaven"! When Luke writes "with different tongues" and later omits "different," the omission is pointed to as proof positive for the fact that there were two entirely different kinds of speaking with tongues. The author has treated the entire subject at length in connection with I Cor. 12:10, and 14:2, etc. Sometimes Luke's sources are questioned. Yet he wrote with full knowledge of the gift of tongues. He had been in Corinth and may well have witnessed this gift in operation. He had Paul at his side who knew all about this gift. We have every reason to think that Luke also met other apostles, certainly Peter, to say nothing of some of the very disciples who here at Pentecost spoke with tongues and still others of the 3,000 who were there to hear that speaking. Still more, the Spirit who bestowed this gift of tongues guided Luke in producing his account.

The gift of tongues is one of the proofs for divine Inspiration. The Spirit who put the words of strange languages into the mouths of the disciples wherewith to speak the great things of God had no trouble in attending to the words of the holy writers so that they recorded what he desired and in the way he desired it.

Many have thought that the confusion of tongues at Babel was counterbalanced here at Pentecost, and that is the chief import of this part of the miracle. Rocholl, *Philosophie der Geschichte,* 275, beautifully states this view: "The speaking with tongues by the witnesses of the Mediator celebrates the resurrection of the unity buried at Babel. . . . It was the first full chord, struck by a higher hand on the discordant giant harp, the strings of which are the nations of the earth," etc. An attractive thought; and yet the diversity of languages has continued unchanged. Even Greek, a world language, did not endure. We must go deeper than Rocholl. The miracle of tongues maintains the diversity but points out into all lands, nations, and tongues exactly as Jesus does in 1:8. The miracle is prophetic, the first full chord of that symphony of confession, testimony, prayer, and praise that was soon to rise to the throne of the Redeemer from the tongues of all the nations of the world.

The gift of tongues was one of the miraculous gifts of the apostolic church and as such, together with other miraculous gifts, served its purpose in attesting the presence of the Spirit at a time when such attestation was needed. Hence it was transient and disappeared when the church grew to such proportions that its very presence and power attested the Spirit's presence within it. The gift was not intended for preaching, and none of the believers in the apostolic church used it for that purpose. The one apostle who preached to so many nationalities did this without the gift of tongues. God had providentially prepared the vehicle of Greek, the world language of that time, for this purpose. Wherefore the New Testament also appeared in Greek.

As they have done in the case of the gift of healing, men have tried to regain the gift of tongues. The last abortive effort started in California, leaped to Scandinavia, ran its course there and in Germany as a Pentecostal movement, and died suddenly when its chief exponents openly confessed that they had been hoaxed by devilish spirits. Those "tongues" had been gibberish, their translation pure imagination. The devilishness consisted in no small measure in attributing this folly to the Holy Spirit.

5) **Now there were dwelling in Jerusalem Jews, men devout, from every nation of those under heaven. And when this sound occurred, the crowd came together and were confounded because they kept hearing them speaking, every single one, in his own language. And all were in amazement and kept wondering, saying: Lo, are not all these speak-**

ing Galileans? And how do we on our part hear, every one in our very language in which we were born?

Luke is concerned only with this class of Jews who were born or reared in foreign parts but had now permanently settled in the Holy City in order to end their days there. They, of course, knew and spoke Aramaic, but they knew, in some cases even still better, the native language of the land where they had dwelt so long. How dearly these Jews loved Jerusalem is evidenced by expressions such as this: "Everyone who is buried in the land of Israel is in as good case as if he were buried under the altar." "Men devout" brings out this idea, earnest and sincerely religious Jews who wanted to spend their last years near the Temple and join in the worship at this great sanctuary. Εὐλαβής, "one who takes hold well," is regularly used in this religious sense. "From every nation," etc., is not as hyperbolic as might be supposed. Few cities and towns, to say nothing of countries in the great Roman empire, were without a contingent of Jews. In his great oration in Josephus, *Wars*, 2, 16, 4, Herod Agrippa states only facts about the Jewish diaspora: "There is no people upon the habitable earth which have not some portion of you (Jews) among them."

6) It was the mighty sound that brought the crowd together at the place where the disciples were gathered. The sound identified the place. We know how quickly crowds gather. Natives of Jerusalem and pilgrims from afar may have been in the crowd, but Luke has already drawn our attention to the great number of foreign-born Jews who are of special importance in this connection. They were utterly confounded "because they kept hearing them speaking, every single one, in his own language." The imperfect brings out the continuousness of the action. Each

foreign-born Jew heard his own foreign language uttered, not once or twice, but for a considerable time. After the plural verb the singular "every single one" individualizes as this is frequently done. Luke means "in his own language" and not "dialect" just as the word used in 1:19 means "language." The list of nations following also excludes the idea that the disciples, whose own Aramaic was the Galilean dialect, were now speaking a number of other Aramaic dialects. Compare v. 11.

7) Luke heaps up the verbs describing the effect upon the hearers. The aorist συνεχύθη states the first impression: the crowd "was confounded." Then two imperfects describe the condition that followed: "they were amazed," dazed by the astounding thing they were witnessing, "and kept wondering" what it could mean and how it could be explained. So the questioning began, first as to the identity of these disciples, secondly as to how they could speak as they did, the two questions belonging together. Luke states only briefly the questioning that went through the crowd.

We need not ask how the disciples were known to be Galileans. The first inquiry, no doubt, was: "Who are these people?" And someone who knew them quickly supplied the information. The question is one of astonishment as the interjection shows. So all these speaking in all these languages were Galileans! That, of course, meant neither "Christians" nor "unlearned," connotations which "Galileans" never had; but it did mean that the disciples were not residents of Jerusalem, and it identified them as what they were. We also have no reason to think that some were not from Galilee.

8) But the fact of their being Galileans shed no light whatever on the miracle. Note that ἡμεῖς is in contrast with ἅπαντες οὗτοι. These foreign-born Jews could certainly understand Galilean Aramaic, but how

could Galileans speak all these different languages, they say, "in which we were born"? To be born "in a language" means to claim that language as one's mother tongue.

9) The list of nationalities is in apposition to the emphatic ἡμεῖς in v. 8, and should be read: "we Parthians," "we Medes," and so on down the list, each group exclaiming about itself. **Parthians and Medes and Elamites; and the Jews inhabiting Mesopotamia and Cappadocia, Pontus and Asia, both Phrygia and Pamphilia, Egypt and the parts of Libya, those along Cyrene; and temporary residents, Romans, both Jews and proselytes, Cretes and Arabians, we hear them telling with our own tongues the great things of God.**

This list is neatly arranged in three groups: 3 + 8 + 3; the group of 8 in 4 pairs. The countries mentioned describe a great circle about the Holy Land, starting on the east and swinging around westward to the north and ending in the south. A map is instructive also for some of the distances. The two articulated participles head the second and the third group.

The reading Ἰουδαίαν τε has always been a conundrum. How could "both Judea and Cappadocia" be so closely linked together? How could "Judea" occur in this list at all, which is to name only foreign-born Jews? Rather unsatisfactory explanations have been offered. Emendations have also been suggested; Syria, Armenia, Idumea. To Zahn belongs the credit for having cleared up this *crux*. Following an old Latin version, he drops τε and changes Ἰουδαίαν into Ἰουδαῖοι "Judea" into "Jews." Thus those in the second group (Mesopotamia to Cyrene) were Jews; but the third group consisted of "both Jews and proselytes." This emendation makes the grouping symmetrical and at the same time reveals how easily the corruption of the text could have crept in. "Asia" is the great province of which Ephesus was the capital. The first group names nations, the second group countries, the third again nations.

10) Egypt is paired with "the parts of Libya, those down along Cyrene." Simon, who bore the cross of Jesus, was a Cyrenian. Josephus, *Ant.* 14, 7, 2 cites an interesting passage from Strabo that shows how numerous the Jews were not only in Egypt but also in Cyrene.

The third group, like the second, is introduced with an articulated participle and presents temporary residents in Jerusalem (οἱ ἐπιδημοῦντες): Romans, Cretes, and Arabians. The participle must refer to all three. We do not think, however, that these were only pilgrims who had come for the festival, for this lasted but one day, and that they would come from a place so remote as Rome for so short a time seems improbable. These, too, "were dwelling in Jerusalem" (v. 5) but, as Luke carefully indicates, only for a time. After the 3,000 had been converted, it was an easy matter to gather the exact data that Luke records.

It seems that the apposition "both Jews and proselytes" belongs only to "Romans" and not also to "Cretes and Arabians," most certainly not to the entire two preceding groups as some have supposed. The Jews had two kinds of proselytes: "proselytes of the gate" who were not bound to submit to circumcision, who observed only the seven Noachian commandments against idolatry, blasphemy, disobedience to magistrates, murder, fornication or incest, robbery or theft, eating of blood (Gen. 9:4), and were restricted in taking part in the worship; and "proselytes of righteousness," Gentiles who became complete Jews. The latter seem to be referred to here.

11) When Luke records in regard to all these different nationalities: "we hear them telling with our

own tongues," he intends to repeat and thus to emphasize the statement made in v. 8. The emphasis is on the dative of means "with our own tongues," our own because we were born in them. In v. 8 the question was raised as to how this could be, here the fact is asserted that it, indeed, is. The persons heard are put into the genitive, the things heard into the accusative. The latter are added, namely "the great things of God." While this is a summary, we are safe in saying that the great deeds of God in Christ are referred to, plus the attributes displayed in these deeds.

In this description, which presents merely the essentials, we must retain the idea of order. All these disciples did not shout together in a Babel of foreign languages, but one spoke here, another there, and each was understood by the nationality whose language he spoke. The foreign-born Jews heard what was spoken, understood what was said. From the account it cannot be ascertained whether one disciple spoke more than one foreign language. Nor can we determine whether the disciple himself understood what he uttered and could have translated it into Aramaic. This speaking was also not preaching the gospel to this crowd. Peter did the preaching. The tongues were just what Paul states in I Cor. 14:22, a sign to those who did not believe and, as he further states, one that should be followed by prophesying (preaching), even as Peter also presently began to preach and to explain this sign to all these Jews.

12) **And all were in amazement and were in perplexity, saying one to another, What does this intend to be? Others, however, scoffing, were saying, They have been filled with sweet wine!**

"They were all in amazement" is repeated from v. 7, and emphasizes this condition. Again an imperfect is added which describes the condition of perplexity which could not get beyond the question as to what this thing could intend to be. Some texts have the optative with ἄν, potential: "What this might intend to be?" The indicative is assured and far better, for it implies that it intended to be something although the hearers could not as yet understand what. Ἄλλος πρὸς ἄλλον is not quite reciprocal (R. 747), a Latinism (R. 692). The great bulk of the hearers were sensible; they stopped with their question, gave no hasty answer, were willing to wait for the true and satisfactory answer. They were in the presence of a great miracle that transcended all reason and all experience and deeply felt the effect of it.

13) But among these foreign-born Jews were others who were of a different character (ἕτεροι, R. 749). They, too, heard the great things of God. But they passed the whole thing off with scoffing; they called the disciples tipsy with γλεῦκος, "sweet wine," not "new wine," since the last vintage was four months in the past. Ἔλεγον is descriptive; they passed this scoffing remark on. The perfect "have been filled" is intensive (R. 903) and means that they have reached the point where they are full. Wise men, sensible men! When God works, and the thing is too plain, these fellows appear with their slur. But what they say reveals only themselves and the baseness of their hearts.

PETER'S PENTECOSTAL SERMON

14) We may say that the speaking with tongues continued until the maximum effect had been attained. Then the Spirit ceased to speak through the mouths of the disciples. **But Peter, after stepping forth with the eleven, lifted up his voice and spoke exaltedly to them: Jewish men and all inhabiting Jerusalem, let this be known to you, and give ear to my utterances! For not are these drunk, as you suppose, for this is the third hour of the day. On the contrary,**

this is what has been declared through the mouth of the prophet Joel:

> And it shall be in the last days, saith God,
> I will pour out of my Spirit upon all flesh;
> And your sons and your daughters shall prophesy,
> And your young men shall see visions,
> And your old men shall dream dreams;
> Yea, and on my men slaves and on my women slaves in those days
> Will I pour out from my Spirit, and they shall prophesy.

Σταθείς is not ἀναστάς, "having arisen," as though all this occurred while the apostles and the disciples had been sitting. Peter "stepped forth," "took his stand," and the eleven with him, out in front of all the disciples, at some place where he could preach to this crowd and be heard by it. "With the eleven" means that Peter was only the spokesman for them. Matthias was with them. That the apostles should assume this leadership was the intention of Jesus when he appointed them to their office; moreover, the Spirit was now directing and empowering them. Peter had been but an ordinary fisherman, but here Luke's sketch of his sermon shows that it was a masterly, masterful, most effective discourse that was delivered without preparation or premeditation at the decisive moment on this day before an audience of thousands. This was possible only by the aid of the Spirit. Luke indicates the dignity, the solemnity, and the exalted tone when he says that Peter stepped forth with the eleven, lifted up his voice, and spoke exaltedly (the same verb that was used in v. 4) to the great assembly.

Peter uses the form of a complete address. Ἄνδρες is just as difficult to render here as it was in 1:16, and is just as respectful and dignified with Ἰουδαῖοι as with ἀδελφοί; but note the gradation and see how Peter draws nearer and nearer to his hearers as he continues to speak, advancing to "men and Israelites" in v. 22, and finally to "men and brethren" in v. 29 (see 1:16). "Ye men of Judea" in our versions is incorrect, for Ἰουδαῖοι = Jews, those identified with the entire Jewish nation. The Twelve were such Jews although not all were "of Judea." Nor is it correct to say that Peter took no cognizance of the proselytes in the audience when he said "Jews," for every proselyte of righteousness was no longer a Gentile but an out-and-out Jew.

The addition "and all inhabiting Jerusalem" should not be understood so as to exclude those who were living only temporarily in the city (οἱ ἐπιδημοῦντες in v. 10) but so as to include them. Nor is the idea of this expression such that those living in Jerusalem form a class that was distinct from other Jews who resided elsewhere, transient visitors in the city. What would be the object of such a distinction; and does not what Peter here says apply to all Jews, irrespective of residence, as explaining the Pentecostal miracle? "Jewish men" and "all inhabiting Jerusalem" are the same; the latter is only an apposition. It is added in the sense of the "men devout" used in v. 5. The exclamations uttered by these men showed that they were foreign-born Jews, yet their devoutness had impelled them to transfer their homes to the Holy City. Even those residing here temporarily were here because of the same motive. Peter's address makes that plain and honors them by the statement: "All you who love Jerusalem so much as to have come here to live." A participle in apposition has the article even when it does not occur in an address (R. 1107).

Peter, however, speaks to these devout Jews with all authority: "Let this be known to you and give ear to my utterances!" Note the same authority in 4:10

when he is facing the Sanhedrin. Here is no timidity, no uncertainty but only solid certainty and full warrant. Peter is stating divine realities and makes no apologies for them. "This" = "my utterances" = all that follows in the sermon. Peter uses excellent psychology, he meets the questioning of his auditors squarely, without circumlocution. His authoritative tone is enforced by the full impact of what he says.

He even uses excellent homiletics. He states his theme clearly: "This is what has been declared by the mouth of the prophet Joel." Stating it in advance of his text is proper; you may do the same. Then comes Peter's tremendous text. He marks the two parts of his sermon most distinctly, at v. 22 and at v. 29. They clearly expound the vital point of this text for these particular hearers — no homiletics was ever better. The conclusion is brief, direct, and powerful, v. 36. In order to get the full effect of this sermon put yourself into Peter's place and think how you would have met the situation that morning before that audience.

15) With one stroke Peter quashes the scoffers. Only a few readers get the full force of Peter's reference to "the third hour of the day," our nine o'clock in the morning. Following Exod. 16:8, the Jews ate only bread in the morning; the Targum says, not until after the morning sacrifice, hence at about ten; and meat only in the evening at the δεῖπνον or main meal of the day. They drank wine only when they ate meat, which means at this evening meal. This is the sense of Eccles. 10:16, 17. The godlessness of the princes "who eat in the morning" consists in this that they eat all sorts of food, especially also meat, and with it drink wine already in the morning, hence "for drunkenness"; but godly princes "eat in due season," meat, wine, etc., in the evening. "It is the third hour of the day." Yet these scoffers claim that all these

disciples had already partaken of a great meal, not only with wine, but with far too much of it! The very keenness of this one word of reply shows the full clarity of Peter's mind. Peter speaks for "these," pointing to them; he does not need to speak for himself. Note how οὐ is placed far forward in the sentence, putting it in the strongest possible opposition to ἀλλά.

16) The idea of a drunken jargon becomes even blasphemous when Peter states the reality back of this speaking with foreign tongues: "on the contrary, this is what has been declared through the mouth of the prophet Joel," i. e., this that Peter's hearers have seen is the fulfillment of Joel's great prophecy. Many times we read "it has been written," and now in the same sense "it has been declared or spoken," the perfect tense always has its strong present connotation: once spoken (written) the thing stands so now and forever. The speaker implied in the passive is God (v. 17: "saith God"), and διά here, as in every other case of quotation, states the medium or instrument used by God, the prophet or the mouth of the prophet. This passive plus διά, wherever they occur in Scripture, state in brief the entire doctrine of Verbal Inspiration, to wit, that in all Scripture the real speaker is God, and that the holy writers are only his media, instruments, mouthpieces.

17) Joel prophesied about 870 B. C. Peter quotes Joel 2:28-32, compare the A. V. for the Hebrew; the LXX and Peter have a few longer statements. Thus "in the last days" = "afterward," Hebrew; "after these things," LXX. Peter's wording, however, is interpretative, explaining what the Hebrew "afterword" really means, namely the last period of the world which is ushered in by the first coming of Christ and continues until his second coming for judgment. It is with this time in view that God made his promise

regarding the pouring out of the Spirit. So also Peter inserts "saith God" in order to make plain that it is he who promised, "I will pour out of my Spirit upon all flesh." It is this pouring out that had just occurred (v. 33). "Upon all flesh" is universal but not absolute; v. 38 shows both, "everyone" may receive the Holy Spirit but only by repentance and faith. "Flesh" = men as distinguished from angels by having flesh or a body (Rom. 1:3; John 1:14); but men in their sinfulness and their frailty. Here σάρξ is not in contrast with πνεῦμα in the ethical sense. With abstract words "every" and "all" flow together, hence ἐπὶ πᾶσαν σάρκα needs no article in order to mean "upon all flesh." "I will pour out" implies the full gift of the Spirit and thus extends as far as "all flesh." The Spirit who came upon a few disciples at Pentecost has filled others of all languages in all lands the world over and is still extending his activity to more of them. Once confined to the narrow limits of Judaism for such operations as were preparatory to Christ's redemption, the Spirit, now that redemption was accomplished, went out to men generally and extended the church to the ends of the earth (1:8) and symbolized this at Pentecost by letting the disciples speak in many languages.

The chief effect of the Spirit's activity is always prophesying, not in the narrow sense of foretelling future events, but in the broad and far more important sense of voicing the saving and blessed will of God to men everywhere. In I Cor. 14 Paul speaks of this as the best and highest gift of the Spirit; and Luther writes: "What are all other gifts together compared to this gift, that the Spirit of God himself, the eternal God, comes down into our hearts, yea, into our bodies and dwells in us, rules, guides, leads us! Thus now, as concerning this passage of the prophet, prophesying, visions, dreams are *all one thing,* namely the knowledge of God through Christ, which the Holy Spirit kindles and makes to burn through the Word of the gospel." The fact that Luther is correct is shown by Peter when in v. 18 he adds to both the Hebrew and the LXX texts: "and they shall prophesy." This is interpretative and repeats "they shall prophesy" from v. 17.

"Your sons and your daughters" is amplified by "your young men" and "your old men," the possessives referring to the Jews to whom the Spirit first came through the apostles. The three lines of Hebrew poetry are parallel and synonymous statements, which means that all the predicates belong to all the subjects, sons, daughters, young men, old men. So the three predicates form a unit, each predicate saying the same thing with variation, as each subject is only a variation. All shall prophesy, confess, and tell the gospel, and thus the young men shall see glorious visions of its progress and its victories, and the old men shall dream dreams of its blessedness and its power, literally: "dream with dreams," a Hebraism in the translation and not a case of a Greek cognate object.

18) In καί γε the particle is climacteric or ascensive, which we try to render by "yea and," meaning, "on top of all that has been said." This emphasis applies to the two phrases: "on my men slaves and on my women slaves." In v. 17 the four ὑμῶν refer to the Jewish nation. What a blessed thing it is to have *their* sons and *their* daughters prophesy, etc. But they also have a relation to the God who made this promise and fulfills it with reference to them: they are *his* slaves, etc. And "slaves," δοῦλοι, brings out the idea that they belong wholly to God, are wholly subject and obedient to his will. Jesus himself was the ʽEbed Yahweh, "Servant of Jehovah," and all believers are in a similar position.

Are these still only Jewish believers? Some think so. Yet "all flesh" precedes, the Spirit was to reach out into all the world. Hence we are inclined to think that this "yea and" introduces all who belong to God by faith in Christ, Gentiles plus Jews combined into one. All of them shall have the Spirit and shall prophesy. The Hebrew has: I will pour out "my Spirit" (the accusative); the LXX and Peter the partitive: "of or from my Spirit." We take the sense to be the same, for to have the Spirit is to have some of his power and his gifts, no man can assimilate all of them.

A peculiar question arises as to the difference between the Hebrew and Peter's quotation. The Hebrew has this gradation: your sons — your daughters — your old men — your young men (these two in this order) — the (men) servants — the handmaids. The last two seem to refer only to the Jewish servants. Delitzsch calls them slaves and says that in the Old Testament no slave had the gift of prophecy. He states that the translators of the LXX could not understand how slaves should have this gift and therefore added "my," making them God's *douloi* and *doulai*. But this does not remove the difficulty. For most of these slaves of the Jews were Gentiles, and for even these to receive the Spirit implied that the Gentile world would be blessed. And Peter is right: these persons would no longer be just slaves but *my* (God's own) slaves, even as all believers, whether they are Jews or Gentiles, are purchased and won by Christ in order to be his own and to live under him.

19) Peter must quote Joel's prophecy in full because the second part of it states how long the Spirit, poured out at Pentecost, will continue his work in the world, and because the last line opens the door of salvation to everyone who, in repentance and faith, **calls on the Lord** (v. 38).

> And I will give wonders in heaven above
> And signs on the earth below,
> Blood and fire and vapor of smoke;
> The sun shall be turned into darkness,
> And the moon into blood
> Before the Lord's day comes,
> The one great and manifest,
> And it shall be, everyone who shall call on the name of the Lord shall be saved.

It must be well understood that the prophets always viewed the two comings of Christ together without having the interval between the two revealed to them. We have a clear example in the Baptist who in Luke 3:16 speaks of Pentecost and in 3:17 of the final judgment. This also caused a difficulty for him. When he saw Jesus doing works of grace only and none of judgment he wondered whether another was yet to come to perform the work of judgment. Joel's description recalls that of Jesus given in Luke 21:9-11, 25, 26. Joel combines the two, "wonders in heaven above and signs on the earth below," and Peter adds the words "signs," "above," and "below" in an interpretative way.

Τέρας = "wonder," a startling, amazing portent or prodigy. The pagan world also had such portents. It seems that for this reason the New Testament never uses "wonders" alone but always conjoins the word with "signs" or with "miracles." Many of God's signs are, indeed, also portentous wonders, but they are never wonders alone, they are divine indications and thus lie on a far higher plane than pagan portents. "Sign," σημεῖον (σημαίνω, to make known by a σῆμα), is always used with a strong ethical connotation by pointing to the significance of the occurrence and not merely to its strangeness. Hence the word is also used alone. In the parallelism of Hebrew poetry the wonders are not restricted to the heavens, nor the signs to the earth, but in both spheres both shall occur and shall at the same time be astonishing and very significant. The sign language of God cannot be misunderstood, every startling and disquieting phenomenon proclaims that heaven and earth must pass away and all their affairs be wound up.

"Blood," etc., are only specifications, a few of the arresting signs that occur on earth. "Blood and fire and vapor of smoke" appear together at the time of wars and in great calamities in nature. As far as bloody wars are concerned, we have seen this sign often enough, and the Scriptures hold out no hope that it will not be repeated until the very end.

20) The turning of the sun into utter darkness and of the moon into a blood-red glow until its light, too, is extinguished, is the ushering in of the end of the world itself as Jesus described it more fully in Matt. 24:29. In Joel's prophecy this is indicated by the final phrase; πρίν is best regarded as an adverb-preposition, and the infinitive as a noun (R. 1091; B.-D. 395 has the older explanation). "The Lord's day" is the final day of the world, it is peculiarly his because it is the day on which he shall judge the world. But it is no longer a mundane day of so many hours by the clock. The whole universe shall be utterly changed, and time shall have ceased. It is called "day" (the genitive "Lord's" making it definite) because human language supplies no better word. The two adjectives are added by the article and are like an appositional climax (R. 776): "the one that is great and manifest." "Great" in the absolute sense, the positive being stronger than a superlative would be; "manifest" as revealing what this day is to be to the whole universe. The Hebrew adjective is "terrible," and this was translated "manifest" by the LXX. The Spirit allowed Peter to retain the latter because it was satisfactory and appropriate. In fact, the ἐπιφάνεια of the Parousia is emphasized repeatedly, II Thess. 2:8. Κύριος = *Yahweh*; it is his

day in which he will judge the world through Christ, Acts 17:31.

21) The really important statement in Joel's prophecy is the final one which declares that during all this time, from Pentecost to the Lord's day at the end, everyone who calls on the Lord shall be saved. It is this promise that Peter applies in v. 38. Καὶ ἔσται, as in v. 17, is the Hebrew *vehayah* and needs no connective to link it with what follows (R. 1042). "It shall be" is a promise that cannot be broken. What it includes has already existed for nearly two thousand years. "To call upon the Lord's name" (the verb is the middle) means to call him to our aid, i. e., in our spiritual need. The ὄνομα or "name" is that by which the Lord alone is known as the One who has the help we need. This name is his gospel which must first be brought to us in order to reveal the Lord in all his grace in Christ and thus to kindle in us the desire for that grace and help and cause us to call upon his gracious name.

Note the universality in Joel's "everyone who," etc., and ὃς ἄν (ἐάν) indicates expectancy, it is assumed that many will call on the Lord's name. Here is the commentary on "all flesh" mentioned in v. 17. Here grace flows out also to all the Gentiles. "Everyone who" and all similar expressions of universality are like blank spaces in mighty bank drafts which are signed by the Lord and into which he invites us to write our own name by faith. If we do, the draft will without fail be honored by him. Here we meet the great verb "shall be saved," the passive implying the Lord as the Savior. In this verb as in all its derivatives (Savior, salvation, those that have been saved) lies the idea of mortal danger, a mighty act rescuing from that danger, and then also the blessed power that continues to keep in safety forever. The verb has its full meaning here. Its future tense is not to be dated at the last day, but this salvation begins the instant the sinner calls upon the saving name of the Lord. Peter's sermon, as here sketched by Luke, brings to his hearers all the actuality of this great prophecy of Joel as on this Pentecostal day and hereafter applying to his auditors for their own personal salvation.

22) Israelite men, hear these words! Jesus, the Nazarene, a man accredited from God to you by power works and wonders and signs which God worked through him in your midst even as you yourselves know, him, delivered up by the determinate counsel and foreknowledge of God, you, through lawless men's hand fastening up, made away with; whom God raised up by loosing the pangs of death for the reason that it was not possible that he be held by it.

On the address compare v. 14 and note that the apposition "Israelites" is a name of the highest honor for Jews which recalls Jacob who prevailed and had his name changed to "Israel," contender with God. So "Israel" and "Israelites" involved the covenant and the highest hopes of Judaism. To call his hearers "Israelite men" was an appeal that they now show themselves worthy of that name. "Hear these words" with its decisive aorist imperative for hearing that actually grasps continues the tone of authority from v. 14.

In one masterly sentence Peter presents Jesus who is back of the Pentecostal miracle and back of the whole prophecy of Joel. The directness, completeness, conciseness with which the essentials about Jesus are combined into one sentence deserve fullest appreciation. The name is put first: "Jesus, the Nazarene." It is the ordinary name by which he was commonly known, the personal name "Jesus" with "Nazarene," from the town of his long residence, added in order to distinguish him from others who had the same personal name: for

Yᵉhoshuʻa, later *Yᵉshuʻa* (Joshua = Jesus), was a name that was frequently chosen for sons and meant "*Yahweh* is help," i. e., on or through whom *Yahweh* effects salvation. So also Peter says "a man," his object being to recall Jesus to his hearers as they had seen him so often during his earthly life.

"Even as you yourselves know" appeals to the knowledge of the hearers of the tremendous fact that was so prominent in the case of Jesus: his miracles. Peter purposely uses three terms when referring to them, the three applying to each miracle, yet the three accentuating the great number of the miracles. They were δυνάμεις, τέρατα, σημεῖα, works of supernatural power, creating wonder and amazement but full of heavenly, divine significance as works of divine grace. The whole Jewish world rang with the story of these miracles. By them, Peter says, this man "has been accredited from God to you," and he fortifies this by stating that "God wrought them through him in your midst," οἷς being attracted from ἅ. This no honest and sincere Jew would or could deny (John 3:2; 9:31-33), and when the Pharisees attempted it by claiming they were wrought by Beelzebul, Jesus showed the senselessness of their falsehood.

The fact that God wrought the miracles does not place Jesus on the same level with the apostles who also wrought miracles. It is equally true that Jesus wrought them by his own power as no other man ever wrought a true miracle. All the *opera ad extra* are ascribed equally to the divine Persons. The point of here ascribing the miracles of Jesus to God is not to indicate the source of their power but to bring out their purpose in regard to Jesus: they accredited him to the Jews, for which reason also they were wrought in their midst, so all of them might accept them as accreditations. The perfect participle "having been shown forth or accredited" has its usual strong present force, "still standing thus accredited." Note the juxtaposition: "from God to you." As what Jesus thus still stands accredited to all Israelites worthy of the name the statement itself makes declaration, namely as sent to Israel by God to be for Israel all that he claimed to be and was.

23) The emphatic τοῦτον, "him," "this one," sums up all that has been said: this man so mightily and publicly accredited from God — *him* the Jews murdered! That was their answer to God's seals and accreditations. Here Peter preached the law with its crushing power in order to bring about the conviction of sin and genuine contrition. He in no way softens his words since this would only defeat their purpose. He states the cold, damnable fact: "him, through lawless men's hand fastening up (namely to the cross), you made away with," which means murdered. The ἄνομοι are pagans who are without the Torah or νόμος and follow their pagan gods and heathen ideas. "Through the hand" is Hebraistic for "by means of." The aorist participle προσπήξαντες is used in an absolute sense and may be rendered "having crucified"; ἀναιρέω is often used in the ugly sense of to kill, murder, make away with one. The killing of Jesus by the Sanhedrin through Pilate was an act of the Jewish nation (Matt. 27:25) that involved every Jew who, when the act was made known to him, did not completely disavow and disallow it. Until Peter's hearers did this, he had to uphold the charge: "him you made away with."

But Peter has far more to say; he had to insert the claim that this bloody deed did not happen accidentally or only by the damnable will of the Jews. God could have prevented it in a second. This murder of Jesus happened only because Jesus was "delivered up (handed out to the Jews) by the deliberate counsel and foreknowledge of God." God abandoned Jesus to the murderous Jews in order that they might wreak their hatred upon him (John 19:11); this God did for his own mighty purpose: by the death of his Son to redeem the world. Peter wisely takes his hearers step by step and leads them carefully to faith. Any sincere Jew had to agree that no one such as Jesus was could have been killed as Jesus was unless God were in some way back of his death. Nor would any Jew use this fact in order to absolve his nation of blame for the killing. Ἔκδοτον is a verbal adjective from the aorist stem of δίδωμι and is equal to a passive participle.

In what way God delivered Jesus up to die on the cross is indicated by the weighty datives of means. The success of the betrayal by Judas, which placed Jesus into the power of the Sanhedrin, was due to no cunning or power of men (Matt. 26:53, 54; Luke 22:53b). The death of Jesus was due to "the determinate counsel and foreknowledge of God"; the perfect participle ὡρισμένῃ, "having been fixed or determined on," places the counsel of God back into eternity. God formed his plan of salvation, which involved the sacrificial death of his Son, in eternity and therefore alone gave him over to the murderous Jews. The divine counsel comes first, and on it rests the divine, infallible foreknowledge. The relation of the two is not one of time — in God no before and after exists — but of inward connection. When we consider the actions of men, this relation is reversed; what God determines in eternity regarding them rests on his infallible foreknowledge. "Counsel" and "foreknowledge" are not identical; to make them one and the same is to misunderstand both. The "foreknowledge" is misunderstood when it is regarded as an action of the will, a determination to do something and thus knowing it in advance. Such is the idea of C.-K. 256: *im voraus gefasster Beschluss*, "a decree formed in advance"; for according to C.-K. 226 βουλή means *Ratschluss*, and the fact that this resolve or decree was formed in advance need not be said

24) Here we have the first apostolic preaching of the resurrection of Jesus. Although it is couched in only a relative clause, its force is tremendous. You made away with him — God raised him up! You did it by crucifying him — God did the opposite by loosing the pangs of death! These were hammer blows of the law. So directly were these Jews opposed to God, and God to them. The genitive in "pangs of death" is subjective; ὠδῖνας are birth pains. The idea is that, when Christ died, death was taken with birth pains and suffered them until God delivered death of Christ by raising him up, thus "loosing the birth pains," ending their strain. "The birth pains of death" is generally regarded as being cited from Ps. 18:5, and Ps. 116:3, where the LXX translated *cheble maveth*, "snares of death," "birth pains of death" (the English of Ps. 116:3 also has "sorrows of death"). In the plurals occurring in these two passages the word "snares" and "pains" are indistinguishable, *chêbel* = snare; *chĕbel* = birth pain. But Peter is not quoting either psalm; he is using this expression of his own accord, and no one can prove that he borrowed it from a psalm, or that Luke translated Peter's "snares of death" with the LXX's "birth pains of death." We need scarcely add that for Christ these pains ended at the moment of his death. A few texts have the reading "hades" instead of "death."

Luke alone uses καθότι which here has the force of διότι, "because," "for the reason that." Peter states merely the fact that it was not possible that Jesus should be held by death; he then proceeds to prove this from the prophecy of David and thus once more proclaims the resurrection of Jesus and along with it his exaltation, which also is proved from David's prophecy. Thus Peter reveals the contents of the counsel and foreknowledge of God which gave Jesus into death in order to destroy death by atoning for sin in which lies the power of death. The deity of Jesus becomes evident in this exaltation which enabled Jesus to send down the Holy Spirit with those miraculous results which Peter's hearers see and hear (v. 33).

25) First, then, the proof that, according to the Scriptures, Jesus could not be held by death. Peter is speaking to Jews, hence he quotes a word of David's from the Scriptures. The proof lies in the fact that what God foretold regarding Christ must come to pass. Some critics place Ps. 16 later than the time of David. Peter here contradicts them: "David says," etc.; Paul does likewise in Acts 13:35. The testimony of Delitzsch is to the same effect. The external marks as well as the internal ("David" in the title; the language, tone, poetical fervor, etc.) point to the Davidic authorship of this psalm. Just what situation in the life of David this psalm pictures cannot be historically determined. It was most probably recovery from a severe sickness which prevented David from entering the reconstructed castle on Zion (cf. Delitzsch on Ps. 30).

The LXX is quoted quite exactly which agrees with the Hebrew and expands only a phrase here and there for the sake of clearness. On the general subject of quotations we may say the following: Where it seems necessary the New Testament writers translate the original, or correct the LXX according to the original, or translate interpretatively, and often use the LXX without change. The Holy Spirit guided them throughout, and he has full and free power to deal with his Word in the way that best suits his purposes. He may restate in other words, add to, abbreviate, interpret, etc. We do the same, not only with our own words, but also with those of others and even with Scripture. To demand mechanical, literal exactness of the Holy Spirit and the New Testament writers is to set up for them alone a peculiar canon against which all sensible writers must rebel. The quotation from Joel in v. 17, 18 is reproduced with greater freedom than the one now cited from David. This fact alone shows how well the writers knew their Old Testament even when they did not quote it according to the very letter. See *Introduction to the Critical Study and Knowledge of the Holy Scriptures*, Thomas Hartwell Horne, 7th Ed., II, 281, where the Hebrew, LXX, and New Testament passages are printed in parallel columns, in the original and in translation, together with other helpful material.

> **For David says regarding him,**
> **I saw the Lord before me always**
> **Because he is at my right in order that I shall not be moved.**
> **Because of this glad was my heart, and jubilate did my tongue.**
> **And besides also my flesh shall tent on hope**
> **Because thou wilt not abandon my soul unto hades**
> **Nor wilt give thine Holy One to see corruption.**
> **Thou didst make known to me ways of life;**
> **Thou wilt fill me with gladness in the company of thy countenance.**

In προορώμην, the middle voice, the imperfect tense, and the preposition πρό each contribute their part so that we have no equivalent in English: for himself, all along, every time he let his glance move in front of him, David saw the Lord ἐνώπιόν μου, right before his eyes, and that "always." Nor had he the least difficulty, "because he was at my right" as advocates used to sit at the right side of the clients they supported, "in order that I should not be moved," made to toss to and fro in uncertainty and in fear. The same thought is found in Ps. 23:4: "Thou art with me; thy rod and thy staff they comfort me." The phrase ἐκ δεξιῶν is idiomatic, has no article, always has the plural, and extends "out from" his own right side to where he saw the Lord (*Yahweh*) with the eyes of faith. The aorist speaks of actually being moved. All that this vision meant for David he now unfolds.

26) His heart, in the Scriptures always the center of the personality, was filled with gladness, the same verb that is used for making merry at a celebration in Luke 15:32; and his tongue jubilated, exulted in songs and expressions of praise. The Hebrew has "my glory jubilated." But we question whether the Hebrew "heart, glory, flesh" is identical with the triad found in I Thess. 5:23:."spirit, soul, body." From the abundance of the heart the mouth speaketh; heart and tongue go together. Spirit and heart are not the same. It seems that the LXX translated "my glory" "my tongue" because "my glory" was used with reference to any illustrious bodily member, especially where this glory is said to jubilate.

Both ἔτι and δέ indicate that what is now added about "my flesh" is the counterpart to both previous statements; heart and tongue are combined as one concept, flesh is the other. "Besides" (ἔτι) what he had to say about his heart and tongue David has something great to say about even his flesh (καί), and this is naturally of a different nature (δέ) than what he had to say of his heart and tongue. His flesh, meaning his body, "shall put down its tent on hope." The verb means "to put down a tent," "to camp in order to rest," and thus simply "to rest awhile." This verb implies only a transient sojourn; a tent is not a permanent structure. "Rest" in the A. V. is more correct than "dwell" in the R. V. The temporary tenting comprises both the bodily life of David and the stay of his body in the grave. In both conditions his flesh makes its tent and camp "on hope," on this as the ground (ἐπί). What that hope contains follows in the next line. The point to be noted is that making camp matches hope, both continue only for a time; when hope reaches its fulfillment, it becomes joy and gratitude.

27) This hope of David's has solid reality under it and thus cannot end in disappointment as do the hopes of the ungodly which have no other foundation than the desires of the ungodly themselves. Jehovah, who has ever been at David's right to keep him from being shaken by doubt and by fear, will never forsake him at the time of death. His hope is sure: "Because thou wilt not abandon my soul unto hades." When David comes to die, *Yahweh* will not abandon his soul or permit it to sink into hell, the place of the damned. *Denn nicht preisgeben wirst du meine Seele dem Hades*, Delitzsch, who also correctly defines the Hebrew verb of which ἐγκαταλείψεις is a correct translation: the abandonment here denied is not merely one which leaves a person in a terrible place after he has fallen there, but one which never even permits him to get into such a place. "It is thus the hope not to die or, dying, not to die, which David utters."

Here ψυχή is in contrast with σάρξ, "my flesh," and not with πνεῦμα or "spirit" and thus refers to the soul as the entire immaterial part of man which in life animates the body and also contains the spirit and personality. Thus body and soul constitute the entire human being. When *psyche* and *pneuma* are paired, the former refers to the immaterial part only as animating the body (translated "life"), the latter to the same immaterial part as representing the ἐγώ or personality and as being able to receive impressions from the divine *Pneuma* or Holy Spirit. From this lower sense of ψυχή the Greek derives its adjective ψυχικός for which we have no equivalent derived from "soul," since the English does not use "soul" in this lower sense of the Greek but only as almost the equivalent of "spirit";

thus we are compelled to translate the adjective "carnal," for it means disregarding the higher nature of the *pneuma* and yielding wholly to the promptings of the animated body. David says, Jehovah will not permit his soul, when at death it is separated from his body, to fall "into hades," εἰς ᾅδην (the better reading), or εἰς ᾅδου, supply δόμον, "into the house of hades."

Sheol is here translated "hades." The word *sheol* is used in a wide sense: at death all men go into *sheol*, and around the word in this sense cluster all the dark, painful, dreadful things that we still associate with death, leaving this bright world, and entering the grave. Neither the Greek nor the English has a true equivalent for *sheol* in this sense; the Greek used its "hades," we use our "grave." It was the best that translation could do.

Sheol is, however, used also in a narrow sense. It is applied peculiarly to the wicked, and all connotations and descriptions are according. The second use complicated matters still more as far as translation is concerned. The Greek again used "hades," but the English could not again use "grave," it used "hell," the place of the damned. As translations of *sheol* both "grave" and "hell" are interpretative and as such perfectly proper. But here confusion sets in. Some retain the Hebrew *sheol* in all passages of the English Old Testament where this word occurs, and "hades" in all the New Testament passages. Pagan ideas are introduced. We are told that the Hebrews had no clearer ideas than their pagan neighbors. Their *sheol* was uniformly "the nether world," the *Totenreich*, the realm of the dead. It was thought to consist of two parts, an upper and a lower part, the one being less terrible than the other. Everything in the Old Testament that clashes with this idea is ignored. This procedure is carried into the New Testament, where it begins with Dives and Lazarus in Luke 16:22, etc. "Hades" is retained in the sense of *sheol* and is now an intermediate place between heaven and hell. Hither all the dead are still said to go, the godly into the upper part, for which the term "Paradise" is appropriated from Luke 23:43, the wicked into the lower part which is not specifically named. Again, all that disagrees with this view — and there is very much, indeed, in the New Testament — is ignored or left as a contradiction.

Fancies go still farther. At his death Jesus is thought to have entered the Paradise part of this intermediate place in order to stay there until his resurrection. Some call this his descent into hell (hades). It is also stated that he opened this place and released all the souls in it so they might enter into heaven; as a consequence this place is now vacant, the godly now going directly to heaven. But the ungodly still enter the nether part. It is not hell but only like hell. But some extend the idea still farther: in this lower part of the intermediate place conversion is still possible. A kind of infernal missionary work is said to be in progress. Jesus himself is thought to have started it in I Pet. 3:19; 4:6.

Not only David's hope is thereby darkened, but the entire Christian hope as well. Two places, and only two, exist in the other world, heaven for all believers, hell with its damnation for all unbelievers. The only difference between the two Testaments is this: the New is clearer than the old on this subject as on all others. In Peter's sermon the New is made to bring out the full reality contained in the Old.

The translation of our versions is unfortunate: *"Thou wilt not leave my soul in hell (hades)."* This reads as though David's soul would, indeed, enter hell (hades), but that God would eventually remove his soul from this place. Even a scholar like Zahn attempts to maintain this sense of the verb. He weakens the force of the Hebrew *'azab* by saying that it *might* mean "abandon" but claims the Greek verb *must* mean "to leave." David is thus thought to say of himself and of Christ that at death their souls would enter, not heaven, but the realm where all the dead are and would be released from this place by means of the resurrection. But did Christ, according to this notion, not take all the souls of the Old Testament saints out of the upper part of this realm of the dead? And David would have been released ahead of his resurrection! And does not the Old Testament itself teach with all clearness the resurrection of also the ungodly, Dan. 12:2? And what about the parallelism? If David's soul entered hades (hell), then Jehovah's Holy One saw corruption. Οὐ — οὐδέ are decisive in negating both lines and not merely the main verbs but also their objects. The soul of David did not enter hell as little as Jehovah's Holy One saw corruption. He preserved both from both.

God, indeed, "gave out" (implied in ἔκδοτον in v. 23) Jesus to be made away with through death, but David already said, "He will not give him to see corruption." He will be dead, indeed, and entombed as one dead, but no corruption, decay, putrefaction would touch his holy body while it lay in the tomb. Recall how the women hurried to the tomb on Sunday morning, fearing that even then they might find corruption too far advanced to handle the body. "To see" corruption means to experience it. Delitzsch notes the major sense of sight which is figuratively employed as the sensus communis by which all experiences, active and passive, are perceived. In his *Biblische Psychologie*, 234, he shows how by this verb and by the singulars eye and ear (not plurals) the Scriptures go back to the unit *sensorium* underlying all perception and all experience. We need not puzzle ourselves about *shachath* and its translation διαφθορά, "corruption." The Hebrew means both "pit" and "corruption," the noun being a derivation from two verbs (Ed. Koenig, *Hebraeisches und aramaeisches*

Woerterbuch, 495). Note the contrast: Holy One — corruption.

Note the far more important contrast: *my* soul — *thy* Holy One. Let us admit it that the former refers to David and to Christ, the latter only to Christ as Peter also proceeds to explain. David's body decayed; not even the slightest bit of decay touched the body of Jesus. "Holy One" (*qadosh,* ἅγιος) is often applied to God, especially by Isaiah; also to Christ in Mark 1:24; Luke 4:34; Acts 3:14; I John 2:20; here and in Acts 13:35, ὅσιος (Trench: opposite of "polluted") is used. "Holy One" thus predicates the holiness of deity of Jesus; it was thus that he did not see corruption. The body of the incarnate Holy One could not be touched by the decay which touches even the bodies of the saints because they are still sinners. David thus prophesied in regard to Christ and his stay in the tomb. And now we see the "hope" on which his flesh rested. Death would bring corruption to his body, but at death his soul would escape hell and enter heaven because Jehovah's Holy One would not see corruption when he would be given into death (v. 23). The body of Jesus, untouched by corruption, would arise on the third day, sin and death being conquered forever. David's body, living or dead, thus rested in the hope, in the hope of its resurrection at the last day, and at death his soul would enter glory.

28) It is thus that the Lord made known "life's ways" to David (the Hebrew has the singular), and we may take the genitive in either sense: "the ways that belong to life," are characteristic of it, or "that lead to life," i. e., life eternal. These ways are repentance, faith, obedience, and hope; and "life" (ζωή, so often in John) is the life principle itself, life in God, with God, in and with Christ who is "the Life," i. e., the fount of life for us. "Didst make known" goes far beyond the intellect; no one can have the knowledge of life's ways

except by having that life and in its living power walking in those ways. The thought is not merely reaching that life hereafter, but having it, enjoying it, walking in its ways now.

The Hebrew: "Satiation with joys is with (or at) thy countenance," i. e., is had where the light of Jehovah's countenance or presence is felt, is rendered in the Greek: "Thou wilt fill me with gladness in company with ($\mu\epsilon\tau\acute{a}$) thy countenance." The thought is the same as it is in the Hebrew. The future tense "wilt fill me" means already now and, of course, vastly more after death.

29) Peter adds an exegesis of the main point of David's prophecy. **Men and brethren (1:16; 2:14), it is permitted to state with openness to you concerning the patriarch David that he both died and was buried, and his tomb is with us to this day. Therefore, as being a prophet and as knowing that God swore to him with an oath to seat one out of the fruit of his loins on his throne, foreseeing it, he made utterance concerning the resurrection of the Christ that he neither was abandoned unto hades nor did his flesh see corruption.**

Peter first of all makes very clear that David's words were not fulfilled in his own person but were prophecy and dealt with the resurrection of the Messiah. He is deferential: "it is permitted," etc. = "permit me to state openly to you" as my brethren who know that I mean nothing derogatory when I say "concerning the patriarch David," whom I revere with you as a patriarch, the progenitor of a royal line in Israel, first "that he both died," ended his life, "and was buried," these two going together, and secondly, as well-known evidence of the fact, "his tomb is with us to this day." Neh. 3:16 mentions David's tomb; Josephus speaks of it several times. It was about a thousand years old at this time, and Dio Cassius 64, 14 reports that it fell into ruins during Hadrian's reign in the year 133, after which it is no longer heard of. It was at Jerusalem — mute but incontrovertible evidence that Ps. 16 was not fulfilled in David. David's body saw corruption. It was dust.

30) The possibility that David could have been mistaken in his psalm is not for one moment entertained. The conclusion (οὖν) to be drawn is far otherwise, one to which all of Peter's hearers at once agree: "as being a prophet . . . he made utterance," and that "concerning the resurrection of the Christ." The verb ὑπάρχω is often used in the sense of "to be." But Peter must add an important point, the one on account of which he already called David a "patriarch." When David wrote that psalm he did it "knowing that God swore to him with an oath to seat one out of the fruit of his loins on his throne." The form of the participle εἰδώς is perfect, but the sense is always present. "Swore with an oath" may be pleonastic but it is stronger than the verb without this dative of means (R. 1205, 531). See II Sam. 7:12; Ps. 132:11. The phrase ἐκ καρποῦ is partitive: "one out of the fruit," etc., and should be regarded as the object of καθίσαι and not as the subject (R. V.); the additions found in the A. V. have far too little support to be considered. Peter needed to say no more for Jews. They knew that "one out of the fruit of his loins" (the Greek for "loins" is always singular) referred to the Messiah. They, indeed, conceived his throne to be one of earthly grandeur only and had to be taught Luke 1:32, 33.

31) "Foreseeing it," Peter says, David made utterance as he did. He foresaw what he recorded in Ps. 16. This psalm is quoted by Peter, and thus Peter says that David made this utterance "concerning the resurrection of the Christ." As a prophet he spoke by revelation and by inspiration; hence ἐλάλησε, "he made utterance," is the fitting verb. How fully David himself compre-

hended his own utterance is quite immaterial. It is Peter himself who tells us how far beyond the comprehension of the prophets some of their utterances were, I Pet. 1:10-12; II Pet. 1:20, 21. We have no interest in reducing this comprehension to a minimum or in searching out and speculating on its degree. The point is that we ourselves see and believe the literal fulfillment. In the case of David the word was half fulfilled, namely only the clause that his soul would not be abandoned unto hades. In the case of the Christ both were to be fulfilled, this statement and the other that his flesh should not see corruption. Note how Peter repeats the double statement, retaining the sense but not the identical words. Most important, he uses aorist tenses where David had futures: "that he neither was abandoned unto hades, nor did his flesh see corruption." These historical aorists are in place, for they declare that the fulfillment has come in the resurrection of the Christ who is Jesus.

32) **This Jesus God raised up, whereof all we are witnesses.** In "this Jesus," who is presented fully in v. 22 as to his accreditation and his death according to God's counsel, the prophecy of David, which was unfulfilled in his own case, was truly and completely fulfilled: "This Jesus God raised up." It is he and he alone whose flesh did not see corruption. He is the Holy One of *Yahweh* in David's prophecy, the One out of David's loins, "the Christ," fully and gloriously proved so by God's raising him up. By this act God sealed him as the Christ. Note that in this its very first presentation the entire apostolic message centers in the resurrection of Jesus. God centered it there already in David's prophecy, then again in fulfilling that prophecy in the case of Jesus, I Cor. 15:13, etc.

All that Peter needs to add is the clause: "whereof all we are witnesses," namely the whole body of the disciples, all of whom had seen the risen Lord, 500 at one time in Galilee; οὗ must be "of which," of the act of raising up Jesus, and not "of whom," of his person. In order to see the force of this clause for all these Jews, dwellers in Jerusalem, we must recall the full publicity of the death of Jesus (v. 23), plus the report on his empty tomb which the Sanhedrists tried to explain away (Matt. 28:11-15), thereby aiding the publication in the city of what had occurred in Joseph's tomb. The lie that disciples had stolen the body from under the eyes of the Roman guard was too shallow. All that Peter needed to do was to flash the truth on those hearers in connection with David's prophecy. To this day that empty tomb establishes the resurrection of Jesus and the fulfillment of the prophecy. "All we" recalls I Cor. 15:4-8, and what the risen Lord himself expounded to them regarding the prophecies of Scripture as recorded in Luke 24:27; 44-48.

33) But Peter cannot stop at this point. His hearers themselves are witnesses this very day. **Therefore, having been exalted by the right hand of God and having received the promise of the Holy Spirit from the Father, he did pour out this which you yourselves see and hear.** Right here and now Peter's hearers were both seeing and hearing the great effects of the resurrection of Jesus, the miracles of Pentecost. They reveal what the resurrection involved, the exaltation of the risen Jesus, his pouring out the spirit, the miraculous evidence of which all were seeing and hearing. Peter thus goes straight to his goal: he lays up stone on stone with perfect, swift mastery until the arch is complete.

The fact that the resurrection of Jesus as the Christ was not intended to bring him back from the dead for a continuation of his former earthly life did not need to be stated. The resurrection miracle was far too great for so small an effect. Another act accompanied that of raising the incorruptible body of Jesus from the dead: he was exalted by the right of God, οὖν presenting this and what follows as resting on the resurrection. The participle presents this act of exalting Jesus as being preliminary to what follows. "Having been exalted" includes both the glorification of the body at the time of its resurrection and the ascension of that body to heaven. Peter does not say regarding this exaltation that the disciples constitute the witness of it. They saw some of it in the appearances, and the eleven saw the first part of the ascension, but none saw the exaltation in heaven. Peter will offer the other, the Scripture, proof.

The dative is called ambiguous by R. 543: to — at — by the right hand, and some puzzle about the choice to be made when interpreting. But the ambiguity is only abstractly grammatical and not exegetical. This is the dative of means: "by the right" (supply "hand"); and it has been well said that, when the right hand exalts, it does not place on the left side. In all the passages which speak of God's right hand his omnipotence and his majesty are referred to; by these the human nature of Jesus was exalted; Eph. 1:20-23 offers the fullest description.

A second participle is added with the close connective τε which is stronger than καί and indicates that the exaltation and the reception of the Spirit are a double act. The exalted Jesus "received the promise of the Holy Spirit from the Father." Here we have the Holy Trinity, for "Father" implies Jesus as the Son. The fact that the exalted Jesus receives the Spirit from the Father in order to send him forth to the disciples appears in John 15:26; 16:7; compare Acts 1:4. It is thus that the three Persons unite in working out our salvation; we may also compare Luke 3:22. On this centering of all these acts in the Father nothing beyond the fact itself can be offered. "The promise of the Holy Spirit" = the promise which is the Spirit; the genitive is appositional (R. 498). In 1:4 we, therefore, have simply "the promise of the Father." The Spirit is the Promised One, promised as the result of Christ's redemption, to convey that redemption to men and to appropriate it unto them.

And now Peter is back where he began in v. 16: "he did pour out this which you yourselves see and hear," ἐξέχεεν the aorist to express the fact. While τοῦτο might refer to Πνεῦμα, the relative speaks of what Peter's hearers are seeing and hearing, which is not the Spirit himself but the effect of his presence, the miraculous manifestations. They are poured out by the pouring out of the Spirit. Since the Spirit is a person, it is a striking expression to say that he is poured out. In v. 17, 18 we have the partitive "from or of my Spirit," which helps to explain the figure of pouring out. The Spirit is the source and fountain of all spiritual gifts and blessings; where the Spirit is these are richly distributed and bestowed like heavenly streams of grace. Thus both the Spirit himself is said to be poured out and all the gifts which we still see and hear. Compare the literal presentation in I Cor. 12:7-11.

34) Peter offers far more than his own assertions, true as they are. He at the same time offers the proof that is decisive for his Jewish hearers by again quoting the prophet David, this time Ps. 110. **For David did not go up into the heavens, yet he himself declares,**

> Said the Lord to my Lord, Sit thou at my right
>
> Until I place thine enemies as a footstool of thy feet.

With assurance, therefore, let all Israel's house be realizing that God made him both Lord and Christ, this Jesus whom you on your part crucified.

The one thing it was necessary to prove was the exaltation of Jesus. The other needed no proof, for the miracles of the outpouring of the Spirit Peter's hearers themselves saw and heard. They also beheld the fact that these effects of the Spirit were observable only in the disciples of Jesus who were assembled before them. The connection with Jesus was thus plain. David is merely called on to reveal just what this connection was. But this is set aside by the critics who deny that David wrote Ps. 110 by attributing it to an unknown and much later writer. Here again we have the parting of the ways, on the one side these critics with their hypotheses, on the other hand Christ and his testimony. Matt. 22:41-46; Mark 12:35-37; Luke 20:41-44 report an untruth if the declaration of Jesus that David wrote this psalm is not reliable. The very words Peter here uses are elsewhere used in the same sense: I Cor. 15:25; Heb. 1:13; 10:13. Other passages of the psalm are likewise used with reference to the Messiah: Heb. 5:6; 7:17, 21. If anything is Scripturally certain, it is that David penned this psalm.

He did not speak of himself in what he said in this psalm but again, as in v. 27, of another who was vastly greater than himself. Peter at once points that out. With γάρ he introduces the proof for the exaltation of Jesus. "David did not go up (ascend) into the heavens." He died and was buried, and the tomb that contained his body was nearby when Peter spoke, had been there for a thousand years. Peter renders the Hebrew dual *shamayim* with the word "heavens." "Did not go into the heavens" refers to the body of David. David ended as every other human being ends. Death separated his soul and his body, the latter rotted in the tomb, and since David was a believer, the former went to heaven to await the last day and the resurrection. In connection with v. 27 we have treated the claim that David's soul went to hades.

And yet this very David says this wonderful thing which cannot refer to himself, which must refer to the Messiah, and which is now seen to be fulfilled in Jesus. "The Lord said unto my Lord," *Yahweh* unto David's *'Adon*. David was king and had no earthly lord above him. Who, then, was this "Lord" of David, this *'Adon*, this mighty dignitary, whom Jehovah seats at his right in eternal triumph over his enemies? All Jews knew that David was here speaking of the Messiah and by calling him "my Lord" was confessing and worshipping him. But the great point of the revelation which David makes lies in what *Yahweh* says to this Messiah Lord: "Be sitting (present imperative, durative) at my right," etc. This is divine exaltation (Heb. 1:13). To only One did *Yahweh* ever say this.

On the idiom ἐκ δεξιῶν see v. 25. God's right and right hand (v. 33) are anthropomorphitic expressions which signify his might and his majesty; and sitting at God's right is to exercise all this might and this majesty. Need we say that this is impossible for one who is only a human being? Need we add that it could not be said of the Son as the Second Person of the Trinity, he who in his very being is already of equal might and majesty with the Father? This was said to the Son as man. In his human nature he was exalted to rule forever with divine might and majesty.

It is as the incarnate Son that he has "enemies" (Luke 19:14). Had they not carried him to the cross? But *Yahweh* says he will place them all as a footstool of the feet of this Lord of David's. The figure matches this *'Adon's* sitting at Yahweh's right. In this way conquering kings showed their triumph by placing a foot upon the neck of some conquered king. But here the figure is magnified — *all* the enemies as a unit, as a permanent footstool of the exalted Messiah. This does not imply that the Messiah rests on the heavenly throne while the Father crushes his enemies for him. Ps. 2:9

makes that plain. The Persons join in all works. Nor is this crushing a strain. God laughs at these enemies and their silly rage against his Anointed. Delitzsch writes: "Temporal history shall end with the triumph of good over evil but not with the annihilation of evil but with its subjugation. To this it will come when absolute omnipotence for and through the exalted Christ shows its effectiveness."

By citing this prophecy Peter accomplished two things: he explained from David's writings how the miracle of Pentecost occurred after having shown from Joel's prophecy *that* it must occur; and he placed David before his hearers as calling the Messiah "his Lord" together with the enemies who would be made the Messiah's footstool. These were *Jesus'* disciples upon whom the Spirit promised by Joel had come with such miraculous manifestations; from whom could this Spirit have come upon them except from Jesus and except from him as exalted at God's right even as David had said? But what about these hearers of Peter's? Were they among the enemies of whom David, too, had prophesied? Peter struck home in the hearts of these hearers with his quotation.

36) The summing up is so masterly that it could have been made only by inspiration from the Spirit even as the entire sermon bears the plainest marks of the Spirit. It has been well said regarding this last sentence: *Tot verba, tot pondera.* Note the same tone of authority in the imperative that was evident at the beginning (v. 14) and in the progress (v. 22) of the sermon. This final οὖν draws the deduction from the entire presentation. Take Jesus (v. 22-24), the Pentecostal miracle, the prophecy of Joel and the two prophecies of David — what do they put beyond question? "That God made Jesus both Lord and Christ," and "let all Israel's house be realizing it with assurance." Any other deduction is false to both the facts and the

prophecies. Note the durative present "be realizing," γινωσκέτω. This is more than mere knowing, it is a knowing that is realization and complete conviction that grows deeper the longer it continues. "Assuredly" or "with assurance" fits this realization; note the noun in Luke 1:4, "the certainty" for Theophilus.

Peter looks far beyond his immediate hearers when appealing to "all Israel's house." No article is needed after πᾶς to have it mean "all" and not "every"; better than the explanation of R. 772 is that of the older grammarian Winer: οἶκος Ἰσραήλ is a proper name. "House of Israel" makes all Jews one great family of the patriarch Israel, all of whose members ought to share his faith. Israel is the third great patriarch, the one from whom the whole people of Israel branched out. The reference is to the human nature of our Lord when Peter says that "God made Jesus both Lord and Christ," this nature, of course, in conjunction with the divine. And "made" includes everything from the incarnation to the final exaltation. "Lord" is divine Lord, David's *Adon*, the Κύριος (1:6) and ὁ Κύριος Ἰησοῦς (1:21) of the apostles. The word contains power and majesty but always coupled with grace and the highest magnanimity, for this Lord is our Savior. Here the title is joined with "Christ," Χριστός, the verbal adjective from the superior verb χρίω, "to anoint," hence "the Anointed," the Hebrew *Mashiach*. The word refers to an office. As the Anointed, Jesus is our Prophet, High Priest, and King, and in all these offices brings us salvation.

This Lord and Christ had been the great hope of the Jews, but they had converted their expectation into one of a grand, earthly Deliverer and Ruler who would lift the Jews above all nations in supreme power and glory. Therefore they rejected "this Jesus," Peter adding: "whom you on your part (emphatic ὑμεῖς) crucified." *God* made him Lord and Christ, *you* crucified him. On their guilt compare v. 23. The contrast between "God" and "you" is the same as in v. 23, 24, but terser and thus stronger. Peter minced no words. He preached plenty of gospel but drove straight home with the law. And he was content with that. There was no sentimental pleading, belaboring, begging, which so often defeats itself. No sinner does God a favor by accepting Christ. Peter preached the divine truth in all its power; the effect took care of itself.

THE EFFECT OF PETER'S SERMON

37) **Now on hearing it they were pierced through as to the heart and said to Peter and the rest of the apostles, What shall we do, men and brethren?** Δέ is metabatic or transitional, carrying the account farther. The effect of Peter's preaching was the one intended. His sermon consisted of law and of gospel, and in normal cases it is always the law that first takes effect; yet the gospel must accompany the law, otherwise the law will effect only despair instead of contrition. It is not merely the repeated statement that these hearers of Peter's were involved in making away with Jesus that pierced their hearts but their whole previous attitude toward this Jesus whom God had sent them as "Lord and Christ." They had not accepted him thus, they had treated him as a mere man, many perhaps with indifference, others joined in the hostility of their Sanhedrin. Their eyes were now opened to the wickedness of their previous attitude toward Jesus. All the guilt of their unbelief was revealed through Peter's sermon. This shows us how we must today preach the law in connection with Jesus, the Lord and Christ of God. We must reveal the guilt of unbelief. Unless the sinner is pierced in heart with this guilt, conversion will not be wrought.

The second passive is followed by the adverbial accusative: "they were pierced through as to their hearts." Like a sharp spear the law penetrated their hitherto hard and impervious hearts. The Greek καρδία is always the center of the personality, psychologically the mind plus the will. Far more than the feelings of the hearers were stirred or hurt. "Pierced through" means in a deadly way. By the exposure of it which Peter had made their entire previous attitude of unbelief was struck a deadly blow. These men felt utterly crushed. They were not only hurt but hurt so that they could not rally against the hurt. Their conscience was smitten so that they could not fend off the blow. They had been in opposition to God in their treatment of his grace in Jesus. Denial on their part was impossible. The question they asked is a full admission of their guilt.

They use the plural "men and brethren," for they realized that Peter spoke for all the apostles. On "men and brethren" see 1:16, and 2:29, and note the appeal in "brethren," which asks the apostles to help them as brethren. They use the deliberative subjunctive in their question, thereby indicating that they are utterly at a loss as to what to do in their terrible situation. The question was not intended in a synergistic sense nor was it less than the one asked in 16:30 because "to be saved" was not added. These men were not thinking of doing something *of themselves* to remove their guilt. Their question implies the contrary: 1) a complete confession of their guilt; 2) a complete confession of their helplessness in regard to this guilt; 3) complete submission to the apostles in order that they who have produced the consciousness of their guilt may lead them also to deliverance from this guilt. Peter does not correct their question, nor did Paul do so in 16:30. He would have been in the wrong to answer, "*You* cannot do anything!"

38) **And Peter to them** (the verb is to be supplied from v. 37): **Repent and be baptized, everyone of you, in the name of Jesus Christ for re-**

mission of your sins, and you shall receive the gift of the Holy Spirit. For to you is the promise and to your children and to all afar off, as many as the Lord, your God, shall call to himself.

Peter gives direct answer and tells these men exactly what to do. But this doing is nothing more than the divinely intended reaction of the gospel in the hearts of these men. *They* must repent, *they* must come to baptism, but only as drawn by the gospel and its power of grace. It is our will that moves and acts and yet only because God's grace makes it move.

In μετανοεῖν and μετάνοια we have one of the great concepts of the Bible. The word originally signified to perceive or understand afterward (μετά), i. e., too late; then it advanced to the idea of a later change of mind and thus came to mean "repent." But throughout the New Testament the word has been deepened to mean an inner change of heart that is decisive for the whole personality, one away from sin and unbelief with their guilt unto Christ, faith, and cleansing through Christ. When it is used without modifiers as here, "to repent" includes the entire inner change or contrition and faith (like ἐπιστρέφειν, "to turn," "to be converted"); but when "to believe" is added, contrition alone is referred to but as accompanying faith. So "repent" here = turn wholly to Jesus as your Savior ("Lord and Christ," v. 36) and accept him as such. In order to effect this change of heart Peter had placed so fully before them just who and what Jesus is. It is this Jesus who is thus to draw them to repentance.

The aorist imperative is one of authority and demands a decisive act that is to stand once for all. A present imperative would imply that the repentance is to be renewed daily even as Luther calls the Christian's entire life a repentance.

"Repent" is plural, but "be baptized" has the distributive singular subject "everyone of you." The two acts, however, always go together in the case of adults, and all difficulty disappears when we properly conceive them as a unit. Let us not separate them. The pathological cases of possible repentance without baptism need not concern us. Peter's hearers knew about baptism through the work of the Baptist. Jesus continued John's baptism (John 4:1, 2). This baptism was not only symbolical. As practiced by both John and Jesus and then as being appointed for all nations it bestowed the remission of sins and was thus a true sacrament. The Twelve, as far as we know, had been baptized only with John's baptism.

"In the name of Jesus Christ" for the first time uses "Jesus Christ" as a personal designation, combining the personal "Jesus" with the official "Christ." This later became the regular usage. As in v. 21 and in all these expressions, ὄνομα, "name," designates the revelation by which Jesus Christ is known so that we rely on him. To be baptized "in his name" means to be baptized "in connection with the revelation he has made of himself," the application of water (as instituted by him) placing us into union with him by means of his name or revelation. Baptism seals us with this name and revelation and gives us all this name and this revelation contain, and by receiving baptism we accept it all. A refusal of baptism would be a repudiation of Christ and of all the gifts contained in his name. He who wants a piece of property wants and accepts the deed to it: if he will not have the deed he may be quite certain he does not really care for the property, especially since both property and deed are a gift.

The church has never considered "in the name of Jesus Christ" the formula to be used when baptizing; it employs only the words occurring in Jesus' own command: "in the name of the Father and of the Son and of the Holy Spirit." The εἰς is static and does not mean "into" but, as so frequently in the Koine, "in." What words are we to use: some selected by ourselves, one person using this, another that formula? Would our words be better than Christ's own? The holy name is like a signature and deeds to us all that the revelation centering in this name intends to convey. Are signatures to deeds something immaterial, to be changed *ad libitum?* Banks certainly do not think so. When we baptize, all doubt as to the genuineness of the act is always to be excluded. That is done by the use of the name Jesus gave; it is not done by substituting words of our own even though these be other words taken from Scripture.

"Everyone of you" makes repentance and baptism personal in the highest degree. Salvation deals with each individual. Note the universality: "everyone," no matter what his condition or position may be. One door is open to all, one only. Baptism is pure gospel that conveys grace and salvation from God through Christ; it dare not be changed into a legal or legalistic requirement that is akin to the ceremonial requirement of Moses such as circumcision. God does something for us in baptism, we do nothing for him. Our acceptance of baptism is only acceptance of God's gift.

This is emphasized strongly in the addition: "for or unto remission of your sins." It amounts to nothing more than a formal grammatical difference whether εἰς is again regarded as denoting sphere (equal to ἐν), R. 592, or, as is commonly supposed, as indicating aim and purpose, R. 592, or better still as denoting effect. Sphere would mean that baptism is inside the same circle as remission; he who steps into this circle has both. Aim and purpose would mean that baptism intends to give remission; in him, then, who receives baptism aright this intention, aim, and purpose would be attained. The same is true regarding the idea of effect in εἰς. This preposition connects remission so closely with baptism that nobody has as yet been able to separate the two. It is this gift of remission that makes baptism a true sacrament; otherwise it would be only a sign or a symbol that conveys nothing real. In order to make baptism such a symbol, we are told that Peter's phrase means only that baptism pictures remission, a remission we may obtain by some other means at some later day. But this alters the force of Peter's words. Can one persuade himself that Peter told these sinners who were stricken with their terrible guilt to accept a baptism that pointed to some future remission? Had he no remission to offer them now? And when and how could they get that remission, absolutely the one thing they must have? And how can Ananias in 22:16 say, "Be baptized and *wash away* thy sins!" as though the *water* of baptism *washed* them away by its connection with the Name?

Ἄφεσις, from ἀφίημι, "to send away," is another great Biblical concept: "the sending away" of your sins. How far away they are sent Ps. 103:12 tells us: "as far as the east is from the west, so far has he removed our transgressions from us." Measure the distance from the point where the east begins to the point where the west ends. Nor does David say, "as far as the north is from the south," lest you think of the poles and succeed in measuring the distance. Again Micah 7:19: "Thou wilt cast all their sins into the depths of the sea." Even today the sea has depths that have never been sounded. The idea to be conveyed is that the sins are removed from the sinner so as never to be found again, never again to be brought to confront him. God sends them away, and he would thus be the last to bring them back. When the sinner appears before his judgment seat, his sins are gone forever. This is what our far less expressive "forgiveness" really means. Nor does the guilt remain, for sin and guilt are one: sin **gone**, guilt gone!

"And you shall receive the gift of the Holy Spirit" means in and by repenting and being baptized. The genitive is appositional; as in v. 33 the promise is the Holy Spirit, so here the gift is the Holy Spirit. In Peter's sermon the Spirit came to work upon the hearers from without, but by bringing them to repentance and to baptism he would actually enter their hearts, be their heavenly gift, and thus put them into actual communion with God. This gift is bestowed upon each and every repentant and baptized soul and cannot, therefore, refer only to charismatic gifts of the Spirit, speaking with tongues, healing, etc., but denotes the gift of grace and salvation which is always present in the heart which the Spirit enters. We do not read that any of the 3,000 spoke with tongues, yet they all received the Holy Spirit.

Here again we must not separate repentance, baptism, the Spirit. Not at some later time were these people to receive the Spirit; not in some later sudden, mysterious seizure; not as a later "second blessing" that would produce a total sanctification or sinlessness by a sudden transformation. Luther wrote against the Anabaptists: "This doctrine is to remain sure and firm, that the Holy Spirit is given through the office of the church, that is through the preaching of the gospel and baptism. There must seek him all who desire him, must not despise the little band in which the preaching of the gospel resounds, but must hold to that band, gathered and staying together in Christ's name."

39) In order to draw all his hearers unto repentance and baptism Peter assures them: "For to you is the promise and to your children," to them first as Jews. "The promise" is the Holy Spirit, "promise" occurs in this sense in 1:4, and in 2:33. It was the intention of God to bestow his Spirit upon the Jews

first. "To you" is emphatic and thus stresses the thought that, if God so graciously purposed to bless them with his Spirit, they should surely not despise his intention. "And to your children" is a most significant addition when we bear in mind that the Old Covenant included children. Certainly, the New Covenant would include them likewise. But how are children to receive the Holy Spirit except by baptism? "Your children" allows no restriction as to age. How the Holy Spirit enters their hearts by baptism is his concern only, ours is to administer that baptism, in no wise doubting, otherwise we could not answer to God.

"And to all afar off" includes all other nations and, of course, also their children, εἰς μακράν (ὁδόν), a phrase that is made a substantive by the article with εἰς being static (R. 593). These "afar off" cannot be restricted to the Jewish diaspora, especially not in view of "all flesh" in v. 17; compare Isa. 49:1, 12; 57:19. "As many as the Lord, our God, shall call unto himself" in no way limits the universality. These are not persons who are chosen by a mysterious decree of election but those who are called by the gospel. Others, too, are called but reject the call in permanent obduracy; these are won by the call and its grace. The aorist subjunctive is futuristic and views the entire calling as a unit that includes all those won by the call as one body. Κύριος ὁ Θεός = *Yahweh Haelohim*, and ἡμῶν means that this covenant Lord and omnipotent God exercises his power in favor of Israel. By means of this possessive Peter unites himself with his Jewish hearers; the God of the Old Covenant is also the God of the New. It is worth noting, both here in Peter's words and beginning with the Baptist, that the Three Persons are mentioned with utmost freedom, and all Jews accepted this Trinity of God without a question.

40) **And with many other words he adjured and kept urging them, saying, Be saved from this**

crooked generation! Luke himself tells us that he is reporting only the essentials. Perhaps Peter had to answer questions and make further explanations literally "with other more words (statements)," more than the ones recorded. The verb is strong: "to protest earnestly," "to adjure," the aorist to express the fact. But the imperfect "he kept urging them" (thus M.-M. 484) describes the chief point of this adjuration, the urging: "Be saved from this crooked generation!" The aorist imperative is passive, and there is no reason for not regarding it so. Some passive forms are to be taken in a middle sense, but scarcely this passive. One might make it permissive, "let yourselves be saved," but scarcely the reflexive middle, "save yourselves."

Here "generation" is to be taken in an ethical sense as the adjective "crooked" plainly shows. The Hebrew *dor* and the Greek γενεά are often so used although this has often been denied in connection with Luke 21:32. The generation here referred to is the entire succession of unbelievers with the Sanhedrin at its head. From it Peter's hearers are to be saved by repenting and by being baptized. "Crooked" is made emphatic by means of a second article (R. 776); σκολιός (Deut. 32:5; Ps. 78:8 = LXX 77:8; Phil. 2:15) is used figuratively. It refers to a warped piece of timber which the carpenters must throw out as being useless. "Be saved" implies that the crooked generation is bound for destruction.

41) **They, accordingly, who received his word were baptized; and there were added on that day about three thousand souls.** Οἱ μὲν οὖν is clearer here than in 1:6; for the article is to be construed with the participle: "those receiving his word" and not all those present on this occasion. Receiving, "consenting to the word, giving it entrance" (C.-K. 281), was one act, hence the aorist participle; "his word" (λόγος)

is the substance of what Peter said. All these "were baptized."

This leads us to a consideration of the question of baptism by immersion. When Luke writes, "They were baptized, and about three thousand were added on that day," he certainly intends to say that they were added by baptism on that very day and not that they were added that day but were baptized later on. Those who accept the plain sense of Luke's statement must show where 3,000 could be immersed in Jerusalem in about half a day. Some speak of the brook Kidron or of one or the other of the pools, but Kidron is bone-dry the greater part of the year, and the pools are not ponds. For several reasons none of the pools that have been mentioned in this connection can be considered. Those who are informed regarding the water facilities of Jerusalem, therefore, regard Luke as saying that the reception took place "on that day," but that the baptizing took place later, namely at the Jordan. But we may wonder why Luke did not then write: "Those who received his word were added on that day, and there were baptized about three thousand." Even this might well mean that they were also baptized on that day. Luke, however, wrote as he did: baptized — added that day. Even the long journey to the Jordan is taken for granted although Luke should then have written, "were baptized in the Jordan," which he, however, did not add.

The question at issue is, however, much more extensive. It involves all other baptisms mentioned in the New Testament beginning with that of John. We have treated the latter in the Gospels (which see). Neither John's nor any other baptism mentioned in the New Testament was administered by immersion. All the evidence is to the contrary, often overwhelmingly so. The issue in regard to the 3,000 who were baptized at Pentecost is vital. This grand baptism, the first in the Christian Church, undoubtedly established the mode also for all future baptisms. Soon the membership in Jerusalem rose to 5,000 men (not counting women and children, 4:4); then Luke loses all count and says only that further "multitudes" were added (5:14), and after that "the number of the disciples were multiplied" (6:1), and again "multiplied," even "a great company of priests" believing (6:7). Were all these thousands also taken to the Jordan for baptism? The claim is often made that all the men among the 120 or more disciples helped the Twelve to baptize the 3,000. This is done in support of immersion, especially when the baptism is placed in Jerusalem and when Luke is thought to say that it occurred "on that day." Immersion requires so much strength that many men would be needed for immersing 3,000. But who alone stepped forth to deal with this multitude? In v. 14 it is "Peter with the eleven," and in v. 37 the multitude speaks to "Peter and the rest of the apostles." This is Luke's answer. Here the apostles functioned in their high office for the first time.

How, then, were the 3,000 baptized? We do not know. The Spirit has withheld the answer. Why? Because the mode is not essential. In order to make it essential the Spirit would have had to state it in plain terms. One mode, however, was not used: immersion. Why, then, should we use it? The church has selected the simplest mode, one that is probably much like the one that was employed in Jerusalem. To insist on one mode and to condemn all others is rather presumptuous. We may add that all the pictorial and the archaeological evidence regarding the mode of baptism in the early church has been gathered by Clement F. Rogers, M. A., *Baptism and Christian Archaeology*, Oxford, Clarendon Press. This man approached his investigation with the conviction that immersion was the primitive and original mode. He found the exact contrary to be true. The most ancient tracings and carvings portray the act of baptism as being carried out by pouring. In this way John baptized Jesus, and in this way other baptisms were administered. All the fonts found in ruins and in excavations are shallow, a few steps down. In some of these immersion could have been possible, but only by laying the person down flat in the font, and then he dared not have been very corpulent. This mass of evidence invalidates the assumption, so often met with, that immersion was the mode of baptism in the early church.

To this day it is by means of baptism that people are added to the church. In the Greek "were added" is enough and needs no phrase which states to whom they were added; the same is true in regard to v. 47. Luke's ψυχαί are "souls" in the sense of "persons." The statement that all of these were men must be denied in view of 4:4, where Luke counts only "men," ἄνδρες, and omits women and children. "Souls" does not exclude children, especially in view of "your children" in v. 39 and of the entire Old Covenant which included children. In 7:14, where the family of Jacob is mentioned, "souls" positively includes every child. The effort to take "your children," τέκνα, in the sense of adult descendants only is ineffectual. All these details, however, must not dim the tremendous fact which Luke here records. Think of 3,000 coming to faith and to baptism on one day, the very first day of what may be called the Christian Church! Thus on one day the great mother church of all Christendom was founded. The first Christian congregation starts off with 3,000 members.

THE FIRST PICTURE OF THE MOTHER CONGREGATION AT JERUSALEM

42) Luke gives us several of these pictures in due succession, and each is intensely interesting. The

Spirit begins his saving work, we are subject to it today. Jesus labored for three years and at last had only some 500 disciples (I Cor. 15:6); here 3,000 were added at one stroke, fulfilling John 4:37, 38. **And they continued steadfast in the teaching of the apostles and in the fellowship, in breaking the bread, and in the prayers.**

The entire sketch is presented by means of descriptive imperfects, thus painting the picture. Προσκαρτερέω means "to adhere with strength" to something, the periphrastic imperfect stressing the continuance. We have four datives in two pairs and do not regard the last two as a unit apposition to "fellowship."

The fundamental activity of the first congregation is this firm, continued adherence "to the teaching of the apostles." They were the called teachers and preachers and they began their work at once, there being about 300 hearers to each apostle. This work went on continuously, and all these people not only attended the meetings faithfully but also earnestly adhered to what was taught. Διδαχή is both the work of teaching and the doctrine taught. In this case both meanings flow together.

The deduction should not be made from this passage that people may be received into the church only on their willingness to enter it and that teaching may be postponed until later. These converts were Jews who were fully conversant with the Scriptures as Peter's quotations from Joel and from David show. The one thing they needed was the conviction that Jesus was the Christ. That Peter wrought in them on Pentecost. Thus they were fully prepared for baptism and for membership; they had what we must now first give to those who have never been properly instructed. This teaching after Pentecost was that which we now perform Sunday after Sunday, the teaching and the preaching in public worship.

They adhered "to fellowship," and Luke adds no genitive, nor is "of the apostles" to be understood; this is the fellowship of all the members with each other as well as with the apostles. They were one spiritual body, inwardly one by faith in Christ, inwardly and outwardly one by confessing Christ and by adhering to the one doctrine of Christ that was taught by the apostles. And so they kept together as one body and treated each other accordingly. One faith and one teaching, and thus one body in one fellowship. No parties, schisms, inwardly. Κοινωνία is here *communio* and not *communicatio* or impartation of alms. That point Luke also notes later; it would be out of place so far forward in this account. Already that fact settles the question as to the next two datives; they are not appositions to *koinonia*.

They adhered "to breaking the bread." There is no necessity for stressing the article in the sense of "their bread," that eaten at a joint meal. Even then the Sacrament of the Lord's Supper would be involved, since at this early time it was always celebrated at the end of a meal (I Cor. 11:33, 34 in connection with what precedes). Luke is speaking of the greatest things done in this first congregation and characterizes the celebration of the Lord's Supper by use of the expression that was common at that time: "breaking the bread." To stress this phrase so as to exclude the cup from the Sacrament is just as unwarranted as to have the phrase mean only partaking of a joint meal. The apostles cannot be charged with mutilation of the Sacrament. I Cor. 11:23-29. "Breaking" has been made an essential feature of the Sacrament, yet there is no counterpart for the wine. Breaking was practiced only for the purpose of distribution, the bread of that time never being cut in our fashion. Krauth, *Conservative Reformation*, 723, shows the impossibility of letting the breaking of bread symbolize the killing of a man; see the words of institution in the Gospels and in I Cor. 11.

They adhered "to the prayers," i. e., to the worship in their own gatherings, 4:24, etc., and to the stated devotions in the Temple, 3:1, etc. It seems that this word is used to designate the entire service or worship and not merely the praying. We thus see how Luke first pairs teaching and the fellowship it involves and secondly the Sacrament and the worship which parallels it.

Here we have a brief description of the religious life of the first Christian congregation. All the essentials are present and are in proper order and harmony. The church has always felt that this is a model. One wishes that Luke had said more. Where did this large congregation assemble, for it grew tremendously (4:4; 5:14; 6:1, 7)? Many think of the halls of the Temple. But this was scarcely the case. The one thing certain is that no difficulty was encountered regarding a meeting place. Were these "prayer meetings" in the modern sense of that term? We shall see that only on special occasions were gatherings for the purpose of praying held. The dominating feature is the teaching (Word) and the Sacrament.

43) **Moreover, on every soul fear kept coming; and many wonders and signs through the apostles kept occurring.** Here and again in v. 44 δέ adds something different. The reason for referring "every soul" to non-disciples who came into contact with the congregation is the contrasting subject in v. 44, "all those believing." These outsiders kept experiencing "fear" in the sense of awe. They felt that higher powers were at work among the disciples. It is one thing to have such impressions, quite another to act properly upon them. With the close connective τέ Luke adds the "wonders and signs" that were connected with this fear; see v. 19 regarding the two terms. The miracles

were intended to impress those that were on the outside. The statement is summary and is placed at the head of the activity of the apostles because Luke does not intend to recount these miracles but to confine himself only to notable instances. Let us not overlook the fact that these were "many," astonishing as τέρατα and significant as σημεῖα. But the apostles were only the instruments (διά) through whom One who was far higher wrought. This differentiates all the apostolic miracles from those of Jesus. God, indeed, wrought those of Jesus (v. 22) but only as the divine Persons work together.

44) **And all those believing kept together; and they were having all things as common and were selling their possessions and goods and distributing them to all according as anyone had need.** This translation reproduces the correct reading. "All those believing" (present participle) "were," in the sense of "kept," together (the phrase is to be understood as it was in 1:16). The imperfect ἦσαν is iterative; the believers made a practice of meeting together. Remember in what different countries they had been born. The Temple had drawn them to live in Jerusalem, and now their believing drew them together in a different, deeper, and far truer way. Faith in Christ was the bond which made one body of these believers even outwardly. This must be added to "the fellowship" mentioned in v. 42. Some think that these thousands lived together, others reduce the number. Both views are unacceptable. The fact that they all found room for their frequent meetings Luke considers it unnecessary to explain.

45) As they were thus drawn together, so they treated each other. "They were having or holding all things as common," κοινά is predicative. This states the main idea, namely how they considered and treated their possessions, not as belonging to the owner only,

but as something in which the rest were to share as need arose. This was not communism but the product of something that communism does not understand. The following imperfects are iterative (R. 884): this selling and this distributing took place from time to time and was individual and wholly voluntary as 5:4 plainly states. It occurred "according as anyone had need." The use of a conjunction with ἄν (or ἐάν) with the iterative imperfect is the classic construction, which is, however, retained in the Koine only in subordinate clauses (C.-K. 367; R. 922). As needy cases arose they were taken care of in this manner. It is a fair conclusion that most of these Jews who had moved to Jerusalem from distant lands and were now believers were well off and were living on their wealth. Yet they had changed their entire attitude toward their wealth and were now using it in fine Christian charity. Volunteers came forward, such as Barnabas mentioned in 4:37, sold some possession or goods, and placed the proceeds at the disposal of the apostles. The fact that among so many believers instances of need occurred is only natural.

The old Mosaic law provided ways and means for taking care of all cases of poverty among the Jews; but the number of beggars referred to in the New Testament shows that these laws were no longer enforced. This old spirit was revived in the first congregation in Jerusalem and chose this means for letting no fellow believer suffer need. It is unfair to say that the Christians thought that their property was insecure because of the hostility of the authorities and therefore gave it away, or that they expected Christ's return in the immediate future and therefore dealt so lavishly. So also the poverty of the mother congregation which was found there at a later date is often attributed to what Luke here records, but this was due to the fact that the Herodian persecution scattered this first congregation to the four winds while famine and hard times set in and caused distress. What Luke describes is a fine display of Christian charity. The same motive is still active in the church today. Many rich still offer large sums, and the rest still bring their portion, and Christian need never waits long for relief.

46) Day by day both continuing steadfast with one accord in the Temple and breaking bread house by house, they were partaking of their food in exultation and simplicity of heart, praising God and having favor with the whole people. Moreover, the Lord kept adding together day by day the saved.

The descriptive imperfects continue. Luke sketches the daily life of the first congregation. The three κατά phrases are distributive: "day by day," "house by house"; τε . . . τε correlate the first two participles (R. 1179), "both . . . and." The believers both visited the Temple and broke bread house by house at home. The daily visits to the Temple were made for the purpose of participation in the Temple worship; we see Peter and John thus engaged in 3:1. The separation from the Temple and the Jews generally developed gradually and naturally. Until it was effected, the Christians used the Temple which Jesus had honored and which typified him (John 2:19-21) as they had used it before. Its spacious colonnades and halls afforded them room for their own assemblies.

Many think that "breaking bread" again refers to the Sacrament, but in a brief sketch such as this Luke would scarcely repeat in this fashion. The addition "house by house" would add nothing new since it is self-evident that the Temple was not the place for the Sacrament. "Breaking bread" also refers to all the meals and not merely to such as might precede the

Sacrament as an agape. "House by house" is like "day by day." It does not mean merely "at home" but in each home. Wherever there was a Christian home its residents partook of their food "in exultation of heart," with high delight in the grace vouchsafed them, and "in simplicity or singleness of heart," rejoicing in the one thing that filled their hearts with such joy. This noun is derived from an adjective which means "without a stone," hence perfectly smooth and even, metaphorically, a condition that is undisturbed by anything contrary.

47) "Praising God" was the natural expression of their hearts for the supreme blessing they had found in Christ. So also they enjoyed "favor with the whole people." Taken as a whole, the people of the city thought well of all these disciples. Their fervor in the Temple worship commended them, and their happy conduct with praise to God on their lips made the Jews like them. What a beautiful picture of this morning hour of the church! The goodness of the Lord gave his disciples this period of undisturbed peace in which to grow and increace. The favorable disposition of the populace helped to bring many to faith. So the Lord often gives his church days of peace — do we always use them as did the first church in Jerusalem? Soon the skies would become clouded and the storm of persecution descend to scatter the flock.

In v. 41 we have the passive "they were added," here we see the agent in that passive: "the Lord kept adding together," ἐπὶ τὸ αὐτό occurs in this sense (1:16). The Lord alone can add new members. Those who lay stress on numbers bring in many in ways which they devise. We want numbers, but such as the Lord adds and records in his book, and none, if we can help it, whose names would be only on our books. He adds only by filling the heart with the gospel. "Day by day" in a brief space of time the congregation grew from

3,000 souls to 5,000 men, or some 10,000 souls (4:4). Those added are significantly called "the saved," οἱ σωζόμενοι. The substantivized present participle is timeless and expresses quality or condition and nothing more. "The saved" are those who are in a saved condition. "Such as should be saved" (A. V.) is incorrect and introduces a wrong idea; "those that were being saved" (R. V.) is also incorrect, for it suggests the thought that salvation was still in the future; "those that were saved" (R. V., American Committee) is still faulty in so far as it introduces the past tense. An aorist participle would point to the saving act, and a perfect participle (and this is at times used) to that act and the saved condition resulting. The present participle stops with a statement of the quality or condition: "the saved." On the readings found in the A. V. see 3:1.

CHAPTER III

PETER AND JOHN HEAL THE CRIPPLE IN THE TEMPLE

The miracle is notable in itself but is recorded chiefly because of its effect. It aroused the Sanhedrin to its first opposition against the apostles. Luke has no indication as to the time that intervened between Pentecost and this miracle. For doing good Peter and John receive evil.

1) **Now Peter and John were going up into the Temple at the hour of prayer, the ninth. And a man, being lame from his mother's womb, was being carried, whom they were placing day by day at the door of the Temple, the one called Beautiful, to ask alms from those going into the Temple, who, on seeing Peter and John about to go into the Temple, began requesting to receive alms.**

We follow the preferred reading which has ἐπὶ τὸ αὐτό concluding 2:47, and not opening 3:1. The A. V. does the reverse and therefore concludes 2:47 with τῇ ἐκκλησίᾳ, a dative that is found in several texts. The textual evidence is in favor of the reading translated in the R. V. To put the phrase at the head of 3:1 makes it too emphatic, since the very mention of "Peter and John" shows that they were "together." We are prepared to find them so. In his list in 1:13 Luke has grouped them together (correct the A. V.); they act together in Luke 22:8; John 13:24, 25; 18:16, 17; 20:2, etc.; 21:21, 22. So we repeatedly find these two together in the story of Acts. A close friendship unites them. By nature they were entirely different. Peter was impetuous, John serene. Thus they supplement each other.

124   Interpretation of the Acts of the Apostles

Diamond polishes diamond, writes Rieger, and it may well happen that each enhances the luster of the other. God often uses the friendship of believers for the good of the church, especially the friendship of highly gifted men; witness the working together of Luther and Melanchthon.

These two were in the act of going up into the Temple at the hour of prayer. In 2:15 we find mention made of the service held at 9 A. M., here the one held at 3 P. M. is referred to. The Jews counted twelve hours for the day, starting with 6 A. M.; so their ninth hour was 3 P. M. which was called the evening sacrifice. Already in 2:46 we see how the disciples adhered to the Temple and its services. They continued this practice until the Lord himself eventually made it impossible. The Jews always spoke of going "up" to or into the Temple, no matter what the elevation was from which they started. This was said in an ethical sense. The Temple did not occupy the highest elevation in the city.

2) Simultaneous with their going into the Temple, as a second imperfect informs us, a lame beggar "was being carried" into it on some sort of a litter; τις is only our indefinite article "a" man. "Lame from his mother's womb" states that he was born lame, had never walked during the forty (4:22) years of his life. He seems to have been injured at birth so that his ankle bones (v. 7) had not developed or were misshapen. His congenital lameness, especially at the age he had now reached, rendered him incurable. The first two imperfects are descriptive of actions in progress. Peter and John overtook the men who were carrying the beggar in. This very likely occurred somewhere in the large court of the Gentiles. The imperfect in the relative clause expresses customary action as the added phrase shows: "whom they were placing day by day," etc. Relatives or friends did this, and it was

quite a task to carry the beggar such a distance and back home again. Israel was to have no beggars (Deut. 15:4), but the Jews were omitting the weightier matters of the law such as judgment, *mercy*, and faith, Matt. 23:23. We meet beggar after beggar.

This one had his regular station at the gate called "Beautiful," Ὡραία (θύρα or πύλη), from ὥρα, "timely" and thus "blooming," "beautiful." Josephus, *Wars*, 5, 5, 3, describes it as being much higher than the other gates and as being adorned with magnificent silver and gold plates. The Talmud calls it Nicanor's gate after its donor. This great gate was the only one that led from the court of the Gentiles surrounding the Sanctuary and the Temple buildings proper into the court of the women and through this to the court of the men. Opposite this gate was Solomon's Porch, a colonnade. Fourteen steps led up to a gallery, that ran around the three sides of the women's court, and five more steps from this gallery to the gate "Beautiful"; on two sides of the women's court other less imposing gates afforded entrance. We at once see that, while it was work to carry the beggar so far and also up those steps, he certainly had the most promising place for begging. The infinitive with τοῦ denotes purpose.

3) Not waiting until he was deposited in his usual place but already when Peter and John were about to go into the Temple, perhaps before they ascended the steps, this beggar "began requesting to receive alms." This imperfect is not iterative (R. 884) but inchoative: the beggar "began to request," and the tense also holds us in suspense as to the outcome of what he began which was anything but what he expected. The verb itself expresses respectful asking. There is no reason for connecting this request with the liberality manifested toward fellow believers by the Christians described in 2:44, 45, as though the beggar knew all about that and expected some of that liberality

to be shown him. This man was begging in his usual way and was accosting people even before he got to his regular station. "Began requesting alms" would be enough; "to receive" is circumstantial and indicates the outstretched hand that is anxious to take whatever might be offered. Luke draws the picture well.

4) **Now Peter, earnestly looking on him, with John, said, Look on us! And he began to give heed to them, expecting to receive something from them.** Δέ continues the story but introduces a new action which was so different from that which the beggar usually experienced. Peter is the spokesman and later performs the miracle, but John is with him in both. This earnest look of the apostles does not mean, "looking through to the innermost bottom of the heart in order to discover the proper receptivity." Interpretations such as that are due to the view that miracles require faith in advance. This view is here carried to the point of making Peter and John look into the beggar's very heart, which would itself be a miracle. The simple fact is that Peter and John saw only a poor, pitiable cripple and his outstretched, begging hand before them. But why this earnest and intent look? We know of but one answer. The apostles had often seen this cripple begging at the gate "Beautiful," they may even have dropped him a coin now and then. To heal him had not entered their minds. Why not? Because the Lord had not put it into their minds to do such a thing. The apostles did not perform miracles just when and where they thought advisable. In every case they were moved to do so by the Lord and by his Spirit. It is because the Lord so moved them that they now fixed their full attention on the cripple whom they had seen so often on previous days.

Hence also their order to the beggar to look on them which was uttered with the peremptory **and** authoritative aorist imperative. This beggar must pay close attention to the apostles.

5) And he does. "He began to give heed to them," ἐπεῖχεν (supply τὸ νοῦν), but only in the same way as any man might do when his attention is thus aroused. So little was the thought of faith of any kind in his mind that he supposed only that something would now be given to him, something more than the ordinary small coins he usually received. This is one of a number of plain cases in which faith does not and is not intended to precede but rather follows the miracle.

6) **But Peter said: Silver and gold is not mine; but what I have I give to thee. In the name of Jesus Christ, the Nazarene, be walking! And having grasped him by the right hand, he raised him up, and at once his feet and ankles were made firm. And leaping up, he stood and began to walk. And he went with them into the Temple, walking and leaping and praising God.**

Peter speaks of "silver and gold," the more valuable coins, because the beggar evidently expected an unusually valuable gift from them and because he thought them wealthy. It is a rather hasty conclusion on the basis of this word to suppose that the apostles were themselves dependent on alms; for John had a home and was able to support Jesus' mother (John 19:27). Peter means, "I have no wealth." But the cripple has no time to be disappointed, for Peter immediately adds, "But what I have I give to thee," leading the cripple to wonder what that might be. He had his gift from the Lord — miraculous healing as the seal of the gospel message, that definite form of healing for this particular person as it was indicated to both these apostles by the Lord.

Without adding a single word of explanation, without doing anything to awaken or to increase faith,

Peter utters the command that conveys its own power of compliance: "In the name," etc. Here again is this pithy and significant phrase ἐν τῷ ὀνόματι κτλ., which is so often interpreted in inadequate ways. It does not mean "by the authority of," etc. (R. 649); nor does it mean this in some places and something else in others. See ὄνομα in 2:21 and this phrase in 2:38. Here, as always, the sense is: "in connection with the revelation of Jesus," etc. In addition to what has been said when considering 2:21 and 38 we may state that "name" in the sense of "revelation" not only comprehends Jesus and all his power and grace but also conveys him to us for our apprehension. Paul is acquainted with the phrase "in Christ" or "in the Lord," and uses it often; in the expression "in the name of Jesus Christ" "name" stresses the vital connection with the person Jesus Christ. The power and the grace that make him "Jesus Christ" ("both Lord and Christ," 2:36) are revealed in all that truly makes us know him, that shines out from him, and that is his NAME, the source from which all blessings, also this miracle of healing, flow. On "Jesus" see 2:22; on "Christ," 2:36; the two combined in 2:38; on "the Nazarene," 2:22. "In the name of Jesus Christ, the Nazarene," suddenly brought to the cripple's mind all that he had ever heard about this wonderful person.

"Be walking!" is the present imperative to express enduring action; he is to have the power of walking now and always. Here is no "if" or "but"; here is no process or slow mending. We all know that even when limbs are sound, no human being can at once walk, leap, caper, jump, who has never done so before. The thing must first be learned. But the cripple is not to learn, he is to walk perfectly from the very first instant. Let that feature of the miracle have its just due. In no way did the miracle depend upon the man's faith or will or understanding. Of course, he was to know, to believe, and to act, but all these came about as a result of the healing, they were not conditions or requisites to the healing.

7) Peter grasped him by the right hand, the very hand he was holding out for alms, only in order to raise him up, to make him stand and to walk at once. If Peter and John had walked away, the cripple would have discovered that his feet and his ankles were normal and that he could walk. But no interval was to occur. Peter's effort raised the man from the ground; instantly his limbs were firm, sound, strong, ready to serve their natural purpose. The member grasped is properly in the genitive: took hold "of the right hand."

8) Peter did not need to exert much effort, of himself the restored cripple, "leaping up, stood and began to walk" (inchoative imperfect). Luke's description is vivid. R. 1116 writes: "It is not clear why the present participle occurs, ἐξαλλόμενος, unless it is to note that he kept on leaping and walking alternately." One would expect the aorist, "having leaped up, he stood." The aorist "stood" is constative: without falling he stood upright. Then the imperfect notes that he began to walk, to do just what Peter had told him to do.

He accompanied the apostles as they proceeded up the steps and on through the gate Beautiful, walking, of course, but also leaping and jumping every now and then, overjoyed at the blessing given him even without his asking, praising God who had made him so rich in Jesus' name. But what about us who have enjoyed sound limbs all our lives? So many blessings, so little realization and gratitude! The cripple's first walk took him into the Temple, the very purpose for which we should use our feet, keeping them always in the paths of righteousness for his name's sake.

9) And all the people saw him walking and praising God; moreover, they kept recognizing him that this was the one sitting for the alms at the Gate Beautiful of the Temple, and they were filled with amazement and excitement at what had come to him. But he holding to Peter and John, all the people ran together to them at the porch called Solomon's, dumbfounded.

It seems that v. 9, 10 describe what occurred before the Temple service, and v. 11 what occurred after it was over and the people had dispersed. When Luke says that all the people saw him "walking and praising God" he tells us that the man drew general attention to himself. Even after the restored cripple had come to the men's court he continued walking around instead of standing still like the other men and kept calling out words of praise to God. Thus everybody saw him.

10) For a man to act thus was unusual, yet in itself such conduct would not have attracted so much attention. People would only have wondered as to what made him act in this way. By means of the iterative imperfect Luke tells us that, as he thus moved about, group after group recognized him as the very man they had so often seen "sitting for the alms," the article to indicate the alms they had given him from time to time at the Gate Beautiful. They had not seen him sitting thus with his deformed feet and ankles this afternoon — here he was among them, walking around and praising God. Luke uses two nouns to convey the effect; both are strong: θάμβος, "amazement" that came with a shock, and ἔκστασις, "excitement" that throws the mind off its balance. They stared uncomprehendingly at the change that had come over the man.

11) What happened when the service and the worship were conducted is not stated. But these are evidently now over, and all the men pass out of the Temple through the court of the women. Instead of making

Acts 3:11, 12

their exit by one of the side portals, all those present stream through the main eastern portal called "Beautiful," down the steps to the court below, "at the porch called Solomon's," ἐπί with the dative, not into this porch, but in front of it. This *stoa* consisted of a span of roof which rested on magnificent pillars extended along the entire eastern outer wall of the Temple area. It was named after Solomon, because this side of the Temple area perhaps rested on the old massive foundation walls which rose several hundred feet from the valley beneath and had been left undemolished since Solomon's time. As they went out, the healed cripple clung tightly to Peter and to John. The three got no farther than this court facing Solomon's porch. Everybody ran out to this and surrounded them in a packed crowd. And ἔκθαμβοι, "dumfounded" with amazement, describes the state of their minds; the "greatly wondering" of our versions is far too weak.

12) The beggar clings to Peter and to John. Attention is centered on all three. Amazement with its silent questioning looks to them for an answer and an explanation. The Lord had timed this miracle so as to bring this whole audience before Peter, literally compelling him to preach to these people. His words are straight to the point: Not we have done this but the risen Jesus. While the question seems to be one that is wholly about the beggar, Peter turns it into a matter that is entirely personal to everyone of his hearers. God is attesting this Jesus whom they crucified as the Savior promised by prophecy. Let them repent and share in his blessings! And again we see the authority, the mastery, the effectiveness of this sermon, which strikes straight home into the consciences and the hearts of Peter's hearers.

Now on seeing it, Peter made response to the people: Israelite men, why are you marvelling at this man, or why are you gazing on us as though

by our own power or godliness we have made him to walk? The verb "made response" is used with reference to any situation that requires an explanation, and here certainly was such a case.

Ἄνδρες is used as it was in 1:16, and 2:14, and "Israelites" as in 2:22 which employs the religious name of honor for the Jews with its appeal to their highest hopes and motives. They are to view this miracle as true Israelites should. Thus they are not to marvel at this man and to stop with their amazement — they are to let their thoughts go much farther. The neuter "at this thing" is out of place because τούτῳ is in contrast with ἡμῖν, persons. So also they are not to gaze on the apostles "as though" (concessive ὡς, R. 1140) they had made this man walk (object infinitive with τοῦ, R. 1168) by their own power (effective cause) or with their godliness (meritorious cause, John 9:31, 33) The power did not emanate from the apostles, nor was power given them as a reward of their godliness. To understand that power these people will have to look elsewhere.

13) **The God of Abraham and of Isaac and of Jacob, the God of our fathers, glorified his Servant Jesus whom you delivered up and denied before the face of Pilate, he having judged to release him. But you denied the Holy and Righteous One and asked for yourselves that a man, a murderer, be granted unto you, but the Author of life you killed, whom God raised up from the dead, of which we on our part are witnesses. And on the basis of the faith of his name this man, whom you behold and know, his name made firm; yea, the faith, that through him, did give to him this entire soundness in the presence of you all.** This true explanation of "what has come to this man" (v. 10) all Israelites should know, for it means everything to them personally.

Peter is speaking to Israelites, hence he employs the great covenant name which God gave himself in Exod. 3:6, "the God of Abraham," etc. It is no mere heaping up of words when Peter adds the apposition, "the God of our fathers," for he intends to designate God as the God also of all the descendants of the patriarchs who in times past shared the covenant and the faith with them. "Our" links also Peter and John with all these "fathers." It is to sink into the minds of Peter's hearers that he whom their nation worshipped in all past ages in their covenant relation with him, he it is who as this God and in this covenant of his "glorified his Servant Jesus." It is the same glorification which Peter preached on Pentecost in 2:30-36, namely the resurrection and the exaltation at God's right hand. Not only the miracle is referred to and the fact that God gorified Jesus in and by that. For in v. 15 Peter himself specifically mentions the resurrection, and in v. 16 the miracle is ascribed to the name of Jesus, i. e., to the name of this glorified Jesus. Παῖς is never used in the sense of "Son of God"; this thought is always expressed by the words υἱὸς Θεοῦ. The marginal note of the R. V., "Child," should be cancelled here and in all other passages where it occurs. This παῖς is the great *Ebed Yahweh* of Isaiah, chapters 40-66, the mighty "Servant" of Jehovah, who is his Son, indeed, but the Son who by his incarnation became "his Servant" to work out our salvation.

Now comes the personal turn of Peter's words which is sudden and startling, direct and crushing. On the one side, God and what he did, namely glorified Jesus; on the other side, these Jews and what *they* did, namely denied, rejected, disgraced Jesus. Note the emphatic ὑμεῖς: "whom *you on your part* delivered up and denied before the face of Pilate, he having judged to release him." Note the balance in μέν and δέ (v. 14).

134 Interpretation of the Acts of the Apostles

Peter is a master in making these terrible contrasts between God and the Jews; compare 2:23, 24, 36; 4:10, 30, 31. When stating the terrible action of his hearers Peter names only the chief points and these in the order in which they occurred: "they delivered Jesus up" to the pagan governor with the demand that he be crucified, they wanted him made away with forever; then "they denied him before the face of Pilate," boldly, shamelessly, to his very face, declaring that he was not their King (Luke 23:2; John 19:14, 15), disowning him utterly. And this they did after Pilate "judged" or declared his verdict that he would release him, ἐκείνου is far stronger than αὐτοῦ and places pagan Pilate into contrast with the Jews. God glorified Jesus, Pilate wanted at least to release him, but the Jews demanded his death. Even pagan Pilate was better than the Jews. See 2:23 as to how it was possible for Peter to blame all the Jews.

14) Now follows another and a different contrast which is suggested by the word "deny." Jesus they denied, Barabbas they chose in his place. "The Holy and Righteous One" they rejected "and asked for themselves that a man, a murderer, be granted unto them." Being murderers themselves, that was the man they wanted. Note the chiasm which brings the two verbs that have a similar sound but an opposite sense strikingly together: ἠρνήσασθε — ᾐτήσασθε. Compare what is said in 2:27 on "thine Holy One." Holy and righteous are often found together in the sense of separate from sin and pronounced guiltless by the divine Judge. Him who in all his life and his work was spotless and approved of God the Jews denied and thereby declared that they would have nothing to do with him; but they considered it a favor that a vicious murderer be released for them. The middle of αἰτέω is used in business transactions. Here and in Matt. 27:20, and Luke 23:25, the middle brings out the idea

Acts 3:15

that the custom gave the Jews a right to ask for Barabbas, while in Matt. 14:7 this form emphasizes the right of request because of Herod's oath.

15) The word "murderer" leads to another still mightier contrast (δέ). Over against this murderer Peter places "the Author of life," τὸν ἀρχηγὸν τῆς ζωῆς, life's cause and originator (Heb. 12:2; also C.-K. 179). A murderer takes life although it be only the earthly life; this Author of life has divine life in himself and has thereby become the fountain of spiritual and everlasting life for us. The contrast rises to a tremendous climax: the one destroys the lower life, the other bestows the highest life. To this climax there is added the paradox, "you killed the Author of life." How can life's own Author be killed? One might ask further, "How can Jesus become the Author of life by being killed?" This is one of those great Scriptural statements that cannot be brushed aside by calling it a *praedicatio verbalis*, mere verbal play. "The Author of life" is a divine name for the person of Jesus, yet something human is predicated of him. The Scriptures also have the reverse. And this means that everything human as well as everything divine may be predicated of Jesus, no matter how his person is designated, whether by a human or by a divine name. This can be done because in Jesus a communication of natures and also of their attributes exists — he is the Godman.

Luther points out the practical value of Peter's word for us: "We Christians must know that if God is not also in the balance and gives the weight, we sink to the bottom with our scale. By this I mean: If it were not to be said, God has died for us but only a man, we should be lost. But if 'God's death' and 'God died' lie in the scale of the balance, then he sinks down, and we rise up as a light, empty scale. But, indeed, he can also rise again or leap out of the scale; yet he could not sit in the scale unless he became a man like us so that it could be said: 'God died,' 'God's passion,' 'God's blood,' 'God's death.' For in his nature God cannot die; but now that God and man are united in one person, it is correctly called God's death when the man dies who is one thing or one person with God." *Concordia Triglotta*, 1029, etc. In brief, the entire value of Christ's being killed for us lies in his being the Author of life, God.

Peter now returns to his original contrast: the clash between the deed of the Jews and the act of God. *They* killed the Author of life "whom *God* raised up from the dead." And this divine act is more than a contrast to the deed of the Jews; at one stroke God nullified all that the Jews had done. He contradicted and condemned all that they had done; he approved and sealed his great Servant as being in fact the Author of life, the destroyer of death. God accepted all of Christ's work and sacrifice as being full, complete, sufficient and crowned Jesus with infinite glory.

The phrase ἐκ νεκρῶν, like so many other fixed Greek phrases, needs no article. The absence of the article also stresses the noun. The expression never means "out from among the dead" so that all the other dead are regarded as still lying in their graves. The idea expressed by this combination is one of separation alone, R. 598. The phrase occurs thirty-five times with reference to Christ, a few times with reference to other individuals, and also in a figurative sense. Two of these passages refer to the resurrection of a number of the dead, and in them this standard phrase can have no other meaning than the one indicated. No wonder that the phrase is never used with reference to the ungodly; such usage, to say the least, would be gravely misleading. When they are called from their graves, this return to life is not an escape of their bodies from death but an entrance of their bodies into a state that is far worse than decay in the grave. The idea of this expression is not that, when Christ arose, he left all the other dead behind. God took Christ out of death and returned him to life. That is what the phrase means literally and actually.

"Of which we on our part are witnesses" is the same statement found in 2:32 with the pronoun being neuter (not masculine); compare 1:8. The mighty evidence that the power of the crucified Jesus was still operative was before Peter's hearers in the person of the miraculously healed beggar. No personal power of Peter's and of John's had wrought this miracle. It was like so many that were wrought by Jesus prior to his crucifixion. How was it wrought? Here are the witnesses to testify as to the how. By the power of the risen and the glorified Jesus.

16) Peter is even more explicit. Besides clearly stating the ultimate cause of the miracle, he states also the intermediate, or we may say, mediate cause: "his name made this man firm," made his feet and his ankles strong and firm to bear his body, the verb being used as in v. 7. And united with this "name" is "faith" in the name. Hence both name and faith are mentioned twice and are thus made emphatic. This takes us back to v. 6, "in the name of Jesus Christ," and we must recall what was said regarding "name" as designating the revelation which brings Jesus to us. Name and faith are correlatives, the name (revelation) is intended for faith, intended to awaken trust, to be received and held by confidence of heart. And faith needs the name or revelation as the sure ground on which to rest. All other ground is sinking sand.

We thus get Peter's thought. He gives all the credit to "his name" for making firm "this man whom you behold and know." The power that wrought the miracle lies in the name, for it reveals him who himself is in and with his name. Yet the name is not suspended in the air, the revelation must reveal to some heart, somebody must hold to the name and revelation by faith. So Peter adds the thought that the beggar was healed "on the basis ($\epsilon\pi i$) of the faith of his name" (the objective genitive); and again, "the faith, that (faith) through him" gave the man "this entire soundness in the presence of you all." So the object of this faith is the name and revelation; but this faith is "through him," mediated and brought about by Jesus who is revealed by his name. Peter says that only in this way are he and John connected with the miracle. It certainly ought to be clear that the faith which Peter is here speaking of is that which he and John have and not a faith which the beggar had. We have discussed this point when considering v. 4. Yet the view is held that this beggar had to have faith before he could be healed; that his believing was essential; that his faith cooperated with that of the apostles, etc. But the whole account, v. 1-7, places this healing into that class of miracles where faith is intended to follow, and not to precede the miracle. The view that faith must always precede a miracle is a deduction from only a fraction of the facts.

Note the emphasis on "this man whom you behold and know." The man is physical, visible, tangible evidence of the power of the glorified Jesus as mediated by his name and by faith in him and his name. And this man is but a sample of what that power of the risen Christ does in the hearts of men to this very day. It is a continuation of the miracle by which he attested his power and his grace throughout his own ministry. These attestations, once made, stand for all time. To demand their constant repetition is to declare that the recorded attestations do not fully attest, that the seals which the Lord deemed sufficient are not sufficient. We note, too, that the miracle justified the faith of Peter and of John, justified the faith of all who through it came to believe (4:4), justifies our faith today. It is unwarranted to regard Luke's account as a myth, to assert that the early church added its own ideas and conceptions to some perfectly natural occurrence. If Luke's account portrays only the fancies of Peter and of John or those of the early church, then our faith is as vain as theirs was, and the sensible thing to do is to drop the whole matter and to be satisfied with our ethics.

17) Peter plainly marks the transition to the second part of his address. The first part is objective and states the great facts and, of course, includes also those of the rejection of Jesus; the second is subjective and reaches into the hearts of the hearers in order to win them to repentance. Yet the second rests on the first and could not exist independently. **And now, brethren, I know that you committed it in accord with ignorance as also your rulers.** "Now" is not temporal but logical: taking the situation as it is. The word of address, "brethren," marks the turning point in the sermon and voices the love that now accompanies its appeal. "Brethren" is to be taken in the sense of "*our* fathers" in v. 13, "fellow Israelites," and not as "Christian brethren."

Peter says that he well knows that what these hearers of his as also their rulers had committed ($\pi\rho\acute{a}\sigma\sigma\omega$ is often used with reference to evil acts) was done "in accordance with ignorance." But he does not thereby retract his previous statement regarding the ungodliness of their action (v. 13-15). It was directly against God, and not one particle of the damnableness of it all can be subtracted. Κατὰ ἄγνοιαν refers to the Old Testament distinction between sins for which sacrifices can be made (Num. 15:27-29) and sins for which the sinner's soul is cut off (Num. 15:30, 31); sins done "ignorantly," sins done "presumptuously" ("with a high hand"). On the former note Lev. 4:2, 27; 5:18; 22:14; and notably Heb. 9:7 compared with

10:26. Jesus made this distinction when he hung on the cross, Luke 23:34; Paul repeats it in I Cor. 2:8; Peter speaks of the sins committed prior to conversion as being done in ignorance, I Pet. 1:14. The point to be noted is that pardon is possible for such sins; and of that Peter intends to assure his hearers. The popular notion that ignorance excuses sin so that it is without guilt is wholly un-Biblical.

18) **Moreover, what things he announced in advance through all the prophets' mouth that his Christ suffer, God did thus fulfill.** This presents another consideration for Peter's hearers, hence δέ, "moreover." He restates in other words what he has said in 2:23. Not by accident did God's Christ suffer. If the Jews did not know what they were doing by making Jesus suffer, God knew what he was doing when he gave "his Christ" as a lamb for the slaughter, as the sacrifice for the sins of the world. In fact, God had announced in advance "through all the prophets' mouth," making them all speak with one mouth and voice, that the Messiah was to suffer. Only thus could his Messianic work and purpose be accomplished. And what God had thus announced this he, indeed, did fulfill in just that way. The Jews acted in ignorance, God with full intelligence. Peter states the facts as they are. God did not cause the ignorance. But God's grace and wisdom work in spite of human ignorance, yea, in and through that wicked ignorance they bring about its cure and deliverance from its guilt. On "Christ" see 2:36; "his Christ," sent by God and wholly his, is used in 4:26; Luke 9:20; Rev. 11:15; 12:10. The Greek prefers to place οὕτως in the emphatic position at the end. God gave Jesus to suffer as his Christ and thus also glorified him (v. 13).

19) This rich gospel and effective law lead straight to the gospel call: **Repent, therefore, and turn again for the blotting out of your sins, in order that**

there may come seasons of refreshing from the presence of the Lord, and that he may send the Christ who has been appointed for you, Jesus; whom heaven must receive until the time of the restoration of all things, of which God made utterance through the mouth of his holy prophets from of old.

The double command, to repent and to turn again, points to the necessary result (οὖν) of Peter's address. He had dispelled the ignorance of his hearers, they saw the wickedness of their killing Jesus and the blessedness of God's making him their Messiah. This should surely draw them to repentance unless they intended to continue their opposition to God in full consciousness and thus place themselves beyond pardon. "Repent!" is explained in 2:38. "Turn again" merely re-enforces "repent"; it is our "convert" which is used to indicate the change from sin to pardon in conversion.

The clause with εἰς τό states what the immediate purpose of repentance is: "for the being blotted out of your sins," the passive denoting God as the one that blots out the sins. See the same figure in Col. 2:14; Ps. 51:9; Isa. 43:25. The aorist indicates one erasure. The figure conceives the sins as being written into a record, which charges them against the sinner. The reality back of the figure is God's recalling to mind the sins and bringing them to judgment; blotting them out means that he forgets them so that all trace of them is removed. On "remission" see 2:38.

The clause with ὅπως ἄν states the purpose of repentance that follows upon the blotting out of the sins; ἄν is seldom used with this conjunction (B.-D. 369, 5), and its presence here in no way modifies the sense as the older grammars suppose. "Seasons of refreshing or cooling from the presence of the Lord (*Yahweh*)" are longer or shorter periods of spiritual enjoyment when men who repent and are justified are given times in which to feel the sweetness of God's grace in Christ Jesus without disturbance. They come from God's presence or countenance like sunshine and pleasant breezes. The old legalism of Pharisaism knew nothing about such seasons, for all work-righteousness is like the drive, heat, and sweat of slavery. Difficult times, even fiery trials, alternate with such pleasant seasons. Chiliasts think that these seasons are the millennium, and the absence of the article with both nouns is overlooked by them: *Erfrischungszeiten,* "refreshment seasons." Nor do they notice that Peter makes these seasons the proximate purpose of repentance and not one that is remote.

20) The ultimate purpose is that the Lord (*Yahweh*) "may send the Christ who has been appointed for you, (namely) Jesus." The participle means, "to take to hand" and thus "to appoint" (M.-M. 556); the perfect passive states that, once having been appointed as the Messiah, he remains so. "Jesus" is an apposition which states who this appointed Christ or Messiah is. Compare 2:36. The Lord will send Jesus at the end of the world, and what that means is next stated. Peter also shows how the purpose of our repentance centers in the great Parousia of Jesus. Chiliasts overlook the fact that Peter places the refreshing seasons ahead of the sending of Jesus for his great return (1:11).

21) Peter makes the matter plain by means of the relative clause. The Greek ὃν οὐρανὸν δέξασθαι may, however, be understood in two ways, the accusative being either the subject or the object: "who must receive heaven," or, "whom heaven must receive." Luther chooses the former, our versions the latter. Some think that the latter translation conveys the idea that heaven received Christ's human body and nature in such a manner as to confine them to that place and thus to make it impossible for him to be present any-

where else. It is said that he was like Elijah who, when he is in heaven, is nowhere else and who, when he came to Jesus on the mount, was there only and not in heaven. But the thought is that heaven had to receive Jesus until the day of his return and not that he received heaven for that period of time. Δεῖ stresses the necessity of God's plan which glorified Jesus, permitted him to work with divine power on earth until the consummation is reached, and then sent him as appointed for us (ὑμῖν, as believers).

Thus Christ rules from heaven in glory "until the times of the restoration of all things," those times (ὧν = χρόνων) of which all the prophets of old have spoken. Ἀποκατάστασις means placing things back into their former condition: "in the regeneration, when the Son of man shall sit on the throne of his glory," Matt. 19:28. Compare Rom. 8:18, etc. II Pet. 3:13. "We look for new heavens and a new earth, wherein dwelleth righteousness." Rev. 21:1, 5: "I saw a new heaven and a new earth." "Behold, I make all things new." Paradise will be restored. Here again ἄχρι χρόνων has no article, but the plural does not speak of separate times with intervals between them but refers to eternity but speaks of it in a human way as "times"; for after the restoration has been effected, it will remain forever.

Peter's expression has been misunderstood. Although the Greek terms "seasons" (periods) and "times" always have distinct meanings, these two words have been identified in this passage and referred to the millennial era. At least the term "times" has been referred to this era. So also not only are the seasons placed after the sending of the Christ, but this sending is placed after the times. The old fancy of Origen has also been revived that "all things" must include even Satan and all the damned.

If ὧν refers to πάντων, it becomes restrictive: "only all those things which." It must refer to χρόνων: "those times which the prophets have made utterance about"; the genitive is due to the antecedent and is attracted from ἅ. God mentioned (ἐλάλησεν) these times of the consummation through the mouth of the old prophets, compare Isa. 11:6-9; 35:1-10, etc. Here, as in v. 18, we have διά which is so significant for the Biblical conception of Verbal Inspiration. God is always the speaker, the prophets are always the media or instruments "through" whom he speaks. It is the "mouth" of the prophets which God uses, for the very words they speak are those desired by God, and the "mouth" is mentioned although the written word is referred to. The prophets are called "holy" as being set apart and belonging to God who makes them his mouthpiece.

The neat Greek phrase ἀπ' αἰῶνος, literally, "from the eon," means all along during the past era of the world. The noun denotes an age or eon and includes both the time and what transpires in and distinguishes that time. The R. V. gives a long circumscriptive translation: "which have been since the world began"; far better is that of the American Committee, "from of old."

Peter opens a grand prospect to his hearers which is far beyond his own former conception and that of all other Jews and their earthly Messianic kingdom. Repent, etc., and there shall follow cancellation of all sins, then seasons of spiritual refreshing, finally Christ's glorious return, and the fulfillment of all prophecies concerning the final restoration. The apostles were never afraid to place their admonitions on the mightiest possible base or to appeal to the most powerful motives.

22) Peter instances Moses, Deut. 18:15, 18, 19. **Moses said: A Prophet will the Lord God raise up for you out of your brethren like me. Him shall you**

hear according to all things whatsoever he shall utter to you. Moreover, it shall be, every soul which shall not hear that prophet shall be utterly destroyed from the people.

This is not μέν *solitarium* (R. 1151), for δέ follows in v. 24, which balances Moses and all the prophets since Samuel. In v. 23 δέ is a part of the quotation. The quotation is freely reproduced from the LXX by slightly changing the order of the words in the first part and following the Hebrew in the second part. On quoting see 2:25. Moses had special importance for Peter's hearers. This passage of Deuteronomy was well known and was also by the Jews referred to the Messiah. Peter quotes it for two purposes: as presenting Jesus the Prophet-Messiah foretold by Moses, and as emphasizing the admonition to repent, this being what the Prophet-Messiah has to say to all Israelites. Moses "said" means in his writings.

"The Lord God" is used for the Hebrew as in 2:39 and implies his covenant relation and his power. What God told Moses about the Prophet, Peter repeats as being told to the Israelites by Moses. "Out of your brethren" has peculiar force. When did God ever raise up a prophet for the Israelites from any people except their own brethren? Why, then, add the words that this future prophet would come "out of their brethren"? This is a reference to the human nature of Jesus, but by mentioning it in such a peculiar manner God implies that there will be something about him that is far higher than his Jewish birth. The phrase points to this Prophet's deity. Therefore also he will be only like Moses and not like all the other prophets. Moses was a mediator-prophet, the mediator of the covenant made on Sinai, for which task a man was sufficient. The promised Prophet would also be a mediator but of a still higher covenant, the one that superseded the first and centered in Golgotha. The Jews kept looking for this prophet although in their own way, John 6:14; Luke 17:16. Jesus himself referred to this prophecy of Moses' in John 5:46, 47.

Hence also the gravity of the command and the threat. "Him shall you hear!" the genitive of the person after a verb of hearing, the future tense with the imperative sense of laws: thou shalt; thou shalt not. The sense is "hear and obey" by doing exactly what he says. Peter adds the next phrase and clause as interpreting what this command includes: hear "according to all things whatsoever he shall utter to you." The aorist is constative and sums up all his utterances into a unit, while "all things as many as" distributes them as to their number. The indefinite ὅσα ἄν conveys the thought that, no matter what this Prophet may say, unquestioning obedience is demanded. Certainly, all of God's prophets must be obeyed; yet of none is this said with such peculiar emphasis as of this supreme Prophet.

23) Hence also the threat is made prominent in the same strong manner. Ἔσται, like ἐγένετο, is used without a connective; and "every soul" is to be taken in the sense of "every person." In ἥτις ἄν with the subjunctive there lies the idea that someone may, indeed, not hear that Prophet, may dare to reject the message that he brings by the disobedience of unbelief. Such conduct shall be fatal for him. His doom is sealed in advance. The Hebrew reads, "I will require it of him"; the LXX, "I will execute vengeance upon him." Instead of either of these expressions Peter uses the strong formula which occurs frequently in the Pentateuch beginning with Gen. 17:14: "shall be utterly destroyed from the people." He shall be sundered from the λαός, from God's people, by the death penalty without forgiveness, to be cast out and rejected forever in the final judgment. The threat could not be made stronger   The moment we realize wherein all

the things Jesus came to proclaim centered, namely in faith and forgiveness, we see how absolutely fatal the rejection of unbelief necessarily is.

24) And, on the other hand, all the prophets from Samuel and those in succession on, as many as made utterance, also announced these days. After μέν in v. 22 we now have δέ, for which "on the other hand" is cumbersome yet reproduces the idea. Moses on the one hand, and not merely one but all the others on the other hand. In one grand chorus they proclaimed "these days," those of the great Mediator-Prophet foretold by Moses, who would grant the seasons of refreshing until the times of the restoration of all things, the days of the entire Messianic era. Peter attributes to all the prophets a vision of the New Testament era up to and including the Parousia. All their prophecies related to these days in one way or in another; for none of them would have prophesied if these days had not been promised.

The prophets after Moses are reckoned from the time of Samuel and his school of prophets. Samuel was not only himself great, he also founded a school of prophets, for which reason the Talmud calls him *magister prophetarum*. The adverb καθεξῆς, "successively," "in succession or due order," is made a substantive by the article. If "those in succession" are Samuel's pupils, the construction is quite regular. Samuel and his pupils in order after him would justify Peter's making the count begin with them and their great teacher, "as many as made utterance" would include the rest. The alternative is to find a mixed construction here: 1) "all the prophets from Samuel on, as many as have spoken"; and 2) "all the prophets, Samuel and those in order, as many," etc. The two statements would be combined into one, which is not satisfactory. I Sam. 2:10 contains a notable prophecy which names "his Anointed." When we are thinking of Samuel we should not forget his anointing of David, the type of Christ, and his relation to the kingdom that began with Saul.

25) All that has been said about Moses and the prophets Peter now drives home. **You yourselves are the sons of the prophets and of the covenant which God covenanted with your fathers, saying to Abraham, And in thy seed shall all the families of the earth be blessed.** This appeal to the highest motives is powerful. Nothing could be more effective psychologically. The pronoun "you" is emphatic, and the predicate with the article makes it identical and interchangeable with the subject (R. 768); in other words, there are none others who are sons of the prophets. The connotation in "sons" as compared with "children" is that of legal standing, of heirship, and thus of succession in carrying on that for which the fathers stood. Peter says, "you are the sons," meaning that this honor and this high position now rest on these his hearers. All that the prophets gave them as sons is theirs to have, hold, and pass on. In all the world none others are found who have a right to this position. The prophets are the spiritual fathers of the Israelites and even the physical fathers of their blood.

"And of the covenant" is added in order to bring out the idea of the full blessedness, greatness, and nobility of this sonship. The position which was once occupied by the prophets as their fathers they now hold as their successors. More than this, the fathers had only the promises of the covenant, these sons are to have the great fulfillment of those promises. Being sons and heirs, the inheritance is now to be paid out to them. Διαθήκη is the Hebrew b^{e}rith, noun and verb being the same: "the covenant which God covenanted." The middle voice also corresponds with the noun: God disposed of what was his, disposed of it as he saw fit (ἧς is attracted from ἥν).

Always it is God who covenanted and never Abraham. It is always God's covenant and not Abraham's; nor are the two ever coordinated. God did the bestowing, Abraham only received. This covenant was "with your fathers," πρός being used to indicate living relationship and intimate intercourse (R. 625.) Since it was made with Abraham, the covenant included all the fathers, for they were Abraham's sons and heirs even as Peter's hearers now are.

Peter quotes the words of the covenant from Gen. 22:18, but deviates from the LXX by placing "in thy seed" first and by substituting "all the families" (πατριαί) for "all the nations" (ἔθνη), which is evidence that Peter translates the Hebrew independently. Gal. 3:16 establishes the vital point that τὸ σπέρμα of this covenant promise is Christ; in that passage Paul stresses the use of the singular rather than the plural σπέρματα. God said "seed," not "seeds." The great covenant blessing of redemption and salvation was in connection with (ἐν) Christ and not in connection with all the descendants of Abraham. That Seed, that great son of Abraham, had now appeared, and all the blessing promised in him was now actually present. Abraham and the fathers had died in the faith and the hope of it, seeing it from afar and thus appropriating it; Peter's hearers have it right before them. The healed beggar is a sample of that blessing; Peter's sermon is the offer of all the spiritual riches of that blessing. With πατριαί Peter echoes πρὸς τοὺς πατέρας in its connection with οἱ υἱοί. The word refers to families in the widest sense as being derived from one father as the head. We might translate "tribes or clans." But "of the earth" extends the covenant promise and blessing beyond Judaism (1:8), and this universality is intensified: "all the families of the earth."

We challenge the claim that Gal. 3:16 does not apply, and that "seed" is a collective term for the descendants of Abraham, so that they bring the blessing to all the families of the earth. That is the contention of the Jews today: they, the Jews collectively, are the Messiah for all nations, Judaism is the salvation of the world. Isaiah's *Ebed Yahweh,* Servant of Jehovah, is Jewry. The commentators do not, of course, have this in mind; they refer to Christ but associate him with the Jews as a nation. Not only is salvation of the Jews (John 4:22), it is still bound up with the Jews. Zahn writes "that the redemption of humanity depends on whether Israel after its errings will yet finally reach the goal of its destiny," i. e., in a final, national conversion. We, of course, cannot agree with such views.

26) **To you first God, having raised up his Servant, sent him blessing you in turning each one from your wickednesses.** After the strong ἡμεῖς at the head of v. 25 we now have the equally strong ὑμῖν at the head of this verse: *"you,"* what you are by reason of God's past grace — *"to you,"* what comes to you by means of God's present grace. Note the three great words placed together: "to you — first — God." "First" places Peter's hearers at the head of the vast host and the procession of "the families of the earth." They alone had the "Seed," the great "Servant" of Jehovah in their midst, παῖς as in v. 13. "Having raised him up" refers to the entire ministry and mission of Jesus as God's Servant and is thus construed with "sent him to you."

The present tense εὐλογοῦντα causes the grammarians some difficulty. R. 1116 and 1128 regards it as expressing purpose and assumes that the context makes this clear. Such a significance would seem to call for the future participle or the present infinitive. The present participle is descriptive of αὐτόν, "him," and is durative because he blesses continuously. Its present tense is without relation to the aorist of the main verb. Ἐν τῷ with the infinitive is a favorite usage of Luke's although it is Semitic (R. 1072). It is usually temporal, "while," but also has other meanings: *indem, dadurch dass* (B.-D. 404, 3). Here we translate, "By turning each one," etc. This is the turning of repentance as in v. 19. The supreme blessing for any sinner is that Christ turn him "from his wickednesses."

Ἀποστρέφειν is regarded as intransitive by B.-D. 308: "in that each one turn from your wickedness." But this gives the sentence the unsatisfactory sense: Christ blesses when each one turns. The infinitive is transitive: Christ blesses by turning each one. Peter individualizes, for conversion is a personal matter; Christ turns us, but so that we ourselves turn, Jer. 31:18. Peter is using Old Testament phraseology when he speaks of turning from wickedness; note Ezek. 3:19; 18:27; 33:14; Jonah 3:10. With πονερά Peter uses no soft words; it is "wickednesses" in the sense of *Bosheiten, Schurkerei*, active and vicious evil. The plural leads us to think of all the fruits of unbelief. To turn from them means to turn to Christ in a new life. At this point Peter is interrupted by some of the very wickedness against which he was warning. Yet he had said enough to bring a host of his hearers to faith.

CHAPTER IV

Peter and John Before the Sanhedrin

1) News of what had occurred (the healing) and of what was now occurring (the preaching) reached the Sadducees, and they at once interfere with strong measures. **Now while they were speaking to the people, there suddenly stood by them the priests and the commander of the Temple and the Sadducees, thoroughly vexed because they were teaching the people and proclaiming in connection with Jesus the resurrection from the dead. And they laid hands on them and put them in ward for the morrow; for it was already evening.**

Peter did the speaking. "They speaking" means that he acted also for John. The address was just about completed. Before anything further could happen such as happened in 2:37, the authorities swoop down on the scene and arrest Peter, John, and the beggar. The verb denotes sudden, unexpected appearance and is used with reference to the sudden standing of angels beside someone. So absorbed was everyone that the approach of the authorities was not noticed.

Luke names in order: "the priests, the commander of the Temple, and the Sadducees." But this mention of "the priests" in the first place, and the fact that they were few, in no way debars us from thinking that they were the ones who had charge of the service on this afternoon. Their authority was less than that of the commander and of the Sadducees: To think of these "priests" as priest police, and to assume that there were two kinds of police: one that was composed of priests and another of Levites, on no stronger evidence than the appearance of ἱερεῖς in first place in this passage of Acts, is venturesome thinking. These were the regular priests, one of the twenty-four groups that had been selected by lot, whose time of service had been appointed for this day. Somebody had reported to them, and they, in turn, had informed the higher authorities, and so it came about that they were present with these authorities.

"The commander of the Temple" called the *sagan*, was at the head of the entire police force of the Temple which was composed of Levites. In the story of the arrest of Jesus these Levite police are called ὑπηρέται, "underlings"; they went about armed with clubs. Luke uses the plural στρατηγοί (Luke 22:4), from which we conclude that the commander had several lieutenants under him. The chief commander, Zahn claims, ranked next to the high priest, but that he, too, was a priest we decline to believe unless convincing evidence is furnished. Josephus mentions the commander in *Ant.* 20, 6, 2; *Wars*, 6, 5, 3. On an errand such as this present one this commander would not appear without a detachment of Levitical police. That is so self-evident that Luke does not need to mention these "underlings" when he names the authorities that appeared.

"The Sadducees" were members of the Sanhedrin, such as happened to be at hand when Peter addressed the people. They are the persons that instigated the arrest. This Jewish sect rejected the mass of oral tradition taught by the popular schools, claimed that this life was the whole of existence, that there are neither angels nor spirits, and that there is no resurrection of the dead. Although they were few in number, the Sadducees wielded a tremendous influence because they commanded wealth and social position and because the family of the high priest and a number of other priests belonged to their group. "The doctrine of the

Sadducees is this, that souls die with the bodies; nor do they regard the observation of anything besides what the law enjoins them; for they think it is an instance of virtue to dispute with these teachers of philosophy whom they frequent. But this doctrine is received but by a few, yet by those still of the greatest dignity," Josephus, *Ant.* 18, 1, 4. They were the aristocrats, the freethinkers and skeptics among the Jews. They were coarse in manners and lived in Epicurean luxuriousness.

2) What brought them to the scene was the fact that they were "thoroughly vexed" because Peter and John were teaching the people and proclaiming the very doctrine they were opposing, and were doing this ἐν τῷ Ἰησοῦ, "in connection with Jesus," namely by proclaiming that Jesus was risen and by furnishing as evidence of his living power the miracle wrought on the lame beggar. Peter had not yet preached the general resurrection, but these Sadducees drew the correct conclusion that, if Jesus was risen, their whole contention about the impossibility of the resurrection was null and void. Jesus had already answered them, Matt. 22:23-33, but his answer had left them obdurate. Now, when right here in the Temple, under their very eyes, the resurrection was being taught "in connection with Jesus" whom they had brought to the cross, they rise up in their might to decree a summary stop. Note that Luke adds ἐκ νεκρῶν with a second article so that this phrase receives the emphasis (R. 776): "the resurrection, that (namely) from the dead." The dead, no, they cannot arise! On the phrase itself see 3:16.

3) Luke's account is summary. Whether any charges were preferred, whether an altercation ensued, whether the people took the matter quietly, is not said. He states only that these authorities made short work of it, arrested and locked up Peter and John and the beggar. The Greek has the expressive phrase, "they

threw their hands on them," meaning, of course, that not the authorities themselves did this but their "underlings" at their command; so in 3:15 Peter said to all the people, "You killed the Author of life." Strong men took them by the arms and hurried them away.

Τήρησις is "custody," "ward," "imprisonment." Zahn has located the place of confinement on the basis of statements found in the Mishna and places it in one of the vaulted halls above a certain portal; but all we can say is that the place was not the same as that mentioned in 5:18. Evening had come, not, indeed, sunset but late afternoon. Thus it was too late to summon a session of the Sanhedrin in the hope of having it take care of the business on hand. The Jewish law forbade trials at night, a law that was most flagrantly violated in the case of Jesus but was here observed.

4) **But many of those that heard the Word believed; and there came to be a number of men about five thousand.** The aorists are historical and register only the facts. Peter's success was phenomenal. This is a fine example of apostolic evangelization. But remember that these were Jews who knew their Scriptures and not Gentiles or people to whom the true religion is still unknown. Even these Jews needed further instruction, 2:40. The apostles always laid a thorough foundation. Note that "they heard the Word," Rom. 10:17. Thus early "the Word" signified the sum of the apostolic doctrine; in 2:42 it is called "the teaching" or "the doctrine."

Luke says that the entire number of believers in Jerusalem increased from over 3,000 souls (2:41) to 5,000 men, not counting women and children of whom there was, of course, a due proportion. A count must have been made so that Luke could obtain this figure. It was too difficult to count all the souls, at least Luke could obtain only the figure he here recorded. He might have made an estimate of the souls. But his aim is accuracy with no intention of making the figure as large as possible.

5) Now it came to pass on the morrow that there were brought together their rulers, and the elders and the scribes in Jerusalem and Annas, the high priest, and Caiaphas and John and Alexander and as many as were of high-priestly kindred.

Luke's Hebraistic ἐγένετο may be followed by καί and a finite verb, by a simple finite verb, or, as here, by the accusative with the infinitive as the subject. The Sanhedrin was brought together by a summoning of its members. Only those "in Jerusalem" were summoned and not those living in country places outside of the city. The phrase modifies the nouns. The Sanhedrin is often designated by naming only two of its constituent groups; a little more impressive is the naming of all three: "the high priests, the elders, and the scribes." Here Luke refers to the high priests in a special way (v. 6) and thus varies the designation by calling the first group οἱ ἄρχοντες, "the rulers." He surely has in mind the group that is otherwise called by the general term "the high priests." "Rulers" befits them in a special way since they had the leadership in the Sanhedrin, Caiaphas being the presiding officer who had the executive power in his hands. There is no reason for including lay rulers who were not priests in this first group. These were classed as "the elders." They were important laymen who had been elevated to a position in the Sanhedrin because of their standing and their experience in judicial matters. The scribes were the rabbis, graduates of the schools, who were chosen because of special ability in interpreting the Tora, i. e., the Law, the Old Testament. All or nearly all of them were Pharisees as were also the elders. The entire number that made up the Sanhedrin was 70 or

72 although not all members were needed for transacting business.

6) Καί particularizes by naming four of them individually and by summarizing the rest of this special high-priestly group. This is an exceptional construction in Luke's writings but becomes almost necessary after the statement in v. 1 that "the Sadducees" had brought about the arrest; v. 6 tells us who the chief Sadducees were, namely all those of high-priestly connection.

Here, as elsewhere, Annas is mentioned as being especially important. He is named first because of his age; Caiaphas was his son-in-law. Annas had been high priest from the year 6 to the year 15. Then several other high priests followed in quick succession. After these Caiaphas held the office from 18-36. Having been high priest, this title was still accorded to Annas, no doubt also because he continued to wield great influence personally and through his family. His son Eleazar had been high priest after him, his son-in-law now held this office, four other sons attained the high priesthood at a later time (Josephus, *Ant.* 20, 9, 1), so that a regular dynasty of the house of Annas was established. The name Annas was common, hence an addition was needed to mark the Annas here referred to. He also had a son by the name of Annas. Caiaphas was a rare name; we know of only this one individual who bore it; hence no further distinctive mark was needed. The Talmud also laid down the principle, that one might promote an individual to a sacred office but not demote him. This idea may well have been operative already at this time when the Romans interfered with the high priesthood so that the office was no longer held for life.

We really know nothing definite about John and Alexander. Zahn identifies John with Jonathan, the son of Annas, high priest after Caiaphas in 36, who was soon replaced by his brother Theophilus, was offered the same office again but declined in favor of his brother Matthias, and was finally murdered in the Temple by bandits. When Luke wrote, all this was history (recorded by Josephus), and this circumstance would explain why "John" is placed third by Luke, if he is, indeed, this Jonathan and son of Annas. All that can be said about Alexander is this, the fact that a Sadducee bearing such a name reveals the foreign influences at work among the sect.

Luke mentions still others who belonged to the high-priestly γένος, "kindred," which some take in a wide sense as referring to relatives of former high priests, but which seems to refer to relatives of the present high-priestly family. These, Luke suggests, were the real leaders of the Sanhedrin, all of them Sadducees, all of them foes of the resurrection and of any preaching about Jesus as having risen from the dead. These most powerful judges, whose verdict was absolutely determined in advance, the two former fishermen from Galilee had now to face.

7) **And having stood them in the midst, they began to question, In connection with what power, or in connection with what name did you do this thing?** The judges sat cross-legged in a half-circle on a raised platform. Temple police brought in Peter, John, and the beggar. They were compelled to stand on the lower floor "in the midst," the judges facing them from all sides. This was the exact manner in which and the exact place where Jesus had stood when facing this court. What memories, what anticipations must have crowded into the apostles' minds! Caiaphas must have presided as he had done when Jesus was tried. But no crime is charged against them, no row of witnesses confronts the disciples. This is only a judicial investigation; the apostles are asked to make a statement regarding themselves. All present know

what that statement will be, one that gravely incriminates themselves together with this court, most especially with its dominating members, the high-priestly Sadducean connection. The imperfect "they began to question" is descriptive and at the same time holds us in suspense as to what the answer will be.

The English cannot reproduce the pointed τοῦτο ὑμεῖς at the end of the question: "this thing — *you*," fellows like you. The pronoun has an emphasis of scorn. "This thing" declines to describe it in any way, for that would bring into prominence the greatness and the beneficence of the deed of the apostles. Not *what* they had done is asked about, for who could condemn the restoration of a congenital cripple; the *way* they had done what they had done, the *means* by which they had done it, are assailed. Sometimes ποῖος is qualitative, sometimes it is not (R. 740). We may here render: "In connection with what kind of power, or in connection with what kind of name?" The Sanhedrists know that the apostles will be compelled to say that the power and the name have reference to Jesus. Now also the Jewish exorcists claimed to do wonderful things by using the formulas of their day, the names of the patriarchs or the name of Solomon, and this procedure was considered proper and orthodox. The question thus implies that, if some other power and especially some other name was used by the apostles, they lay themselves open to the most serious charge. Jesus of Nazareth was regarded as a rank blasphemer in the eyes of the Sanhedrin because he had called himself the Son of God. To use his power and his name for healing, no matter what the blessed result, was using the power and the name that were as blasphemous as this blasphemer himself.

The question with its repeated and thus emphatic "what kind of" is shrewd; it is like a noose thrown around the necks of the apostles. The end certainly does *not* justify the means. Damnable means dare not be used even if, through them, good or apparent good is done. That is the point of the double question. The Sadducees could not, of course, unlike the Pharisees in the Sanhedrin, claim that Beelzebul was the source of Jesus' power and name, for they denied the existence of angels and of spirits. Yet Josephus, *Ant.* 18, 1, 4, informs us that they were base enough, when it served their purpose, to "addict themselves to the notions of the Pharisees because the multitude would otherwise not hear them." The question is here put in a shrewd way so as to gain the support also of all the Pharisees who had their own view of the wickedness of Jesus' power and name. Note that here and in 2:38 and in Peter's answer ἐν ποίῳ ὀνόματι means "in connection with" what name?

8) **Then Peter, filled with the Holy Spirit, said to them: Rulers of the people and elders, if we on our part this day are judicially examined on a good deed to an impotent man, in connection with what this man has been saved, let it be known to you all and to all the people of Israel that in connection with the name of Jesus Christ, the Nazarene, whom you crucified, whom God raised up from the dead, in connection with this One does this man stand here before you whole.**

Peter again speaks for himself and also for John. It was not necessary to state explicitly that on Pentecost Peter was filled with the Holy Spirit when he preached as he did; nor was there need to state that he spoke by the Spirit to the multitude before Solomon's Porch. But here this fact must be noted because it is the first fulfillment of the Lord's promise given in Matt. 10:19, 20. Peter's wonderful defense is not to be credited to his keen powers and his great courage. He and John had not lain awake all night planning what to say. They had not even known what turn

Acts 4:8, 9   161

things would take. It is the Holy Spirit who puts this telling defense into Peter's mouth. Peter merely uses a shorter formula when he names only the rulers and the elders when addressing the Sanhedrin. Both are most honorable terms; in fact, either could be used alone as a designation of the entire court. Like Jesus, the apostles acknowledge and submit to the authority of the Sanhedrin. Peter used even the most respectful form of address.

9) In the conditional form of the answer: "if we this day," etc., there lies a fine intimation that no just grounds exist for instituting the examination now being made. The emphatic ἡμεῖς, "we on our part," takes up in a dignified way the emphatic and scornful ὑμεῖς of the question. The verb ἀνακρίνω is used in a forensic sense to indicate a preliminary judicial examination on the result of which further legal action may depend. Peter thus tells the Sanhedrin what it is doing; its president had failed to do so. The latter had used only τοῦτο, "this thing," in his question of examination; Peter is proud to state what "this thing" really is because of which he and John are being subjected to judicial probing: "a good deed to an impotent man" (the objective genitive, R. 500). The articles are purposely omitted in order to emphasize the quality of the terms and to generalize the phrase. Any good deed done to any helpless man, a restoration of such a man, speaks for itself. Not only this good deed but any and all like it ought to be beyond criminal suspicion and inquiry by any court. The Sanhedrin should investigate crimes and not good deeds. Yet if this high court must know "in connection with what this man (pointing to the beggar) has been saved (and thus now stands before them as saved," Peter is certainly ready to furnish the fullest information, and this high court may then decree whether any criminality attaches to the means used for the man's wonder-

ful restoration. Ἐν τίνι is neuter because it includes both "power" and "name" in the question; the R. V.'s marginal translation "in whom" is inexact. All five ἐν, beginning with those in the question, are identical in force and mean neither "through," "by," nor "in," but, "in connection with," which is the original sense of this preposition. This sense also gives it so wide a range. Sphere illustrates its idea, for ἐν draws a circle around two concepts.

10) We have noted Peter's tone of authority in 2:14, 36; here it appears again and is expressed with the same imperative: "let it be known to you and to all the people of Israel." So little is there to hide that Peter courts the utmost publicity and would have the world of Judaism know the exact facts regarding this beggar's restoration. The Sanhedrin wants the name stated that is involved in this miracle; triumphantly Peter complies: it is "in connection with the name of Jesus Christ, the Nazarene," that this man stands here before their very eyes ὑγιής, sound, whole, no longer crippled. By naming this name Peter does not need to specify the power in regard to which he also had been asked. All Palestine knew about that power because of the miracles which Jesus himself had wrought.

The old view is still held that in these "name" phrases ὄνομα means "authority," R. 649, or that the phrase is a mere circumlocution. It is, of course, the Hebrew b⁰schem, B.-D. 206, 3; but in these phrases and in other connections NAME always denotes revelation; see the discussion in 2:21, 38; 3:6. We believe "in or on the name." The name is inserted before the person as making him known to us, as the means for apprehending him, of connecting ourselves with him. Note the resumptive ἐν τούτῳ in this verse: "in connection with this One" as named and revealed. "Nazarene" is repeatedly used to identify Jesus in the popular way (2:22); and, as in 2:38, "Jesus Christ" designates him as the Messiah (2:36, "Lord and Christ").

The two relative clauses name Jesus as Christ more fully, and the asyndeton makes them the more striking by presenting clashing opposites: "whom *you* crucified, whom *God* raised up from the dead." Here we have the same bold contrast we noticed in 2:23, 24; 3:14, 15, which appeals to the conscience when the divine law reveals the sin. Here again God is shown as nullifying what the Sanhedrin had done. It had intended to abolish Jesus forever, God raised him up and established him forever. Here Peter does not add as he did in 2:32; 3:15: "of which we are witnesses." Their testimony regarding the resurrection of Jesus would be scorned by the Sanhedrists. Peter points to the testimony that even these vicious haters of Jesus cannot deny, namely the healed beggar standing there before their eyes: "in connection with this One," whose name and revelation he has just presented, "this man stands here before you whole." The perfect παρέστηκεν is always used as a present, and παρά, "stands beside," means, "stands here."

Peter says this to men like Annas and Caiaphas here in the midst of their Saducean following. The whole Sanhedrin had tried to hush up the resurrection of Jesus, Matt. 28:11-15. Here it faced them with even stronger evidence than that which the Roman guard brought from the tomb. No dead Jesus could work a miracle such as this; the risen and glorified Jesus alone could do that. So Jesus had healed when he was alive; lo, so he had healed now after this Sanhedrin had crucified him!

11) Why did Caiaphas and those Sadducees not leap up and denounce Peter in blazing wrath? Did the truth thrown into their faces, hurled at their consciences with such unexpected power dumbfound them

for the moment? Peter continues: **This One is the stone, the one considered as nothing by you, the ones building, the one become corner head. And the salvation is in connection with not a single other; for there is not another name under heaven as having been given among men in connection with which we must be saved.**

Peter was not defending himself and John. There was nothing against which to make a defense. He is doing his part of witnessing (1:8), preaching Jesus Christ to these Sanhedrists as to any other sinners through law and gospel. What this court would do with him and with John mattered not at all; his one concern was to glorify Jesus as the Savior, and in this the Holy Spirit directed his words In his witness he uses Ps. 118:22, yet not as a quotation but in order to recall to the Sanhedrists what Jesus himself had told them on the basis of this psalm in Matt. 21:42-44. Jesus had warned them that this prophecy would be fulfilled; Peter points out that it has now been fulfilled, both parts of it, viz., what they had done, and what God had done. But he centers attention on Jesus, on the unbelief of the Sanhedrists in rejecting him, and on the deed of God in making him the Savior.

"This One" is resumptive and repeats all that Peter has said about Jesus. The article with the predicate "the stone" makes it identical and interchangeable with the subject, R. 769. The figure refers to the spiritual temple of God. In their office as spiritual leaders of the Jewish nation God had appointed these Sanhedrists builders of this temple. How they would function as builders the psalmist had foretold, and Peter now repeats the thought of the psalmist in connection with this stone, Jesus Christ, "the one considered as nothing" by them, unfit to be used anywhere in a building such as they proposed. They rejected Jesus and crucified him. But this very stone is "the one become corner head," the one supreme stone which, laid at the head corner, governs every other corner and every angle in the entire spiritual temple and thus determines the angle at which every other stone is to be laid. How Jesus became this wonderful stone Peter has already stated, namely by God's raising Jesus from the dead. Note that εἰς is predicative: *geworden zum Eckstein*, Hebrew, *l^e*, R. 481. "Corner head" is without articles and thus stresses the concepts themselves; it is almost a compound.

Sometimes Christ is viewed as the entire foundation (I Cor. 3:11), then again as the cornerstone, as distinct from the foundation (Eph. 2:20). The latter is not the former. Peter loved this passage about the cornerstone (I Pet. 2:4, etc.), for his own name Peter (rock) always reminded him of this Stone. Will these blind Sanhedrists at last see their terrible sin and repent?

12) In plain, literal language Peter presents the fulness of the gospel with its mighty call to salvation. The Greek may or may not use the article with an abstract noun, so that here ἡ σωτηρία is usually translated "salvation," *Heil* (Luther); yet here the article specifies. Peter means "the salvation," that promised in the Messiah. It is this salvation that exists "in connection with not a single other"; ἐν is used like the five ἐν in v. 7 and 10. No second, no substitute, no alternate to Jesus exists so that by connecting with (ἐν) this other we could secure salvation. The noun "salvation," to which the verb "be saved" is added, denotes the act of deliverance plus the resultant state of safety; both are wrought by the Σωτήρ, Savior; see the participle in 2:47. Peter uses the same verb when speaking of the deliverance of the beggar in v. 9, just as Jesus, too, had used it in the case of persons healed in Luke 8:48; 18:42; and with reference to the deliverance from sin in Luke 7:50. The word can be used in

either sense, but here, where Peter speaks of the supreme work of the Messiah Jesus, salvation and saving are to be taken in the spiritual sense.

With γάρ Peter explains by restating more fully and explicitly what he had said. Because of γάρ, οὐδέ cannot mean "neither," this is true also because no other οὐδέ follows. The entire previous sentence is expanded. Elucidating and fuller restatements are generally introduced with explanatory γάρ. Instead of "not a single other" (person) Peter says, "not another name under heaven as having been given among men." Here he again uses "name" as he did in v. 10 and as he used it with such emphasis in 3:16, there adding the correlative "faith" with equal emphasis; see the remarks on that passage.

Name" is again the revelation by which the saving person becomes the possession of the person to be saved. It is the objective means of saving and implies faith in that name or revelation as the subjective means. Jesus comes to us by means of his name; that name awakens faith; and by faith in his name he saves us. Ἄλλος and ἕτερος are often used without a special difference in meaning; and R. 749 thinks that here the latter means only no "other at all." This absoluteness, however, lies in the added phrase "under heaven" and not in ἕτερον itself. We are certainly entitled to retain the difference here; "not a single other" who is in any way *like* and comparable to Jesus brings us salvation; and, excluding the other possibility, "not another name under heaven" that is *different* from his and works on us in a different way.

Instead of a relative clause we have the articulated perfect participle, articulated because otherwise the participle would be combined with ἐστίν and form a periphrastic perfect verb form. This participle adds the very important thought that, to do us any good, the "name" must be given to us, namely by God or by

Christ. Only of a name thus given among men is Peter
speaking, any other name would reveal and convey
nothing to us. Names are intended as distinctions by
which others know us, and the better they know us,
the better they can trust us. The perfect participle
"having been given among men" implies that, once
given, the name remains as our means of salvation.

And here again is universality: "among men," par-
alleling "on all flesh" in 2:17, and "to those afar off"
in 2:39. The name has been given "among men" in
order to attract and to draw them with its saving
power: "in connection with which we must be saved,"
ἐν is for the sixth time used in the same sense. This
"we" is not a retraction of "among men," not a limitation of the universality. It appeals to Peter's hearers
and joins him with them; for he is not offering an aca-
demic or abstract proposition which one might debate
and regarding which one might hold different opinions
but an absolute fact of necessity on which hangs eternal salvation or eternal destruction. Since "to be
saved" includes the act plus the condition, Peter can
freely include the apostles with the Sanhedrin; the
infinitive is constative. The necessity implied in δεῖ is
that of the fact: Since salvation is possible only in connection with Jesus, all who desire to be saved *must*
embrace his name.

13) **Now, beholding the boldness of Peter and
John and having perceived that they were people
uneducated and ordinary, they were marvelling, also
they were recognizing them, that they had been with
Jesus. Seeing also the man standing with them, the
one having been healed, they had nothing to say to
the contrary.**

The imperfect tenses are descriptive of the situation of the Sanhedrists. Two things made them marvel: the παρρησία of the apostles, the free, assured way
in which they bore themselves and spoke, and yet the

fact that they were "uneducated," never having attended a rabbinical school, and besides that they were ἰδιῶται, ordinary, common people who had nothing but their own little personal affairs to which to attend. They held no public office of any kind that might give them some training. They understood that the apostles had neither the advantage of rabbinical schooling nor that offered by any other kind of prominence. Associated with this was their recognition of the fact that they had been with Jesus, and that this experience in some way accounted for the effective way in which they spoke and acted. Many, no doubt, had seen these two apostles with Jesus during the Passover week, then, however, paying little attention to them. The Greek retains the tenses of the direct discourse when it expresses what one perceives and recognizes, hence εἰσί and also ἦσαν; the thought of the Sanhedrists was: "they are uneducated" — "they *were* with Jesus."

14) Associated with all this they saw standing beside the apostles the man that had been healed, whom, of course, they had for a long time known as the most hopeless cripple but who was now standing on his feet completely healed — eloquent attestation of every word Peter had spoken. All of this was too much. They were checkmated, "they had nothing to say to the contrary," there just was nothing that they could say. Note how the two τε used in these verses bind the three statements into one compact whole.

Here we have a shining exemplification of the manner in which the Holy Spirit conducts the cases of persecuted disciples. Even the Sanhedrists perceived that a power was sustaining Peter and John. The point to be noted, however, is not the fact that the apostles escaped but that, irrespective of this, they so perfectly maintained the cause of Christ and the gospel. The very judges who compelled them to appear were converted into an audience for the apostles' preaching, and they preached to this audience without the least timidity or restraint and with all power and effectiveness. Such scenes occur throughout the Acts; in this way the gospel reached out to the highest authorities to win rulers, governors, kings for Christ.

15) But having ordered them to go outside of the council chamber, they conferred with each other, saying: What shall we do to these men? for that a known sign has occurred through them is manifest to all those inhabiting Jerusalem, and we are not able to make denial. But in order that it may not spread farther to the people, let us threaten them no longer to speak on the basis of this name to any man.

This was a painful situation. The Sadducees, who had caused the arrest, had not expected to find themselves at such a disadvantage. Nothing is left to them but to order the prisoners to step outside and to confer in private. Here συνέδριον designates the hall where the session was held, where the judges "sat together"; the word is also used to designate the Sanhedrin itself. The Greek is picturesque: "they threw together" (words, λόγοι), R. 1202, and thus conferred in private, each giving his opinion. We need not ask how Luke obtained the results of this conference, for since so many were conferring, it was impossible to keep things secret.

16) Luke reports only the gist of what was said and decided. "What shall we do to these men?" is a question of deliberation and doubt, hence the subjunctive is employed. Having arrested these men, they felt that they must do something to them; but what could they do? The honest thing to do was to acknowledge their wrong in having made the arrest; yea, to admit their crime in crucifying Jesus, to repent, and to accept him as the Christ. But their very question implies that these things they will *not do*. They must in some

170   Interpretation of the Acts of the Apostles

way maintain their opposition, the only question being in what way.

They admit that they cannot deny the reality of the "sign" wrought through the apostles. It is a "known sign" and by this time "manifest to all those inhabiting Jerusalem." The crowds that saw the healed beggar and heard Peter's address in the Temple court spread the news over all the city; the Sanhedrists admit this to each other. With φανερόν supply the copula ἐστί.

This is the blindness of unbelief. The fact that a known and notable sign has occurred, a sign that signified something, one that had been wrought "through the apostles," they being only the medium (διά) of a higher power, means absolutely nothing to these Sanhedrists personally. They would deny the miracle if they could; the only thing that prevents such a denial is the fact that it is already known throughout the city. This to their great regret. We see how old the motives and the policies of unbelief are. The circumstance that facts are facts and signs are signs means nothing; deny them, get rid of them in some way; it is deplorable that they should be known at all, and they must be kept from becoming better known lest still more people believe them.

17) Ἀλλά corresponds to μέν in v. 16. The only thing left to be done under the painful circumstances is to take effective measures to prevent the further spread of the knowledge of this sign "to the people" (εἰς, not. "among"). The Sanhedrists agree that proper threatening will accomplish this; yet we must remember that they were sorely perplexed to find anything they might do. The subjunctive is hortative: "let us threaten them," aorist to express the one act. They have in mind a threatening command "no longer to speak on the basis of this name to any man." Note λαλεῖν; not "to make utterance" is to keep still. The

apostles are not to mention "this name" nor anything depending "on this name," no matter what it may be. The Sanhedrin intends to muzzle the apostles completely. The phrase "on the name" has the same force as "in the name," the preposition varying only the relation by using the idea of basis instead of that of connection. "Name," however, has the same meaning it had in v. 7, 10, 12; compare 3:16; and the previous passages 2:21, 38; 3:6. They purposely say "this name" without mentioning "Jesus." It has been well said: *sie wollten ihn totschweigen*. (They would kill him by silence.) This significant aversion to pronouncing even the name still exists to this day.

18) **And having called them, they passed the order all through not to make a sound and not to teach on the basis of the name of Jesus.** The threat was implied. To disobey a strict order of the supreme Jewish court was at that time a more serious thing than contempt of court is now. The order is summary and permits no exception of any kind. "All through" is to be construed with both infinitives, but τό modifies only the compound adverb καθόλου by regarding this as an adverbial accusative. The present infinitives are linear and refer to all time to come. They are not even "to make a sound," *etwas verlauten lassen*, on the basis of the name of Jesus. This includes the teaching, but that is also specified because the apostles had been teaching.

"Jesus" is here added, and the usual explanation given is that the Sanhedrin was compelled to mention this name when issuing its order; yet these are Luke's own words, and there is no evidence that "Jesus" was even here uttered by the Sanhedrists. One cannot be sure that they did so. Thus the apostles were no longer to be apostles, the witnesses (1:8; 2:32; 3:15) were no longer to testify. The Sanhedrin nullifies the order and the appointment of Jesus. The whole work of the gospel is to be nipped in the bud.

19, 20) But Peter and John, making answer to them, said: Whether it is right in the sight of God to hearken to you rather than to God, judge ye; for not able are we on our part not to utter what things we saw and heard.

The circumstantial participle (aorist of simultaneous action), "making answer to them," intends to mark the importance of the answer to this court order. The answer is very brief but perfect. No man could have given a better one. Peter and John act as a unit. The perfection of the answer lies in the turning of the question at issue back upon the judgment of the Sanhedrin itself; in the formulating of that question in the simple way in which it ought alone to be formulated; and then in the giving of the only answer the apostles on their part are able to make. The whole answer is designed so as to focus on the real issue and to cut off any opportunity to quibble about irrelevant points. The Holy Spirit prompted this answer even as to its wording.

From the Jewish supreme court the apostles appeal to God's own court, to which even the Sanhedrin was amenable: "whether it is right in the sight of God." As the highest religious court of the nation the Sanhedrin itself was always assembled as being in the very sight of God, and its every act was to have the full sanction and approval of God. Peter struck home when he said "in the sight of God." The forensic point in the words employed by the apostles should not be overlooked, for both δίκαιον and ἐνώπιον τοῦ Θεοῦ refer to God as the Judge who pronounces what is δίκαιον, "just," "righteous," in harmony with the divine δίκη or norm of right. The one thing the Sanhedrists need to dread is that the divine Judge should pronounce an action of theirs unjust, contrary to his norm of right.

So the alternative before the apostles is, "whether to hearken *unto you* rather than *unto God,*" or negatively, "whether to disobey men rather than God." "Judge ye" means that, as far as the apostles are concerned, the alternative is decided, and they are ready to abide by the consequences. Elucidative γάρ explains that their position has been taken: "not able are we not to utter what things we saw and heard." This is a litotes which puts negatively what is intended very positively, namely that they are bound to utter these things. The οὐ and the μή cancel each other, B.-D. 431, 1. The inability of the apostles to remain silent about all that they have seen and heard (the Greek uses aorists to express the facts, the English prefers perfects to express the relative time of the facts) of Jesus is moral, spiritual, due to the compulsion of conscience. In the four Gospels we have a survey of what the apostles saw and heard. The emphasis is strongly on ἡμεῖς, both because it is written out and because of its position, verb and subject are reversed: "unable are we," stressing both. The Sanhedrin may judge for itself, what the apostles judge they here declare. Where God is involved, every man must judge for himself, and he is entitled to do so.

There was not a moment's hesitation, not the least trace of fear, but complete outspokenness. The apostles do not leave the impression that they may possibly obey while in their hearts they resolve not to obey; nor do they evade the issue by saying that they will think the matter over. They face the issue like men, squarely, openly.

Compare 5:29. No wonder Luke devotes so much space (chapters three to five) to the events which evoked these declarations that are of the highest moral import regarding human and divine authority. In John 7:48, 49 this very Sanhedrin operated with the directly opposite principle, a principle which now receives its supreme challenge. All human authority must yield to divine authority. It is, indeed, a divine command that we obey the government (Rom. 13:1), but this obedience is never absolute. When the government or any human authority commands what is contrary to God, we are bound to obey God alone. The first members of the church who suffered for this principle were the Twelve, cf., 5:40; the history of all the martyrdoms that followed extends from that time until the present. Tears and blood have ever anew sealed this great principle in this wicked world.

Some individuals have gone too far by having this principle justify rebellion and revolution. The apostles offered only passive resistance and not the sword. Like them, we may use all legitimate means to change the wrong demands made on us, but beyond that we suffer in patience any infliction that may result. It is this great principle that makes for the separation of church and state, that keeps each out of the domain of the other. This is the principle underlying true civil and religious liberty and the liberty of conscience. Endless are the means by which this principle is assailed, endless the efforts of human authority to supersede the divine. The author has treated the entire subject in *Kings and Priests*, see especially pp. 101, 104, 116.

21) **But they, having made further threats, released them, finding nothing as to how they should punish them on account of the people, because all were glorifying God for what had occurred. For the man was of more than forty years on whom this sign of the healing had occurred.**

So the whole proceeding ended in failure. Luke adds the reason that the Sanhedrists found nothing chargeable: "on account, or in consideration, of the people." They dreaded the effect which harsher methods might have on the people, for these glorified

God because of what had occurred. The insincerity and the inner dishonesty of the Sanhedrin is in glaring contrast with the openness of the apostles. Chrysostom has a fine passage in which he compares the two: the Sanhedrists at a loss, the apostles joyful; they afraid to say what they think, these speaking out openly; they dreading to have the report spread, these unable not to say what they saw and heard; they not doing what they wanted, these declaring what they wanted. He ends by asking, "Who, then, were in bonds and in dangers?" The article before the indirect question of deliberation with πῶς merely substantivizes it as being the object of the participle, R. 766.

22) It may well be possible that as a medical man Luke adds the notable detail of the man's age although one need not be a doctor in order to be impressed by this feature of the miracle. The people, no doubt, remarked about the beggar's age when they told the story of his instantaneous healing. With πλείων (and ἐλάσσων) ἤ, "than," is omitted when these occur before numbers, B.-D., 185, 4. The perfect participle is proper in the phrase in v. 21; "what has occurred," which states the viewpoint of those praising God; here, in the relative clause, the past perfect states the standpoint of the reader. The genitive "of the healing" is appositional to "this sign," R. 498.

THE PRAYER OF THE APOSTLES

23) Luke adds the sequel, which incidentally gives us an insight into the prayer life of the apostles. **Now, having been released, they came to their own and reported what all the high priests and the elders said to them.**

There is a question as to who are referred to by "their own?" Many interpreters answer, "The believers." But in v. 31 we learn that *all* were filled with the Holy Spirit and continued to utter the Word of God;

and in v. 32, we read of the multitude of those that believed. And this multitude, no doubt, includes more than the "all" of v. 31. Nor did "all" mentioned in this verse preach the Word. Peter and John came to their fellow apostles; if a few other persons were present, they are not considered in Luke's narrative. The Sanhedrin is usually designated by naming only two of its classes as is done here where "the high priests and the elders" are named. And these are "their rulers and the elders" which were mentioned in v. 5. Stress is laid only on what these foes of Christ and the gospel "said" and not on what Peter and John replied, because the prayer that now follows deals with what these foes ordered, namely, the cessation of all preaching. The apostles pray that God may grant them the ability to go on preaching with boldness (v. 29).

24) **And they, on hearing it, with one accord lifted voice to God and said: Lord Almighty, thou art he that madest the heaven and the earth and the sea and all the things in them, the One that through thy servant David's mouth didst say:**

> **For what purpose did Gentiles snort,**
> **And people put care on empty things?**
> **The kings of the earth stood in array,**
> **And the rulers were gathered together**
> **Against the Lord and against his Anointed.**

For there were gathered of a truth in this city against thy holy Servant Jesus, whom thou didst anoint, both Herod and Pontius Pilate with Gentiles and peoples of Israel to do what all thy hand and thy counsel foreordained to occur.

Instead of launching words of indignation against the Sanhedrin and its unjust demands, the apostles automatically turn to God, the Omnipotent, lay the case before him, and ask him to enable them to resist those demands. A great critical moment has come: all their preaching and teaching must henceforth be done in open violation of the highest legal power and authority of their nation. They must, therefore, depend wholly upon the still higher power and authority of God. "They lifted up voice and said" certainly does not intend to exclude Peter and John. Here we again meet the significant adverb "with one accord." There was no coward among the apostles, no one wavered, all as one man resolved to disobey the Sanhedrin and to rely and to call upon God.

The view that the plural conveys the idea that all those present actually spoke the prayer aloud in unison is as untenable as to think that in v. 19 Peter and John spoke in unison. Some even state that this prayer had been composed and committed to memory some days before, and that it was a general prayer without special reference to what had just occurred. But this view is plainly contradicted by v. 29: "look upon their threats," which clearly refers to v. 17 and 21; and by v. 30: "while thou stretchest forth thy hand for healings," which certainly refers to the healing of the lame man on the previous afternoon. No; we discard such literalism. Luke evidently means that one of the apostles uttered the prayer, and that all the apostles lifted up their voice and spoke through his voice and his words. We pray in the same manner. The pastor's voice is the voice of the entire congregation speaking to God.

Δεσπότης is our "despot," one who rules with absolute and unrestricted power by his will alone, but the Greek word does not have the connotation of arbitrariness and tyranny which we associate with the word despot. In spite of Prov. 11:26 where the LXX used the term as a translation for 'Adon, it is a question whether 'Adon was the Aramaic word here employed. The word evidently refers to God's omnipotence, and we might translate it "Lord Almighty." When deciding between the A. V. which inserts the copula: "thou art (God is not in the text) he that made," etc., and the R. V. which omits the copula, we prefer the former. To make all that follows in v. 25, 26 an apposition results in an unwieldy anacoluthon. We then have an extended subject without the sign of a predicate, and the construction continues with a γάρ clause in v. 27. By inserting the copula a construction such as this is avoided. The omnipotent power of God is sketched by describing him as the Creator of heaven, earth, sea, and all things in them, and the mind dwells on each of these tremendously great created objects somewhat as in Neh. 9:6; Jer. 32:17; Rev. 14:7.

25) Although it is supported by four great uncials, the reading ὁ τοῦ πατρὸς ἡμῶν διὰ Πνεύματος Ἁγίου στόματος Δαυεὶδ παιδός σου εἰπών is unacceptable both as to form and to substance. It seems to be an old Jewish-Christian gloss that found its way into the text. Linguistically it is impossible to construe both the Holy Spirit and David after the one διά, to say nothing of the genitive "our father" which precedes this preposition; nor has anyone discovered why David should here be called not only God's servant but in addition "our father," the latter being placed forward for the sake of great emphasis. The A. V. renders in a sensible way, "Who by the mouth of thy servant David hast said," or more literally, "the One that through the mouth . . . didst say." Παῖς = "servant." It is so used with regard to Jesus in 3:13, 26; 4:27, 30. Διά, especially when it is used in connection with "mouth," describes Verbal Inspiration. R., W. P., supposes that a second διά dropped out in the longer reading given above, but this still leaves that reading unacceptable.

The critics reject this apostolic testimony to the Davidic authorship of Ps. 2, and seek to find some other far later author. The testimony of the apostles is rejected although it is inspired (v. 31). Like the Sanhedrists, the critics still regard them as ἀγράμματοι καὶ ἰδιῶται, v. 13. The Old Testament has no superscription for this psalm, and the critics draw the conclusion that therefore David could not be the author of it and thereby ignore the old warning that it is dangerous to conclude anything *e silentio*. The fact that the psalm is nevertheless, ascribed to David is explained by some on the supposition that the term "psalm" was regarded as equivalent to "song of David" although this is contradicted by the fact that many psalms are ascribed to other writers.

We may well regard David himself as a type of Christ, so that the psalm refers to David's ascending the throne of Israel and maintaining that throne by the help of Jehovah in spite of all his enemies. But this is described in a way that is so grand and comprehensive that it plainly reaches out beyond David's person and extends to the Messiah whom David typified also in this respect. Meyer paraphrases the words of the psalm here quoted as follows: "Why do the Gentiles rage" against Jesus, namely the Romans, "and the peoples," Israel's tribes, "imagine vain things," such as they cannot successfully carry into effect, namely the destruction of Jesus? "The kings of the earth," represented by Herod, "set themselves in array" against Jesus, "and the rulers," with Pilate, "were gathered together" with the ἔθνη and λαοί "against the Lord," Jehovah who had sent Jesus, "and against his Anointed." This psalm, of course, goes beyond the opposition that was evident at the time of Jesus and the apostles and includes all opposition down to the end of time. The greatness of the psalm is evident from the fact that it is repeatedly quoted in the New Testament.

26) The ἔθνη, heathen and Gentiles, are paired with λαοί, the plural to denote the tribes of Israel (the

singular is regularly used as a designation of the people of Israel). The question introduced by ἱνατί is one in regard to purpose ("in order that what may occur?") and here inquires as to what possible sensible purpose the heathen could have in snorting against Jehovah and his Anointed. What end had they in view? This verb is used with reference to the snorting of horses and thus denotes the pride and the scorn of strength. These pagans rear, paw, and snort like wild stallions who show their power as though nothing could control them. What for? For nothing.

What is the end to be accomplished by these λαοί by bestowing care, thought, and diligence on things that are κενά, empty, without inner reality or substance? The senselessness manifested by devoting effort to things that are void and hollow ought to be apparent. The whole scheme of abolishing Christ is an empty dream, an insane delusion, and yet ceaseless effort is put forth to realize that dream. These two lines are full of divine scorn and irony.

The psalm advances to the kings and the rulers who stand at the head of their people, and in whom this opposition centers. Παρέστησαν, "stood by," is well rendered, "stood in array." They ranged themselves in line for battle. In the same way the rulers "were gathered together" (ἐπὶ τὸ αὐτό as in 1:16 and repeatedly) for the same opposition. Two great κατά phrases ("down against") state the focus of all this tremendous though vacuous hostility: "the Lord (*Yahweh*) and his Anointed (Χριστός, Luke 3:22)." They will not have this man to reign over them, Luke 19:14. And yet he will reign even over them, over all of them, if not in grace (which they scorn) then in judgment (which none can scorn), Ps. 2:9. It is one of those odd fancies that still find occasional favor (as in R., W. P.) that all present sang the lines of the psalm, and that Peter then applied them. Luke, however, records a prayer.

27) What the psalm depicted found one of its most notable fulfilments as to both Gentile and Jewish opposition in the death of Jesus. The conjunction γάρ frequently specifies by introducing an example; it is like our "for instance." Note that the verb "there were gathered" is repeated and put into the emphatic forward position. For the striking feature of the killing of Jesus was this very coalition of his foes, notably Herod and Pilate, who actually again became friends in this strange way. Who would have thought it possible? But it occurred "of a truth" — it actually did. And "in this city," the last place in the world where one would have thought it possible for Jews and pagans, a Jewish king and a pagan ruler, to combine against Jehovah and his Messiah.

'Επί, "on thy holy Servant Jesus," fits the idea of the trial to which Jesus was subjected. This monstrous and unholy alliance was directed as the psalm states, "against Jehovah's Anointed" who is fully designated in the prayer. "Servant," the great *'Ebed Yahweh*, is explained in 3:13. He is here significantly called "holy" in order to manifest how monstrous and damnable this combination against him was. "*Thy* holy Servant" shows how Jehovah was involved as the line of the psalm last quoted states. Instead of saying "Jesus Christ," the prayer expands, "Jesus whom thou didst anoint" and lays fuller stress on this point in the psalm and again shows that Jehovah is involved. It is enough to mention the king and the governor, for all the rest that were implicated in the murder of Jesus are included in the phrase "with Gentiles and peoples of Israel." Yes, "of Israel," a poignant genitive!

28) The purpose of this coalition is expressed, not from the viewpoint of Herod and of Pilate, but

from that of God. The enemies of Jesus did not assemble to do what God had foreordained but to carry out what their own wicked will intended; and yet they thereby carried out exactly what God had determined from eternity. Behind their violence in attempting to destroy Jesus there stood "thy hand," the power of God designated concretely and anthropomorphitically, and "thy counsel," the will and plan of God regarding Jesus, his Anointed, which through his very passion and death made him the Savior of the world.

The things these enemies did were κενά, "empty," as far as *their* purpose and intent were concerned; but in God's hand and counsel these vicious things were made to serve *his* purpose and intent. Neither God's hand nor his counsel compelled these enemies to make Jesus suffer and die; their own wickedness did that. But God's hand and counsel foreordained in all eternity that what they did should serve the divine purpose and end, defeat their purpose and accomplish his. It is thus that God rules in the midst of his enemies, and when they do their own wicked will most perfectly, they become mere tools for his high and blessed will. The depth of thought here so tersely expressed is the product only of divine revelation.

29) **And as to things now, Lord, look upon their threats and give to thy slaves with all boldness to go on uttering thy Word while thou stretchest out thy hand for healing and in order that signs and wonders may occur through the name of thy Servant Jesus.**

Acts alone has the form τανῦν, "as to things now" or simply "now," here referring to the situation that has just developed. In regard to the threats of the Sanhedrin the apostles ask only that God "look upon" them, i.e., take them into account in what he does for the apostles. They do not ask for punishment of the Sanhedrin, nor that God should make its threats null and void; they do not ask for protection against the execution of these threats, nor for anything regarding their own person. All they plead for is the gift of boldly uttering the Word, irrespective of what the Sanhedrin may do. Peter and John had shown this boldness (v. 13), but the apostles realized that this consisted in more than just manly courage, that it was a spiritual virtue and thus a gift bestowed by God. The emphasis is on the phrase "with all boldness."

By calling themselves δοῦλοί σου they bow in humility before God but also state that they have no will but his, that they are wholly dependent on him and wholly bound to his service. The aorist is used in prayers because of the urgency and the intensity it expresses. As true apostles, men sent and commissioned, they merely "utter" the Word, λαλεῖν; it is laid upon their lips and is not the product of their own minds. And here again, as in v. 4, "the Word" is used in its comprehensive and specific sense as designating the gospel of Christ. If God will help them to keep sounding forth (durative infinitive) the Word, all will be well.

30) When they ask for signs, no second request is made, for these naturally accompany the apostolic Word as its seal even as Jesus had also promised; hence also there is no καί or coordination but only ἐν τῷ, Luke's favorite idiom, which certainly does not here indicate means (R. 1073) but has its usual force, "while." Here we have a plain statement by the apostles themselves that a miracle is wrought only when God wills "to stretch out his hand" in omnipotent power. In every case (as noted when explaining 3:4) the apostles waited until God bade them act; they never depended merely on their own judgment. "For healing" is a special reference to the miracle performed upon the lame beggar.

184 Interpretation of the Acts of the Apostles

"Signs and wonders" include all miracles of every kind such as the Lord's hand may choose to work. His hand (power) works them but does so through the medium of (διά) "the name" of Jesus; on ὄνομα see 2:21, and the phrases found in 2:38; 3:6; 3:16; 4:8, 10. "Thy holy Servant" is added as it was in v. 27. Some interpreters construe the infinitive γίνεσθαι with ἐν τῷ and coordinate it with ἐκτείνειν, but the subject of the latter is personal, that of the former neuter. Others construe it with εἰς, but this makes the infinitive clause coordinate with a mere man. We construe it as a purpose clause that is dependent on "in that thou stretchest out thy hand"; thus it is parallel with the phrase εἰς ἴασιν, which expresses purpose.

31) And when they had petitioned, the place was shaken in which they had been gathered, and they were all filled with the Holy Spirit and continued to utter the Word with boldness.

The answer to the petition was immediate and miraculous. We are helped in understanding this when we remember the great issue (v. 19, 20) with which the petition dealt. God put his sanction and his seal upon the principle uttered in this prayer, did it for all time to come. Δέομαι is the common verb to express begging for something either from men or from God. The shaking of the place is sometimes assumed to have been due to an earthquake; but when an earthquake occurred, as at the death and at the resurrection of Jesus, this is stated, see also 16:26. This shaking had no natural cause but, like the manifestations at Pentecost, was due only to the Holy Ghost. The sign was one of omnipotent power in the divine presence. The verb "they had been gathered together" may be considered the periphrastic past perfect (R., W. P.) or the imperfect plus a perfect participle: "they were," namely "as having been gathered" and thus still being together.

A new measure of the Holy Spirit was bestowed on them. The wider we open our hearts, or the wider God is able to open them, the more of the Spirit we receive; verbs of filling are followed by the genitive. Although it is added only as a coordinate fact by means of καί, it is the result of this being filled with the Spirit that they all "continued to utter the Word with boldness," the very thing asked for in v. 29. The imperfect tense is not inchoative (R., W. P.), for they had been speaking with boldness all along, and the test was now whether they would allow the threats of the Sanhedrin to intimidate them or not. By the Spirit's help they continued their public preaching openly and freely as though the Sanhedrin had never made a threat. They obeyed God rather than men and committed the consequences to God. This was spiritual heroism.

The Second Picture of the Mother Congregation at Jerusalem

32) Compare 2:44-47. After the first great influx of members Luke describes the excellent condition of the congregational life; now after a second great influx and after a notable victory over their opponents he again shows us the condition of the church. **Now of the multitude of those that believed there was one heart and soul; and not one was saying that anything of his possessions was his own, on the contrary, for them all things were common.**

Viewed outwardly, the congregation consisted of a great πλῆθος or "crowd" that was made up of a vast variety of people, old and young, rich and poor, with many differences in occupations, gifts, temperament, inclinations, etc. The 3,000 won at Pentecost came from many lands and had different native languages. Luke's last count was about 5,000 men (4:4). Make your own estimate of the total membership when the women and the children are included. What held all these people together was their one faith; they were "those that believed," the aorist participle stating only the fact of their believing.

Faith is the inner and essential bond of union in the church. The Communion of Saints is such by faith alone. Mere outward connection with a church body does not constitute true membership although it may lead to that. This is a spiritual state in the soul and not a matter of outward arrangement. Faith, of course, produces many visible results, for those who believe show their faith in many ways, and all these manifestations are valuable, but valuable only as evidences and fruits of the inner state, the precious saving faith itself.

The outstanding feature which Luke can report is that of this host of believers "there was one heart and soul." As in a living body only one heart beats, and as it is animated by only one ψυχή, so it was true of this great body of believers. Καρδία and ψυχή naturally go together as the pulsing heart and the breath of life. The Greek word for the heart designates the center of the personality, the seat of thought, feeling, and volition; in English the word heart connotes chiefly the feeling. The Greek ψυχή characterizes the soul in so far as it animates the body, it is the "life" of the body. Luke presents the fact that this great outward body of the congregation had one living personality in it. Its whole active life was one in thought, feeling, and will. "They all wanted one thing: to be saved eternally; they all thought one thing: only to be faithful to the Lord Jesus; they all experienced one thing: the comfort of the Holy Spirit." Besser. This means that, despite the great number, no divisions, no factions, no contentions existed.

In this regard the mother congregation of Christendom serves as a model for all time, a rebuke to all her daughters who followed heresies and errors and caused rents in the church, and a rebuke likewise to all members in any congregation that cause strife and disturbance; but a shining example for all congregations that hold in unity to the one faith and doctrine (2:42) and in one mind to the things that make for peace. The condition of the first congregation was one that made for healthy inner and outer growth.

We have already discussed how "for them all things were common," see 2:44, 45. Here the additional feature is added that even in this matter "not one was saying or claiming that anything of his possessions (literally, of the things belonging to him) was his own." Everyone regarded his possessions as not being intended for him alone but to be employed for all as need required. Even in the matter of personal possessions all were one heart and soul. This is truly remarkable, especially in so large a body. "Not one" — usually one or at least a few are opposed to such an arrangement. This is especially true where money is concerned. Selfishness shows itself, often in shameful ways, and will not let true generosity and Christian love flourish. We have already shown that even here in Jerusalem no communism was practiced and have answered the attempts to misconstrue the motives that animated these first Christians; see 2:44, 45.

33) **And with great power the apostles continued duly to give the testimony of the resurrection of the Lord Jesus, also great grace was upon them all.**

In v. 31 the uttering of the Word with boldness refers to the preaching before the general public in the city in order to win new believers. We have, pointed out that Luke says this regarding the apostles and not regarding any and all of the believers. The fact that these latter also testified in their private capacity is taken for granted. When Luke now adds that "the apostles continued duly to give the testimony of the resurrection" we again see that this was their official task; ἀπό in the verb always denotes a giving that is due to an obligation that is to be met. The obligation is indicated by the word "testimony" or witness, which recalls the fact that the apostles were the divinely appointed "witnesses" (1:8). We know that many others had seen the risen Lord; yet here the apostles alone act as the public witnesses. The fact that the others testified in private is self-evident. Yet we are not friendly toward the restriction which some introduce at this place by claiming that the testimony here mentioned was given only to the congregation — why not also to others? The answer usually given, that Luke here writes only regarding the believers, overlooks the fact that the apostles had the appointment "duly to give the testimony" in all Jerusalem, etc. To be sure, as in 2:42, they diligently testified and taught in the congregation; but they also reached out beyond it.

About this testimony the believers had gathered, about it new believers would gather. From it sprang their faith and their love. They needed to have it preached to them ever anew. The resurrection is the crowning work of God in accomplishing our redemption. It was the final proof of the deity and of the Messiahship of Jesus. It attested the full efficacy of his life, his suffering, and his death in removing the barrier that separated us from God (sin) by satisfying every claim of his holiness and righteousness. It showed also that the glorified Savior lived and ruled as the Head of the church to keep and to bless it to eternity. To this day it is Sunday, the day of Christ's resurrection, which assembles the hosts of his believers

Acts 4:33, 34

to the worship of his name. With the close connective τέ Luke unites this preaching with its result, namely "great grace upon them all," namely divine grace through the channel of this testimony, God's unmerited favor which built up the faith and the love of all. In 2:47 we have a different context, and there χάρις means the favor and the good will of the general public.

34) In 2:44, 45 Luke wrote only briefly regarding the manner in which love manifested itself in the congregation; here he returns to the subject and adds an instance of how things were done. **For there was not anyone needy among them; for as many as were owners of lands or of houses, making sales, kept bringing the proceeds of the things disposed of and laying them at the feet of the apostles; and it was distributed to each according as anyone was having need.**

Here γάρ brings evidence of the grace that rested on them: not one in need of the necessities of life. There were many beggars among the Jews. We meet them constantly (3:2 is a sample). The believers had none. The model here given has been followed by the church since that time. Every congregation takes care of its poor and unfortunate, and we need not add how extensive the arrangements are for doing this work through entire church bodies and in regular institutions. Even the world has learned something from the church in this line.

The rich came forward, "owners of lands and of houses." The present participle and the two imperfect verbs are iterative (R. 884) and express what occurred from time to time (R. 1116). The prices or proceeds of the sales were brought into the assembly and deposited beside the feet of the apostles. They seem to be represented as sitting on a platform and at this time managed the distribution of the funds thus voluntarily brought in. The idea to be expressed is certainly not that the rich sold all of their property and thus made also themselves poor. What Luke conveys is that the amounts brought in were large, each seller going to great lengths in disposing of some of his property, and that sales were made only at intervals, when new funds were required.

35) Another iterative imperfect reports the distribution; it is a form of διαδίδωμι, and the passive singular has an indefinite subject: "it was distributed," i. e., by the apostles who still managed everything without assistants. In this simple, though effective, fashion every case of need received proper relief.

36) Luke adds an illustration of this way of giving but singles out Barnabas for the special reason that we may thus early take note of this man, since he came to occupy an important place in the advance of the church. An illustration is in place at this point so that we may properly understand the following narrative which records a flagrant case of deception in this very matter of charity. **And Joseph, the one called besides Barnabas on the part of the apostles, which is, when interpreted, "son of consolation," a Levite, a Cyprian by race, he, having a field, on selling it, brought the money and placed it at the feet of the apostles.**

The elaborate manner in which Luke introduces this man is due to his future importance. His introduction is fittingly connected with a noble act of his that was performed in the early part of his Christian career. He had the common Jewish name "Joseph" which had been given him at the time of circumcision. Since many others had the same name, it is not surprising that he bore also another name. This second name was "Barnabas" and, as we shall find, completely superseded his original name.

Acts 4:36

We restrict ourselves to the main points regarding this second name; those interested may examine Zahn on our passage who has an elaborate investigation. Luke writes ὁ ἐπικληθείς, the aorist participle, and not ἐπικαλούμενος, the present. The latter would mean that Joseph was always called Barnabas, the former means that he got this name from the apostles, and ἀπό is the correct preposition, "from," not ὑπό, "by." One of the apostles must have called Joseph by this name; originating thus, everybody (not only the apostles) called him by this name. Luke translates the name for Theophilus. Why? Because Theophilus is not merely to know its meaning but is at the same time to see how a name that had such a meaning was given this man by the apostles. Luke is the last man to dispense mere etymological information. The interpretation or rather translation of Barnabas is "son of consolation." Luke mentions all this regarding the name in advance of the statement that Joseph was a Levite in order to bring together everything regarding the name. The fact that Joseph was "a Levite" is again no mere biographical item without further relevancy. Joseph was the first Levite to be won for the gospel by the apostles, won immediately after the Sanhedrin had uttered its dire threats to Peter and to John. His conversion was the first breach in the hierarchical walls and, coming at just this critical time, brought great consolation and encouragement to the apostles. That is why they gave him the new name, one which caused his original name to be discarded.

The onomastic debate with regard to "Barnabas" is rather severe and has taken on renewed energy. The charge that Luke mistranslated is rather beside the point since he was for so long a time and so well acquainted with Barnabas himself. And at least some of the Twelve most certainly knew Barnabas intimately. Meanings such as "son of prophecy," "son of a prophet," "son of consolation" in the sense of preaching in a comforting way, or Deissmann's "son of Nebo," an idol whose downfall Isa. 46:1, 2 prophesied, find no support in Luke. If Joseph's preaching gave him his name, why did he preach so early, and why was he called "son" and not, as one should expect, "father of consolation"?

The fact that he was a Cyprian by race is added because he and Paul made their first missionary journey to Joseph's homeland, the island of Cyprus. He was thus a foreign-born Jew. His father seems to have given up his station as a Levite and to have moved to Cyprus; see the list of foreign-born Jews in 2:9, etc. Joseph, however, remained a Hebrew Jew and, like Paul, did not become a Hellenist. The fact that he was at this time in Jerusalem, aside from other reasons, may be explained by the circumstance that his relatives, his sister Mary and his cousin Mark, lived here. It is only a conjecture that Joseph was one of the Seventy, a conjecture that disagrees with all that may otherwise be safely assumed.

37) The genitive absolute, "a field being for him," i. e., "he having a field," shows that he possessed wealth; he was like those mentioned in v. 34. The statement regarding what he did with this field is worded exactly like that in v. 34, 35, and only uses the aorists instead of the iterative tenses. The singular τὸ χρῆμα, instead of the usual plural, seems to signify the sum of money as a whole.

CHAPTER V

ANANIAS AND SAPPHIRA

The deceit of Achan, Josh. 7:1, etc., and his severe penalty, which occurred when Israel first entered Canaan, are recorded as a warning for the entire Old Testament Church. The deceit of Ananias and of Sapphira, which happened when the Christian Church began in Jerusalem, and their severe penalty are recorded as a warning for the entire New Testament Church. The first danger to the young church came from the outside when the Sanhedrin struck at Peter and at John. This had been safely met, and the church continued on in its successful course. Now follows the second attack of Satan from within the sacred circle of the congregation itself: the hearts of two disciples had become false, two hypocrites are unmasked. Rich members, also Barnabas, sold land or property and laid the proceeds at the feet of the apostles to be used for the needy. Ananias and Sapphira do the same, but their act is in reality the absolute opposite, and judgment overtakes them. Here God's attitude toward all hypocrites in the church is recorded whether his judgment strikes them at once or is delayed for a time.

1) Now a man by name Ananias with Sapphira, his wife, sold a property and held out for himself something from the price, his wife also knowing it together with him; and having brought some part, he placed it at the feet of the apostles.

Because of the gravity of the offense the names of the offenders are not withheld; τίς is used like our indefinite pronoun. Throughout the account Ananias is linked with his wife who was not the jewel (sapphire) after which she was named. They both sold the property. It is usually assumed that this parcel of ground (v. 3) was all they owned, but the indefinite κτῆμα, without the article, makes the impression that this property was only one of their possessions. Nor did Barnabas or any of the owners mentioned in 4:34 sell all their real estate for the benefit of the needy.

2) Selling the property and retaining a part of the price were but two elements of one transaction. The whole procedure was planned in advance. In order to place the matter beyond question the genitive absolute, "his wife also knowing with him," is added. We cannot agree with those who think that the idea of retaining part of the price came to these two people only after the parcel had been sold, that perhaps the sight of so much money stirred the cupidity of the couple, that thus an originally right motive went wrong. No sinner should ever be painted blacker than he is, but on the other hand, no sinner should be whitewashed to hide some of his blackness. Here there was no change of mind, no yielding to a sudden impulse. The heart of husband and wife had grown cold and dead in regard to faith. Their sin was not merely cupidity but the worst and the boldest type of hypocrisy. Satan had entered where Christ could not remain.

Husband and wife were "one heart and soul" (3:32) in evil. Whereas the one should have restrained the other, neither did so, but each aided and abetted the other, both were equally guilty. This premeditation, this conspiracy made the sin so terrible. They had to talk the matter over, had to say to each other what was in their hearts, had to tell each other what to do and how to act so that nobody should know. For such conduct calousness is required; theirs were two seared consciences. Neither had scruples or compunctions of conscience. And thus Ananias carried out the deed.

We must imagine that the congregation or a part of it was assembled for worship. The apostles are present to lead and to teach. Ananias has the bag of money with him; and when the time came to make the offerings, he went forward and in the sight of all deposited the bag. "At or beside the apostles' feet" (the same expression used in 4:34, 37) represents the apostles as seated on a platform. To those who looked on, Ananias appeared as a second Barnabas. Words of praise, at least thoughts of commendation, accompanied the act of Ananias. He acted with perfect assurance, certain that no one could possibly detect his deception. He never thought of God or of Christ who were present in that assembly according to their promise. And so the deed was done.

The supposition that Ananias aimed at attaining more than praise, that he aspired to a leadership such as Barnabas had gained, cannot be substantiated from Luke's account. Why Barnabas received his second name is explained in 4:36; that he sold all his possessions is not stated nor is it to be assumed; he became prominent at a later time and only for this reason is he here cited as an example. The mere juxtaposition of Barnabas and Ananias with its contrast of sincerity and base hypocrisy involves no more than is thus indicated, which also is certainly enough.

3) **But Peter said: Ananias, for what reason did Satan fill thy heart for thee to belie the Holy Spirit and to hold back for thyself something from the price of the land? Was it not, remaining (unsold), remaining for thee? and sold, was it not still in thy power? Why didst thou put this affair in thy heart? Thou didst not lie to men, but to God!**

Ananias had just laid down the money and had most likely added a few words that expressed his intention. He, no doubt, expected Peter or one of the other apostles to answer with words of acceptance and personal commendation. Instead of this there came the exposure of his fearful sin like a bolt out of the clear sky. How did Peter gain such complete knowledge about the sin of Ananias? One answer to this question is found in 1 Cor. 12:10, "and to another discerning of spirits." In the case before us Peter had even more, namely the direct revelation of the Holy Spirit concerning Ananias and his wife. Did this revelation include the judgment to be visited upon Ananias? Peter announces the judgment upon Sapphira but not that upon Ananias. We can get the answer by inference only since we do not have a direct statement by Luke himself. It seems that the revelation given to Peter included the judgment awaiting both Ananias and his wife. Why should God have revealed less than this to him? Sin and judgment belong together. Was Peter to be dumbfounded by the sudden, terrible death of Ananias, frightened, perhaps, that he had helped to kill him?

But why did Peter not announce the judgment upon Ananias as he did that upon Sapphira? The explanation is not acceptable that he did not know that Ananias was to die but from his death concluded that Sapphira was likewise to die. So Peter would speak partly as a result of revelation and partly on the basis of deductions of his own. In a matter of life and death that cannot be considered likely. It seems rather that Peter spoke only such words to Ananias that the Spirit inspired him to speak, and that the Spirit withheld the announcement of the death of Ananias in order to make it absolutely clear to all those present that this judgment was wholly a divine act and not one that was in any way due to Peter, or one in which he served even as an instrument. After this was clear from the first instance, Peter could announce the Spirit's judgment in the second case without leaving the slightest impression that he was inflicting the penalty or was the agent in the infliction.

The questions asked by Peter assume complete knowledge against which denial is impossible. Peter's questions are unanswerable. Ananias has no excuse to offer and can state nothing in extenuation of his guilt. So the sinner is always dumb before God: "and he was speechless," Matt. 22:12; or if he should venture a defense he would be condemned out of his own mouth. "Why did Satan fill thy heart?" refers the guilt back to its real source and implies that Ananias could and should have resisted Satan. With διατί Peter asks for the reason — Satan's reason was the damnation of Ananias — what reason could Ananias have had? "Filled" means that Satan took complete control of the man, and that his was done with the full consent of Ananias.

Here again (4:32) "heart" is the center of the personality, including especially the mind and the will. When Ananias became a believer, the Holy Spirit filled his heart and cast out and kept out Satan and his power. But Ananias had turned away from God's Spirit and had once more opened his heart to Satan and to all his devilish suggestions. How a man, once won for God, can again turn to the devil is a mystery no one can solve. We know the fact only too well but we cannot understand how any sane man's will can so turn to his own destruction.

The two infinitives do not denote purpose, do not state the intentions of Ananias; they express result (R. 1089): "so that thou didst belie and didst hold back for thyself." The deed has gone far beyond its original intent, it is fully accomplished (two aorists). "Belie" is followed by the accusative as in the classics: in v. 4

it governs the dative. The sin of Ananias is here truly described. All sins are, indeed, committed against God, and those of believers especially against the Holy Spirit. Ananias permitted Satan to influence him to the extreme and to beguile him to carry out a deed that emanated wholly from Satan and to offer it as a deed that was prompted wholly by the Holy Spirit; yea, to present this deed to the Spirit himself, in the very church where the Spirit wrought, before the special agents, the apostles, through whom the Spirit wrought, a deed which the Spirit was to accept as being wrought by him when it was wrought wholly by the power of Satan. Thus, deliberately, mockingly, Ananias belied the Spirit and attempted to palm off a devil's work on the Spirit and hoped that the Spirit would not detect the deception; yea, he would leave the impression that the Spirit had produced this devil's work!

The second infinitive defines the lying act more clearly: "to hold back," etc. It is dreadful enough to sin and to admit that we followed the evil one; but what shall we say of him who sins and then not only pretends that the Holy Spirit prompted his sin but also that it is a divine work and then proceeds to bring it to God as a holy offering?

4) The sin of Ananias was altogether gratuitous. It was without rime or reason. The double question is so compact in the Greek that we cannot translate it into English with a like compactness. Ananias was entirely free to keep his land for himself or to sell it. The present participle μένον, "remaining," means: "remaining as it was, unsold and in thy possession"; and the imperfect ἔμενε: "was it not remaining for thee," no one asking thee to make a change? The interrogative particle οὐ, here found in its strong form οὐχί, brings out the fact. Ananias was compelled to answer "yes"; he knew that he could have kept his

land. he sinned with full knowledge. The enclitic σοί is accented and placed before the verb because it has a strong emphasis: "was it not remaining *for thee*," wholly and entirely for thee alone.

The question is extended. But now the aorist neuter passive participle πραθέν (from πιπράσκω) speaks of the land as "sold." Although it had been sold, nothing was changed: "Was it not still in thy power?" The imperfect ὑπῆρχε expresses continuance, "still it was in thy control" (ἐξουσία) for thee to do with it in all honesty and uprightness as thou mightest wish. He could have retained the whole sum he had received for the land, and no one could in the least have blamed him; or he could have brought as an offering for the needy any portion of the money, small or large, as he might have desired; the only requirement set was that he make no false pretense about it. Did Ananias know this? Most certainly. Again the deliberateness of his lie is revealed.

"Why didst thou put this affair in thy heart?" the middle ἔθου, "put it there for thyself." Τὸ πρᾶγμα τοῦτο is not merely this idea or plan but the whole transaction as now carried out. "Why," τί ὅτι, *quid est quod*, "what has occurred that" (R. 965), asks about the terrible change that has occurred in the heart which made it possible for Ananias to lend his heart to this deed. To place in the heart means more than "to conceive" (our versions); "heart" includes the will as the center of the personality, and Peter does not refer only to the conception but also to the entire execution of the plan. Something had occurred in this man's heart: Satan had usurped its control. And thus he lied not merely to men but to God himself.

The deed is considered only with reference to God. Ananias is sadly mistaken when he thinks that he is dealing with men; he is dealing directly with God himself. He could and should have known that.

This is in a way true of every sin, especially of every conscious sin; but it is most directly true of every act of hypocrisy, in all matters of worship, wherever God is directly concerned as here in this lying offer to God. Peter's word to Ananias undoubtedly identifies God and the Holy Ghost. This is often denied, and the claim advanced that the lie was made to God indirectly through the Holy Ghost, the latter serving only as the medium. But this virtually declares that the Holy Ghost was as ignorant of the fraud as men were. God is not behind the Holy Ghost as he is behind the apostles and the church so that whatever is done against them is done mediately also against God. The Holy Ghost is God; the sin was committed against him as God. The old dogmaticians and the church are right when they here find a clear expression of the deity and the personality of the Holy Spirit, the Third Person of the Godhead.

5) And Ananias, hearing these words, having fallen down, expired; and there came great fear on all those hearing it. And having arisen, the younger men wrapped him up and, having carried him out, buried him.

With the words ringing in his ears, the λόγοι, the things Peter was saying, Ananias suddenly collapsed and expired (this verb is used only in Acts but is found also in LXX and in Hippocrates). Neither Peter nor the words he uttered killed Ananias. All natural explanations such as a stroke of paralysis, heart failure, etc., that was superinduced by the sudden shock at finding himself exposed, prove insufficient when they are applied to two persons as must be done here, the death of the second being announced the moment before it occurred.

Why was Ananias granted no time for repentance? We have no warrant to inquire into the secret counsel of God in either this or any other case. That question belongs in the domain of divine providence where hundreds of things are beyond our comprehension. God alone knows when and how to interfere with his judgment. He is not accountable to us, and no questioner should forget this truth. His mercy, like his judgment, is beyond question. Even if he were to uncover these to us, our poor minds would not be able to grasp them. Was Ananias lost? "Not to desire to know where the best of all teachers wants us not to know, is a wholesome and faultless ignorance." Gerhard. As far as we are concerned, the object of this judgment upon Ananias is to inspire us with fear that we may guard ourselves against the machinations of the devil. This was the effect produced upon the first church.

The present participle "those hearing" = "the hearers," i. e., those present who heard what Peter said. In v. 11 more is said. This fear was the effect of the power and the judgment of God that were manifested in so sudden a manner. It was awe for faith, fright for the flesh. On the latter, the third use of the law, compare *C. Tr.*, 965, etc., 9 and 19.

6) The dead body must be removed and buried. Why was Sapphira not called to her dead husband's side; why was he buried immediately without her knowledge? The answer appears in the sequel: the same judgment awaited her. But we must remember that all this is an act of God's Spirit and not of Peter nor of the apostles. It was proper that "the younger men" should attend to this sad task. In v. 10 they are called "the young men," and the change of words indicates that no officers of the church are referred to as some have supposed. The next chapter will tell us about the first officers. The two words used do not signify youths or boys but men between twenty and forty years

of age. The implication is that older men were also present as well as the apostles (v. 2) and not merely Peter. The entire account reveals a full assembly.

When bodies are not embalmed in Oriental countries burial is greatly hastened; in the case of the Jews this hasty burial made possible also the early cleansing from the defilement contracted by touching the dead. Burial took place on the day of death or, if the hour of death was late, the next morning. The wrapped body was carried to the cemetery and buried without a coffin. The writer witnessed such a Jewish funeral procession at Jerusalem: men marched in ranks, the body was wrapped in its garments and carried on a bier of two long poles with bands stretched across them. No covering hid the body, several men carried the poles on each side. In a manner similar to this Ananias was carried out.

7) Now there occurred an interval of about three hours, and his wife, not knowing what had occurred, came in. And Peter answered to her, Tell me whether you disposed of the land for this much? And she said, Yes, for this much.

Luke regularly records only the facts and leaves their combination and relation to the reader. It has been well said that this manner of writing expects a good deal on the part of the reader. Our historians are prone to relate everything and to leave very little to the reader. So here we should like to know why both had not come together, why the interval was three hours, why Sapphira came at all, etc. Was she worried because of her husband's long absence? The text supplies nothing. Was it all planned with a view that Ananias should precede her and receive the plaudits of the congregation, and that Sapphira was later to furnish the occasion for a second congratulation? It almost seems so.

The three hours have been regarded as being the interval between the regular Jewish hours of prayer, but this was longer, the morning devotion being held at nine, the evening devotion at three. All that Luke states is that Sapphira was ignorant of what had happened three hours before and came into the assembly in the usual way. She must have known that the meeting was to continue for so long a time or longer. Were there matters other than worship that required so long a time, or did teaching take up so much time? We see no reason for making διάστημα a nominative absolute that is merely inserted to mark the time (B.-D. 144; R. 460), so that ἐγένετο καί plus the finite verb is the idiom Luke often uses; why not let this nominative be the subject: "there occurred an interval," etc.?

8) Sapphira probably looked about the room for her husband. "Answered to her" does not imply that she asked a question to which Peter replied. The verb is frequently used with reference to a statement called forth by a situation. So here it means simply that Peter had waited for Sapphira to enter in order that he might address her as he did. Before she sat down, Peter called to her. "For this much," genitive of price, gives the impression that the sack of coins had been left untouched where Ananias had deposited it on the platform, and that Peter now pointed to it and Sapphira recognized it. One should think that the question, asked in this manner, should have made the woman hesitate. Why did Peter ask so significantly in regard to the actual amount: "for so much"? That question must have struck her conscience since she knew that it was not for so much but for more. But no, Sapphira is not startled. She clings to the agreement made with her husband to say "for so much," and Satan is supporting her as he did Judas when Jesus gave him a final warning. With all positiveness she

affirms, "Yes, for so much!" This was loyalty but of the wrong kind. With this word Sapphira forfeited her opportunity for repentance. This final "yes" to the sin was yes also to her judgment.

9) But Peter said to her: Why was it agreed for you to tempt the Lord's Spirit? Lo, the feet of those that buried thy husband at the door, and they shall carry thee out! And she fell at once at his feet and expired; and, on coming in, the young men found her dead and, having carried her out, buried her beside her husband. And there came great fear on the whole church and on all that heard these things.

Peter's question is an exclamation of grief, τί ὅτι as in v. 4. He reveals some new features of the sin. They had deliberately agreed, had formed this conspiracy with resolute purpose. The impersonal passive may have the dative as it is found with a passive or after σύν. By carrying out their agreement they have deliberately tempted the Lord's Spirit. The aorist infinitive states a result; it is like the two infinitives occurring in v. 3: "so that you tempted." This Israel had done in order to see whether the Spirit would permit its wickedness to pass unpunished, Num. 14:25; Ps. 95:8, 9. We need not say that Ananias and Sapphira intended their act to be such a temptation of the Spirit whom the Lord (Jesus) had sent; it was this, nevertheless.

Sinners often call their sins by mild but untrue names. When the light of God falls upon them, all shams disappear. Every imitation of faith and of love tempts the Spirit, challenges him. Will he know, will our cunning not deceive him? "Be not deceived, God is not mocked."

"Behold the feet," etc., needs no verb to complete its sense for it is an exclamation. The footsteps of the returning young men were heard. Now, only a moment before her own death, Sapphira learns that her husband is already buried. "They shall carry thee out" states only the fact. Why this was said to her and not to Ananias also is discussed above.

10) Her death ensued on the instant. When the young men came in they found another such sad task awaiting them. The first two and the most awful hypocrites in the Christian Church were buried side by side. It is often asked whether they committed the sin against the Holy Ghost. This may be safely denied because an outstanding mark of this sin is blasphemy, a feature that was absent in the case of Ananias and Sapphira.

11) The effect produced by these two deaths that had occurred in the very assembly of the congregation must have been tremendous. Luke again notes the fear and its greatness; not, however, fear of the apostles but of the Spirit before whom the lies found in every heart are open to view, and who is able to smite the sinner in the very midst of his sin. This fear came "upon the whole church."

Here Luke for the first time uses ἐκκλησία with reference to the body of the believers in Jerusalem, whether they were gathered in an assembly or not. It is so used in Matt. 16:18, but in a still wider sense, for it refers to the body of believers of all future time. In Matt. 18:17 the word denotes the local congregation. This double use continues to this day. The term is derived from ἐκκαλεῖν, "to call out," as when a herald calls out the citizens to meet in assembly. The assembly of Israel was called its *ecclesia*, 7:38. "All those that heard these things" were the people who were not connected with the congregation. In v. 5 the present participle denotes the immediate hearers who were present in the meeting; here the aorist participle refers to those who later learned of the matter, and the preceding *ecclesia* restricts these to outsiders.

206 Interpretation of the Acts of the Apostles

THE THIRD PICTURE OF THE MOTHER CONGREGATION IN JERUSALEM

As he did in 2:43-47; 4:32-35, Luke pauses also at this point to present a survey of the congregation and briefly notes the main features of the great and continuous progress.

12) Now through the hands of the apostles there continued to occur many signs and wonders among the people. And they were all with one accord in the porch of Solomon. Yet of the rest no one dared to join himself to them, but the people kept magnifying them.

What has been recorded in the previous brief descriptions holds good for the present account and need not be repeated. Some new, notable features are added, especially the signs and wonders (see 2:19 on the terms) of which Luke records that they were many, πολλά being placed emphatically at the end. These were miracles of grace and of healing, and we note that Luke places them in strong contrast with the one miracle of judgment he has just recorded. The singular "through (the) hand," the phrase being little more than a preposition, denotes only agency in general, but the plural "through the hands" points to the actual placing of the hand or the hands upon the sufferers. In Luke's first description of the congregation signs and wonders were noted (2:43); these have now greatly increased.

The usual meeting place of the entire congregation was "the porch of Solomon" (see 3:11) before which Peter and John had been arrested. Here "all" (ἅπαντες, stronger than πάντες) kept meeting "with one accord." Although they had been threatened never again to use the name of Jesus, the apostles used it right here in the Temple court. Thus far those threats had remained empty. The long, roomy colonnade afforded

Acts 5:12-14

ample space for the assembly of the thousands of Christians. Although all of them were Jews, they now constituted a separate body and thus met "with one accord." This spacious porch was also ideal for the work of the apostles in ever making new converts. Here the Jews gathered daily in multitudes, and the Christians, too, joined in the regular services so that no outward division as yet appeared.

13) Yet the Christians were a distinct body and were recognized as such with the result that no outsider ventured to join himself to them. This concurs with the fact that the people kept magnifying them (compare 4:21 and 2:47) and speaking highly of them. Had it not been for this general favor and praise, undesirables would have crowded in and disturbed the gatherings of the believers in all sorts of ways. To whatever degree the miracles prompted this high regard, the effect here described is not that "the rest," the Jews generally, stayed away from the gatherings of the Christians; they were evidently drawn by the preaching and the teaching that went on diligently here in Solomon's porch.

14) **Moreover, the more were believing ones added to the Lord, crowds both of men and women.** Μᾶλλον refers to this magnifying on the part of the people, and δέ adds the statement as something that went beyond what has just been said. The attitude of the people helped in producing new believers. Many would at any rate have been won, but now this occurred the more. In 2:47 the Lord kept adding; the parallel is now passive, "believing ones kept being added to the Lord." In 4:4 Luke could still state figures, but only with reference to the men, 5,000 of them; but now all count has been lost, no figures could be secured, and all that Luke can write is that "crowds both of men and of women" were added to the thousands already in the faith. Why this manner of expression should be

called popular exaggeration is hard to see; "crowds" does not mean "little groups." A general movement set in which was due to the favorable attitude of the people as such. Luke considers πιστεύοντες and "were being added to the Lord" quite sufficient for the intelligent reader who will understand that these people believed in the Lord (Jesus) and were brought to such faith by the preaching of the apostles. Since 2:41 baptism has not been mentioned, but it certainly is understood that all new believers were, like those 3,000, received by baptism.

A few oddities must be noted. The section from 12b to 14 has been considered an insertion by a strange hand, or a marginal note that was introduced into the text, or a section transposed from 4:31. Why? Not on the basis of textual evidence but because v. 15 is supposed to be a continuation of 12a. Yet v. 15 properly joins v. 14 and could not fittingly be connected with 12a. B.-D. 365, 1 considers v. 14 a parenthesis and calls it harsh because v. 15 is said to match illy with v. 13. There is no parenthesis. At this point, too, we can see how unwarranted is the opinion that in v. 13 κολλᾶσθαι signifies "to join" in the sense of believing, and that "dared not join" refers to a certain party that kept entirely aloof. Here in v. 14 we see how Luke expresses this kind of joining: "were added unto," the same verb he used in 2:41, 47. Verse 13 speaks of intrusions, men fastening themselves on the assemblies of believers in order to harass them.

15) So that they kept carrying the sick even into the street and kept placing them on little beds and pallets in order that, as Peter came, at least the shadow might overshadow some one of them. Moreover, there kept coming together also the crowd from the cities around Jerusalem, bringing sick and any oppressed by unclean spirits, who continued to be healed all.

Ὥστε with the infinitive expresses actual result. The claim that we must connect this verse with 12a overlooks the fact that, the more signs and wonders occurred, the less reason was there to carry the sick into the streets. Luke intends to show that the people magnified the Christians, and that numbers of men and women came to faith, and that the result of this circumstance was that they kept carrying the sick out even into the streets, etc. This, as Lukes states it, was a result of the attitude of the people, of their tremendous confidence; not, as some regard Luke as saying, a result only of the occurrence of many miracles. The present infinitives denote iterative action. With the feminine πλατείας supply ὁδούς. The diminutive κλινάριον denotes a little bed, and κράβαττος (κράββατος) a pallet or camp roll. The sick were carried out into the street and then deposited on some sort of a bed to await Peter's coming. No distinction is here made between rich, soft beds and hard, poor couches.

The sick were arranged in this manner in order that they might be directly in the path of Peter so that he could not avoid seeing them and could heal them without losing time by going to their homes. The idea to be expressed is that he did so heal them. For κἄν (note the crasis for καὶ ἐάν), which has come to be a mere particle (B.-D. 374), states that "at least," i. e., if no more were done by Peter, his shadow might overshadow some one of them here and there and evidently thus transmit the healing. Some texts have the future indicative after ἵνα, a construction which is found in the Koine.

This trust that even Peter's shadow would heal them has been called superstition or faith coupled with superstition. The question has also been raised as to whether healing was actually thus transmitted. If Peter's shadow had not healed, the fancy that it might heal would have at once been dissipated. Many unfortunates asked Jesus to touch them and to heal them in this manner; to ask for the touch is not more superstitious than to look to the shadow. In Mark 6:56 the touching of even the garment of Jesus healed; in Acts 19:12 the handkerchiefs of Paul accomplished a like miracle. The physician Luke describes these effects and in no way suggests that the apostles or Jesus found anything superstitious or wrong in this faith. The important feature in all these healings is the fact that contact was in some way sought with the person transmitting the healing. The διά in v. 12 states that the Lord used the apostles as the personal media for the signs and wonders. It was throughout his power that wrought the healing.

More must be added. All healings emanate from the Lord and his will; the apostles are no more than his instruments. Once this is understood, we shall not lay stress on the will or the consciousness of the apostles. In Matt. 9:20 it was the will of Jesus that healed the woman who touched the tassel of his robe from behind. It is his will that operated through the apostles, through their hands (v. 12) and through Peter's shadow. As far as the will of the apostles was concerned, this was wholly in accord with the will of Jesus. The rich outflow of healing power from Jesus at this time meets the abundant faith that sought this healing power and manifested itself in such striking ways. Here faith in Jesus' power preceded the healing; this was not the case in 3:4 and in other instances — see the discussion on this passage. No man who came to Jesus or to the apostles in faith remained unhealed, and not a few were healed without previously having had faith in order to be brought to that faith. All this, too, was at first faith only in the power of Jesus to heal. That was enough to begin with; but this incipient faith was to advance to the higher faith which would rely on him for healing and for saving also the soul. This subject must be studied in its entirety; those who busy themselves with it merely as they happen upon it here and there will naturally draw inadequate and wrong conclusions.

16) For the first time the history of the church reaches out beyond Jerusalem proper, namely to the towns around the capital ($πέριξ$ is an adverb with the genitive and is like the preposition $περί$). Even from these places the sick were brought in. As he does in his Gospel, so here in Acts Luke differentiates and describes the demoniacs and never for a moment confuses them with people who were suffering from ordinary ailments. Here he mentions them for the first time in Acts and calls them "oppressed by unclean spirits," agitated, vexed. Note that $ὑπό$ points to these spirits as being the personal agents; and "unclean," filthy, vile, points to their unholy character. On the entire subject of demoniacal possession see the comment of the author on Matt. 4:24; 8:28; Mark 1:23; Luke 4:33.

The idea expressed in $οἵτινες$ is "any such," no matter who they were or how severe their case. They continued to be healed *all,* $ἅπαντες$, as in v. 12, is stronger than the simple $πάντες$, "all altogether," without a single exception, the word being placed emphatically at the end. Note the imperfect tenses throughout the entire paragraph, all of them are descriptive and picture what was going on at this time; they are also continuative and iterative. These open tenses at the same time imply that something is to follow that interfered with this grand work and progress. In fact, that is why Luke places this sketch at this point of his narrative.

Peter continues to stand out pre-eminently. This may be due to the fact that the apostles had not as yet scattered but remained together and moved about and acted as one body. Thus Peter spoke for all and in the case of the healings acted for all; note v. 29. The people thus looked to Peter and trusted that even his shadow would cure the unfortunate. Neither the other apostles nor Luke see an undue assumption of authority on Peter's part in this fact, on the contrary, all feel that through Peter they are acting as a unified body, and that is the way in which they intended to act.

Here the promise of Jesus regarding healings and signs was fulfilled in a notable manner; the miracles of the apostles appeared as a direct continuation of the extensive healings wrought by Jesus himself. His power in and through the apostles thus in the most manifest way connects their work with the work he did during the days of his earthly ministry. The success was phenomenal. It now seemed as though the entire population of Jerusalem and that of even the surrounding towns would soon be won for Christ; and once the capital became Christian, what might not be expected from the nation as a whole?

The Twelve Arrested and Miraculously Released

For some time the Sanhedrin tolerated the bold disobedience of its peremptory orders not to speak or to teach in Jesus' name and with growing concern watched the growth of the Christian movement. The members of this body were, however, convinced that this could not be permitted to continue much longer unless they were ready to abdicate their position in favor of the apostles. The tension increased until finally, without an especial cause or occasion, the cord snapped.

17) **Now, having arisen, the high priest and all those with him, the local sect of the Sadducees, were filled with passion and laid hands on the apostles and put them in a public ward.**

These same Sadducees caused the arrest of Peter and of John in 4:1, 2. This time the high priest takes the lead, and he and his following take summary action. "Having arisen" means, "having proceeded from inaction to action"; he and his followers refused to remain inactive. Because in 4:6 "high priest" is appended to the name Annas, it is supposed that this same individual is referred to also in this place and Luke is accordingly charged with inaccuracy. But in 4:6 the names are arranged according to seniority, and "high priest" indicates only the general status of Annas. Neither there nor here does Luke make Annas the ruling high priest, for Caiaphas held this position.

These Sadducees have the leading position in the Sanhedrin and maintain it also in this case by ordering the arrest on their own authority and afterward call a session of the Sanhedrin. Our versions translate, "which is the sect of the Sadducees"; R., W. P., "the sect of the Sadducees" or "the sect which is of the Sadducees." But the high priest and those with him were only a small part of this sect, nor were they a little sect within the sect of the Sadducees. Hence these translations are unacceptable. Moulton (in R. 1107) puts us on the right track when in 13:1 he translates the same attributive participle, "the *local* church"; a papyrus has this participle in the sense, "the *current* month." So Luke means "the *local* sect of the Sadducees." Αἴρεσις means "choice," a chosen opinion or tenet, and thus the party holding that tenet, "a sect"; it often has a connotation of reproach.

First the motive, then the act. They were filled with passion, filled to overflowing, could not longer contain themselves. The noun means "hot steam"; it is derived from ζέω, "to boil." That this was "envy" (A. V. margin) or "jealousy" (R. V.) is a deduction made from what is regarded as the general situation, but this is too narrow. These Sadducees were wrought up because the apostles were boldly continuing their preaching of Jesus. We have their own statement for this in v. 28.

18) On this occasion all the apostles are summarily arrested; of course, by the Temple police on an order of these Sadducees. Where and how this was done we are left to surmise. We have only one clue in v. 26, where the Temple commander and his men proceed alertly because they were afraid of the people present. We thus conclude that the arrest mentioned in this verse was made at a moment when the people were absent. The culprits were placed "in a public ward." Since Luke always writes with great care and exactness, it is fair to conclude that this was not the same place of confinement as the one referred to in 4:3, but was one of the common jails, in regard to the location of which we are left uninformed. Thus at one sudden stroke and without the least warning the leaders of the entire church in Jerusalem were snatched away. Lodgment in jail was no more pleasant or honorable in those days than it is in ours; the procedure seems to be a deliberate attempt to subject the entire leadership of the believers to public disgrace. Criminals are summarily arrested but not decent men. Peter and John seem to have been placed only under guard for the night; the Twelve are now thrown into jail under lock and key.

19) But an angel of the Lord, during the night, opened the doors of the prison and, after leading them out, said, Be going and, having taken a stand, go on speaking in the Temple to the people the words of this life! And having heard it, they went at dawn into the Temple and began to teach.

To say that Luke is less vivid here than he is in the similar account in 12:6-10 is to overlook the great differences in the situations. Peter was to be executed, was fastened in chains and most heavily guarded in a far stronger prison; the Twelve were confined in the common jail. So Luke has less to say here, but what he says is surely vivid enough. We make no apology as far as the veracity of Luke's account is concerned. We find no legendary element in the narrative, no clothing of any fact in symbolical form, no friendly jailor or courageous Christian who released the apostles. Meyer is correct: *Das ist einlegende Schwindelei.*

Some time during the night (the phrase needs no article) an angel appeared in the prison where the apostles were confined, miraculously opened the locked doors from the inside, and himself led the apostles out (note the close connective τε which makes the whole action but one procedure). The guards saw nothing. Twelve men witnessed this act, saw and heard the angel, and were not deceived as to his identity. Some say that this release amounted to nothing since the apostles were promptly rearrested. But the rearrested apostles were in a position that was far different from the one that obtained at the time of their first arrest. The outcome of this affair was turned in favor of the apostles by this miracle; the time of peaceful development for the church was yet to continue.

20) The angel leaves the apostles with specific directions which in point of boldness, were like an open challenge to the Sanhedrists who had caused their arrest. They are to go and to take their stand or position in the very court of the Temple where they had been preaching constantly, and are to "continue to utter all the utterances of this life" to the people. Both λαλεῖτε and ῥήματα· say nothing about the subject matter to be uttered, they make plain only that the apostles are to speak as they did before. The subject matter is contained in the emphatic qualitative genitive "of

this life," the divine ζωή. In John 6:68, Peter had confessed regarding Jesus, "Thou hast utterances of life everlasting." The demonstrative does not refer "in sense" to ῥήματα (R. 497, 706) but is placed correctly: "this life," the one you are preaching in connection with the resurrection of Jesus, the one that is so objectionable to the Sadducees, the one that is salvation indeed. We do not need the capital letter of the R. V. even as it is not needed in John 6:68, nor the appeal to the Aramaic as though the angel had said, "these life utterances," and Luke had misconceived the sense. "Utter the utterances" implies that they were given to the apostles by the Lord, and "of life" that they conveyed this life to men.

21) One text adds: "and each one went home," which is certainly true. It was still night, the Temple gates were still locked, the time still too early to carry out the angel's order. But *sub lucem*, "under the dawn," when the gates were first opened for the early service at dawn, the apostles entered the Temple courts and began their teaching (inchoative imperfect). This was God's answer to the Sadducees. Rejecting "this life" themselves, they were resolved to prevent all others from accepting it even as Jesus had said in regard to the Pharisees, Matt. 23:13.

Now the high priest having arrived and those with him, they called together the Sanhedrin and all the eldership of the sons of Israel and sent to the jail in order that they be brought. But the underlings, on coming, did not find them in the prison; and having returned, they reported, saying, The jail we found as having been locked in all safety, and the guards standing at the doors; but on having opened, inside we found no one.

Granted that the addition of the words "having arisen early" in a very few texts reports a fact, the reason for this very early appearance of the high priest and his coterie would not be due to the fact that the high priest officiated in person at the early morning service; we should rather suppose that this early beginning was made in order to hasten on their way the messengers that were to summon the members of the Sanhedrin. Luke never reports irrelevant matters, and this functioning of the high priest at the early service would be one of these. Παρά in the participial form refers to the Temple which has just been mentioned.

The twofold designation, "Sanhedrin and all the eldership of the sons of Israel," has led to the conjecture that two bodies were summoned, or that the eldership was called in as advisory, in the capacity of assessors. But no historical evidence for such a second body has been found. The Sanhedrin was certainly large enough in itself. We have a similar twofold designation in Mark 15:1. In each instance a plenary session in indicated. Συνέδριον refers to the function of the body sitting together and taking counsel; while γερουσία indicates its dignity as being composed of γέροντες, old and honored men; hence it was also called the presbytery. "Sons of Israel" is only a more dignified term than "of the people." The Sadducees were presenting a case of major importance and they, indeed, had no less than twelve men to present as criminals.

The Sadducees summoned the members of the high court and then also sent a detachment of Temple police to bring the prisoners from the δεσμωτήριον or jail. These Temple police were Levites, were a large body that was generally armed with clubs, were under the orders of a chief commander who, in turn, had lieutenants under him. They are usually termed ὑπηρέται, "underlings." The high priests and the Sadducees imagine that they have everything in their own hands and are fully determined to crush the entire movement. They were due for a rather rude awakening.

22) The detachment of "underlings" proceeds on its errand. Luke states only the facts that they did not find the apostles in the jail and that they returned and made due report to their superiors.

23) Here we learn more although the report, too, states only the facts in the succinct way of military reports. First of all, they report that they found the jail still duly locked in all safety, the perfect participle bringing out the thought that, once locked, it had remained so until these underlings themselves unlocked it. Secondly, they also found the guards standing at the doors. In other words, on arriving, they found nothing whatever amiss — locks and guards were in order. But now comes the shock: "on having opened up, inside no one did we find." The twelve prisoners had vanished into thin air. One can imagine the expression on the faces of the Sadducees when they heard this report.

24) **Now when they heard these words, both the commander of the Temple and the high priests, they were much perplexed concerning them as to what might have occurred. But someone, having come, reported to them, Lo, the men whom you placed in the prison are in the Temple standing and teaching.**

Only the commander of the Temple police and the high priests are named because they had made the arrest; the rest of the Sanhedrists now learned of the matter for the first time. The commander is named first because he was responsible for all his men through whose fingers these prisoners had slipped. The preposition διά in the verb intensifies it: "thoroughly perplexed concerning them," i. e., the words or statements just made. In the indirect question: τί ἂν γένοιτο τοῦτο, we have an instance where a misconception of the meaning may mislead not only some translators but a few grammarians. Neither the sense nor the grammar yield the translation, "whereunto this would grow" (our versions, Luther, R., W. P.). This translation would require the present optative. The aorist optative compels us to translate, "what might have occurred" (B.-D. 299, 2: *was da wohl geschehen sei; wie das zugegangen sei*). The perplexity was caused by what had just been reported and the astonishment as to how in the world such a thing could have happened. It was not as yet caused by a regard for the future and what might happen.

In the New Testament the direct discourse is preferred to the indirect, hence so few examples of indirect discourse with the optative occur, and these occur only in Luke's writings. They represent the potential optative with ἄν which is taken over from the direct question without change, B.-D. 385 and 386. Only the apodosis is used in these indirect questions, the protasis, εἰ with the optative, does not appear.

25) In the midst of this perplexity there comes a messenger with the news that the men whom the Sanhedrists had locked up were in the Temple this very instant, back in their accustomed places, standing there as usual and proceeding with their teaching of the people. This messenger was, no doubt, a Levite, at least someone who knew all about the arrest of the previous day. But note that the news reaches the perplexed Sanhedrists just at this psychological moment as though the Lord had timed it so. If the Sadducees had heard this news sooner they might have kept it to themselves; now it came to the ears of the entire Sanhedrin and certainly had its effect.

The Twelve Before the Sanhedrin

26) The situation had taken on an unexpected complexion. **Then the commander, having gone with the underlings, brought them, not with force, for they were fearing the people lest they be stoned.**
The chief commander had not thought it necessary to go to the prison in person, now he finds it decidedly necessary to go to the Temple court, for the situation has become delicate. He takes with him the Levite police who have just made their astonishing report. The texts with the reading ἦγεν describe, those with ἤγαγεν merely state the fact. From the prison the apostles were to have been brought "with force" like prisoners who are being haled before their judges; nothing of the sort is now attempted, "not with force," but the apostles are brought as men who have been requested to appear. They accompany the commander of their own accord; not a hand is laid upon them. And Luke states the reason (γάρ): the commander and his men feared the people, crowds of whom were again listening to the teaching. That was real fear "lest they be stoned."

We see no reason for being in doubt in regard to the construction of this clause; it is not a purpose clause that is dependent on the phrase "not with force" (R., W. P.); but it is dependent on "they were fearing" and states what was feared. See R. 995; B.-D. 370. Sections of the Temple were still being rebuilt; in fact, this rebuilding was not completed until shortly before the war and the final destruction of the entire Temple. So stones were at hand as in John 8:59; 10:31. The Jews were also extremely excitable, and when they were suddenly aroused knew no limits in their mob violence. Here we see the high esteem which the apostles enjoyed among the common people; it was highly dangerous to make a false move against them in the presence of the people. And all this occurred while the great Sanhedrin was kept waiting.

27) **Now, having brought them, they made them stand in the Sanhedrin. And the high priest inquired of them, saying: With an order we gave orders to you not to be teaching on the basis of this name; and lo, you have filled Jerusalem with your teaching and intend to bring on us the blood of this man!**

While the Sanhedrists were seated on a semicircular platform, the apostles were literally made to stand (the verb is transitive) "in the Sanhedrin." So John and Peter, and so Jesus, too, had stood. Caiaphas presides, and it is he that "inquired." But the form of his address is not a question, it is an assertion in an accusing tone that demands a reply in defense.

28) Not a word does Caiaphas breathe about the manner in which the apostles escaped from the prison — he surely had his suspicions regarding that. It would have been a fine thing for him and for the other Sadducees, who did not believe in angels, to hear it attested by twelve witnesses before the whole Sanhedrin and all the Pharisees who were in it, who did believe in angels, that an angel had opened the prison and had led them out. So not a word regarding that subject. But a strong word regarding the awful crime of the apostles who had flagrantly disobeyed the strictest orders of the august Sanhedrin in no way ever to be teaching ἐπὶ τῷ ὀνόματι τούτῳ, with "this name" and what it stands for and reveals as the basis (see 2:21).

"With an order we gave orders" is the Greek reproduction of the Hebrew infinitive absolute and yet follows similar Greek constructions which, by adding the cognate noun, emphasize the force of the verb: "we issued strictest orders to you," R. 531. The infinitive is properly durative: "not to be teaching." Here we again see the unwillingness of these foes of Jesus even to utter his name "Jesus"; "this name," "this man" is all that they can bring themselves to say. *Sie moechten ihn totschweigen. Fugit appellare Jesum; Petrus appellat et celebrat.* Bengel. The high priest's feeling on that point is correct, for this name will prove his destruction.

But what have the apostles done? "You have filled Jerusalem with your teaching!" No less. And this is true in fact and not an exaggeration. The perfect is extensive (R. 895); it reaches from the past to a point in the present; the accusative indicates what is filled, and the genitive that with which the filling has been accomplished. "Jerusalem" has the article, *das Jerusalem* (German), it is feminine because it is the name of a place. This very teaching, this reprehensible doctrine (2:42) the apostles have spread over the entire city in bold violation of the Sanhedrin's stringent command.

Thus far Caiaphas kept the judicial tone, his words sounded like a stern indictment. Now the judge turns defendant and speaks in behalf of his own personal cause and even in an injured tone. He is recalling the bold words of the people that were, no doubt, first uttered by him personally and then caught up by all of them when Pilate refused to assume the guilt of Jesus' blood as recorded in Matt. 27:25. But he is now thinking only of himself and of the Sanhedrin. When they stood before Pilate they were morally certain that there would be no such guilt and boldly offered to take it upon themselves if such guilt there should be.

Why should that offer and especially the word "blood" have remained in this high priest's mind now to be recalled in the presence of apostles? Why should he say, "you intend (the verb expressing purpose,

R. 878) to bring on us the blood of this man" if no guilt attached to the shedding of his blood and to the part the Sanhedrin had played in that shedding? This is the secret working of conscience which makes a coward of this hardened criminal. He sees frightful intentions in the hearts of the apostles and in the growing success of their work. They were resolved to dethrone the high priest, to overthrow the Sanhedrin, and thus to wreak vengeance on them for "the blood of this man." His blood is haunting this Jew, has gone on haunting Jews ever since; but all they do is what Caiaphas here does: betray the thought and charge men with trying to execute it instead of repenting before God.

29) **Answering, however, Peter and the apostles said: It is necessary to obey God rather than men. The God of our fathers raised up Jesus whom you on your part laid hands on, hanging him on wood. Him as Leader and Savior God exalted with his right hand to give repentance to Israel and remission of sins. And we are witnesses of these things, also the Holy Spirit whom God gave to those obeying him.**

The indictment is met by a perfect defense. The singular "answering" presents Peter as the speaker, and the plural "they said" makes the words of Peter the words of all the apostles. First of all, Peter summarily restates what he had said already in 4:19, 20, with the difference that now the great principle is stated abstractly in the briefest form: "It is necessary to obey God rather than men." The "we" of our versions is due to the awkwardness of the English; the Greek expresses the general idea that "one must obey," the German, *man muss gehorchen.*

This dictum is axiomatic for all except atheists and agnostics. Its tremendous significations have been fully discussed in connection with 4:19, 20. But in any given case of supposed conflict between these two authorities "God" and "men," how are we to determine that God really says and orders what men object to, deny, and forbid? Peter answers this question in a full and direct way for the apostles. The Sanhedrin would readily admit the general principle, but it would deny that, by filling Jerusalem with the name of Jesus, the apostles were obeying God and thus rightly placing his authority above that of the Sanhedrin. This, then, is the real point. Men who have erring consciences convince themselves in some way of their own that they are obeying God, whereas, like the Sanhedrin here, they are not but are, perhaps, doing the very opposite. This is not the case with Peter's defense. We may test it today. The apostles were, indeed, obeying God when they disobeyed the men of the Sanhedrin.

30) *For God did these things with regard to Jesus and made them and the Holy Spirit the witnesses.* They must, therefore, testify and, if men forbid, must obey God rather than men. "The God of our fathers" is a designation that has strong connotations. First, all the hopes and the expectations of our godly fathers rested on God's Messianic promises. Secondly, they were our fathers, and we ought to be their true children by sharing those promises and those hopes now that they have been fulfilled. Thirdly, "our" refers to the Sanhedrin as well as to the apostles; the very pronoun is a call to faith.

The emphasis is on what *God* did, for the apostles are obeying *God* rather than men. And now Peter once more uses two fearful contrasts that were employed so crushingly in 3:13-15, and 4:10: *God* raised up the Jesus *you* killed. *Your* action was directly against *God*; *he* nullified what *you* did, yea, elevated Jesus into his eternal office. Thus, in the most effective way Peter at this very moment does his part by testifying as God's witness and by filling even this hall of the Sanhedrin and the ears of all the Sanhedrists with the name of Jesus.

It is contended that the statement, "God raised up Jesus," does not refer to the resurrection but to the entire act of sending Jesus for his work. Peter cannot mention the resurrection before the crucifixion. Moreover, we are told that we here have the proper chronological order: God raised up Jesus by sending him; the Jews crucified him; God exalted him (by raising him from the dead and by enthroning him in heaven). But this is specious. Peter is not following chronology but is hurling contrasts at the Sanhedrists. The strong asyndeton in v. 31 is not a parallel to the relative ὅν in v. 30; a relative and then an asyndeton do not denote a chronological succession. No; Peter at once announces the mighty deed of God: raising up Jesus from the dead. Everything turns about this central act of God's. As he had done in 4:10, he compels especially the Sadducees in the Sanhedrin who deny the resurrection to face this fact of the resurrection of Jesus. And whereas the Sanhedrists avoided the very name as though even to pronounce it brought defilement upon them, Peter joyfully utters this blessed name and sounds it forth into the ears of these Sanhedrists.

There stands the great fact: *God* raised up Jesus. And here stands its opposite: "whom *you* laid hands on by hanging him on wood," the modal participle which expresses action that is coincident with that of the verb. The verb is expressive of exactly what the Sanhedrists did although they used the hands of others. Moreover, it agrees with the participle: "by hanging him on wood," ἐπὶ ξύλου, which is usually translated, "on a tree." The expression is Jewish for the Jewish thought that is expressed in Deut. 21:23; Gal. 3:13, that one who was executed by being hanged on a beam of wood was by that act declared to be accursed. The Jews suspended the dead body of a criminal after execution; so Christ's dead body hung on the cross. Not only did the Sanhedrin bring about the death of Jesus, a death that was shameful in the eyes of Romans (crucifixion), but they inflicted upon him the death of those who are accursed by God (suspension on wood).

31) The succession of thought is by no means chronological, for with the emphatic τοῦτον Peter in typical Greek fashion resumes all that he has just said about Jesus in v. 30. He is not adding a third act in a series of three but is stating what God's act in raising up the Jesus whom the Jews hanged as one accursed really signifies, namely that "by his right hand God exalted him as Leader and Savior." God's right hand always signifies his power and his majesty; on this dative with the same verb compare 2:33.

Because ἀρχηγόν and σωτῆρα are without articles they are predicative: God exalted him "as Leader and Savior"; the idea is not that of purpose "in order to be a Leader," etc. The two terms, taken together, state what Jesus is. In 3:15 we have ἀρχηγός with a genitive while here this definitive title is absolute. In an effort to find one English term that will fit both passages many translators use "Prince," German *Fuerst*, although the connotation in these translations is not that associated with the Greek word. *Archegos*, like "Savior," refers to what Jesus does for us; he is a fountain, source, author, beginner for us and, as we see from "Savior," the beginner and author of salvation for us. In 3:15 we say "Author of life," here, if we had a similar genitive, we could say "Author of salvation," and this is indeed the sense. "Prince" would indicate that we honor his royal position, that *we* do something for *him*; it may also imply that he is not yet King. On the idea contained in "Savior" compare 4:12 (3:47).

Christ's exaltation always refers to his human nature which is in the *unio* with the divine. The term includes the resurrection which was already a glorification and also the *sessio* in heaven. But only through the medium of the human nature by which Jesus lived under the law, suffered, and died for our sins is he now our Leader and Savior, bringing us to the salvation he has prepared for us.

God exalted him as such an Author of salvation for our sakes, "in order to give (infinitive of purpose, effective aorist) repentance to Israel and remission of sins." This shows how the salvation is made ours. It is wholly by a gift of grace, τοῦ δοῦναι; both repentance and remission are given. The former is wrought in the heart through the Word, the very Word Peter is here preaching so effectively; the latter is given through the divine declaration of justification which absolves the repentant sinner from his sins. The two are simultaneous but always occur in this order and never in the reverse order. The moment repentance is wrought in the heart the act of remission follows in heaven. On μετάνοια and on ἄφεσις see 2:38. "Israel" is mentioned as the recipient of the gift in the sense of 1:8. The gift was intended for Israel in the first place, and Peter had only Israelites before him.

32) These are the profound things that *God* has done for this most vital purpose. "And we are witnesses of these things" or "of these said things." The idea contained in "witnesses" is not only that the apostles themselves saw these said things and could thus testify regarding them. Seeing the nature of these things and their divine purpose, it would be absolutely criminal if they, the witnesses, did not testify and proclaim them to all Israel. Such negligence would certainly be disobeying God in the most wicked way.

When the Sanhedrists attempt to silence them these Sanhedrists disobey God. The apostles cannot permit themselves to be thus silenced, for that keeping silent would imply putting the authority of men in the place of that of God. The logic and the moral rectitude are as clear as crystal.

When Peter adduces the Holy Spirit as another witness in the relative clause, "whom God gave to those obeying him," he intends to state that the testimony of the Spirit is mediate, he using the believers as his media. The idea is not that they are all to preach and to teach as the apostles did, but it is much broader. The apostolic office is kept distinct (1:22). The Holy Spirit is in the hearts as a gift of God to all who by faith in Jesus obey God. All that the Spirit has wrought in these obedient ones is the Spirit's living testimony to Jesus and to what God has made Jesus to be. The fact that Jesus is the exalted Savior is apparent in every believer who has Jesus and his salvation in his heart and confesses these by lip and life. The apostles are not only God's witnesses, their testimony is accompanied by the great fact that is before the eyes of all men, namely that all those who are with the apostles have God's Spirit in their hearts, and that he speaks in and through them. "Those obeying God" include the apostles, although their service as special apostolic witnesses is not excluded. "Obeying" recalls the same verb used in v. 19. What about these Sanhedrists? They are evidently not among those who obey God with the blessed obedience of faith; they have closed their hearts against the gift of the Holy Spirit, against the gift of repentance and remission, against Jesus, God's Savior.

This apostolic address is far more than a defense against an indictment. Peter preaches law and gospel to the hearts of the Sanhedrists, if possible, by God's grace in Christ, to convert and to save them. Note that he speaks to these Sanhedrists about the Holy Spirit as though the Holy Trinity were known to them. This knowledge of the Trinity is assumed already in the preaching of the Baptist and thereafter with never a Jewish objection based on unitarian conceptions of God being uttered. The claim that the Old Testament did not reveal the Trinity to the Jews is without basis in fact.

33) Peter's words reached the heart. **But they, having heard, were sawn in two and were intending to make away with them.** We have the same strong figure in 7:54. We prefer to retain it instead of modifying it: "were cut to the heart" (our versions). The verb is passive and states what Peter's words inflicted. Here the infliction was not salutary, but note a similar passive in 2:37 where it had a salutary effect. The verb states only how pained the Sanhedrists were by the truth concerning their murder of Jesus and their hostility to God; it does not say anything about the rage of these men. The next verb, "they were intending" (to be understood in the same sense as in v. 28 and not "took counsel," A. V.), states that the Sanhedrists were forming the purpose in their hearts to "make away with" the apostles, to murder them. From the treatment accorded Jesus as well as that accorded his apostles we note the type of men that constituted the supreme court and the highest leadership of the Jews: men who had committed murder and were ready again to commit murder.

Would it not have been wiser for Peter to have toned down his words? Many have adopted that sort of wisdom and by doing so have persuaded themselves that they were better witnesses than Peter, more obedient to God than were the apostles. They have never sawn a sinner in two by a preaching of the law. They convert painlessly. Alas, their conversions are only counterfeit. Both verbs are imperfects, both describe conditions, both imply that something definite followed. If the reading ἐβουλεύοντο be preferred to ἐβούλοντο, the former would indicate a little more than intention, namely an openly voiced resolution on the part of some of the Sanhedrists to make away with the apostles. "Were intending," in fact, implies as much, for the intention could not be known unless it was expressed in words.

34) **Now one in the Sanhedrin, a Pharisee, by name Gamaliel, a lawteacher, in honor with all the people, having arisen, ordered to put the men outside for a little while.**

"One in the Sanhedrin" means a member of that body. "A Pharisee" describes him as being a member of the party that was opposed to that mentioned in v. 17 and even more fully in 4:5, 6. This point is of great importance for the sequel. The Sadducees were thwarted by this Pharisee and his followers in the Sanhedrin; a compromise was effected, the apostles were only scourged. "By name Gamaliel," the common dative for introducing names, at once shows to all who know anything about this famous teacher what weight a word of his would have. He was not only "a lawteacher" but one "in honor with all the people" (ethical dative), famous among the Jews. This important personage, as was the right of any member of the Sanhedrin when an executive and private session was desired by him, ordered the prisoners to be taken out βραχύ, "for a little," the neuter adjective used as an adverb.

Φαρισαῖος, from the Hebrew *pharash*, means "a separatist." This designation came to be the name of a member of the Jewish party that is prominent everywhere in the New Testament. Organized after the exile, this party insisted on the strictest outward observance of all legal regulations and also of the tradition that added a mass of rabbinical regulations to the

Mosaic laws. They were extreme formalists who ignored everything spiritual in the Scriptures, under their formalism hid much that was morally vicious, and yet were proud of their holiness. They were honored as being holy by the people generally, were absolutely self-righteous and thus violently opposed to the doctrine of grace and liberty that was proclaimed by Jesus. They are accurately described by Jesus himself in Matt. 23:13-39.

This Gamaliel was the grandson of Hillel who was famous in Jewish tradition. Hillel flourished about 37-4 B. C. We know nothing about his son Simon; but Simon's son Gamaliel, whom Luke introduces here, was one of the seven men who were accorded the title "Rabban." He developed his grandfather's teaching and founded a dynasty of famous men which continued for about four centuries. This Gamaliel, called "the old," to distinguish him from his grandson of the same name, must have been famous for many years before the incident recorded in this passage. Saul was a pupil of his (22:3), and it is just possible that Saul himself was present (but not as a member) at this session of the Sanhedrin and heard Gamaliel's address. Much has been made of this Pharisee in Christian tradition and legend. Zahn loves to trace such things, see his *Apostelgeschichte*, 219, etc.

35) **And he said to them: Israelite men, take heed to yourselves about these men, what you are about to do. For before these days, there arose Theudas, claiming himself to be somebody, to whom there was inclined a number of men about four hundred, who was made away with, and all as many as kept on obeying him were dispersed and came to nothing.**

Gamaliel addresses his colleagues in the same honorable fashion as did Peter the Jews in 2:22, and in 3:12. He counsels caution and advises that his colleagues forget not to consider their own interests in case of any precipitate action into which their passion may otherwise lead them. Many, no doubt, thought that he was referring to the danger from the people (v. 26) who held the apostles and believers generally in high esteem (v. 13), but Gamaliel has a different self-interest. He bids his colleagues look farther. Yet his own view and his conclusions proved to be entirely wrong. The Lord, however, used his spurious wisdom to extend the great work that was going on in Jerusalem with full vigor.

36) He sketches briefly the career of a certain Theudas, who was known to his colleagues, who claimed himself to be somebody, secured a following of 400 men for his rebellion, and was soon killed with the result that those who still adhered to his ideas were dispersed and faded into nothing, *ad nihilum*. His entire movement ran its full course without aid from the Sanhedrin. We see the drift of Gamaliel's argument: this Jesus-movement will most likely fade out of itself. Why should the Sanhedrin dip its hands into the blood of these twelve men who still "keep on obeying" Jesus as the followers of Theudas did even after he was slain?

But this little bit of history recounted by Gamaliel, which Luke records without comment as to its correctness, has become the occasion for considerable debate because of statements made by Josephus. In his *Ant.* 20, 5, 1 he, too, reports about a certain Theudas who incited a rebellion and came to a miserable end; but this man appeared about thirteen years after the time of Gamaliel's address. Gamaliel mentions 400 men as constituting the following of the man whom he has in mind, Josephus writes of this man that "he persuaded a great part of the people." Not a few conclude that Josephus is right, and that something is wrong with Luke's account. To make this conclusion more plausible they date Luke and Acts late enough so that Luke could have read Josephus. And Luke is then thought to have invented this part of Gamaliel's address. Men like Ramsey, Robertson (*Luke the Historian*, 160; W. P.), and others still think that at least a problem exists and themselves propose to wait until it has been solved. There is no problem whatever in regard to Luke who never read a line of Josephus. Any problem there may be pertains only to Josephus whose mistakes and inaccuracies Zahn, among others, has sufficiently pointed out. Whether Josephus speaks about this Theudas mentioned by Gamaliel, confused the dates, or reports about another Theudas who was active thirteen years later, leaves Gamaliel's statements unaffected.

37) After him there arose Judas, the Galilean, in the days of the enrolment and drew away people after him; he also perished, and all as many as kept obeying him were scattered abroad.

This refers to the enrolment for taxation mentioned in Luke 2:1, 2. Gamaliel's expression "in the days of the enrolment" speaks of this as a well-known period. Judas, born in Gamala in Gaulonitis, is called "the Galilean" because of the scene of his revolt which was of far greater proportions than that of Theudas. But he, too, perished, and his following, too, was dispersed so that his efforts likewise ended in nothing.

Usually little is said in regard to Josephus and his account of this Judas, but in this case Josephus' account is worse than that in regard to Theudas. Zahn charges Josephus with *heillose Verwirrung* regarding Judas and other men of like aims as well as in regard to the taxation under Cyrenius in Palestine. Josephus produces a tangle by duplicating Judas, so that he mentions one who was active during the taxation at the end of the life of Herod the Great and another who was active toward the close of the first century. We need not enter into the details which pertain only to Josephus and not in the least to Luke. We add only that the rebellion was of grave proportions, that Judas sought royal honors, and that Josephus, both in the case of Theudas and of Judas, suppresses the Messianic claims that helped to attract the following of these men.

38) In view of these two plain historical instances Gamaliel offers what has become his famous *counsel of indecision*: Be careful — do not decide — wait, wait and see! **And as to now I say to you, stand away from these men and let them be! For if this counsel or this work is of men, it will be overthrown; but if it is of God, you will not be able to overthrow them — lest perchance you be found even fighting God.**

Τανῦν, "as to the things now," as to the present situation, this, namely, in view of the two historical instances that were well known to all present, Gamaliel advises his colleagues "to stand away from these men" and not to think of killing them and "to let them be," which we may also translate, "to dismiss them." Gamaliel then makes plain his method of reasoning. There can be only two possibilities. He takes up each and draws the conclusion. First, if this counsel or this work — call it what you please — is "of men," has its origin and its source of strength only in weak, erring, deluded men, "it will be overthrown." That is undoubtedly true. Every religion that is built and founded on men will go down in failure. The only oversight in Gamaliel's statement is that he did not say *when* it will be overthrown. He and his colleagues may be dead and gone by the time this human thing, if it be human, is finally overthrown. The question for Gamaliel was as to how long he could wait. How long have some pagan religions endured? How old is Mohammedanism? God will overthrow every false religion and every false religious movement in the end, but can we sit down in indecision until this final proof is produced?

39) The other alternative is equally faulty. If it is "of God," has its source and strength in him, "you cannot overthrow it." "Lest perchance" requires that we supply in thought: "Take heed, lest," etc.; and καί is elliptic: "not merely fighting men but *even* fighting God." Shall they, then, do nothing? Shall they sit on the fence and wait and wait, afraid to strike for God lest they strike against God? This counsel has been called wise but it offers only the folly of indecision where decision is imperative. And with its indecision there goes hand in hand the implication that God has not supplied us with means to make the true and safe decision, so that only the final fate of any religion can decide whether it is of God or of men.

Gamaliel belongs to that class of men whom the most convincing evidence does not convince. They still demand other evidence, more and more signs, Matt. 12:39, etc. Their answer to all the evidence furnished by Christ is: "Yes — but!" Gamaliel lacked one thing: the consciousness of sin. The veil of his Pharisaic work-righteousness blinded him to his guilt. Peter's call to repentance did not move him to contrition. So this wise Jew continued in his folly.

R. 1018 compares the two conditional sentences employed by Gamaliel, first, ἐάν with the subjunctive followed by the future indicative (expectance); secondly, εἰ with the indicative followed by the future indicative (reality), and finds that Gamaliel is giving the benefit of the doubt to Christianity. This, however, is not the case. The conditional forms used keep the balance and incline neither way. The reason for using these forms lies elsewhere. In the one case Gamaliel rightly thinks of the future: "if it shall (turn out to) be of men"; in the other case he just as rightly thinks of the present: "if it is of God." Both are suppositions on his part just as all conditions are suppositions and nothing more. In the one case Gamaliel supposes something future with a future result; in the other something present with a future result. He has not a mite more certainty for the one case than for the other — yes, masterly indecision.

40) Now they obeyed him; and having called the apostles, after administering a hiding, they gave orders not to be speaking on the basis of the name of Jesus and released them.

Literally, "they were persuaded to him," the Greek for, "they obeyed." No one of the Sanhedrin arose to point out the fallacy in Gamaliel's argument, and no one called attention to the fact that by rejecting and crucifying Jesus they had already decided that this entire movement was *not* of God. The Sadducees lost, the Pharisees won. This friction between the two parties explains much, particularly also the scourging administered before the apostles were released, δείραντες, literally, "after flaying them." They were stripped and given thirty-nine blows with rods across the back (Deut. 35:3; II Cor. 11:24; compare, Matt. 10:17, and Acts 22:19). This severe treatment was not so much to be a punishment for what the apostles had done but rather an emphasis on the renewed order not to be saying a word "on (the basis of) the name of Jesus" (see 4:17, 18). To be beaten thus was no small disgrace; before Roman judges Roman citizens dared not be treated thus. The Jews had no such restrictions.

41) They, therefore, were going from the presence of the Sanhedrin rejoicing that they were deemed worthy to be dishonored on behalf of the Name. And every day in the Temple and from house to house they were not ceasing to teach and to proclaim as good news Jesus the Christ.

Οἱ μὲν οὖν is Luke's favorite turn of expression, see 1:6; a δέ need not follow. The imperfect with its present participle is beautifully descriptive and pictures the apostles going from the presence of the Sanhedrin and rejoicing as they went. The scourging took place in the presence of the Sanhedrin; Jesus, too, was scourged in the presence of Pilate. Gamaliel also went away, but certainly not rejoicing. If this work was "of God," would not forbidding it and scourging its agents be fighting God? But there was no doubt in the hearts of the apostles.

Note the sharp oxymoron (bringing together contradictory terms) in "deemed worthy to be dishonored." These disgraceful stripes the apostles considered badges of honor. In the great and blessed fight *for* God they had not been undecided and inactive like Gamaliel but had done their part valiantly and as true soldiers of the cross bore honorable wounds to attest their noble loyalty. This was the first instance of what Paul writes in I Cor. 4:9: "I think God hath set forth us the apostles last of all, as men doomed to death; for we are made a spectacle unto the world, and to the angels, and to men." "On behalf of the Name" makes ὄνομα emphatic, for from the beginning (4:7) everything had turned on this "Name," the term being used as explained in 4:2; 2:21. Here it is used in an eminent sense.

42) Never for a moment did the apostles cease their blessed work. "Every day" they continued, and this openly "in the Temple" where the Sanhedrin and the Temple police could see and hear them, and, of course, also κατ' οἶκον, which is distributive, "from house to house," and not merely adverbial, "at home." They continued to fill Jerusalem from center to circumference with the Name. They scorned to work only in secret. They knew no fear. The imperfect, "they were not ceasing," with its complementary present par-

ticiples is still descriptive, and "were not ceasing" (negative) is a litotes for "were ever continuing." The first participle, "teaching," is made more specific by the second, "proclaiming as good news Jesus the Christ"; τὸν Χριστόν is predicative: "as the Christ." Here we have the first instance of εὐαγγελίζεσθαι in the Acts in the full sense of preaching the gospel, and with it the mighty name "Jesus" and its full significance in "the Christ," the Messiah of God (2:36). This "name" fittingly closes the present narrative.

This was the opposite of indecision. This was the divinely wrought certainty that had long ago made the final decision. This was the joy that came from that certainty. The apostles never for a moment complained of the injustice they had suffered at the hands of the authorities; they did not boast of their own courage and fortitude or concern themselves about defending their personal honor against the shame inflicted on them. If they thought of themselves at all, it was only that they might prove faithful to the Lord by working for the honor of his great blessed Name. All else they committed into his hands.

CHAPTER VI

THE ELECTION OF THE SEVEN

In chapters six and seven we have the story of Stephen. There is no reason for thinking that a special document was intercalated at this point by Luke or by some redactor. There is a perfect connection with the preceding. After being told about the great growth of the congregation and of its manner of taking care of the needy, we now learn that this work grew beyond the capacity of the apostles, and thus we come to Stephen, one of the seven deacons who is forever distinguished as the first martyr of the Christian Church. This fact justifies Luke for allotting so much space to Stephen and to his address in this account. At the end of the narrative about Stephen we catch our first glimpse of Saul.

1) Now in these days, the disciples multiplying, there occurred a murmuring of the Hellenists against the Hebrews because their widows were being overlooked in the daily ministration.

Nothing of note occurred after the agitation reported in the previous chapters. The apostles continued their great work strenuously and without interference. The genitive absolute reports their continued great success: "the disciples multiplying." It has been conservatively estimated that at this time the total number of the disciples was between twenty and twenty-five thousand. This vast increase, Luke intimates, occasioned the murmuring, subdued complaint, of the Hellenists against the Hebrews, that the widows of the former were being overlooked in the daily dispensation of support, which is beautifully called the διακονία or "ministration" which freely renders service and help for the benefit of those concerned. Here Luke calls the believers μαθηταί, "disciples," from μανθάνω, "to learn," but not in the sense merely of "pupils" who are still under instruction but rather in the sense of those who have already learned. And even this is not enough, for this learning was not merely intellectual, it involved the acquirement of the very spirit of the teacher. These disciples had become like their Master, they were following in his footsteps.

The Ἑλληνισταί (a word not found until it was used by Luke) were not Ἕλληνες, "Greeks," either by extraction, by religion, or in the broader cultural sense. They were Jews fully as much as the other class that is called "Hebrews." We read of all sorts of Hellenists in 2:9-11 and find their synagogues mentioned in 6:9. They had been reared in foreign lands, had replaced the Aramaic with the Greek language, and thus read their Scriptures only in the LXX translation. In the diaspora the second and the third generations lost their Aramaic to a great degree as the inscriptions on their tombs show. Yet they in every way remained loyal Jews. Among them there were proselytes (2:10), but these had completely adopted Judaism and thus are also designated as Jews. These Hellenists were scattered over the entire Roman world.

The Ἑβραῖοι were the Jews of Palestine and of the great eastern diaspora, Babylon, etc. Their native tongue remained Aramaic, they used the Hebrew Scriptures in their synagogues, their Greek was for the greater part imperfect, and they took a certain pride in being "Hebrews" (II Cor. 11:22; Phil. 3:5). There was, however, no clear dividing line between these two great classes of Jews. Jesus, who lived only in Palestine, needed no interpreter but himself spoke Greek to Pilate. On the other hand, Paul, who who was reared in Tarsus, perfectly preserved his

Aramaic and knew his Hebrew. So also the attitude of the two classes is devoutly Jewish. "To Hellenize" meant to adopt Greek or pagan modes of life, and this corruption had contaminated the Jews, even some of their aristocratic priests, but the Hellenists we read about in the New Testament had not Hellenized themselves in this manner.

The complaint was not directed against the apostles although they must be classed as "Hebrews." It seems as though the majority of the congregation consisted of Hebrews, and that the apostles had used assistants from this class for dispensing the needed charity. How this had been done, and how widows of the Hellenists had thus come to be overlooked, we are unable to say. We see only that the complaint was justified. How much party feeling between Hellenists and Hebrews was involved is difficult to say.

2) **And the Twelve, having called to them the multitude of the disciples, said: It does not please us that we, having forsaken the Work of God, keep ministering to tables. Look out for yourselves, therefore, brethren, seven attested men from yourselves, full of the Holy Spirit and of wisdom, whom we shall appoint for this need. But for our part, we will continue steadfast in the worship and in the ministration of the Word.**

The apostles function as the leaders of the congregation. They act promptly and do not let the case become acute. Although they are apostles, they make no decision of their own a law for the congregation. There is not the least trace of popery; they deal with the members as brethren. The Twelve called the meeting and not Peter. In order to do so they must have discussed the matter among themselves and naturally would offer some proper plan for the congregation to adopt. But this amounted only to making a motion in the meeting and seconding it, after which all voted.

Luke does not need to say that only those who had attained the proper age took part in this meeting in accord with the spirit of the Fourth Commandment, Eph. 6:1; Col. 3:20; likewise, he need not mention the fact that only the men voted in accord with the Jewish practice which was based on Gen. 2:18-23; 3:16, and was for this very reason the apostolic practice, I Tim. 2:12-14. This point has now become controversial, but exegetically neither the apostolic practice itself nor the grounds on which it rests, God's creation and thus nature and the condition produced by the fall, can be controverted.

Perhaps Peter spoke; if this was the case, he did so merely for all the Twelve. The personal pronoun ἡμᾶς lends force to the impersonal οὐκ ἀρεστόν ἐστι, so that this means: "It does not please us." The matter is well stated: "that we, having forsaken the Word of God," i. e., the preaching and the teaching of this Word, the essential task to which the apostles were called by the Lord, "keep ministering to tables," to dispensing food for the needy. We now have διακονεῖν to correspond with the διακονία used in v. 1. The apostles were, indeed, "to minister," but in distributing the Bread of life and not in attending to the distribution of ordinary food supplies. The words are general. Therefore it is impossible for us to learn just how the apostles had been ministering to tables. Yet we may safely say that "tables" does not refer to the love feasts that were taking place at different houses and preceded the Eucharist. The food for these feasts was brought by the participants who readily shared with the needy. Luke has already informed us that this ministry refers to administering and distributing the large sums of money that were derived from the sale of property. From this fund the daily ministration was made.

At first the apostles shouldered this extra task without much difficulty. But now it had grown to undue proportions and interfered with their essential work. The fact that some widows were thus overlooked was only one evil result; the apostles point to one that is still worse; their being forced into a task that really does not belong to their office. This point is worth noting. The theory that all offices in the church are derived from one central office and really constitute parts of it finds no support here. This theory has led to such ideas as that when the janitor rings the bell, sweeps the church, lights the lamps, he is only substituting for the pastor. The apostles have a different view and clearly state what the obligation of the Christian ministry is. Other tasks may arise, but these are extraneous, to be turned over to other hands. The apostles were not delegating a part of their divine office to others — they could not. They were relinquishing tasks that were not a part of this office, that were interfering with that office. To be sure, these tasks, too, need to be performed, but this necessity does not make them a part of the divinely instituted office of apostles and pastors.

3) The selection of the men for this task is left to the congregation. If these men were to serve as assistants to the apostles in their apostolic work, the selection would have been made by the apostles. So Paul selected his assistants, and we know that he declined Mark's services. But these men were to be the aids of the congregation in the ministration at tables, and so the congregation was properly told itself to choose them. The apostles merely make the proposal, suggest the necessary number, and name the qualifications the men should have. And we must note that the congregation freely adopted these restrictions. Just why seven were proposed no one knows. It is, of

course, a sacred number, but here practical considerations evidently governed. If these men were to have been assistants of the apostles, we should expect the number to be twelve and not seven. It is only a conjecture to say that at this time seven special meeting places were used by the congregation. The reason for selecting seven seems to have been obvious to the congregation, but what this reason was we cannot say.

The present participle "attested," "witnessed to," is qualitative and the present tense for this reason. Men who were known for their character and their ability are referred to; this was naturally consented to. Likewise, the requirement that they should be "full of the Holy Spirit and of wisdom." It is well that "wisdom" is added, for this helps us to understand just what is meant by being full of the Holy Spirit. All the disciples had the Holy Spirit, all had received one gift or another from him. The men needed for the task here considered ought to have one notable gift in an especial measure, namely to such a degree as to be recognized by the members generally. This was "wisdom," the ability and the readiness to apply Christian knowledge to the practical affairs of life. We at once see how necessary this gift of the Spirit would be, and how the congregation readily agreed to look for men only of this marked type. Moreover, where the Spirit gives wisdom, other gifts will also be present.

"Whom we shall appoint for this need" has no emphatic "we" and in no way implies anything hierarchical. After the election of the men by the congregation the apostles, who had had this work in their hands thus far, would turn it over to them. The idea that a fitting ceremony would be included was only natural (v. 6).

4) After this arrangement has been made, the apostles expect to devote all their time to what proper-

ly constitutes their divine office which they summarize briefly as "the worship and the ministration of the Word." The term προσευχή is frequently used in this wider sense of worship of which prayer constitutes the prominent part. That the newly created office, like everything else belonging to the life and the activity of the congregation, would be under the guidance and the leadership of the apostles and their divine office, goes without saying.

5) **And the word pleased before the entire multitude; and they elected for themselves Stephen, a man full of faith and of the Holy Spirit, and Philip, and Prochorus, and Nicanor, and Timon, and Parmenas, and Nicolaus, a proselyte, an Antiochian, whom they set before the apostles. And praying, they placed on them the hands.**

We may say, "the proposition" was accepted by vote. The construction with ἐνώπιον is the language of the LXX, and ἤρεσεν is like the Latin *placuit* when a vote is taken. The entire assembly unanimously voiced its agreement. The election was held, but we do not know in what manner except that the apostles do not seem to have made the nominations. The two most prominent men, as the following record describes them, are placed at the head of the list; we know nothing further concerning the rest. Stephen is especially distinguished as "a man full of faith and of the Holy Spirit." If πλήρης is the reading adopted, this word is regarded as indeclinable (B.-D. 137, 1). In v. 3 the order is: "full of the Holy Spirit and of wisdom"; here: "full of faith and of the Holy Spirit." First the source, and then the fruit; again the fruit, and then its source. What Luke means by "faith" we see in the following: the power of personal conviction expressed in most convincing wisdom (v. 10). Stephen's address before the Sanhedrin is the sublime expression of that faith. Philip became the evangelist and is not to be confused with Philip the apostle.

All the men chosen bear Greek names, but it would be a hasty conclusion to state that all were Hellenists when we remember that two of the apostles, who were certainly Hebrews, had Greek names, namely Andrew and Philip. We, therefore, decline to draw the conclusion that, since the complaint came from the Hellenists, the Hebrews generously turned the whole work of ministration over to the Hellenists. Some of both classes of Jews were elected, the only fair and proper course. The one named last was even a proselyte. To select one of this class was also wise. When Luke adds that he was an Antiochian, some think that this manifests Luke's personal interest in Antioch as being the home city of himself and of Theophilus (Robertson, *Luke the Historian, etc.*, 22). The truth lies rather in this that, as he does in the case of Stephen, Luke writes with a view to what follows. Antioch was to become the great missionary center. More serious is the idea expressed by a few of the fathers and by some recent scholars that Nicolas became apostate and founded the Gnostic sect of the Nicolaitans mentioned in Rev. 2:6, 14. He would thus be mentioned last by Luke as a kind of traitor, like Judas. But the sole evidence furnished for this view by Irenaeus, Tertullian, etc., seems to be the name. It ought to be understood that decidedly more evidence is required in a matter of so serious a charge.

6) "Whom they set before the apostles" makes the impression, that it took some time to effect the election, and that the apostles entrusted the election entirely to the congregation. They, too, were the ones to be satisfied. After the election had been held, these seven were certified as the congregation's choice.

Luke continues with a plural participle and a verb, but evidently not the congregation but the apostles laid their hands on the seven and installed them in their office. The word "apostles" is not written because Luke has just mentioned them. The Lord's blessing was invoked upon the elected men, and the hands were laid on them in this Old Testament symbolical act, which transferred the office with its duties and privileges and pictured the bestowal of the divine blessings that were necessary for this important work. Compare Num. 27:18; Deut. 34:9. This rite was freely adopted by the early church; we read of it in 13:3 in connection with missionaries, and in I Tim. 4:4; 5:22; II Tim. 1:6 in connection with elders. We still use it in connection with confirmation and ordination. It was always symbolic and never charismatic.

The entire account shows that these seven men received only the office of deacons, their duty being to care for the poor and the needy as almoners. The preaching and the work of the Word remained wholly in the hands of the apostles (v. 4). The idea, often voiced, that after Pentecost the believers as such preached is without support in Luke's account. So also the idea that, because Stephen argued with the Jews in their synagogues, and Philip became an evangelist, their diaconate included public preaching and teaching, and their installation was an ordination, goes beyond the facts as Luke reports them. These seven were in no sense presbyters of the Jerusalem congregation; they were not elected for that purpose. What is later reported about Stephen and about Philip has nothing to do with their official duties in the congregation. These activities were the result of gifts and of opportunities that extend beyond their special office. The offices that came into being in the apostolic church were not fluid but well defined.

7) **And the Word of God continued to grow; and the number of the disciples went on multiplying**

exceedingly; also a great multitude of the priests were becoming obedient to the faith.

Luke inserts this little account of the progress made in Jerusalem in order to show that neither the attack of the Sanhedrin nor the defect that had developed in the congregation in any way checked its growth. Compare 2:41; 4:4; 5:14, and now 6:7. The imperfect tenses describe and at the same time show steady continuation. "Continued to grow" speaks of the Word of God as a living thing; and it, indeed, grows as it enters and fills more and more hearts. "Went on multiplying exceedingly" is not an exaggeration as the clause with τε proves which adds that "a great multitude of the priests" were won. These had held off the longest but were now coming in numbers. To speak about plebeian priests contradicts the fact that all the priests were on the same level who were divided into twenty-four courses, each taking its turn in the Temple and portioning out the different tasks. There were no ranks or grades among them. "Were becoming obedient to the faith" is an expression similar to the one found in 13:8; Rom. 1:5; 16:26. We see no reason for not understanding πίστις in the objective sense, namely as that which faith holds, Christ, the gospel, salvation in Christ. To understand the word in the subjective sense, faith in the sense of the action of believing, raises unnecessary difficulties.

STEPHEN BROUGHT TO TRIAL

The Lord's hand had restrained the enemy for a long time. Finally the awful blow fell that was to scatter the congregation far and wide. It fell suddenly and in a way that was altogether unexpected: one of the deacons was brought to trial.

8) Now Stephen, full of grace and power, was doing great wonders and signs among the people. But there arose some of those out of the synagogue

called that of the Libertines and of the Cyrenians and of the Alexandrians, and of those from Cilicia and Asia, disputing with Stephen. And they were not strong enough to withstand the wisdom and the Spirit by whom he was speaking.

Once again Luke draws attention to the spiritual qualifications of Stephen, he was "full of grace and power," for Stephen is the first man in addition to the apostles to perform miracles, "great wonders and signs," the two terms being combined as usual (see 2:19). "Many" could not be added, for Stephen's career was cut short; but "great" is added in order to indicate that Stephen's miracles were of the same quality as those of the apostles.

In v. 3 and v. 5 note "wisdom, faith, and the Holy Spirit," two personal effects and their divine source. Now "grace and power" are added. Both are direct gifts of a different kind that are plainly charismatic in their nature and enable their possessor to work miracles. This is not χάρις in the sense of pardoning grace, for that Stephen had when he first came to faith, but the special *favor Dei* that was connected with the δύναμις or power bestowed on him at this time as something exceptional and not granted to the other deacons: the ability to perform miracles. In other words, the Lord singled out Stephen (grace) as his instrument through whom he wrought miracles (power) when and where the Lord desired (compare 3:4). The congregation had made him a deacon, the Lord made something far greater out of him. As stated in connection with v. 6, the latter had nothing to do with his work as a deacon. We add that Luke does not say a word about Stephen's being a preacher or a teacher. He had neither a mediate nor an immediate call to that work.

9) From Luke's account we gather that Stephen was assailed by a number of Hellenistic Jews because

his wonders and signs drew especial attention to him. Why they did not attack one or the other of the apostles but selected Stephen is not indicated. Luke states only the fact. The usual view is that Stephen made bold to invade the synagogues of these Jews and thus forced disputes regarding Jesus as the Messiah. The opposite is true. These Jews arose against Stephen and forced a dispute upon him, not in a synagogue of theirs, but in such a place where they were able to meet Stephen, probably in the court of the Temple or somewhere on the street. Stephen was a Hellenist as were his attackers, and this may have caused them to single him out although Luke does not say this.

We must note that τινες τῶν ἐκ . . . καὶ τῶν ἀπό indicates two general groups, and that "synagogue," although it is often used as a designation for a building, must here have its original meaning: "gathering, congregation, mob." The word is applied only to the first group; the Libertines, Cyrenians, and Alexandrians formed a congregation, not so "those from Cilicia and Asia" — at least Luke does not say so. The fact that Luke does not refer to a building appears also from the circumstance that no synagogue would be called by a name that included three nationalities; on the other hand, no grammarian has supplied "synagogue" with either the first three nationalities alone or with all five. How R., W. P., can say that Luke may have referred to five synagogue buildings, is rather difficult to understand. By using ἀπό Luke excludes a reference to even two synagogues. The Talmud speaks of 480 synagogues in Jerusalem, but if there had been that many or even a thousand, this would not affect what Luke here states.

Luke uses the aorist: "there rose up some" in dispute. This aorist cannot be constative as speaking of a series of acts. It follows an imperfect and is in turn followed by an imperfect, and, therefore, if a series of disputes were implied, we should have an imperfect and not an aorist between imperfects. Moreover, the subject of this aorist is "some," a group made up of five nationalities. These arose in dispute. This does not mean that now the Libertines arose, now the Cyrenians, and so forth, today in this synagogue, tomorrow in that?

Some commentators draw on their imagination and ask: "Was not Saul from Cilicia, would he not be in the synagogue of the Cilicians, and would not this brilliant pupil of Gamaliel's be the first one to oppose Stephen when he invaded this synagogue?" R., W. P., regards this story as "practically certain." As to Luke, he reports that "some" who were possibly chosen for this purpose from two groups (the one composed of three, the other of two nationalities), all of them Hellenists, on one occasion engaged Stephen in a decisive dispute.

The Libertines were freedmen and their descendants, the Latin *libertini*. This term ignores the earlier distinction between *liberti* as a designation for freedmen and *libertini* as a designation for their descendants. This term is geographical like the rest, and to hear it mentioned was to think of Rome, whither two generations before, in 61 B. C., Pompey had taken many hundreds of captive Jews who were then sold as slaves. Numbers of them and of their descendants gained their liberty and were considered Romans. They were rapidly Hellenized. Zahn draws attention to the inscriptions on tombs and to the fact that only one of the seven synagogues found in Rome is called that of the Hebrews. The circumstance that numbers of these freedmen migrated to Jerusalem is most natural, for, like other Jews of the diaspora, those listed here and in 2:9-11, they felt drawn to their great sanctuary in the Holy City. It is entirely probable that some of the *libertini* were among the "Romans" mentioned in 2:10, even some who refused to believe at that time and now withstood Stephen. On the Cyrenians see 2:10. The Alexandrians were from Alexandria in Northern Egypt, two of whose five divisions were inhabited by Jews. Alexandria was the main seat of Hellenistic Jewish learning. Cilicia is a province in the southeastern corner of Asia Minor, while Asia (here without the article) is the province by this name, whose capital was Ephesus. All these Hellenistic Jews, like Stephen himself, had their present permanent homes in Jerusalem.

10) Luke follows with imperfects that are descriptive but not ingressive (R., W. P.). They are open tenses and imply the definite action expressed by the following aorists. These Hellenists were many against one, but despite their number they had not the strength (imperfect) to resist successfully (aorist infinitive) "the wisdom" (see v. 3) and the Holy Spirit granting that wisdom, by whom Stephen kept speaking in this debate. "By whom" = by whose assistance. Luke pictures the situation.

11) Now the result that followed. **Then they suborned men, (these) stating, We have heard him uttering blasphemous utterances against Moses and God. And they stirred up both the people and the elders and the scribes; and having come upon him, they snatched him and brought him to the Sanhedrin, besides they set up false witnesses, (these) saying: This man does not cease uttering utterances against this holy place and the law. For we have heard him saying, This Jesus, the Nazarene, will destroy this place and will change the customs which Moses gave to us.**

When fair means fail, unbelief is prone to resort to foul means, thereby condemning itself. The nar-

Acts 6:11, 12 253

rative proceeds by using aorists, all of which report the outcome of the action described in v. 10. "They suborned men," etc., literally, "threw under," is the regular term for securing perjured witnesses. There is no reason why these "men" could not have been selected from the disputants named in v. 10. It is also plain that these men were to serve as witnesses at the trial to which these opponents of Stephen hoped to bring him — a plan which succeeded. These very men were the ones put forward as the "false witnesses" referred to in v. 13; the idea that they were not the same men lacks support.

Λέγοντας introduces what these men are to say, namely to charge Stephen with "blaphemous utterances against Moses and God." This greatest Old Testament prophet and mediator of the covenant is combined with God as the object of one preposition which practically makes "Moses and God" one concept; for whatever would be uttered against Moses would *eo ipso* be spoken also against God. What these utterances were to be we hear presently; only their general character is stated in advance.

12) With this devilish plan in mind, the Hellenists begin operations. They inaugurate a violent agitation throughout the city and soon succeed in stirring up "both the people and the elders and the scribes," τε — καί, "elders and scribes," being a unit and meaning as much as Sanhedrists. Since so many Hellenists started on a definite campaign simultaneously, it is little wonder that a great agitation resulted. It certainly lasted more than a day or two. The idea of blasphemy against Moses and God stirred up the most violent passions in almost any Jew. The fact that such a charge was prefered from many quarters certainly made it appear to be true. The Sanhedrists, no doubt, responded most readily although it was not an apostle

that was being accused; they must have become more alarmed than ever because so many priests accepted Jesus (v. 7).

Luke simply relates the facts in the briefest fashion. With τε he closely connects the arrest with the successful agitation. This means that, as soon as preparation was well under way, Stephen was to be apprehended and put to trial. This, too, succeeded. How and where his foes captured him is immaterial to Luke. Perhaps it was in his own home or when, upon some occasion, he ventured into the street that they accosted him, caught him, and led him away to the Sanhedrin. The verbs make one think of a wild animal leaping on its innocent prey, burying its fangs in the flesh, and carrying it off.

One of the remarkable features of this story is the circumstance that these vicious and bloodthirsty Jews do not plan simply to capture and to kill Stephen without further ceremony. No; they plan on a trial, prepare witnesses, then secure Stephen and place him before the high court. They just *will* have the legal machinery! It was so in the case of Jesus. Although their motives were insincere and all the means criminal, this show of legal right seems in some way to hush their consciences.

13) We have no reason to think that the Sanhedrin was assembled and waiting when Stephen was brought in. All that Luke wishes to convey to us is the fact that Stephen was placed before this high court to be tried for the worst crime known in its criminal code. How long a time was required to assemble the Sanhedrin is an immaterial detail. So also the proceedings previous to the calling of the witnesses. We have heard the indictment in v. 11; Luke needs to report only its substantiation by means of testimony. The accusers (v. 9) have their witnesses ready. Luke at once calls them "lying" or "false"

witnesses and by the use of that expression intends to indicate that they consciously testified falsely and thus perjured themselves. The proof is furnished *in extenso* in Stephen's own address which shows what he did say in his dispute (v. 9) and at any and all other times.

First the preamble: "This man does not cease uttering utterances against this holy place and the law." Not once or twice but without changing his utterances he assails "this holy place and the law." The view that by "this holy place" the witnesses referred, not to the Temple, but to the city of Jerusalem with its Temple, is unsatisfactory since it cannot be shown that this designation was ever so used. If a holiness of the city might be spoken of, this emanated only from the Temple; and any utterance against the city would be blasphemous only because it was really spoken against the Temple. As far as destruction is concerned, the Temple would be the last structure to be destroyed; its destruction would thus involve that of the city. Far more important is the combination of "this holy place" with "the law" which refers to Mosaic regulations that centered in the Temple (not in the city save as the Temple in that city is referred to). Of necessity the two belong together, for any derogatory utterances against either would involve the other. God (v. 11) was behind both.

14) The actual testimony is introduced with γάρ: "We have heard him declaring, 'This Jesus, the Nazarene, will destroy this place and will change the customs which Moses gave us.'" This sentence purports to be a direct and verbatim quotation from Stephen's own lips; but in reality it is only a restatement of what these witnesses claimed Stephen had said. The case is quite analogous to that of Jesus who was alleged to have said about the same thing (John 2:19-22; Matt. 26:61; 27:40). In both cases no effort

is made to understand what the person charged actually said, and what his words really mean, but only to use his words against him by making him say or imply what he never actually said or really implied. Luther makes the application: "We ought on this account raise no high complaint against such unfair accusations. The devil knows no other way than to lie and pervert and interpret in the worst fashion what has been said well and properly. This we must look for and must wait until God comes and proves whether they have spoken truth or whether they have lied. In the meanwhile we must content ourselves that, together with beloved Stephen, we have the testimony of our conscience that we are not trying to blaspheme or teach people wrongly and mislead them."

After one fashion or another commentators endeavor to determine exactly wherein the lie of these false witnesses consisted, and some of them pare down the lie to very moderate proportions. Fortunately, we have Stephen's own reply. He takes up these charges in detail and first refutes the charge that he blasphemed God; secondly, that he blasphemed Moses and the law; thirdly, that he blasphemed the Temple. In fact, he proves that he does the very opposite, and that in the true sense of God's own Word, that Word which these Jews constantly resisted and whose prophets they killed. Nor was Stephen, as little as Jesus, condemned on the basis of this false testimony but because he spoke the truth, especially the truth about his own accusers and judges.

15) After the depositions of the perjured witnesses had been received, all eyes turned upon Stephen. **And all those sitting in the Sanhedrin gazing earnestly on him, saw his countenance as an angel's countenance.**

What made the entire Sanhedrin gaze thus at Stephen? Was this only a look of interest which is apt to be manifested when a defendant reaches the dramatic moment for his own defense? No; it was what these Sanhedrists saw: Stephen's face like an angel's face. Aorist participle and aorist verb express simultaneous action. Did Luke mean only that "with beaming countenance" and "unafraid" Stephen "enthusiastically" entered on his defense? Then Luke, the great historian, used extravagant, not to say false, language. Even great joy and exalted expressions on a man's face would not make a body of men think they were seeing something "like an angel's face."

We must recall the promise of Jesus given to the disciples that at their trials before tribunals the Holy Spirit would inspire them (Matt. 10:19, 20; Mark 13:11-13; Luke 12:11; 21:14, 15). This was Stephen's supreme hour. That Spirit now filled him to such an extent that his countenance shone with supernatural radiance, light, and power, which were comparable only to those that appear on an angel's countenance. The Sanhedrists gazed in astonishment. They were struck by this phenomenon — struck but not moved. They who were proof against the angelic truth Stephen uttered would certainly not be moved by his angelic face. They had seen other phenomena, for instance, the restored cripple (4:14) and the miracles of Jesus, and had become more obdurate than ever. The appearance of Stephen's face had a purpose with reference to the Sanhedrin and all who witnessed the trial. A hush fell upon them; they were gripped by that light on Stephen's face until his address reached its climax. How did Luke know all this about Stephen? There were witnesses enough, and one especially, Luke's dearest friend Paul.

CHAPTER VII

Stephen's Defense

1) **And the high priest said, Are these things so?** On εἰ introducing a direct question see 1:6; ἔχω with an adverb is practically our "to be." German: *Verhalten sich diese Dinge also?* But this question is by no means equivalent to the procedure followed in our courts when the judge asks the prisoner whether he pleads guilty or not guilty. Here the prosecution had closed its case, and the high priest Caiaphas who is presiding over the court turns the case over to the defense. We should also say that the question of the high priest was *not* abrupt but the expected and necessary question, and that neither this nor anything else "broke the evident spell of the angelic look on Stephen's face." The radiance continued; and its hushing effect continued until v. 54, when it was dissipated by rage.

2) **And he said, Men, brethren and fathers, hear!** Stephen intends to speak at length, hence the command to hear. Ἀδελφοί are all those present, πατέρες the members of the Sanhedrin in particular. The address is dignified, respectful, from the standpoint of one who belonged to the Jewish nation ("brethren") and was under Jewish authority ("fathers").

Stephen's defense has often been underestimated and even criticized. It has been stated that, if it had not been for the impression made by Stephen's bearing and his eloquence, he would have been called to order after the first few sentences for digressing from the point at issue. Such statements are unwarranted. Why should an address that was not pertinent, or that

Acts 7:2

was faulty in other ways, have so much space allotted to it in Acts? Stephen spoke by direction of the Spirit, in later years Luke recorded his words by the prompting of the Spirit. Such an address must show the marks of the Spirit. It certainly does.

Things were at passion heat, the charge lodged against Stephen was the most heinous crime known to Judaism. If you had been in Stephen's place, what would you have offered in defense? Stephen begins in a quiet tone and proceeds with studied deliberation. Accused of speaking against Moses, God, the Temple, and the law and customs, he speaks of them in due order and at some length and reveals just how he does speak of these subjects, namely in the closest connection with God's own Word. Apparently not making a special defense at all or with one syllable referring to his accusers and their false witnesses, he is yet utterly refuting them and making the most effective defense. What could be blasphemous about a man who spoke as reverently and as Biblically as this man did? Yet into his address Stephen weaves the old disobedience and unbelief of Israel. Joseph is sold by his wicked brothers (v. 9), Moses is scorned (v. 25-28), the very Moses whom God made a deliverer (v. 35), the very Moses who spoke the great Messianic promise about the Prophet like himself (v. 37), and whom the whole nation refused to obey (v. 39, 43). It is thus that the final invective is prepared for a ringing denunciation of Israel's vicious unbelief as a call to repentance; it is uttered in the very tone and manner of the old prophets. Beginning so calmly, the defense ends so powerfully and turns the tables completely by putting accusers, witnesses, and court itself on the hopeless defense. To date no one has offered to outline a better defense for Stephen.

How did Luke secure this address? It was delivered in public, followed the Scripture story in simple fashion, may have been recorded by the secretaries of the Sanhedrin, was certainly heard by Paul. The one thing to be noted is that the address differs markedly from Luke's own manner of writing and contains points that were entirely beyond Luke's knowledge. In other words, Luke could not have invented this defense, or made up this address for Stephen, or developed it from a general report of its contents. Luke had a rather exact report of this address; and this helps to establish the exactness and the reliability of all the briefer addresses he records. The theme of the address is not formulated by Stephen himself but is apparent:

GOD'S GRACE IS MET BY ISRAEL'S DISOBEDIENCE

I. *God's grace manifested in Abraham and the disobedience of the patriarchs.* The emphasis is on God.

II. *God's grace manifested in Moses and the disobedience of Israel.* The emphasis is strongly on Moses.

III. *God's grace manifested in David and in Solomon.* The emphasis is on *the Temple.*

Conclusion: The present disobedience.

The God of the glory appeared to our father Abraham, being in Mesopotamia, before he dwelt in Haran, and said to him, Go out from thy land and from thy kindred and hither! into the land which I will show thee. Then, having gone out of the land of the Chaldeans, he dwelt in Haran.

The first words strike the keynote: "*the God of the glory*," (LXX Ps. 29:3). That does not sound like blaspheming God. The genitive is qualitative: the God who is distinguished by the glory, not by glory in general, but by his own specific glory (note the article), the radiant revelation of his divine attributes, of any or of all of them as God permits them to manifest themselves.

It is charged that Stephen misarranged his data when he placed this appearance of God *before* Abraham's residence in Haran and when he locates the previous residence of Abraham (which was Ur) in Mesopotamia. But this charge is unwarranted. It rests solely on the claim that Stephen quotes the words of Gen. 12:1. These were, indeed, spoken in Haran, but their utterance there may have been only a repetition of the original command given in Ur. That this supposition is true may be judged from the omission of the phrase "and from thy father's home," which omission shows that Stephen is not merely quoting Gen. 12:1, but knows exactly what he is saying. In Gen. 11:31, Terah and his family do not leave Ur of the Chaldees of their own will, for already at that time their final destination is said to be "the land of Canaan." Why? Because of the divine revelation. We have the same thought in Gen. 15:7 (see Neh. 9:7): God brought Abraham out of Ur of the Chaldees. To make the measure more than full: Philo and Josephus (*Ant.* 1, 7, 1) corroborate Stephen. In regard to the location of Ur, Stephen located it where it was.

Stephen spoke before an audience that was thoroughly versed in Scripture and he would have made a frightful impression if his first sentences had contained two palpable errors. His critics in the Sanhedrin would have halted him right then and there if his statements had, indeed, been erroneous.

3) We have no reason to think that God spoke only to Terah in Gen. 11:31, and not also to Abraham, or that he did speak words that were similar to those

he repeated in Gen. 12:1 to Abraham alone. The original word was one that combined a command and a great promise. By obeying the command Abraham displayed his full faith in the promise. Stephen points out the fact that Abraham's faith began already in Ur. He speaks of Abraham only because he is the father of believers who rose to tremendous prominence in contrast with all his disobedient and unbelieving descendants. Already in Ur, God began to establish with him the covenant that culminated in Christ, the very covenant the accusers and judges of Stephen were rejecting by repudiating Christ and by now bringing Stephen to trial for his abiding in that covenant by obeying and believing in Christ. John 8:56-59. The address shows its perfect approach by thus beginning with God and Abraham and the promise of the covenant. Were Stephen's hearers still the sons of Abraham?

4) Abraham obeyed, left the land of the Chaldees, and went to Haran. He thus set out for the land that God would show him. The reason for his stopping in Haran is now indicated. **And thence, after his father died, he caused him to migrate into this land in which you are now dwelling, and he did not give him an inheritance, not a foot's space. And he promised to give it to him for a permanent possession and to his seed after him, he not having a child.**

The residence in Haran was temporary; it continued only until Abraham's father Terah had died. But here again, Stephen, like Philo, the celebrated Jewish contemporary of Christ, seems to be in conflict with Genesis. Terah is said to have been 70 years old when Abraham was born (Gen. 11:26), and he died in Haran at the age of 205 years (Gen. 11:32). Abraham was 75 years old when he left Haran (Gen. 12:4). Thus $70 + 75 = 145$; and 60 years must be added to make the total 205. Then Stephen would be wrong: Abraham did not leave *after* his father's death but 60 years before he died. Philo, the Jewish tradition, and thus Stephen are said to have followed an older report which attempted to save Abraham's filial piety toward his father. Over against the Samaritan Pentateuch, which makes Terah's age only 145, the Jewish text must stand that his age was 205. The view that in Stephen's address "died" refers to a spiritual death is without foundation. The solution lies elsewhere. In Gen. 11:26 Terah is said to be seventy years old "and begat Abraham, Nahor, and Haran." Abraham is mentioned first because of his greater importance and not necessarily because he was born first. He was the founder of the chosen nation, Nahor was the grandfather of Rebecca, and Haran was the father of Lot. Now Abraham's son Isaac married the granddaughter of Abraham's brother Nahor. It is fair to conclude that Nahor was much older than Abraham, i. e., that in Gen. 11:26 the names are not arranged according to ages but according to importance. Aside from the inspiration by which Stephen spoke and Luke wrote, it does seem that in the simple matter of adding a few figures Stephen (Philo, too) would not have made such palpable errors.

From Haran God transferred Abraham ($\mu\epsilon\tau o\iota\kappa i\zeta\omega$) to "this land in which you are now dwelling" (static εἰς, and this εἰς is not repeated after the verb as R. 566 thinks), namely Palestine. The emphatic ὑμεῖς intends to connect Stephen's hearers with God and Abraham and the covenant.

5) But the remarkable fact was that God gave Abraham no "inheritance" in this land, not as much as "a foot's space," on which to plant a foot. The field purchased by Abraham in Gen. 23:9-17 was not a gift of God to him, in fact, was only a burial place. All

that Abraham had received from God was the promise that God would give him the land as a permanent holding (εἰς κατάσχεσιν) and to his seed after him — but Abraham had no child. It was all grand and good, but it all required faith, an immense faith on Abraham's part. Not seeing, he yet believed. In the genitive absolute, "a child not being for him," the negative οὐ instead of μή is more decisive (R. 1138) as marking the actual fact at that time.

6) **Moreover, God spoke in this way, that his seed will be a foreigner in an alien land, and that they should enslave it and ill-treat it for four hundred years. And the nation to which they shall be slaves I myself will judge, said God; and after these things they shall go forth and shall serve me in this place.**

Transitional δέ adds another feature, a statement concerning a matter that taxed Abraham's faith still more: 400 years would elapse before his descendants would come into possession of the promised land. "In this way," in this strange manner, did God speak. This is a reference to Gen. 15:13-16. Abraham's seed was to be a πάροικος, one dwelling beside another without right of citizenship "in an alien land," one belonging to others. "They shall enslave" Abraham's seed "and shall ill-treat it," the plural subject needing no further definition.

Stephen quotes the 400 years mentioned in Genesis while Exodus 12:40 has 430 (Gal. 3:17); Josephus gives both figures. It is best to regard 400 as a round number instead of trying to devise two ways of counting the years. To be enslaved and ill-treated was not a pleasant prospect but an added burden to Abraham's faith. Yet Canaan afforded no room for a second nation to develop beside the Canaanites; in Egypt there was abundant room and thus also much less danger of contamination by idolatry. God knew

Acts 7:7, 8   265

what he was doing; we now see it after the event; Abraham could not foresee it and had to rely on faith.

7) Indirect discourse is never long sustained in the New Testament; so here Stephen turns to the direct and continues his reference to Gen. 15. Not with indifference will God view this treatment of Abraham's seed in Egypt. He lets his people suffer, but in his justice he always reckons with the oppressors and the persecutors. He did so in the case of these Jews who were spending their time of grace by persecuting the apostles, now Stephen, and presently the entire congregation of believers. Note the emphasis on ἐγώ, both because it is written out and because it is placed after its verb which stresses both. This judgment came upon Egypt in the form of the ten terrible plagues. Δουλεύω is used transitively in v. 6: "to enslave"; intransitively in v. 7: "to be a slave." The former use is found in the dictionaries.

The indefinite relative ᾧ ἄν (or ἐάν) leaves the guilty nation unnamed. At the time appointed, however, Abraham's seed (now the plural) shall go forth out of this bondage, out of that foreign land, "and shall serve me in this place." The last phrase is possibly an allusion to Exod. 3:12, "in this mountain," but is not a quotation (R., W. P.). Λατρεύω is used with reference to the divine service of worship which all should render while λειτουργέω designates official service. This promise was spoken in Canaan, and "this place" is thus definite.

8) **And he gave him the covenant of circumcision; and thus he begot Isaac and circumcised him on the eighth day; and Isaac, Jacob, and Jacob, the twelve patriarchs.**

In addition to the aforementioned promises God gave to Abraham "the covenant of circumcision." This is almost an appositional genitive but is probably qualitative since circumcision was considered the sign and seal of the covenant, the latter consisting of the promise that Abraham should be the father of many nations (Gen. 17:5). The ordinary word for covenant was συνθήκη, but the LXX translated bᵉrith διαθήκη, apparently because it has less of the idea of mutuality even as it is also used in the sense of "testament." For the covenant was wholly one-sided: God "gave" it to Abraham, and it is always called God's covenant and never Abraham's. Here there were not two equals making an agreement; here there was no exchange of this for that. Here there was only a giver and a recipient, only a great blessing and the obligation properly to receive and to use it.

The seal of this covenant was circumcision, περιτομή (from περί and τέμνω, "to cut around"), the cutting off of the foreskin. It was performed by the father on the eighth day (even if this occurred on a Sabbath); today it is performed by the rabbi or by a special officer (*mohel*). Associated with it was the giving of a name. The religious idea embodied in this act was the placing of the child into and under the covenant with all the blessings, promises, and obligations resulting therefrom. Involved in this is the idea that the child be spiritually renewed as now being in the covenant in that the removal of the foreskin sanctified procreation among the covenant people.

In order to understand why this act was limited to males we must disregard our modern ideas of individualism and of the equality of the sexes and go back to the creation of man and note that Eve was made for Adam. All girls were in the covenant through their fathers, for the covenant line was transmitted only through the men. We may call circumcision an Old Testament "sacrament," but it was such in a modified sense even as the covenant was altogether promise with the ultimate fulfillment coming in Christ. The circumcision found among other ancients has another significance, that of Mohammedanism being only an imitation of the Jewish rite.

"Thus," in this covenant, Abraham begot Isaac and circumcised him on the eighth day, and the line of covenant bearers was continued from Isaac through Jacob (not Esau) and then branched out through all of Jacob's sons who were called the twelve patriarchs as being founders of long lines of descent.

We thus see how Stephen thought of God, how Scripturally he connected him with Abraham and the chosen nation to which all the Jews belonged by virtue of the old covenant and its seal. What a hopeless undertaking to prove that Stephen was a blasphemer of God (6:11)! Where in the Sanhedrin itself was there a man who could honor the God of Abraham, Isaac, and Jacob more?

9) When Stephen sketches the story of Joseph he does it as one who is still speaking of God, and he adds how God fulfilled the promise to Abraham (v. 6, 7) by raising up a nation from Abraham's seed and finally establishing it in Canaan. Another feature is interwoven with this: it was God who made Joseph the savior of the patriarchs and did this despite their hatred of their brother. Joseph thus appears as a type of the eternal Savior Jesus. Such a reading of Israel's patriarchal history glorifies God by a true spiritual insight and makes this section a genuine link in the historical apology of Stephen. **And the patriarchs, having envied Joseph, sold him into Egypt. And God was with him and took him out of all his tribulations and gave him grace and wisdom before Pharaoh, king of Egypt, and established him as governor over Egypt and his whole house.**

Here there is the first defection from the covenant: the patriarchs were filled with envy toward one of their number, the aorist participle stating only the historical fact. But God used this evil unto good, yea, unto good for the very ones who perpetrated it. In this way Stephen thought of God. In ἀπέδοντο the preposition implies the sale; compare 5:8. The patriarchs duly gave from themselves (middle) their brother in the bargain in which they were duly paid. They got rid of Joseph; so the envious Jews (Matt. 27:18; Mark 15:10) got rid of Jesus. Joseph was sold into Egyptian slavery.

10) "And God was with him." In this significant flash Stephen emphasizes the contrast between God and the wicked patriarchs. What God did with Jesus was also the very opposite of what the Jews did; Peter drove this home in 4:10-12; 5:30, 31. God was with Joseph in a most effective manner: he took him out of all his afflictions (θλῖψις, from the verb that means to press or compress); he gave him χάρις, undeserved divine favor, and wisdom before Pharaoh for interpreting the king's dreams, etc.; and thus he established him (set him down) as governor over Egypt and the whole house of the king: "governor" in the sense of grand vizier, prime minister, second only to the king himself; over his whole house like the Frankish *Major Domus*. He raised him from a slave to a vice-king. Pharaoh is the title of all Egyptians kings, *per-'o* = "great house." God is still the subject of "established" and not Pharaoh (our versions), which translation is not necessitated by "his" (Pharaoh's) house, at least not in the Greek. Stephen is reciting all that *God* did by nullifying what the patriarchs had done and by working out *his* plans for Abraham's seed.

11) **Moreover, there came a famine over the whole Egypt and Canaan and great tribulation; and the fathers were not finding provisions. But Jacob, on hearing that there was grain in Egypt, sent out our fathers the first time. And at the second time Joseph was made known to his brothers, and Joseph's family became manifest to Pharaoh.**

And Joseph, sending, called to him Jacob, his father, and all his kindred, in all seventy-five souls. And Jacob came down into Egypt, and he himself came to an end and our fathers; and they were transferred to Shechem and deposited in the tomb which Abraham bought for a price of silver from the sons of Emmor in Shechem.

The story is continued with δέ which adds the great chapter on Joseph, the deliverer, and on the faith of the patriarchs in Egypt. "There came a famine" reports the fact; "they were not finding" describes the situation. Being herdsmen who had numerous flocks, this famine made their situation trying, indeed.

12) Egypt was the great wheat country of the world, in later times the granary of Rome (Acts 27:38). Why Egypt had wheat throughout the seven years of famine is not stated, but it was due to Joseph. Verbs of perception have the complementary participle in the accusative when this refers to what is perceived, hence ὄντα after ἀκούσας (B.-D. 416, 1); another explanation is that of indirect discourse, the participle retaining the tense of the direct (R., W. P.). The diminutive σιτίον is rare. Grain was all that the fathers secured on the first journey to Egypt.

13) But on the second journey Joseph was made known to his brothers, or, taking the passive in the middle sense, made himself known to them (B.-D. 191, 2). Καί adds the effect with which Stephen is here concerned, namely that Joseph's γένος or family became manifest to Pharaoh, i. e., he now knew all about it. In Gen. 41:12, Joseph was introduced as a Hebrew, but now Pharaoh learns much more. Note that "Joseph" is repeated because of the importance and the dignity in his name.

14) It was this knowledge, brought to Pharaoh, that enabled Joseph to transfer his father and his entire relationship from Canaan to Egypt and to take

them out of the famine-stricken land to one that was well supplied with food, with one of the family serving as vice-ruler. But this move was a fulfillment of the word spoken to Abraham in v. 6. Here in Egypt God intended to let Jacob's family grow into a nation. On ἐν used with figures see R. 589: "amounting to," or "in all." Winer called this construction Hebraistic, but the papyri have this construction in all its varieties. In Gen. 46:27; Exod. 1:5; Deut. 10:22, the number of "souls" (persons, as in 2:41, which certainly included every child) is only seventy, while in the first two of these passages the LXX has seventy-five. This is a mere matter of counting. The descendants of Jacob that went to Egypt were sixty-six in number (Gen. 46:26), but counting Joseph and his two sons and Jacob himself (Gen. 46:27), the number is seventy. In the LXX all the sons of Joseph whom he got in Egypt were counted, "nine souls," which, with the sixty-six, made seventy-five. Various other ways of counting are suggested in order to explain this number; the one indicated is correct.

15) Thus Jacob completed his life (τελευτάω) in Egypt, both he and the fathers, including Joseph — far from the land of promise.

16) Yet we see their faith in the promise. They only sojourned in Egypt, their real home was Canaan, and so they were all eventually buried there. Jacob was at once buried in Abraham's tomb Machpelah in Hebron. Read about his grand funeral in Gen. 50:1-13. Stephen is brief and speaks only of the fathers and states that their bodies were eventually transferred to Shechem. We know this only in regard to Joseph, for we learn that his body was embalmed (Gen. 50:26) and, according to the oath he had exacted from the children of Israel, was buried in Shechem after the Exodus (Josh. 24:32). The Old Testament reports nothing in regard to the brothers of Joseph.

It is Stephen who here tells us that they, too, were buried in Shechem together with Joseph. Jewish tradition, no doubt, preserved this information, and there is no reason for doubting it.

There is a difficulty in the statement that *Abraham* bought the tomb in Shechem from the sons of Emmor in Shechem. In 33:19, etc., it is *Jacob* who buys a piece of ground from these owners in order to erect an altar in that locality. Two solutions are offered. Perhaps some scribe wrote "Abraham" instead of "Jacob" in this passage; many are satisfied with this solution. Yet in Gen. 12:6 Abraham is in Shechem long before Jacob was there; and it is not at all improbable that Abraham made the original purchase, but after his departure from this place the land was again occupied by its original owners until Jacob repurchased it as Gen. 33:19 reports. "Sons of Emmor" are the tribe; the term is like "sons of Israel."

---

17) We come to *the second part* of Stephen's defense. The emphasis on God continues; but now Stephen refutes the charge that he is blaspheming *the law and Moses, the lawgiver*. Most emphatically he acknowledges that both were sent by God. Yet Stephen tells this part of the history so as to bring out all of the old opposition to Moses and to the law and thus to God himself, an opposition that finally culminated in the rejection of God's Anointed. Thus the faith of Abraham waned; yea, the faith of the fathers suffered an ominous decline.

Now as there was drawing nigh the time of the promise which God communicated to Abraham, the people grew and multiplied in Egypt until there arose a different king over Egypt who did not know Joseph. This one, by using fraud on our race, ill-treated our fathers so that he was causing

their babes to be exposed that they might not go on living.

The time set for the fulfillment of the promise as it had been told to Abraham (v. 7) was now drawing near; ἧς is attracted from ἥν. The aorists report the fact of the great increase of the Israelites in Egypt. It was this increase that worried the new king.

18) The statement that this king "arose" and that he knew nothing about Joseph points to a dynastic change in Egypt. "The previous dynasty had been that of the Hyksos; the new king was Ahmes who drove out the Hyksos." Knobel. The statement implies that until the time of the rule of this king the Israelites had flourished unmolested; but now their troubles began. Until this time the memory of Joseph and of all that he had done for Egypt brought favor to the Israelites; but this king neither knew nor cared for Joseph, he looked at the Israelites with cold, political eyes and saw that, if they continued to increase, their power would endanger the kingdom.

19) Thus the affliction began. The fraud used on the Israelites was the ill-treatment that the king ordered their babes to be exposed in order to cause them to die. This fraud broke the old agreements and promises originally made to the Israelites. Stephen contents himself with mentioning only the worst part of the ill-treatment visited upon the Israelites, the destruction of their male children. As long as "the fathers" is regarded as the subject of τοῦ ποιεῖν, there will be wavering between the consecutive (A. V.) and the final (R. V.) idea of this infinitive. But when no new subject is expressed with an infinitive, its subject is the subject of the main verb, here οὗτος, the new king. Through his decrees this Pharaoh made those babes ἔκθετα (verbal adjective from ἐκτίθημι), "exposed ones," exposed to die; he did this regularly, present infinitive, by enforcing his decrees.

The infinitive is consecutive. But εἰς τό with its present infinitive expresses purpose: "for them not to go on living," litotes, "for them to die."

20) This was the terrible situation obtaining when Moses was born. **At which season there was born Moses, and he was fair unto God; who was nourished for three months in his father's house. But having been exposed, the daughter of Pharaoh took him up for herself and raised him up for her own son.**

Stephen intimates that God is with Moses from the very beginning. His birth occurred at this terrible season, καιρός, a period that is marked by what distinguishes it. "Fair or beautiful to God" is not a Hebraistic superlative (R. 671); the dative is ethical and has a distinct personal flavor (R. 537). Here and in Heb. 11:23 ἀστεῖος is taken from the LXX translation of Exod. 2:2; it really means "citified" but is used widely in the sense of refined beauty. Note how Stephen connects Moses with God even when Moses was still a babe. The Greek loves to construct his sentences in an unbroken chain; hence these relatives: "at which season" — "who was nourished." For three months only could the babe be kept at home.

21) Finally he had to be exposed to death; but he was saved in a most remarkable way and was reared as the son of Pharaoh's own daughter who, as Josephus, *Ant.* 2, 9, 7 reports, called him παῖς μορφῇ θείος, "a lad divine in form." Both verbs are middle: "she took him up for herself," i. e., appropriated him, and "nourished him up for herself for her own son," i. e., adopted him. R., W. P., following Vincent, thinks that the idea of adoption is expressed by the first verb, but that is evidently not the case, for then the second verb and its phrase would be superfluous. Pharaoh's daughter first appropriated the baby and eventually adopted him as her own son. Moses became a member of Pharaoh's own family.

This is one of the many instances in which God seems to play with his enemies: Pharaoh's own daughter saves, adopts, rears, educates God's great deliverer of his own enslaved people. Ah, if she could have known what God was having her do! And here we have another type of Jesus who also nearly perished as a babe, who also was saved even in Egypt, and who also became a deliverer, yet one who was far greater than his type Moses. This typical feature in the child Moses could scarcely, however, have been known to Stephen.

Sometimes it is thought that the act of taking up the child as here described was equivalent to that of the Oriental father who, on the birth of a child, took it up in his arms in order to signify that he acknowledged and intended to rear it, whereas, if he had refused to do this, the child would have been rejected by him and left to perish. It is certainly stretching the point to present Pharaoh's daughter as thinking of herself as performing such a paternal act.

22) **And Moses was educated with all the wisdom of the Egyptians; and he was mighty in his words and deeds. And when a time of forty years was being filled for him, it came into his heart to visit his brethren, the sons of Israel. And on seeing one being wronged, he defended and exacted vengeance for the one being abused by smiting the Egyptian. Now he was supposing that his brethren were understanding that God through his hand was giving salvation to them; but they did not understand. And on the following day he appeared to them while fighting and tried to reconcile them for peace by saying, Men, you are brethren! Why are you wronging each other? But the one wronging his neighbor thrust him away from himself, saying: Who established thee as a ruler and judge over us? Thou, dost thou want to make away with**

me the way thou didst make away yesterday with the Egyptian? And Moses fled at this word and became a foreigner in the land of Midian where he begot two sons.

Even the mighty man Moses, having arrived at full manhood and being a man of power in every way, was an utter failure without God. No divine work can be done without God. Stephen tells the story at length in order to follow it with the glorious story of what Moses accomplished for Israel when God was with him. Was there any man present who could speak more Scripturally about Moses and show more clearly how God brought the Old Testament mediator to his great office?

The priestly cast of the Egyptians was famed for its knowledge of science, mathematics, astronomy, and medicine, and constituted the nobility about Pharaoh. Compare I Kings 4:30. In all their wisdom was Moses educated; with abstract nouns "every" and "all" flow together, hence πάσῃ σοφίᾳ "all (every) wisdom." And this magnificent education and training were not wasted; they produced a man who was powerful in word and deed, mightily equipped for leadership. Note the similar expression in regard to Jesus in Luke 24:19. Power is referred to and not mere readiness of tongue which explains Exod. 4:10, 15.

23) Moses, too, felt this urge of leadership. He was now reaching the age of forty or full maturity. Men lived longer in those days, and we must reckon accordingly. So although he was without a call from God, with the thought just arising in his own heart, as Stephen carefully states, he proceeded to see for himself, with his own eyes, "his brethren, the sons of Israel," as to what he might do for them.

It is difficult to render the Greek idioms into acceptable English. Thus the clause: "when there was being filled up for him a forty years' time" = when he was about forty years of age. A thought or idea that arises in the heart is in Hebrew said "to go up upon the heart." To think about its going up "out of the lower deeps of one's nature" is a misunderstanding; for in Isa. 65:17, and Jer. 3:16 the expression is used in a good sense with regard to the memory of former glories; and in I Cor. 2:9 it is used negatively with regard to great glories. With reference to Moses the expression is not used in a bad sense but indictes only that the idea was his own conception. "To look for one's self upon" = to visit with the connotation of help. It is thus used with reference to God in Luke 1:68, 78; 7:16: Heb. 2:6; also with reference to judicial visitation (C.-K. 999).

Here the act of Moses is entirely beneficent. For he intends to look upon "his brethren," his own blood and kin, "the sons of Israel," the heirs of God's covenant. Both terms are highly significant. Although he was reared and had grown to manhood in the pagan court, Moses had not become an Egyptian in heart and soul. These enslaved Israelites were his real brethren, he was one of them. Yes, one of them as "the sons of Israel," not merely nationally but spiritually. Moses had not lost his faith, he shared Israel's hopes and Israel's spirit. The fact that they were nothing but slaves did not alienate him. One wonders at the man. How had he escaped all the idolatry in the midst of which he had been reared? How had the faith of Israel been put into his heart and been preserved there?

24) Living at the capital and at the king's court, Moses must have gone some distance in order to see the Israelites in their oppression as slaves. Only two striking instances of what he found are preserved. He saw an Israelite being wronged by an Egyptian in some shameful way, a taskmaster lashing the defense-

less slave. Not only did Moses come to the Israelite's defense, but he also exacted vengeance for the oppressed by smiting the Egyptian, and that fatally. In Luke 18:7 we find ποιεῖν ἐκδίκησιν used in the sense of to do what the law of right exacts, hence to avenge; see the verb alone in Luke 18:3. We at once see the love and the loyalty of Moses to his brethren, but also note that his tremendous power and energy are badly misdirected. He is by no means as yet ready for the great task of which he is dreaming. He acts without a call or direction from God.

25) A parenthetical δέ indicates his thought and his motive: "Now he was supposing that his brethren were understanding that God through his hand was giving salvation to them." Note the durative tenses. Νομίζω has the accusative with the infinitive, and the indirect discourse retains the present tense of the direct: "God through my hand is giving," etc. Note that "God" and "through his hand" are placed close together. The astonishing thing is that Moses already feels himself to be the deliverer of his people, an instrument of God. "Through his hand" = through his agency. We are unable to see how Moses arrived at this idea concerning himself. He even supposed that his brethren were understanding this, and that, when the one he had rescued would tell about the mighty Moses who delivered him, they would all look up to him. Much is veiled here. It seems as though Moses had left the Egyptian court for good in order to become the great deliverer (σωτήρ) of his own people. But he was sadly mistaken: his people understood nothing of the sort.

26) This truth was brought home to Moses on the very next day. "He appeared," suddenly stood beside two of them who were engaged in fighting (present participle) and tried to compose them (conative imperfect) for peace by appealing to them that

as brethren they ought not to wrong each other. In the question ἱνατί asks "to what purpose" they were doing each other wrong. The rebuke was perfectly proper and mild, Moses did not even take sides. What, indeed, could either gain by hurting the other?

27, 28) Then Moses had his eyes opened. The one who was wronging the other, that very one, thrust Moses away with a sharp question: "Who established thee as ruler and judge over us?" And with the accusing question: "Certainly *thou* dost not want to make away with me what way thou didst make away yesterday with the Egyptian?" This is the force of the question with μή which strongly demands a negative answer. In v. 21 the aorist ἀναιρέω is used in its neutral sense, simply, "to take up"; here, as in 2:23 and so often, it is used in its evil sense, "to make away with," "to murder." Note how με σύ are abutted, and the emphasis is on "thou"; ὃν τρόπον, the adverbial accusative, has the antecedent drawn to the relative. These questions must have come as a shock to Moses. The castle Moses had erected out of his own suppositions came down about his head. He was usurping the place of "ruler and judge over his brethren." God had not appointed him. His whole proceeding was wrong. His own brethren considered his deed of yesterday plain murder — and it was that. They thrust him away.

Pharaoh also heard of it and sought to bring Moses to account. When, in Heb. 11:27, Moses is said to have left Egypt "by faith, not fearing the wrath of the king," this means that the did not seek to remain in Egypt, to placate the king's wrath, who, of course, was more wrathful than ever because Moses left; but now he places both his people and their deliverance as well as himself entirely into God's hands. This was a mighty act of faith.

But Stephen has a purpose in bringing out so pointedly the fact that Moses' own people did not understand, and that the very Israelite who was in the wrong thrust Moses away. Stephen returns to this in v. 35. So far is he from blaspheming Moses that he views Moses as a type of Christ. Both were denied, both were thrust away by Israel, and God made both the deliverers of Israel but he made Christ such in a far higher sense.

29) Ἐν τῷ λόγῳ, "in connection with that word" (which B.-D. 219, 2, however, makes *wegen*, and R. 589 the occasion, the preposition being used in its original sense) "Moses fled." He became "a foreigner" (πάροικος as in v. 6) in Midian; but despite his long stay in Midian he did not become a Midianite. During those forty long years he remained a true Israelite and waited for his people's promised liberation (v. 6). The fact that he married and "begat two sons" in Midian makes his remaining a foreigner in the land only the more significant.

The plans of Moses had failed swiftly, utterly; God's plans were moving with perfect success. Moses needed not only the forty years of Egyptian schooling but forty more of desert schooling in order to make him the man God wanted.

30) **And forty years having been fulfilled, there appeared to him in the wilderness of Mount Sinai an angel in a flame of fire of a thornbush. And Moses, on seeing it, wondered at the sight; but as he came near to observe it, there came the Lord's voice: I, the God of thy fathers, the God of Abraham and of Isaac and of Jacob! And become trembling, Moses dared not observe. And the Lord said to him: Loose the sandal of thy feet, for the place where thou standest is holy ground. Seeing, I saw the ill-treatment of my people in Egypt, and**

their groaning I heard; and I came down to take them out for myself. And now hither! I will send thee to Egypt.

The life of Moses may be divided into three periods of forty years each. While he was pasturing his flock in the wilderness of Mount Sinai he suddenly saw a thornbush on fire which was burning intensely but not burning to ashes. On "Mount Sinai" see R. 760. Ἐν φλογὶ πυρὸς βάτου is exceedingly compact, the nouns without articles being stressed in their own meaning: "in a thornbush's fire flame," the two genitives being descriptive (R., W. P.). Since βάτος is any thornbush, it is impossible to determine its variety botanically, and quite unnecessary.

The bush is symbolical of Israel, which, too, was a lowly bush and not a towering tree like the Egyptians. The flame of fire in the bush symbolizes Israel's fiery affliction which, although it was due to the Egyptians, had Jehovah back of it. The fire burned with hot flame but did not consume the bush; so Israel's affliction burned but did not destroy.

The ἄγγελος here mentioned is called both *Yahweh* and *Elohim* and is thus God himself. This is the *Maleach Yahweh* who is mentioned again and again in the Old Testament but never in the New; compare Gen. 22:11, etc., and 48:15, etc. In order to determine with exactness who is referred to all the passages that treat of him must be combined and compared. Thus he will appear as the *angelus increatus* and never as a created angel although some contend for the latter. Other angels are always representatives of a class, this angel is always the specific revelation and personification of God himself.

Regarding the identity of this *Maleach* with *Yahweh-Elohim* there is not the slightest doubt. The question whether we may say more, namely that this *Maleach* is the Old Testament appearance of the Son, the Logos, and thus an anticipation of the Incarnation, is answered by two observations: 1) In some passages this *Maleach* speaks and acts like God and is yet distinguished as a separate person; 2) All his activity is the mediation of salvation so that Malachi 3:1 calls him "the Angel of the Covenant." When this is compared with the New Testament revelation of the Logos and of his Incarnation, the deduction is sound that the great Maleach of the Old Testament was, indeed, this same Logos. When C.-K. will not make this deduction because he thinks that the New Testament revelation in Christ was wholly new (Gal. 3:19; Heb. 2:2), he is answered by John's Prolog, by John 8:56-58, by Heb. 3:1, "the Apostle" Christ Jesus, and by every similar passage. In this as in many other respects the Arian inclinations of von Hofmann have influenced some exegetes and theologians. When C.-K. finally introduces the apocalyptic Jewish literature, we see the source of much of the confusion regarding the Old Testament manifestations of God and must reply that these revelations will never be seen in their clear reality when they are viewed through the medium of such Jewish literature and will be lost altogether when it is thought that even these Jewish apocalyptic ideas originated in Persian and other pagan sources.

31) Attracted by this astounding phenomenon, Moses was in the act of approaching it in order to inspect it more closely when "the Lord's voice" rang out from the burning thornbush. The ὅραμα or "sight" was the strange fact that a bush should be on fire here, where there was no one to set it on fire. Vastly stranger it was that it should burn and burn without consuming itself. This was not an ordinary fire but a miracle of God. Moses saw only this flaming fire from which the voice spoke and no form of any kind in the fire. The voice alone indicated that the Lord was revealing himself by means of this fire.

32) The Lord at once makes himself known by proclaiming his full covenant name: "I, the God," etc. From "the fathers" God goes back to Abraham, Isaac, and Jacob and thus strongly expresses the truth that this appearance has a connection with his great covenant. He appears here on Sinai because here he will renew and advance his covenant with the children of Israel when Moses, through God's mighty hand, has freed them from Pharaoh and brought them to this place. No wonder that Moses was trembling and dared not raise his eyes to look at those flames. Behold, this is how Stephen thinks of God and of Moses!

33) The order to remove "the sandal of thy feet," a distributive singular, is to induce Moses to realize fully that he is standing in the presence of God himself, which makes the entire place "holy ground." The perfect ἕστηκας is always used in the sense of the present: "thou standest."

This is an Oriental idea: to remove the sandals in the presence of a superior, to walk in bare feet in any sanctuary. Thus the priests did in the Temple, thus must all who enter Mohammedan mosques do today, thus the Samaritans do on Mt. Gerizim. See how Aaron and his sons were sanctified, Exod. 29:10; Lev. 8:23. Entrance into the mosques, even that on the site of the Temple in Jerusalem, is now compromised. All the author had to do was to put on huge slippers over his shoes. These were furnished at the doors by an attendant, but these slippers were imperative unless one entered in his stocking feet. The keepers of the synagogue of the Samaritans at Nablous did not require this, but their great sacrifice on Mt. Gerizim is another matter.

34) And now at last Moses receives his divine commission to deliver Israel. God condescends to speak in a human way about his looking down on the

ill-treatment of his people in Egypt and hearing their pitiful groaning. The ἰδών εἶδον is a reproduction of the Hebrew infinitive absolute after the fashion of the LXX, which emphasizes the verb by means of its participle: "I surely saw"; it is found in the New Testament only in quotations. The Greek is content with the mere past fact, "I saw — heard," whereas the English requires the time relation of the perfect, "I have seen — have heard." Thus also we have "I came down" and the infinitive of purpose, the middle from ἐξαιρέω, "to take them out for myself," i. e., to effect their deliverance (effective aorist). Thus Moses receives his commission: "And now thither!" We must connect the adverb δεῦρο with ἀποστείλω (R. 932): "come, I will send thee," and the verb means, "send with a commission to execute," and thus means more than πέμπω although both are generally translated "to send." Stephen thus exalts Moses.

35) But he is not merely reciting the Old Testament story of Moses. He has a purpose in his selection. From the divine commission of Moses, Stephen proceeds to what this commission really implied regarding Israel. He reads the Old Testament with the clear, deep insight of Paul. **This Moses, whom they denied when they said, Who established thee as a ruler and judge? this one God has commissioned both as ruler and ransomer with the hand of the angel that appeared to him in the thornbush. This one led them out by doing wonders and signs in Egypt and in the Red Sea and in the desert for forty years. This one is the Moses who said to the sons of Israel, A prophet will God raise up from you out of your brethren, like me. This one is he who came to be in connection with the assembly in the wilderness, in company with the angel who was speaking to him in the mount of Sinai, and (in company with) our fathers; he who received living say-**

ings to give to us; he to whom our fathers did not will to become obedient but thrust him away and were turned in their hearts unto Egypt when they said to Aaron, Make us gods who shall go before us! For this Moses who brought us out of Egyptland, we do not know what happened to him.

The entire passage is one chain: five emphatic "this" terminating in two "he who (to whom)." It is like a grand pyramid, and the capstone is Israel's idolatrous unbelief.

The trouble lay not with Stephen and his treatment of Moses, it lay with the treatment Moses received from Israel at the beginning and continued to receive, yea, was receiving right now from Stephen's accusers and judges. Stephen's defensive is turning into an offensive. Not he is on trial, but his judges are. Stephen, however, is not judging them, he is letting God's Word, Moses himself, do that just as Jesus did in John 5:45-47. So in the very first place it was "this Moses" whom they denied and repudiated at the beginning as not being a ruler and judge for them, whom in spite of them God made both ruler and vastly more than judge. We have the same verb "denied" that was used with regard to the rejection of Jesus in 3:13. The aorist participle εἰπόντες refers to the one statement that is requoted from v. 27. Only one man uttered it, but it is rightly attributed to all the Israelites, for their whole history shows that very attitude. This repudiated Moses who was made the old covenant mediator is the very type of Jesus who was also repudiated by the Jews and yet was made the everlasting Mediator.

Although he was repudiated as "ruler and judge" (the two functions always going together in ancient times), God commissioned Moses as "ruler and ransomer" to operate in this vastly higher function with the help and agency (σὺν χειρί, compare the phrase in

v. 25) of the angel that appeared (aorist to indicate the one appearance) to him in the thornbush, whose name and identity that angel himself declared (v. 32). Ἄρχων is rather general: "ruler," prince, author, and the like; here it means the head and leader of the young nation. But λυτρωτής is far superior to "judge." This title is purposely chosen in order to bring out fully the parallel with Christ who was a "ransomer" in the supreme sense. Although it is rare, the term is made plain by its cognates in the Greek. All of these involve a λύτρον or ransom price of some kind; in Christ's case the price of his own blood and death. Our word "redeemer" tends to lose this definite sense, "ransomer" retains it. The tendency to reduce this term to "liberator" (the cognate terms similarly) must be resisted. Moses, too, paid a great price in leading Israel out of its bondage. The burden which often crushed his soul, the fearful sins of this people are indicated in part in the following. The perfect ἀπέσταλκε is not a mistake for the aorist (B.-D. 343, 2), nor is it a perfect in a chain of aorists; it is the vivid perfect in narrative (R. 897), and we may add that it conveys the idea of the permanence of the appointment.

36) Another "this one," which emphasizes the previous ones, tells Stephen's hearers that this repudiated leader accomplished the liberation of Israel. And how did he accomplish this? By all the "wonders and signs" (see 2:19) in Egypt, the Red Sea, and the wilderness "for forty years" (accusative of extent of time). In these many signs connected with Israel's release Moses again typified Christ.

37) "This one is the Moses" intensifies all these demonstrations by adding the name "Moses" because of the greatness of what is now predicated of him. He, yes, he it is who prophesied so distinctly about the Christ "to the sons of Israel," sons and thus heirs

of the covenant and the faith of Israel, all of whom ought to be true sons in that covenant and that faith. On the prophecy itself see 3:22, and note that "like me" again and more decidedly than ever makes Moses the type of Jesus, each being a mediator, Jesus being the supreme one.

38) The fifth "this one" brings out this mediatorship of Moses which made him the type of the eternal mediator. For in connection with, ἐν, the assembly (ἐκκλησία, see 5:11) of the children of Israel in the wilderness, namely on Mount Sinai, he was in company (μετά) with both the Angel Jehovah who spoke to him on Sinai (v. 30-34) and with our fathers. Note that μετά has two objects: "in company with the angel and our fathers"; to be with both made him the mediator of the old covenant (in this respect surpassing all other prophets) and the great type of Jesus. It conflicts with the line of thought followed by Stephen when Gal. 3:19; Heb. 2:2; Josephus, and "a well-defined Jewish interpretation" concerning angels (plural) in connection with the giving of the law, are introduced; for Stephen carefully refers back to v. 30, etc., to the one ἄγγελος or messenger who was God himself. He is not to be confused with created angels.

A signal feature of this mediatorship is briefly mentioned in the first relative clause: "he who received living sayings to give to us," received them from God in order to bestow them on us, Stephen regarding himself as one of them. The reference is to the divine law. Since Moses was the medium of its transmission, this law in a signal manner made him the mediator of the old covenant (given to Abraham, v. 8). Δόγια are simply "brief sayings," here those of the Decalog. Any other use of the word, pagan, Biblical, or ecclesiastical, means no more even when the "oracles of Delphi," the "Logia" that Papias said Matthew wrote, or the "Logia of Jesus," extracanonical sayings of Jesus from the Oxyrhynchus papyri, are referred to.

More important is the question as to how Stephen could call the Ten Commandments "living." That view is too narrow which fails to connect them with the entire old covenant and forgets that this covenant was entirely gospel, God's grace in the promise of the Messiah and salvation. We have those "living logia" in connection with the new covenant and its fulfilled promises in Christ. The living power of God is in them. They are even "unto life," Rom. 7:10, 12, 14; Gal. 3:12; but not to the sinner (Gal. 3:21). For him they are only an aid to the gospel in restoring him to life.

39) Once more, and with another relative, Stephen points his hearers to Moses but now he points to him as once more being rejected by these false "sons of Israel": "he to whom our fathers did not will to become obedient but thrust him away (significantly repeating the verb from v. 27) and turned in their hearts (in the very center of their being) unto Egypt." "Did not will" is the very verb Jesus used in Matt. 23:37. There is where the seat of unbelief is always found; and this will is in the heart. Not the bondage in Egypt attracted the Israelites but, as the following shows, the feasts of Egyptian idolatry.

40) Stephen does not speak only in general terms when he thus charges the fathers with the rejection of Moses at Sinai. With εἰπόντες (aorist as in v. 35) he specifies; the Israelites demanded that Aaron make them an Egyptian idol: "Make us gods!" The enormous guilt of this demand needs no emphasis. The relative clause with the future tense denotes purpose (R. 960): "who shall go before us" on our way back to Egypt. The living God led them out with omnipotent miracles; the dead idols of Egypt, manufactured in the desert by their own hands, are to

nullify all this and to lead them back. In the plural "gods" the one true God is denied. The plural is one of category, hence the manufacture of one idol was sufficient.

The excuse for turning from God is the fact that they do not know what has become of "this Moses," the contemptuous use of οὗτος (R. 697). The relative clause may be concessive: "who (although he) brought us out of Egypt-land"; again it may be derogatory: "this Moses, who (we are sorry to say) brought us," etc. The subject is a pendent nominative (R. 459) which is often used in popular language. Moses remained on the mountain peak with God for forty days; hence the light and slighting statement: "We do not know what occurred for him," i. e., what has become of him. He was no longer a concern of theirs. Thus again Moses was repudiated, the covenant cast aside, the faith of Abraham spurned, the omnipotence and the miracles of God regarded as nothing. Why is Stephen bringing these histories forward so prominently? Because he is preparing for his climax: in their rejection of the mediator Moses these disobedient, unbelieving fathers were the type of Stephen's present hearers in their still more vicious rejection of the Mediator Jesus.

41) **And they made a calf in those days, and they led up a sacrifice for the idol and went on making merry in connection with the works of their hands.**

Right here at Sinai the Israelites staged a regular idol festival. The verb "made a calf" is found only here but is a clear compound. This μόσχος is a ταῦρος, a calf that has grown, but not to full maturity, the bull god Apis of the Egyptians. The writer visited the Tomb of the Bulls which is underground and in the desert. It has a long passageway with chambers on each side, and each chamber contains a granite sarcophagus weighing tons and a lid to correspond. The embalmed, mummified bulls were not there, but the monstrosity of such worship of brutes still stared one in the face. Stephen mentions the two chief acts: bringing up the burnt sacrifice (θυσία) for the idol as he properly names the bull, and then the continued making merry (imperfect, descriptive), the same verb that occurs in Luke 15:23, in the parable of the Prodigal. They did not only "rejoice in the works of their (own) hands" (our versions), in the idol they had made, but also "made merry," celebrated a grand feast with dancing, singing, etc., "in connection with the works of their hands," the idol with all its paraphernalia.

42) Stephen passes over the rest of the story and mentions only the punitive act of God, his turning from Israel and giving them up to their idolatries, as Amos 5:25, etc., describes it. **But God turned and gave them over to serving the host of heaven even as it has been written in the prophets' book:**

Certainly, you did not offer to me slaughter victims and burnt sacrifices
For forty years in the wilderness, House of Israel?
Yea, you took up the tabernacle of Moloch
And the star of the god Rephan,
The figures which you made in order to worship them.
Yea, I will transfer you beyond Babylon.

"God turned" (the verb is here intransitive). When the sinner determines to follow his wicked course, God punishes him by giving him over to his sin and thus uses sin to punish sin. A downward progression results until the effects of sin destroy the sinner, and he is blotted out. Nothing can be worse than to have God turn and let the sinner who has turned from him go on into judgment. "God gave them over to serving the host (army) of heaven," which is Sabaism, worship of the sun and other heavenly bodies instead of the Lord of hosts. "Gave them over" occurs in the same sense three times in Rom. 1:24, 26, 28, where God speaks of abandoning the heathen to their lusts, three times "like clods on a coffin in a grave" (R. W P.). Λατρεύειν refers to religious service as in v. 7.

Instead of quoting more from the Pentateuch or alluding to its expressions, Stephen lets the prophet Amos speak for him and uses the regular formula of quotation γέγραπται, "it has been (and thus remains forever) written." The twelve minor prophets were regarded as one book. The μή in the question in the first two lines of Amos' words demands a negative answer: Israel did *not* bring its sacrifices to God during the forty years in the wilderness. What sacrifices were still brought God could not accept. The following lines show that idolatry filled the hearts of the nation. Even circumcision, the sign of the covenant, fell into disuse. The two Hebrew words denote burnt offerings and meat offerings, but the LXX translated them with two words, both of which mean sacrifices slaughtered and burnt. Stephen follows the LXX throughout with but slight change, and since in the next three lines this deviates so far from the Hebrew, it would seem that he spoke Greek and not Aramaic when making his defense.

Amos prophesied between 810 and 783 B. C. against the Northern Kingdom in the time of Jeroboam II, when Uzziah reigned over the Southern Kingdom. When he points out the sin, godlessness, and idolatry of the Israelites of his time, he refers to the Israelites in the desert during the forty years under Moses. Those old idolatries are still going on and are, therefore, the more worthy of punishment. The forty years may be regarded as a round number. They were in reality thirty-eight, yet forty appears in Num. 14:33, and Josh. 5:6. Moreover, the germs of this defection were found already at the start of this period. In "House of Israel" Amos sums up all the generations of Israel since Moses' time, for this wickedness manifested itself ever anew.

43) The Hebrew reads as follows:
*"Yea, you have borne the tabernacles of your king
And the shrine of your images,
The star of your god which you made to yourselves.
Therefore will I cause you to go into captivity beyond Damascus.*

See Delitzsch on the passage in Amos. The thought of Amos is: the king, whose tabernacle, and the images, whose shrine they bore, was a star which they had made their god, an astral divinity. They made images of their star divinity and carried them in a little casket-like temple which was placed on a portable rack (*Gestell*) of some kind. This method of worship the Israelites copied from the Egyptians among whom sun worship and star worship existed from the earliest times. We need recall only that *Ra* was originally their supreme god, namely the sun, the prototype of all their kings, who was worshipped also as Osiris and in Apis, the bull. *Mentu* and *Atmu* are only the rising and the setting sun, i. e., *Ra* divided; *Phtha* and *Amon* (*Amon-Ra*) were later advanced to first place as gods. The oldest translations show how wrong the transpositions of the LXX are. But worst of all, the LXX read the Hebrew word for "your king": *m l k k m* (omitting the vowel points) as "Moloch"; and made "Rephan" a god out of the Hebrew *kiyun*, "shrine," by misreading two of the unvocalized letters: turning *k* into *r*, and *y* into *ph*. And a great deal of difficulty has resulted from this infelicitous misreading.

There is no god "Rephan." The Israelites knew nothing about Moloch during those forty years, and the effort to identify Moloch with Saturn, the one being worshipped by allowing children to burn up in his heated arms, the other said to devour his children, thus making Moloch a star divinity, is misdirected. When Rephan is identified with Satan, this is only another fancy. We may also note that Deut. 4:19 forbids the very type of idolatry to which Amos refers, the worship of sun, moon, stars, and the host of heaven; and Ezek. 20:7, etc., states positively that the Israelites would not relinquish "the idols of Egypt." All the evidence is in favor of the view that in the wilderness Israel practiced Egyptian and no other idolatry.

The last line is simpler. Amos wrote: "beyond Damascus," so also the LXX; Stephen substitutes "beyond Babylon" because the prophecy had been fulfilled long ago, the people having been carried so far beyond Damascus as to have been scattered even beyond Babylon. Amos speaks of the Northern Kingdom.

The question that is of moment here is how Stephen, speaking by the Spirit, could retain the faulty and baseless rendering of the LXX, especially the terms "Moloch" and "Rephan"? The answer is: "Because these names are negligible for the purpose Stephen and the Spirit had in hand, the bringing home to Stephen's hearers their like opposition to God." Even the LXX left "the star" as a god and an idol. Besides, we have the original Hebrew so that actual error even in so insignificant a matter is obviated.

---

44) The *third part* of the address refutes the charge of blasphemy against the Temple. Stephen briefly reviews the story of the Tabernacle and of the Temple and ends with a quotation from Isaiah that is directed against an overestimation of the Temple. The reply scorns to enter into details, it throws on the screen the Scripture story and view of the Temple as

being also Stephen's view and lets that suffice. The entire bearing of Stephen, as it is reflected in his address, is that of power backed by divine certainty, so that he is in reality not defending himself but rather trying to bring his judges to repentance.

The Tabernacle of the Testimony was for our fathers in the wilderness even as he appointed who spoke to Moses to make it according to the model which he had seen.
Note the contrast between "the tabernacle of your king" (god) in the quotation from Amos and this "**Tabernacle of the Testimony**," by which, in connection with which, and in which God testifies to Israel regarding himself and regarding all his covenant grace. The LXX thus translates the Hebrew "tabernacle of coming together," i. e., where God meets his people and reveals himself. This is not literal but substantial correctness so that Stephen adopts the expression. This was the true tabernacle for the fathers, but all that Stephen can say about it is that Moses made it after the heavenly pattern and that thus the fathers had it. What more could he say when they carried that idol tabernacle with them? "It was for the fathers" is the idiom for "the fathers had it."

Stephen points to its divine origin when he says that he who spoke to Moses (God) ordered him to make it according to the model which he had seen while he was with God on the mountain. The very design was God's so as to connect this Tabernacle entirely with God. Τύπος is "blow," then the mark made by a blow, the imprint, and thus the design, pattern, or model. Stephen tacitly points out the fact that Israel did not always have the Temple which the Jews so fanatically adored at the present; a long time elapsed before they ever thought of a temple — surely a sobering thought.

45) **Which our fathers, having received in turn, brought in in company with Joshua, in connection**

with the permanent possession of the nations which God pushed out before the face of our fathers until the days of David who found favor before God and asked for himself to find a habitation for the God of Jacob.

In the flexible Greek fashion all that Stephen says about the Tabernacle and the Temple, v. 44-50, is one grand sentence. The participle "having received in turn" is to be construed with "brought in in company with (μετά) Joshua." The Tabernacle was delivered to them by Moses when Joshua brought the fathers into Canaan. This was "in connection with the permanent possession (κατάσχεσις as in v. 5) of the nations," the Canaanite tribes, "whom God pushed out," etc. The genitive "of the nations" is not subjective so that the phrase would mean: "at the time when the nations held permanent possession"; the genitive is objective: Israel came into permanent possession of these nations, i. e., of their land, they having been driven out by God (ὧν is attracted from ἅ). "Which they brought in . . . until the days of David" indicates briefly that for a period that covered hundreds of years this Tabernacle was all that Israel had.

46) Another relative clause brings us to the last chapter of the Tabernacle. It was David who found such favor (χάρις) with God that encouraged him to ask for himself (middle), as a special manifestation of that divine favor, "to find (object infinitive) a habitation for the God of Jacob." This infinitive clause is an appropriation of the beautiful language of Ps. 132:5. Besides this psalm read II Sam. 7:1, etc., regarding David's plans. Σκήνωμα is poetical language, as is also εὑρεῖν. David has in mind a permanent place of worship, a beautiful temple, yet he calls it no more than a "tent" and speaks of finding it when he thinks of building a fitting temple. Instead of using a mere pronoun Stephen keeps David's impressive dative "for the God of Jacob."

47) An adversative δέ takes us to Solomon. **Solomon, however, built him a house.** Not before this time did Israel have a temple. Even David had to content himself with the old Tabernacle. Somehow God did not seem to be so anxious about a temple. He even let David ask in vain for the privilege of building one (I Kings 5:3; I Chron. 22:7, etc.; 28:2, etc.) and put this event off until Solomon's time. David was a man of war and blood, Solomon (*Sh^elomah, Friedrich*) a man or prince of peace; the one was a type of Christ conquering foes, the other a type of Christ reigning in peace. Stephen is satisfied to mention only the fact that Solomon finally built "a house for him," nor does Stephen call it any more than that.

48) In fact, over against the Jews who valued their Temple extravagantly, far more than they valued the true worship of God by faith and obedience to him, and desecrated even this "house" with their godless obduracy, Stephen shares Solomon's own conception of the Temple (I Kings 8:27): **nevertheless, not the Highest in things made with hands doth dwell,** nay, not he, whatever creatures may do. The negative is purposely placed with the subject: "not the Highest," and our versions ought to be amended accordingly; for to construe the negative with the verb even alters the sense. See R., *W. P.* For, indeed, all that others can do is "to dwell in things made with hands." That is one difference between them and the Highest, one of the great titles for God. It is because of his infinite exaltation that he is beyond all man-made things. We have only the neuter plural and not "temples" (A. V.) or "houses" (R. V.). So also the contrast between the two is heightened by placing them side by side in the Greek: "the Highest — in things made with hands." When Stephen speaks thus about the Temple, the very one built by Solomon, he has God's own Word to sup-

port him: **even as the prophet states,** namely Isa. 66:1, 2, with only slight verbal difference between the LXX and the Hebrew.

49, 50)   The quotation is exactly to the point.

**The heaven a throne for me,
And the earth a footstool of my feet!
What kind of house will you build me? saith the Lord;
And what a place of my rest?
Did not my hand make all these things?**

Here God himself speaks and declares what he thinks of any and every temple built for him by men. The superstitious reverence of the Jews for their Temple here finds its divine answer. These Jews treat the Highest as though he were some pagan god or pagan idol that had to have some sort of temple for its home. Because Stephen has spoken of God as being exalted above all man-made temples, they are now putting him to trial. Because he will not make God an idol that needs must have a temple, they are ready to condemn him for blasphemy of their Temple. We must note the full force of what Stephen says, in particular how his words regarding the Temple naturally merge into the denunciation of v. 51, etc., without either break or pause.

Even the heaven is only God's throne, a royal seat for him. Heaven itself is not a house or a temple for him; it is only one of the things he has made. As for the whole earth, it is vastly less, nothing more than a footstool for his feet, so far beneath him, one of the insignificant things he has made. Why does Isaiah say these tremendous things to the Israel of his time and to the future Israel that would return from its seventy years of captivity in Babylon to build him another temple? Because of their wicked and obdurate hearts.

That is exactly why Stephen, too, hurls these same words at his present hearers, whose hearts are of the same kind. What kind of a house is it that people such as this will build for *Yahweh* who is here confronting them? The Herodian Temple was even now in the process of being rebuilt. And what a place of his rest are they trying to provide, where he may enter and abide among them? They have forgotten his infinite greatness which Solomon remembered, II Chron. 6:18. They do not draw the proper conclusions from the fact that it is he who made all these things, even heaven and earth and all that is therein. They no longer know that God looks only to him who is of a contrite spirit and who trembles at his Word lest perhaps he fail to observe it (the continuation of Isa. 66:2, then also v. 3). When they build with hearts like that, every offering in their Temple so builded is an abomination to *Yahweh*, the blood of every ox like that of a murdered man, every lamb like a dog with his head cut off, every oblation like swine's blood, and their burning incense as though it were intended to bless an idol. Stephen does not add these statements of Isaiah, but these words help us to understand the lines which he quotes.

Neither the Lord speaking through Isaiah, nor Jesus (John 2:19; 4:23, 24), nor Stephen say that no temple and no places of worship shall be built. God vouchsafed his presence in the ancient Tabernacle and in Solomon's Temple (II Chron. 7:1-3). How, by whom, and in what spirit temples are to be built Solomon and Isa. 66:2b show us. But to build temples and churches, to make them grand and imposing, to fill them with crowds for great services while hearts are without contrition, obdurate before God's Word, is to treat God as an idol to whom we may dictate as we please, to invent what his will and word is to be to suit our own perverted hearts. That is the kind of house many still build, a place where they offer rest to the Highest. The view of critics that Isaiah's words refer to a temple which the Jewish exiles proposed to erect in Babylon, or refer only to the Samaritan Temple on Mt. Gerizim, need not be refuted at this place. Compare Aug. Pieper, *Jesaias II*, 653, etc.

---

51) What follows must be called *the conclusion*, for while it continues the account without a break, it pertains to all that precedes. Like one of the prophets of old, in the very spirit of Isaiah from whom Stephen has just quoted, he hurls the countercharge of wilful obduracy against his judges. He wields the law on the conscience of his hearers with the boldness and the fearlessness of a Peter (2:36; 4:10-12; 5:29-32) in order to crush these wicked Jews in repentance.

Stiffnecked and uncircumcised as to heart and ears, you on your part always fall against the Holy Spirit; as your fathers, also you! Which of the prophets did your fathers not persecute? And they killed those who made advance announcement about the coming of the Righteous One, whose betrayers and murderers you on your part have now become: people such as received the law on dispositions of angels and did not observe it!

The invective is deliberate, measured, with not a word too much, like a surgeon who cuts deep in order to let the fearful corruption out. "Stiffnecked" = with a neck or a back ($\tau\rho\acute{a}\chi\eta\lambda$ος) that will not bend; obstinate. "Uncircumcised as to hearts and ears" = bearing the covenant sign only outwardly and not inwardly in its intended force, which involves the cutting off of all opposition to God and to his Word. The dative is neither locative nor instrumental but a dative of relation (B-D. 197): "in regard to hearts and ears." As to their hearts and their ears these Jews were no better than the uncircumcised heathen. John 8:44. The ears are the organs for hearing God's Word and his will, the heart the organ for receiving, believing, obeying that Word and that will. The hearts are mentioned first because they control the ears and in the obdurate make them deaf to God.

Although it is added only coordinately (καί), we now have the proof for these designations: "you on your part (emphatic ὑμεῖς) always fall against the Holy Spirit," which uses the idiomatic Greek verb for opposition and resistance. "Holy Spirit" is in place because it is this Person who comes to us in the Word in order to work contrition and faith. To resist him is to cut ourselves off from the very means by which alone we can be saved. This resistance begins with individual acts and eventually becomes a fixed *habitus* which permanently closes the heart so that the Spirit can no longer have his work in us. This is hardness of heart or obduracy.

Why the Word melts some hearts while others deliberately and permanently harden themselves against it, no man knows. The former is due wholly to God's grace, the latter is due wholly to man's guilt. No one cause for both exists. When synergism or determinism are taken to be such a cause, the fact is overlooked that both are non-existant. Man cannot aid the Spirit with his unregenerate or natural ability, nor is the *gratia* of the Spirit *irresistibilis*. The conversion of the sinner is easy to explain, for the *gratia* is *sufficiens* to work conversion in him; the obduracy remains a mystery because of this very sufficiency of grace, which, as was the case in these hearers of Stephen, secures only the opposite effect. In this respect Stephen's hearers proved to be true sons of their fathers: "as *your* fathers (Stephen takes care not to say *our* in the present connection), also you." Israel's history reveals a damnable ancestry, and the descendants are still multiplying rapidly.

52) Stephen fully establishes this connection of evil spiritual descent; Jesus did the same in Matt. 23:29-32. What did "your fathers" do? They persecuted every one of the prophets through whom the Holy Spirit spoke to them. Stephen's question which asks them to name one who was not so persecuted is not a rhetorical exaggeration. "Who even today, according to the statements of the Old Testament, is able to name a prophet who was received with approval and enthusiasm as other nations received their great spirits and prophets? From Moses and Samuel until Malachi and John the Baptist the true prophets who arose in Israel came to experience ungrateful disregard, haughty contradiction, open rebellion, and, as Jesus also says regarding all the prophets, persecution from the people of their nation, from the princes and the priests, from their own nearest relatives." Zahn. As far as murder is concerned, Stephen does no more than to repeat the charge which Jesus made in Matt. 23:31, 35, 37; Luke 11:47, etc.; 13:34. The fact that the murderous intent did not always succeed, as was the case with reference to Elijah, Jeremiah, etc., made those who had this intent nonetheless murderers. Such, Stephen tells his hearers, were "your fathers."

The words are perfectly chosen when he describes the prophets as "those who made advance announcement about the coming of the Righteous One." That announcing was their chief, their blessed work; they were God's own heralds. What did it, then, mean to persecute and to kill them? "Coming" is the great Messianic term; it is a comprehensive designation of the Messiah's entire life and work. Jesus is repeatedly called "the Righteous One" in the supreme sense; see 3:14, and compare 22:14; I Pet. 3:18. Here this designation is in glaring contrast with "betrayers and murderers." What their fathers did to such an eminent degree these judges whom Stephen faces have exceeded "now," in the recent past. The Greek is content to use the aorist with reference to a recent occurrence: "became," whereas we prefer "have become." By hiring the traitor Judas the whole Sanhedrin made itself "betrayers" of the Righteous One; and by forcing Pilate to crucify him *they* became his "murderers." Note the emphasis on ὑμεῖς and how fully and terribly their connection is established with "your fathers," the persecutors and the murderers of the prophets.

53) R. 728 makes οἵτινες causal (which it often is): "since you are such as"; but B.-D. 293, 2 sees correctly that here (and elsewhere) this relative is used when the general characteristic of definite persons is stated: *you* — "people who," "people such as." Yes, they were this very kind. They received the law in a most heavenly way but did not guard or observe it. All this frightful crime would be bad enough if they had never had or heard of this law of God; but God had made them his chosen people and had given them his glorious law, and they treated it in this manner. The tables are thus completely turned. Stephen stood accused of speaking against the law, but the Sanhedrin itself is convicted of utterly breaking and abandoning the law.

The phrase εἰς διαταγάς is a crux as far as translating and explaining εἰς is concerned. See our versions and the R. V. margin and what they think the Greek means. Many explanations are offered, Zahn is undecided. Fortunately, the sense is clear as Deut. 33:2; Gal. 3:19; Heb. 2:2 show. The angels were active in the giving of the law on Mount Sinai. The genitive "of angels" is subjective: they made "dispositions," shall we say "arrangements," the Germans say *Anordnungen.* Deissmann has found the word used in the sense of an order, a disposition one has made, a testamentary disposition, an imperial or a divine ordinance (*Light from the Ancient East,* 86, etc.). In this case εἰς does not equal ἐν; nor is it "unto," "in accord with," or the predicative εἰς (R. 596), "as" (R. V. margin). It is best to take εἰς in the sense of "upon" or "on," German *auf*. But when "angels" are supposed to include the angel mentioned in v. 30 and 38, or when the plural is identified with this one angel, who is God himself, we cannot agree. Stephen exalts the law: heavenly angels helped in its giving, yet the Sanhedrists disregarded it; Paul's emphasis in Gal. 3:19 is the reverse; *only* angels were used.

STEPHEN STONED

54) It is usually assumed that Stephen's address ends at this point, that it was broken off here, and that he intended to close with some word of gospel. He did close with a wonderful gospel utterance (v. 56); the interruption did not come until after he had spoken it. Luke pauses to tell us about the preliminary effect that was produced by the law Stephen was uttering, which already shows what effect the gospel would have.

Now, while hearing these things, they were being sawn in two as regards their heart and began gnashing their teeth against him. But being full of the Holy Spirit, on earnestly looking to heaven, he saw God's glory and Jesus standing at the right of God and he said, Lo, I behold the heavens having been opened, and the Son of man standing at the right of God!

The imperfects used in v. 54, as the present participle shows, go back to the preceding verses and describe what was happening while Stephen was uttering the severe indictments of the law. No pause occurred at this point. Yes, Stephen's words went home and produced an inner and an outer effect. There are always *motus inevitabiles* when the Word is rightly preached; no man escapes some effect, no man is the same man that he was before that Word reached him.

Here the effect was utterly hostile. Luke again uses the strong verb employed in 5:33, "they were being sawn in two," but here with the dative of relation "as to their hearts," the same dative that occurred in v. 51 (B.-D. 197, who adds that this dative predominates over the accusative of relation). These hearts (the heart is always the center of the personality) did not bend or bow to the law in a manner that indicated contrition; they were stiff and hard like dried wood, and the law could only saw them in two with its sharp teeth. The outward evidence was the fact that, as they sat and listened and heard more and more what Stephen was saying to and about them, they began grinding their teeth at him in suppressed rage. Yet they kept their seats; Stephen could still be heard.

55) And so Stephen spoke his final word. It became an involutary exclamation, for at this moment a wonderful thing happened. Although he had spoken under the Spirit's influence during his entire address, at this moment he became filled with the Spirit and, on earnestly looking up toward heaven (he was in the hall of the court), "he saw God's glory and Jesus standing at God's right." By the help of the Spirit his mortal eyes were enabled to look right into heaven. The words ἀτενίσας, εἶδε, and the following θεωρῶ are an answer to the idea that Stephen saw only mentally, in his own mind or imagination, or, as is usually said, "in spirit." No; this was an outward reality, even as the Holy Spirit is mentioned who gave this ability of sight to Stephen's eyes.

The first martyr of the Christian faith is going to his death; and he becomes the leader of the long, long line of future martyrs. Therefore this sight is granted to him, not as though it were intended for him and his strengthening alone, but through him for all of them. So the glory of God shines for all of them as they near death, so the Savior stands ready to receive them. Through Stephen's eyes they are all to see. "God's glory" is one concept, the Hebrew *k^ebod Yahweh*, all the majesty of God shining in heavenly light. The Spirit enabled Stephen to look at his glory without its blinding his eyes. That glory was over him in the midst of all his enemies.

"And Jesus standing at the right hand of God" (on this phrase see 2:25; this perfect participle is always present in sense) signifies that he had arisen to come to the aid of his confessor, to receive him unto himself. God's "right" or "right hand" is invariably his power and his majesty; and to stand at God's right, like sitting at his right, is to exercise this infinite power and majesty in an unlimited way. This surely refers to the human nature of Jesus as it participated in the divine majesty or attributes (δόξα). To understand this aright one must consider all the passages that speak of God's right plus their contexts. It goes without saying that what Stephen beheld was adapted to his eyes, and at the same time the Spirit gave to his eyes the ability to see this heavenly glory and Jesus.

Strange interpretations have been given to Luke's words. Thus it is said that Jesus is standing and not sitting with God on his throne; that he is not revealing himself as coregent with God but as the servant of the King of heaven, the one who is next to the throne, who is ready to obey the nod of the King and his will in the whole domain of his rule. An older view claims that Jesus' standing thus in heaven means that, when in his human nature Jesus is sitting or standing in heaven, he is closed there so that he cannot at the same time and in the human nature be present on earth (Calvin, *Institutiones* IV, 17, 16), and that we must interpret Matt. 28:20; 18:20; the words of the Lord's Supper, and all similar passages according to the limitation this reasoning places upon the body, the bodily presence, and the human nature of Jesus in his glory. The basic deficiency of these reasonings has often been pointed out. They play one passage of Scripture against another instead of letting one class of passages illumine and interpret the other class. *Scriptura ex Scriptura explicanda est*, always and always, and not by rationalizings of human minds regarding some passage or passages so as to make them conflict with other passages.

56) Thus the Holy Spirit himself completed Stephen's address for him, completed it in a most miraculous way and with the most effective gospel word. Unlike Peter, Stephen did not need to preach to the Sanhedrin the resurrection and the exaltation of Jesus (3:10, 15), here Jesus himself preached it by revealing himself to Stephen in his heavenly glory and causing him to reveal to the Sanhedrin what his eyes were seeing. This was the fulfillment of the very word Jesus himself had uttered before this very Sanhedrin when he was on trial, Matt. 26:64. They now hear that this Jesus whom they crucified is standing in the heavens as the eternal Messiah at God's own right of majesty and power. Stephen is not relating what he saw on some former occasion, but what it is granted him to see at the very moment of his speaking. Far removed and yet not removed is this Jesus; for the heavens stand open (the perfect participle with its present connotation), and he is standing as one who has risen for action. Yes, it was all for Stephen, for his comfort and his assurance. There stood the almighty Son of man whose power maintained his great confessor. But it was intended also for the Sanhedrists. Whom were they opposing? The glorified Son of man, the heavenly, eternal, almighty Messiah of God.

The title "the Son of man" is discussed at length in connection with the writer's interpretation of Matt. 8:20; Mark 2:10; Luke 5:24; John 1:51, to which the reader is referred.

57) While the crushing rebukes of the law were being administered, the Sanhedrists had remained in

their seats although gnashing their teeth; the great gospel testimony of Stephen, although it was produced by a miracle of God, causes the Sanhedrists to rage like wild beasts that are demanding blood. Is it possible that the gospel can affect men's hearts in such a way? It did in this case. **But uttering yells with a great voice, they held their ears and rushed with one accord upon him; and having thrown him out of the city, they began stoning him.**

Pandemonium broke loose. All legal formalities were cast aside as mob rage and violence suddenly came into control. We do not understand how some interpreters can insert into Luke's description the formal passing of a death sentence. According to Jewish law it would have been ineffective because a second session of the Sanhedrin which was held at least a day later was necessary for legal confirmation, and in addition to that the governor's consent to the execution was mandatory. No; a mob storm breaks loose and hurries Stephen to his death forthwith.

The shouting and the holding shut of the ears implies that Stephen's words were considered the most awful blasphemy. Lest they hear another word like that they shout with might and main to drown out Stephen's voice and stop their ears so that no word of his may enter them. Then, as though actuated by one impulse, they dash upon this blasphemer and thrust him outside of the city and there begin to stone him. All this happened without delay. But note that Luke first has a chain of aorists that fall like blow upon blow; the shouting — the holding the ears shut — the rushing upon Stephen — the expulsion from the city; and then uses an imperfect which arrests our attention to view what is going on, the process of stoning, for, before it is finished, something else must be told. This imperfect is repeated in v. 59 and holds us in suspense still longer in anticipation of what is yet to be added. This use of the imperfect is an excellent example of how the tense is employed to hold the reader in suspense.

58) We know that attempts were made to stone Jesus for blasphemy in the very Temple courts (John 8:59; 10:31, etc.). Why Stephen was thrust out of the city in agreement with Lev. 24:14 (Heb. 13:11), we cannot say, unless it was done because of the strange twists of the mob mind which, in the midst of its lawlessness, sometimes clings to legal formality. Points to be considered in reconstructing the story are these: building was going on in the Temple area, and stones were ready at hand there — the paved streets afforded no suitable stones — just where the Sanhedrin met is a question — outside of the city plenty of stones were available.

We are not impressed by the argument that these supreme judges and dignitaries of the Sanhedrin were incapable of the coarseness here described, and that Luke intends to change the subject of all the verbs to other unnamed persons. We know what these men perpetrated upon the helpless Jesus in Matt. 26:67, 68, and in Mark 14:65. They really do less here. But, of course, to the Sanhedrists we must add their Levite police force, into whose hands Stephen must have been given for the trial; we must also add the crowd of Hellenist Jews who had arrested Stephen and brought him in and acted as his accusers, together with their suborned witnesses. Many persons may have been thronging outside of the doors, these were augmented by people who had been attracted to the scene. A force of police rushed Stephen to the scene of execution. Sanhedrists went along, and a crowd that grew as they went followed.

But what about the loss of the Jewish right to execute criminals? Note that the Sanhedrin had not passed a verdict and thus was not legally liable. The whole action was one of mob violence and could be classed as a popular outburst of rage against a fearful blasphemer. Pilate was not eager to do justice in a case such as this, the less so since he himself had grave reasons to fear the Sanhedrin because of outrages he had perpetrated. We need not date this event later than the rule of Pilate, place it into an interim when Pilate had been withdrawn and his successor had not yet arrived. Pilate was at Caesarea at this time.

And the witnesses placed their robes at the feet of a young man called Saul. The witnesses had to cast the first stones in order to attest that they had sworn and witnessed truly (Deut. 17:6); otherwise they would be adding the crime of murder to that of perjured testimony. The long, loose outer robe had to be laid aside in order to permit free use of the limbs in the violent action of throwing stones. The thought is not that some individual, here by chance Saul, was selected to guard these robes lest someone make off with them during the excitement. We must assume that Saul was acting in an official capacity, either alone or in conjunction with others who were superintending the stoning. This is made probable by what is related in the sequel about his prominent activity under the authority of the Sanhedrin. We see what a position he had attained as a disciple of the great Gamaliel who was a member of the Sanhedrin (5:34). "Young man," νεανίας, is not a youth in our sense of the word but a man come to maturity; Saul must have been about thirty years old at this time. This is only an estimate, yet it is based on all the available data.

59) **And they were stoning Stephen, calling out and saying, Lord Jesus, receive my spirit! And having kneeled, he shouted with a great voice, Lord, place not this sin against them! And having said this, he fell asleep.**

The repetition is tragic and is made more so by the imperfect tense. The terrible process of stoning a man

Acts 7:59, 60

to death was going slowly onward. An aorist would mean that the final, fatal stone had been thrown. Note that Luke now adds the name: "And they were stoning Stephen" — yes, this proto-martyr, this first confessor of Christendom to seal his faith with his life. As stone after stone crashed against his body, he raised his face to God and after the pattern of Jesus' own dying prayer (Luke 24:46) asked the Lord Jesus (see 1:21) to receive his spirit. That prayer was heard. Stephen's spirit, the immaterial part of his being, left his body and was received by Jesus into the glory and the bliss of heaven, there to await the last day when his body would be raised up to be again united with his soul and to participate in its heavenly joys. So Paul longed "to depart and be with Christ" (Phil 1:23).

Here there is no "oblivion" for the soul at death. The idea of a *sheol* or hades as a *Totenreich* or intermediate place for souls, lying somewhere between heaven and hell, seems to be foreign to Stephen's mind, who sees only the heavenly glory of God and Jesus at God's right standing to receive his martyr's spirit. *Fecisti me victorem, recipe me in triumphum.* Augustine.

60) Stone after stone struck Stephen. He sank to his knees, literally, "having placed the knees," yet he did not do so in the humbleness of prayer before the Lord but simply because he had been severely struck by well-aimed stones. At the very moment of death, like Jesus, he rallies all his fast-ebbing strength and at the top of his voice so that all in the crowd may hear he shouts his final prayer which asks God not to place this sin against his murderers, the dative of disadvantage. In the aorist negative commands are in the subjunctive and not in the imperative. In prayers, for instance in the Lord's Prayer, the aorist denotes urgency and fervency; so it does here. This prayer for his enemies Stephen had also learned from Jesus. R.,

W. P., regards this aorist as ingressive, it is effective. The verb accords with its opposite, ἀφιέναι, "to dismiss" or send the sin away (ἄφεσις). Stephen's prayer had one most notable fulfillment, namely Saul. Being a young man like Stephen, Saul soon stepped into Stephen's vacant place, took up the martyr's work, and carried it forward with great power.

And so Stephen "fell asleep." This time Luke uses an effective aorist which marks the ending of an action. The two aorists used in this verse thus bring the final outcome of the previous imperfects. Although he experienced a violent and terrible form of death, Stephen "went to sleep." This is not a euphemism which would hide the fearful reality but literal truth. This expression is regularly used in the New Testament with reference to the dying of believers. By the use of this very word for death the resurrection is implied. But only the body falls asleep; the soul does not sleep but is with the Lord, awaiting the awakening of the body.

CHAPTER VIII

The Second Quarter
The Gospel in Palestine, Chapters 8 to 12

THE GOSPEL IN SAMARIA

The stoning of Stephen ushered in the first general persecution. The church had grown extensively; it was to grow more than ever, but now by being spread abroad. Luke's figures and further notes about the growth make the estimate of 25,000 believers in and near Jerusalem at the time of Stephen's martyrdom seem conservative. The persecution aimed to destroy the infant church; in the providence of God it did the very opposite. It started a great number of new congregations especially in all of Palestine, each becoming a living center from which the gospel radiated into new territory even as Jesus had traced its course by adding after Jerusalem "all Judea and Samaria" (1:8).

1) **Now Saul continued to agree with his taking away. Moreover, there arose on that day a great persecution against the church in Jerusalem; and all were scattered abroad through the regions of Judea and Samaria except the apostles.**

It is the strong durative sense of the periphrastic verb form that makes the statement about Saul so important in the present connection. To be sure, he agreed with full approval to Stephen's "taking away," the word that has the sinister meaning of murder; but he continued in this agreement, and it is thus that, starting on the very day of Stephen's martyrdom, a persecution began that Luke rightly calls "great." For so thoroughly did Saul agree to what was done with Stephen that he moved to do the same thing with the entire church in Jerusalem. In other words, Saul became the prime mover in this persecution. That is why the statement regarding him is put here in connection with the word about the persecution.

The A. V. is right in beginning the new chapter as it does. The casual mention of Saul in 7:58 is only preliminary to this more serious statement which connects Saul with the persecution. He was a man of tremendous energy and sound logic. Stephen's death should be followed up, the entire Christian movement should be crushed. Saul placed himself forward in making the effort.

Beyond saying that the persecution began that very day and that Stephen was its first victim Luke reports no details. With the historical aorist he states only the effect that the Christians were scattered abroad all over Judea and Samaria. Τὰς χώρας, "the regions," does not mean that they went only into the country districts and avoided the cities. Samaria became especially attractive to the Christians, for they were losing their antipathy toward the Samaritans, and in this country, so close at hand, the Sanhedrin and its minions could exercise no authority. "All" is to be taken in the popular and not the absolute sense. The apostles, however, remained in Jerusalem. In explanation we may note that Jerusalem was still the headquarters for the work among the Jews, and the apostles were to remain here until the Lord should direct them elsewhere. As far as fear was concerned, they had none as they had already demonstrated (4:8, etc.; 5:30, etc.)

2) **Yet devout men buried Stephen and made great lamentation over him.** This is added lest a wrong deduction be made from the foregoing. In the

Acts 8:2, 3   313

first place, the Jews always buried on the day of death, if possible; and in Stephen's case no delay of any kind was necessary. As soon as the crowd about the dead martyr dispersed, men of the type of Joseph of Arimathaea and Nicodemus took a hand and gave the poor, battered, and bloody body decent burial. Their very act shows them to be "devout" (see 2:5), sincere, and of honest hearts, men who deeply deplored what had been done. Luke's designation can scarcely refer to Christians against whom adverse measures must have been taken that same day.

So also these men made great mourning over him, κοπετός, the beating of the head and the breast while wailing in Oriental fashion. Luke loves contrasts, so he tells us that, while such men were still to be found in Jerusalem, this other man, Saul, began his bloodthirsty work.

3) Saul, however, began to lay waste the church, entering in house by house and, haling men and women, was committing them to prison. They, therefore, on being scattered abroad, went on through, proclaiming as good news the Word.

This is the way in which Saul continued to agree to Stephen's death. The verb indicates the devastation caused by a wild beast, and the imperfect is best regarded as conative. On ἐκκλησία see 5:11. The κατά phrase should be construed with the participle; though the noun is plural and has the article the phrase is distributive as in 22:19 and 26:11 (B.-P. 634). These latter passages refer to different synagogues in which beatings were administered in the different cities and thus cast no light on the proceeding of Saul in Jerusalem where the victims were committed to prison. We are thus not warranted in thinking only of houses in which assemblies were held; these were private homes, the article indicating those in which Christians might be living — these Saul invaded.

Many had to suffer, Luke noting that even women were not spared. The participle "haling them," dragging them with violence, as well as the main statement, "he kept duly giving them over into prison" (thus literally), show that Saul had been given a force of Levitical police by the Sanhedrin in order to execute his orders of arrest in Jerusalem, and that, therefore, Saul was the chief agent of the Sanhedrin in this persecution. In fact, it seems that but for him such strong measures would not have been taken. This ferreting out where Christians lived and then falling upon them with a force of police made all Christians unsafe in the city and necessarily caused the great exodus in harmony with Jesus' own orders, Matt. 10:23 (Acts 14:6).

4) Now a further contrast: Saul ravaging the church, but the dispersed Christians spreading the gospel. Incidentally, we here see how God was turning this persecution to his own great ends. Saul thought he was crushing the Christian movement; in reality, the harder he worked to do so, the more he himself helped to spread that movement. We have οἱ μὲν οὖν as in 1:6, and this subject is modified by the participle: "they, therefore, on being scattered." In whatever territory they passed through "they told as good news the Word," here this verb has an object as in 5:42. Luke uses εὐαγγελίζομαι in its ordinary sense as in Luke 1:19; 2:10; 3:18; and not in the official sense of "to preach." These were ordinary Christians; they did not set themselves up as preachers but told people why they had to leave Jerusalem and thus testified to their faith in Christ Jesus. They fulfilled the duty that is to this day incumbent on every Christian. In 11:19 Luke indicates how far this dispersion reached: to Phoenicia, Cyprus, and Antioch. This does not indicate the use of a separate document; Luke is evidently proceeding in due order by telling us first of what happened in

Samaria and then reporting what happened in more distant places.

5) So we see how Philip came to work in Samaria. **Now Philip, having gone down to a city of Samaria, was proclaiming the Christ to them. And the multitudes with one accord were giving heed to the things being declared by Philip while they were hearing and seeing the signs which he was doing. For many of those having unclean spirits — shouting with a great voice, they kept going out; moreover, many having become paralyzed and lame were healed. And there was great joy in that city.**

After having stated that all the apostles remained in Jerusalem (v. 1), we understand that Luke refers to the deacon Philip (6:5) and not to the apostle Philip (1:13). The congregation at Jerusalem was sadly disrupted; the deacons were no longer needed, and Philip was thus free to leave. We have already indicated why Samaria, so close at hand, offered an attractive refuge to the Christians. We must combine Philip's preaching with his power to work miracles. These gifts of God made him what has been called an evangelist, a missionary preacher. He was thus more than the ordinary Christians who spread the gospel only as a part of their general Christian calling; yet he and his work remained under the authority of the apostles and of the mother congregation in Jerusalem (v. 14) so that he acted with their approval and as their agent. "The Christ" = the Messiah whom the Samaritans, too, expected (John 4:25) although they accepted only the Pentateuch. "The Christ" is the same as "the Word" (v. 4).

On the basis of both textual and other evidence we ought to read: "to a (not the) city of Samaria" (compare the same expression in Matt. 10:5). Even the texts that have "the" seem uncertain, for Aleph has the reading "Caesarea" in place of "Samaria," and B has "Paul" instead of "Philip" in v. 6. Luke never uses the appositional genitive when naming a city so that "the city of Samaria" would be "the city," the one called "Samaria." "Samaria" always refers to the country bearing that name. At this time the city which was at one time called "Samaria" had the name "Sebaste." The usual explanation that we here have an appositional genitive must therefore be dropped. Luke does not name the city. Yet in all probability he has in mind the old city of Shechem, which was later called Neapolis, and at present has the name Nablous, which is located at the foot of Mount Gerizim, the center of the Samaritan worship ("this mountain," John 4:20, 21), and is to this day maintained by the dwindling remnant of Samaritans. In 1925 the writer met their high priest, visited their synagogue in Nablous, and inspected their sacred scrolls. To the Samaritans this city was what Jerusalem was to the Jews. Here the magician Simon would most naturally establish himself. Near this city, at Sychar, Jesus had taught with success for two days (John 4:39-42). When coming from Jerusalem, Philip would reach this city first and have every reason to stop and to work here. Compare the data in Zahn, *Apostelgeschichte*. The temporary order not to preach in Samaria (Matt. 10:5) had been rescinded by Jesus in Acts 1:8.

We thus see why Luke devotes some space to Philip's success in Samaria. It is not just a city such as Sebaste that was won for the gospel but the religious center of the entire Samaritan people. After being driven from one religious center, another such center was promptly being won. Saul was not succeeding in stopping the preaching and the spread of the gospel.

6) The imperfect tenses, starting with v. 5, continue descriptively and picture the remarkable progress until they end in two aorists (v. 7, 8). Supply νοῦν

with προσεῖχον. "Multitudes" were giving heed to the things being declared by Philip, which means that they came to faith. The success of the apostles in Jerusalem was being repeated in the Samaritan religious center. Luke's favorite ἐν τῷ with the infinitive in the sense of "while" reports that seeing and hearing the signs (see 2:19) accompanied the preaching the Samaritans heard from Philip. These signs, like all those wrought by Jesus and the apostles, attested and helped to seal the preaching as being truly a message from God. We may compare Philip with Stephen in this respect (6:8) and remember that every miracle was wrought only by a direct communication from God (Christ), see 5:15.

7) Even many demoniacs were healed. The subject of demon possession is treated in connection with Matt. 4:24; 8:28; Mark 1:23; Luke 4:33. The construction is anacoluthic. It begins with the persons of the afflicted and ends with the demons of these persons as the subject of the verb; and while τὰ πνεύματα which is implied in βοῶντα is a neuter plural, the verb is not made a singular and thus regards the *pneumata* as persons. Luke implies that demoniacs came to Philip, and that all who came found deliverance. These unclean, vile spirits acted just as did those that were driven out by Jesus: they always shouted with hideous cries when they were compelled to leave their poor victims. The witnessing of these miracles which so clearly testified to the complete victory of Jesus over all the power of hell, rightly impressed the Samaritans.

Luke adds the sad cases of the paralytics who had been lamed on one side of the body by a stroke. These, too, appear frequently in the story of Jesus, every one being a hopeless case to this day as far as medical help is concerned. These, too, were healed, and Luke now reaches his aorists which close the story.

8) No wonder the joy in that city became "abundant," πολλή. Jesus had entered it with his gospel to free the souls and with his signs to heal even the bodies.

9) Philip, however, had more to contend with than the perverted Samaritan religion. Here in the old religious center of the Samaritans Simon was holding sway over the minds and the hearts of the people by means of his occult Oriental black arts. His story is introduced by Luke as an indication of the success of Philip in freeing the people from the hold this charlatan had upon them. This is the main object of Luke's account. As far as the man himself is concerned, he is of minor importance, for which reason also Luke closes his account regarding him at v. 24.

Now a man, by name Simon, was already in the city practicing magic and astonishing the nation of Samaria, declaring himself to be someone great; to whom all from small to great were giving heed, declaring, This one is the Power of God, the one called Great! Moreover, they were giving heed to him because he had astonished them with his magical arts a long time.

Δέ turns to the new subject, and τίς is only our indefinite article. When Philip came to the city he found that this Simon had been fully established there for some time and was practicing magic (μαγεύων) and filling the people with astonishment.

He is called Simon Magus and plays a great role in the traditions of the second and the third centuries. None of these reports are worthy of much attention although some commentaries give them space. Zahn discusses them at length. The participle μαγεύων has no connection with the Magi who appear in Matt. 2:1. This Simon belonged to a class of charlatans that were rather common at this period, who practiced occult arts in order to impress the people and to gain a following. Much was plain sorcery which was at times combined with a shrewd use of natural laws that were otherwise unknown. The range of their arts extended from the conjuring of demons, dealing with the dead, influencing the gods, to charms for healing, divination, stargazing, and the like. The more pretentious employed formulae and ideas that were derived from Oriental theosophy and mystic cults, or combined these with Greek ideas. The type of magic employed must be deduced from what Luke himself states. He was certainly successful, for he astonished not only the city but, as Luke says, "the nation of Samaria." It is this power of the man among the people as a whole that shows us what the gospel really accomplished through Philip's activity.

Simon must have performed prodigious feats of conjuring, for in v. 11 Luke uses the noun ταῖς μαγείαις. What these feats were is of less importance than the man's claims and the credence these claims found. He declared "himself to be someone great." This is more than *etwas Besonderes* (neuter), B.-D. 301, 1. He purposely kept the designation of himself indefinite and veiled and thus made a deep impression on the imagination of men who love the mysterious. But there is no evidence that he claimed "to impersonate God." Jerome's report that Simon said: *Ego sum sermo Dei* (the Logos), . . . *ego omnipotens, ego omnia Dei*, is a late fancy that is contradicted by Luke's plain words. Simon kept the people guessing. Even Samaritans who had the Decalog in their Pentateuch, would not have suffered the use of these titles if Simon had, indeed, used them.

10) Simon achieved what he wanted: "All from small to great gave heed to him"; we should say, "both young and old," or, "both high and low." What *he* conveyed by hinting *they* supplied by their own superstitious imagination and declared him to be no less than "the Power of God, the one called Great." This

is not deification. It would be among pagans who had many gods but not among Samaritans. These thought of a manifestation of God's power in the person of the man Simon, of that power which is supreme. The positive "great" is used in the absolute sense and replaces the superlative. Note that, when the predicate has the article, subject and predicate are identical and interchangeable, R. 768. Luke does not report that Simon was identified with God himself, and we have no right to put into his words more than he himself implied. Zahn follows Klostermann in making ἡ μεγάλη the transliteration of the Hebrew participle piel of *galah*: *mᵉgalleh*, and in noting that this Hebrew verb is always translated ἀποκαλύπτειν by the LXX. The people thus esteemed Simon as God's great instrument for revealing everything, also God himself. Thus they followed the hint stated in John 4:25, where the Samaritan woman told Jesus that the Messiah would tell them all things. But Zahn is the only commentator of note who adopts this ingenious explanation of Klostermann's. Both men fail to make clear how Luke's simple Greek adjective could convey the idea to the reader that a Hebrew piel participle is being referred to. Why did Luke not write the corresponding Greek participle ἀποκαλύπτων?

We should not identify this Simon with the one mentioned by Josephus in *Ant.* 20, 7, 2, whom Felix used to seduce Drusilla away from her husband Azizus, king of Emesa. Luke does not make him a spurious Messiah, a rival of Jesus. He is only a notable representative of the superstitious religious imposters, of whom the world was full at this time. He is to be put into the same class with Elymas (Acts 13) and the famous charlatan Apollonius of Tyana, who flourished in the same century. The Satanic influence of these imposters is evident.

Acts 8:11, 12

11) What made the case so difficult for Philip's work was the fact that by means of his arts Simon had held the people "a long time" (dative of time *when* an action takes place; this construction is restricted to words like day, night, year, etc.). The perfect infinitive agrees with this dative. Philip found the man's hold on the people deep and strong. But we already know that Philip broke this hold; even Simon gave way to Philip.

12) **Now, when they came to believe Philip proclaiming the good news concerning the kingdom of God and the name of Jesus Christ, they were being baptized, both men and women.**

We see to what the "giving heed" mentioned in v. 6 led: men and women "came to believe," an ingressive aorist (not a constative, as R., W. P. states), hence it is followed by the imperfect. Πιστεύω with the dative means to believe the person and what he says. So here these Samaritans accepted all that Philip was proclaiming as good news "concerning the kingdom of God (see 1:3) and the name (see 2:21, 38; 3:6) of Jesus Christ (see 2:38)." They came to believe the good news concerning God's rule and reign of grace, pardon, and salvation as this was revealed (ὄνομα) in the person named Jesus and in his office as Christ. Luke gives us a brief summary of Philip's gospel preaching; it centered in the kingdom and in the Name. It does so to this day. The Name is the great door that admits into the kingdom.

And thus Luke states that "they were being baptized, both men and women," the imperfect stating that this occurred continually as they came to faith. We see that Luke makes the account of what happened here in Samaria somewhat of a parallel to what had happened in Jerusalem. At the time of the first ingress of believers, cf. 2:40, their being baptized is recorded; the same is done here at the time of the first influx of

322 *Interpretation of the Acts of the Apostles*

Samaritans. Here, too, no hint regarding the mode of baptism employed is offered. Immersion, however, is out of the question, no place that would be suitable for using this mode is found at Nablous. Yet "they were being baptized" without the least difficulty. Jesus had sown the seed at Sychar in Samaria, Philip was reaping the great harvest (John 4:37, 38). Simon's hold on the people was entirely broken.

13) Moreover, Simon himself also came to believe and, on having been baptized, continued to hold to Philip; and beholding that signs and works of power kept occurring, he was amazed.

He who had amazed others by his magical arts and claims was now himself kept in a state of amazement (imperfect tense) by what he kept seeing (present participle), the miracles that kept occurring (again a present participle, here in the construction after a verb of seeing). Luke does not use the usual expression "signs and wonders" but writes "signs and power works" as emphasizing what Simon saw in the miracles: their significance and their power. On the basis of what is related later it is usually assumed that Simon's faith was only a sham, but Luke uses the same verb and the same tense with reference to him as he does with reference to the people; he even adds that Simon remained in close attachment to Philip. The man did believe. The fact that he later went wrong, and that his young faith was perverted and lost, is something that followed. All that Luke intimates regarding this outcome is the fact that Simon was too much captivated by the miracles he saw. The probability is that he came to regard them as being in the same class with his own magical arts but far superior to what he had been able to produce.

It is unwarranted to claim that in the case of Simon's baptism we have "clear proof that baptism does not convey salvation." The Baptist taught and practiced the baptism of repentance and remission of sins. The 3,000 were told to be baptized "for the remission of sins." Paul's sins were washed away by his being baptized (22:16). Baptism is "the washing of regeneration and renewing of the Holy Spirit" (Tit. 3:5). Baptism is what it is irrespective of its recipient. A gold piece that is treated as being worthless is no less a gold piece. The only deduction that can be legitimately made on the assumption that Simon had only a sham faith at the time of his baptism is that baptism does not work mechanically, as an *opus operatum*, which means that the saving grace it conveys must be apprehended by the heart. The fact that a man does not appropriate something is not a proof that there was nothing to appropriate.

14) It must have been some time after Philip had begun his work and not until his success attained the proportions recorded by Luke that the apostles came to Samaria. **Now, when the apostles in Jerusalem heard that Samaria had received the Word of God, they commissioned to them Peter and John who, having come down, prayed regarding them that they might receive the Holy Spirit; for as yet he had not fallen on anyone' of them, and they had been baptized only in the name of the Lord Jesus. Then they began to lay their hands on them, and they began to receive the Holy Spirit.**

Since the congregation at Jerusalem had been scattered far and wide, the good news that came from Samaria must have brought joy to the apostles who had remained in the city (v. 1). We see nothing hierarchical in their action of sending two of their number to Nablous to Philip to review this new increase of believers.

It is not hyperbole when Luke writes "that Samaria has received the Word" (the tense of the direct discourse being retained), for this does not mean "all

Samaria" but Samaritans as distinct from Jews; note 1:8. The Word was advancing from Jewish into Samaritan territory — a most significant progress. Since the return from Babylonia a gulf had existed between these two peoples and, lo, it was now being bridged by the Word of Christ. And this was being done, not by an apostle, but by one of the former deacons. That certainly concerned the apostles, and they sent the two most important individuals of their number to Philip. The idea to be conveyed is that all the believers constitute one body whether they were formerly Jews or formerly Samaritans. This oneness is expressed by the mission of Peter and of John.

15) Their mere visit to Nablous would, however, have meant too little; that would have made manifest no more than outward oneness between the old and the new wing of the church. On their arrival Peter and John, therefore, prayed for the Samaritan believers in order ($ὅπως$, purpose) that they might receive the Holy Spirit. For it is this Spirit who makes the church one. When he dwells in all believers through the Word and faith, they are all made one spiritual body with Christ as the head and with his apostles as his chief ministrants of the Word.

16) The reason for their prayer is explained by the $γάρ$ clause: the Spirit had not yet fallen upon any of the Samaritan believers (periphrastic pluperfect). The very expression indicates that the charismatic gift of the Spirit is being referred to, which comes in a miraculous way and is apparent to all who might be present. "Had fallen" recalls what had happened at the time of Pentecost. The Samaritan believers had not yet been distinguished by this sign of the Spirit's presence; it had been delayed until this time.

"They had been baptized only," etc. The periphrastic pluperfect with $ὑπῆρχον$ instead of $ἦσαν$, R. 1121, is used, but this by no means intends to say that at this time these Samaritans had received no more than baptism from the Holy Spirit or, as some would say, baptism as a mere symbol so that through the apostles they were now to receive the Spirit himself. They had been baptized as believers, they had received Word and sacrament and all that Word and sacrament bestow, the Holy Spirit in their hearts, and thus regeneration, conversion, justification, the power of a new life, in a word, salvation. They had received the supreme gifts of the Spirit "only," but these are invisible. Baptism was the one gift that was also an outward mark of their having the Spirit.

Still other marks were to be granted them, seals and signs that they were true members of the spiritual body that is created by the Spirit. These were the charismata of the Spirit, those gifts which the Spirit distributes freely in the church (I Cor. 12:7-13). In these earliest days of the church's history he distributed them miraculously, most wonderfully at Pentecost in the speaking with tongues, after that in a less wonderful way here at Nablous; then in 10:44-48 (11:15), in 19:6, and in the congregation at Corinth.

17) So this manifestation of the Spirit was now bestowed upon the Samaritan believers. As was the case in 19:7, this was done through the laying on of hands; see 6:6 for this symbolic rite. On Pentecost, in the case of Cornelius, and in Corinth, the Spirit did not make use of such a rite. Here and in 19:7 its purpose is apparent: the Spirit uses the chosen apostles of Jesus in order to unite all his believers into one spiritual body and to make this apparent. Not two or more churches were to be established: one that was Jewish, another that was Samaritan, others that were Gentile; no, only one, in which all believers were to be on the same level. In order to get the full import

of this fact we must project ourselves backward into those days when Jew, Samaritan, Greek Gentile, barbarian Gentile were as widely separated from each other as the poles. The Spirit had his mighty reason for waiting until the arrival of the apostles before bestowing his charisma in Samaria.

In order to avoid wrong deductions, let us note that none of the 3,000 new believers at the time of Pentecost received the gift of tongues but only the 120 whom Jesus himself had long ago brought to faith; in 10:44-48 the new believers received this gift. After Pentecost, as the church grew by leaps and bounds, speaking with tongues did not occur, but at a far later time this gift reappeared in the congregation in Corinth. It was exactly as Paul states in I Cor. 12:11.

No charismatic gift was bestowed in connection with the baptism administered by the apostles — remember Pentecost;. the baptism of Philip lacked nothing which the apostles had to add. The Spirit's manifestations at the time of Pentecost, here in Samaria, and then in Caesarea had their own special purpose, and this by no means concerned just those who received gifts miraculously but extended far beyond them. As to far more necessary and valuable charismata that were bestowed unobtrusively, note Stephen (6:10) and note Paul's estimate and advice (I Cor. 14:1). Only by strange processes of reasoning could the older view arise that in the coming of Peter and of John to the Samaritans lies support for the rite of confirmation as a sacrament of the church (Cyprian, *Epistle* 73).

18) **Now, when Simon saw that through the laying on of the hands of the apostles the Holy Spirit was being given, he offered them money, saying, Give also to me this power, that on whom I lay the hands he may receive the Holy Spirit.**

When Peter and John came to Nablous, a gathering of all the believers was probably held, and the apostles laid hands on some of them, and these began to speak with tongues. It was this that Simon saw and that made him desire to possess the same ability he thought the apostles had. When it is said that those speaking with tongues were transported into "ecstasy," this is without the support of any passage dealing with this gift. It is likewise exaggeration to suppose that every believer had hands laid on him, and that all spoke with tongues. This view misunderstands the purpose of this manifestation. What was done in the case of some counted for all; this was not a matter that pertained to individuals but to this entire body of Samaritan believers and to all others who might yet come to faith. This manifestation happened once, and that was all. Its significance as a sign for all believing Samaritans was thus established and needed no repetition.

19) Simon was still bound by his ideas about magical acts and thus rated what he saw the apostles doing as something of the same order but grander than anything he himself had been able to do. He had paid out money to learn his feats of conjury and so made bold to offer money to Peter and to John in order that they might teach him how to perform this new and astonishing feat. When estimating the import of this offer the fact is often overlooked that Philip had already been working many signs even on demoniacs and paralytics, and that Simon, nevertheless, had made no attempt to acquire this power. This makes his present offer appear like a relapse into his old life and ways. He believed and was baptized (v. 13) but now fell back into his love for occult arts. The worst feature about this relapse was the fact that he regarded the Holy Spirit as being merely some sort of mysterious effect that could be brought about by

one who understood the secret art. Any derogation of the Holy Spirit is dangerous in the extreme as we see in the case of Ananias and Sapphira (5:3, 9). Simon's offer of money eventually coined the term "simony" as a designation for the purchase of church offices and the revenues connected with them.

20) Was Simon planning to return to his old life by adding this new art to his old ones? He was certainly severely reprimanded by Peter. **But Peter said to him: Thy silver be with thee in perdition because thou didst suppose to acquire the gift of God through money! There is not for thee part or lot in this matter; for thy heart is not straight before God. Repent, therefore, of this thy baseness and beg the Lord if, perhaps, the project of thy heart will be remitted for thee. For I see that thou art in gall of bitterness and bond of iniquity.**

The optative of wish εἴη is construed with static εἰς and = "May thou and thy silver be in perdition!" This is an imprecatory wish. This wish is really a judgment and one that is fully justified, since any man who has the idea that money may purchase the powers of the Spirit is on the verge of committing blasphemy against the Spirit and should, therefore, be damned. Ἀπώλεια, "destruction," is regarded as annihilation by those who wish to abolish hell from the Scriptures, whereas its Biblical meaning is the complete ruin of the sinner in the loss of salvation and life and in the doom of eternal death. "Thy silver with thee," the means of the sin together with the sinner. The use to which we put our money stamps our character upon it.

This judgment of imprecation is at once substantiated, ὅτι, "because." This former conjurer imagined that he could acquire the gift of God through money. Peter says nothing about the insult Simon offered him by the proffer of money in such a deal; he at once points out the worst feature the insult offered to God by imagining that *his gift* was like a conjurer's trick that could be *bought with money*. "The gift" is really generic, for anything that constitutes such a gift is referred to. Here the Holy Spirit is himself the gift; for only one filled with the Spirit would be used by him to convey such spiritual gifts by the laying on of the apostles' hands. Peter is opening the eyes of Simon to the damnableness of his proposition.

We should note that Simon's story is told so fully because it is a parallel to that of Ananias and Sapphira. Both stand out in the first church as glaring examples of the frightful attempt by means of money to obtain what can be obtained only by God's grace. So men still think they can buy honor in God's kingdom, yea, salvation itself, by means of money contributions to some church cause, whether they acknowledge their secret intent or not.

21) "There is not part or lot for thee" = thou hast neither part not lot, the two terms emphasizing the same idea, namely that Simon has completely excluded himself from any participation "in this matter." This meaning of λόγος, the matter under discussion, is well established. But we must not narrow its sense in this statement to the transmission of the Spirit by the bestowal of a spiritual gift. "This matter" includes everything connected with the Spirit and his gifts. Simon was unfit to receive even the gift that so many Samaritans were freely receiving. We must note that he had not knelt down with them to have hands laid on his head so that he, like others, might speak with tongues. He had only stood by and conceived his vicious project of purchase. It was thus that he completely excluded himself from all contact with the Spirit.

This answers the objection that is based on too narrow a view and makes "this matter" refer only to the

330 Interpretation of the Acts of the Apostles

laying on of hands for bestowing the gift of tongues. Those who see that this view is too narrow and that it does not fit the context offer an unsatisfactory remedy by letting λόγος mean "this Word and gospel of Christ" by appealing to the use of "Word" in v. 14 and 25, and also to the context, that Simon's heart is not straight before God. Yet the context does not deal with the gospel Word, its preaching (v. 25) and its reception when preached (v. 14). All is clear and the context fully satisfied when "this *logos*" is taken to refer to this entire matter of receiving anything from, or transmitting anything as an agent of, the Holy Spirit.

From that Simon completely excluded himself in that his heart was no longer "straight," sincere, honest, true, in God's sight. "Heart" is always the center of the personality with all that characterizes it in mind and in will. It is thus that God always looks at our hearts and sees our inmost character. We are unable to judge the heart, and there is no worse vice in the church than what the Germans call *Herzensrichterei*, presuming to judge other men's hearts. Peter was not doing that, for Simon himself had fully revealed the crookedness of his heart, and Peter was judging him on the basis of that revelation.

So we may judge men on the basis of their clear and undeniable actions. Often a pretense of doing no more than that is made when evil motives are attributed to fellow men in attempts to injure them. Then our own hearts are no longer "straight before God." Then we pretend to see a splinter ("mote" is incorrect) in our fellow man's eye the while we carry a beam or plank in our own eye. In the case of Ananias and Sapphira, Peter acted under special revelation from the Spirit, which makes that case entirely exceptional.

22) Simon is shown how he appears in God's eyes. At the same time he is told what to do in order to be restored. He is to repent from this baseness; see this verb in 2:38, and not that it is here used in its narrower sense: true contrition and sorrow of the heart for sin. It is thus construed with the sin from which Simon is to repent and turn, and he is told to seek remission for that sin. Peter rightly calls it "this baseness," κακία, which is not the same as "wickedness" (our versions), the word for that is πονηρία. While the two terms are synonymous, the former is milder, it is the German *Schlechtigkeit*, the opposite of ἀρετή or excellence (C.-K. 558), while the latter is active, vicious wickedness. The idea expressed is that of loss as in good-for-nothingness, here with reference to a spiritual condition that has become spoiled, bad, depraved.

This contriteness is to be combined with the humble, begging prayer for the divine remission of the sin and guilt involved in his ἐπίνοια, the thing that has come upon his mind, his frightful "project." Peter's two aorist imperatives are intended to make Simon see the urgency of Peter's commands. By using δέομαι Peter bids Simon throw himself at the Lord's feet as a beggar; and the εἰ with the indicative expresses expectation (B.-D. 375) which is in this case lessened by the addition of ἄρα: "if, perchance, he will," etc. The implication of this conditional form is not regarding the Lord's willingness to remit but in regard to Simon's contrition and begging as being necessary for enabling the Lord to extend remission. Unless Simon's heart changes, he himself will prevent the Lord's remission. Therefore, too, Peter says, "the project of thy heart," for the seat of this sin is in Simon's heart, and the Lord will see his very heart, and no outward contrite begging will deceive him. In "shall be remitted," literally, "shall be sent away," we have the Biblical term for freeing the sinner from his sin and his guilt; see the explanation of the noun ἄφεσις in 2:38.

23) The γάρ explains to Simon how serious is his condition. His "project" betrays the terrible condition existing in his heart. Peter sees Simon "in gall of bitterness and bond of iniquity," for that is what his project reveals concerning himself. His entire person is concerned; the construction ὁρῶ σε ὄντα is classical, and εἰς is static, "in," not "into," R. 593. Both genitives are appositional: gall that is bitterness, and bondage that is iniquity, the absence of the articles stressing the force of the nouns themselves. On "bitterness" compare Heb. 12:15. The entire expression describes Simon's spiritual state. Bitterness, however, does not refer to "bitter enmity" on Simon's part, not to embitterment and "bitter anger" against the apostles or the Lord. The latter idea has influenced the interpretation of the next verse. As in Heb. 12:15 the "root of bitterness" means a root out of which bitter fruit grows, fruit which the Lord abominates, so here "gall of bitterness" is that fruit. The Lord will not taste it and must cast it away. The next expression is more literal and helps to explain the former: Simon's iniquity is a bond that firmly holds him, wrapped, as it is, all about him.

24) **But, answering, Simon said, Do you yourselves beg in my behalf of the Lord that nothing may come upon me of the things you have mentioned!**

A few texts add the statement that he continued weeping greatly: ὃς πολλὰ κλαίων οὐ διελίμπανεν. Is there anything wrong about this answer? Yet, just about everything about it has been found wrong. Why? Because of the later tradition which presents Simon as the father of heresies, the founder of the first heretical sect, a man who deified himself. Instead of interpreting Luke's words as they stand, they are interpreted in conformity with this tradition, and the matter settled in advance: Simon could not have repented, he did not repent, and all that Luke states is made to conform to this view. What is wrong in his asking for apostolic intercession? If some other sinner had done the same, the commentators would praise him; but Simon is accused of merely referring Peter's command back to him: You apostles go and beg of the Lord if there is begging to do! This is not fair to Simon. Simon asks for the apostlic intercession in his behalf as one who first of all earnestly prays for himself.

Then his desire to escape the things about which the apostles have warned him is regarded proof positive that Simon did not repent and desired only to escape the apostles' threats. No account is taken of the fact that Simon had just recently been brought to faith; in fact, although in v. 13 Luke writes, "he himself came to believe," this plain assertion is interpreted to mean that he only pretended to believe. It is not to the credit of some exegetes that they allow later tradition not only to modify but to reverse the words of the inspired text.

As to fear, shall we forget the warning Jesus himself gave about being cast into hell, Matt. 5:22, 29, 30; 10:28; 18:9? If it was wrong for Simon to fear as he did, was it right for Peter to threaten him as he did? Luke, moreover, leaves Simon at this point as he is pleading for the apostolic intercession. Could he do that if he intended his readers to understand that Simon failed to repent? He could not! Luke's words permit only one interpretation, namely that Simon did repent, that Peter's strong words were not in vain.

Yet Luke's leaving Simon with this petition on his lips has been thought to imply that Simon continued in his evil ways, and that the only reason Luke does not say as much is that he intended to write a third book in which he intended to tell us more about Simon and his wicked heresies. It is certain that Luke intends to say that Simon repented. The next verse corroborates this fact. *If* this is the same Simon who afterward introduced the first heresies, Luke intimates it in no way. All that Zahn, for instance, reports of the later tradition, as he himself admits, is invention, much of it based on Simon's magical arts. It seems as though his former practice of magic is the basis for the traditional connection of *his* name with those old heresies and fictions. And Luke is not responsible for these views.

25) They, therefore, after testifying and uttering the Word of the Lord, began to return to Jerusalem and were proclaiming the good news to many villages of the Samaritans.

In regard to Luke's favorite "they, therefore," see 1:6. We should note that both aorist participles fit the idea that the Word was altogether that of the Lord, and that the apostles merely uttered it as being his. With this they supported all that Philip had done and did all they could to strengthen the faith of the Samaritan believers. Then, as the imperfect states, they began their return to Jerusalem, left the whole work in Philip's hands, and thus acknowledged his competence. It was still their place to be in Jerusalem. But they proceeded slowly and evidently traveled about here and there and thus "evangelized many villages of the Samaritans" (the verb is here used with the accusative of the persons). Peter and John thus helped materially in winning Samaria for the gospel.

The Ethiopian Eunuch

26) Only one man is concerned in this account, but his conversion is of the utmost importance for the early history of the church, hence the space devoted to him by Luke and the place assigned to this account, being introduced between the conversions in Samaria and the conversion of the apostle to the Gentiles. The unnamed Ethiopian eunuch is *the first Gentile* converted to the Christian faith. He was, indeed, not a pagan but a proselyte of the gate and thus, however, still regarded as a Gentile by all Jews. It is by the Lord's own direction that the gospel is thus beginning to reach out into the great Gentile world; and it is the evangelist Philip who is distinguished as the man who, besides opening up Samaria to the gospel, brought in also the first Gentile convert. Through him the gospel first entered Africa, and that not in lower Egypt among the many Jews in Alexandria, etc., but in the more distant interior land of the Ethiopians who were a type of Negroes.

Now an angel of the Lord spoke to Philip, saying, Arise and be going toward the south on the road that goes down from Jerusalem to Gaza; this is desert. And having arisen, he went.

It is decidedly noteworthy that the Lord employed the service of angels for bringing the first Gentiles into his kingdom, here the Ethiopian eunuch, and in chapter 10 Cornelius, the centurion of the Italian cohort. We have no details about the appearance of the angel to Philip; only the great fact that this heavenly messenger gave directions to Philip, who promptly obeyed them, is recorded. "Arise" simply means that Philip is to make ready for his long journey; compare 5:17. "Be going" is the durative present imperative to indicate an act that will take some time. When the persecution broke out in Jerusalem, Philip had gone north to the Samaritans; he is not to continue in that direction but is to return to Jerusalem and from there to go "toward noon," i. e., southward, in an altogether unexpected direction. The Lord does not call one of his apostles in Jerusalem. He chooses his own instrument for the task he himself maps out. Philip is to take the road that goes down from Jerusalem to Gaza, the old Philistine city on the coast. The data regarding this city need not occupy us as it is mentioned only to designate the road that Philip is to take.

The remark, "this is desert," refers to the road. While the feminine demonstrative might refer to Gaza, a remark about its condition would be irrelevant since Philip was not to go to Gaza, nor was the city ἔρημος at this time. The angel designates which one of the roads Philip is to take: not the one that leads through the more populous sections of the country but the one that leads through the rather uninhabited parts. We are unable to determine which road this was. Any road would pass through uninhabited territory after leaving the hills; and we do not know how far toward Gaza Philip had to go. The claim that this clause is not a part of the angel's directions but only a remark made by Luke, leaves Philip to conjecture which road to take and has Luke write as though there was only one road and that one desert.

The fact that Philip is thus shown just where to go is plain, but we cannot see the force of the objection which denies that the eunuch chose this road, chose it because it permitted him to be more undisturbed in his study of the Scripture roll he had recently acquired. On this road Philip, too, encountered no interruption in dealing with the eunuch.

But why did the Lord not send the angel to instruct and to baptize the eunuch and leave Philip in his successful work in Samaria? We have an answer to this question. The Lord bestowed the office of the ministry upon men and not upon angels, and we find that the Lord in every case makes use of the men he has called and honors their office and their work accordingly. So Philip is off on his long journey afoot; the time and the effort spent in winning the eunuch are not too great.

27) **And lo, a man, an Ethiopian, a eunuch, a lord under Candace, queen of the Ethiopians, who was over all her treasure, who had come to Jerusalem in order to worship; and he was returning and sitting on his chariot and was engaged in reading the prophet Isaiah.**

Luke may well utter an exclamation at the thought of the man Philip found travelling on this lonesome road. He merely reproduces the astonishment that Philip himself must have felt. Luke immediately records all the details although some of them Philip did not learn until a little later when he conversed with the man. He was an Ethiopian, a black man! Αἰθίοψ, from αἴθω, "to burn," and ὤψ, "countenance," points to race and nationality and not merely to residence. Thus the idea of his being a Jew who had risen to great power in Ethiopia is at once excluded. In fact, the entire narrative points to the fact that this man was a Gentile. Philip's first glance at the man put him face to face with the question of receiving Gentiles into the church. The apostles had not as yet encountered the question: "On what terms and in what manner are Gentiles to be received?" Yet in this case Philip was relieved of hesitation or difficulty. The Lord had sent him through the word of an angel and was even now directing him.

This man was a eunuch, which must be taken in the literal and not in the official sense, since his official position is described in the following. We learn only the fact and not how he became a eunuch. Yet he was a δυνάστης, a man of authority and power, "a lord." We translate the Greek genitive "of Candace" with the idea "under" this queen of the Ethiopians. This intermediate title is explained by the relative clause which states that this man was the royal treasurer, γάζα being a Persian word for "treasure" which is used in both the Greek and the Latin (γαζοφυλάκιον, "treasury," a place where the treasure is kept, Mark 12:41 and elsewhere).

In Ethiopia the royal descent was by way of the mother. The queen mother transmitted the inheritance to her son but herself exercised the rule, and though the son was regarded as king and given divine honors, he was confined to the palace while his mother reigned. In the year 25-21 B. C. a one-eyed Candace fought the Romans and saved her kingdom by a favorable peace.

"Candace" is only a title like Pharaoh, Sultan, Czar, etc. The history of missions has made this title famous. In 1853 Pastor Louis Harms, of Hermannsburg in Hannover, Germany, a small inland town, had a vessel built with funds he collected, and sent the first missionaries he had prepared to their destination in Africa. He called the vessel *The Candace*. This missionary enterprise was highly successful and stands out as one of the great monuments of faith in the history of modern mission endeavor.

The kingdom of the Ethiopians was not Abyssinia, the old kingdom of Aksum (Axum), but a domain whose boundaries shifted at times. It began at Assuan on the Nile and extended beyond Chartum and since the eighth century B. C. was known as "Ethiopia" to the ancients. It was inhabited, not by semitic, but by hamitic, Negro-like tribes. This powerful kingdom had two great royal cities: Meroë on the island in the Nile by the same name, and one farther down on the river Napata.

When Luke adds that the eunuch had come to Jerusalem to worship (future participle, denoting purpose, R. 1128) he informs us that this Gentile was a proselyte of the gate. In 2:10 we read about proselytes of righteousness; these had become completely Jewish and had really been absorbed into Judaism and had lost their character as Gentiles. No eunuch could be more than a proselyte of the gate, since because of his mutilation he was debarred from entering the inner Temple courts (Deut. 23:1). Yet read the great and special promises of the Lord to godly eunuchs as recorded in Isa. 56:4, 5. These second-class proselytes, who were exceedingly numerous in the Jewish diaspora, did not submit to circumcision and were bound only to the so-called Noachian commandments (Gen. 9:4-6) against idolatry, blasphemy, disobedience to magistrates, murder, fornication or incest, robbery or theft, and eating of blood. They were quite generally open to the gospel and received it with great readiness; in the New Testament they are designated as σεβόμενοι or φοβούμενοι τὸν Θεόν.

Recently discovered papyri, dating from the fourth and the fifth centuries B. C., mention a Jewish military colony that was at first under Pharaonic, then under Persian, later under Ptolomaic, and finally under Roman jurisdiction. It was located at Syene and the island Elephantine which were close to the boundary of Ethiopia. By way of business and financial contacts the treasurer of the queen could easily come into contact with these and perhaps also with other Jews.

The sincerity and the devotion of this proselyte are evident when we note that he undertook a journey of some 200 miles that was difficult at best and not without danger in order to visit Jerusalem and the Temple although he was debarred from entering beyond the court of the Gentiles. He is after a fashion the counterpart to the Queen of Sheba who came from southern Arabia on a similar long journey. Tradition reports his name as Indich or Judich.

28) Verse 27 is minus a verb and is to be regarded as an exclamation — such a man is awaiting Philip! On his return homeward after his visit in the holy city he is riding in his chariot with his driver, absorbed in reading a newly acquired parchment roll of the prophet Isaiah. The imperfect tenses picture him as Philip saw him. He might have chosen a more interesting road homeward. It is fair to conclude that he chose this lonely road in order to read the roll which he had recently acquired and was now eager to study and to absorb. It was surely the Lord's providence that had placed Isaiah, the evangelist of the Old Testament, into this devoted proselyte's hand and had led him to turn to the very choicest part of the book of this prophet at the time of Philip's approach. God had prepared this pupil for his new teacher. He was reading aloud, perhaps with some difficulty, for the ancient manuscripts did not write the words separately, had no punctuation, no breathings, and no accents. His copy must have been made from the Greek LXX, and Philip conversed with him in Greek, the language everywhere current.

29) **Now the Spirit said to Philip, Go to him and attach thyself to this chariot. And having run to him, Philip heard him reading Isaiah, the prophet, and said, Dost thou understand what thou art reading? And he said, How, then, could I unless one shall guide me? And he besought Philip to come up and sit with him.**

The Spirit never has difficulty in communicating with a person so that the latter knows from whom the communication comes. All *ifs* and *buts* are removed for Philip in regard to the important personage who is evidently a Negro, riding in his stately chariot. To Philip the Spirit speaks and not to the eunuch when the way of salvation was to be expounded to the latter. "Therefore we ought and must constantly maintain this point, that God does not wish to deal with us otherwise than through the spoken Word and the Sacraments." C. Tr. 497, 10. In the preaching of the gospel God adheres to the means and to the office he himself has given us; dreams, visions, voices, and the like he may use for other purposes but not for this one. We may translate the aorist passive imperative, "be joined," or as a middle, "join thyself."

30) The chariot seems to have been moving slowly ahead of Philip so that by hastening his steps he soon came to walk beside it. It is rather farfetched when R., W. P., says that "probably Philip jumped on the running board on the chariot." Walking thus, without intruding, Philip heard the man reading from Isaiah and, perhaps as the man paused and looked up, Philip asked the question whether he understood what he was reading. The ἄρα is a word of interrogation, γε is strengthening and lends a touch of doubt.

31) The eunuch not only acknowledges his inability but states that he needs a guide. The sentence is a mixed condition: in the apodosis it has the optative with ἄν (potentiality): "How then could I"; in the protasis ἐάν (= εἰ) with the future indicative (reality): "unless one shall guide me," and γάρ is added like the German *denn* (B. D. 452, 1) so that the force is: "No, for how could I," etc. And promptly the eunuch beseeches Philip (the verb is strong) that "having come up (into the chariot), he sit with him," to guide and to instruct him. All three aorists, verb, participle, infinitive, imply that the request was granted (B.-D. 328); a verb in the imperfect would imply that something else followed.

32) **Now the section of the Scripture he was reading was this:**

**As a sheep to the slaughter he was led;
And as a lamb before the one shearing him is dumb**

So he opens not his mouth.
In the humiliation his judgment was taken away.
His generation who shall recount?
Because taken from the earth is his life.

The passage that caused the eunuch difficulty was Isa. 53:7, 8, which Luke records for his reader from the LXX. The chief variation from the Hebrew is in the fourth and in the last lines:

"He was taken from prison and from judgment;
. . .

For he was cut off out of the land of the living."
A glance at the text shows that even these are but variations in form and not in thought. Both Delitzsch and Aug. Pieper (*Jesaias II*), each in his own way, vary from the translations found in our Old Testament according as they read the Hebrew and construe the last line. These intricacies need not detain us; for the eunuch had no difficulty in reading the words and the sentences in his LXX copy of Isaiah, his difficulty was vastly greater, namely what the prophet really meant by this entire section.

For ourselves we note cursorily that Isaiah is depicting the great '*Ebed Yahweh*, τὸν παῖδα τοῦ Θεοῦ Ἰησοῦν, "the Servant of God, Jesus," (Acts 3:13, 26; 4:27, 30) in his suffering and his death. Patiently, silently, without resisting, the great Servant of Jehovah, "was led as a sheep to the slaughter." Pieper: "Maltreated was he; but he — he bowed himself." His silent submission is emphasized: "And as a lamb," etc. Delitzsch and Pieper translate the Hebrew in the same way.

33) "In his humiliation his judgment was taken away," the judgment executed upon him as our substitute. He rendered full satisfaction and atonement; all claims were satisfied. Delitzsch translates the line

Acts 8:33 343

as it is found in our Old Testament (see above); but Pieper lets the Hebrew preposition *min* mean, not what it usually does, "from" but "by means of." He does this for internal reasons, but his reason is by no means satisfactory. The rendering of the LXX which the eunuch had is thus substantially correct.

There is disagreement in regard to the next line: "His generation who shall recount?" In both Isaiah and here in Acts the sense is that the suffering and dying Servant of Jehovah shall have a vast progeny, a generation (the word is used in an ethical sense, as a designation of those who become his own by faith), *dor*, γενεά, that no one can number. Delitzsch: "And among his cotemporaries who considered: Torn away was he out of the land of the living"; Pieper: "And as to his generation — who mourned, that he was torn," etc. Those internal reasons again obtrude themselves: the idea that Isaiah could not speak of Christ's deliverance and the fruit of his death so early, namely ahead of a narration of his death. Why could he not? Especially since he is writing poetry? The moment we remember this, the matter is cleared up.

The Hebrew verb is *siach*, German *sinnen* (Delitzsch, *bedenken*; not Pieper's *beklagen*), LXX διηγέομαι. And in the Hebrew as well as in the Greek the accusative "his generation" is the object of this verb. Why must we read it adverbially, "as to his generation" (Pieper), or "among his cotemporaries" (Delitzsch)? The same is true in regard to the next line. Why must *ki* be "that," recitative or otherwise? Why not leave it "because"? And so we are in the clear. This *dor* or generation is not the contemporary Jewish nation. Why let it deal so prominently with what it failed to consider or lament? The prophet says: "His generation who considered?" and then states why the question is asked: "Because taken from the earth was his life." Taken from the earth, how could he have a generation? Yet behold, what a vast generation is his, all these believers in all the ages! And the LXX is about correct: "Who shall declare, recount, set out in detail his generation?"

34) Wonderful these words of the prophet! So and yet a mystery! **And answering, the eunuch said to Philip, I beg thee, concerning whom does the prophet say this? concerning himself or concerning someone else?**

The Greek "answering" is often used in a wider sense with regard to any statement that meets a situation. The eunuch had, indeed, struck the heart of the matter. Who was this wonderful person of whom the prophet was speaking? Could it be the prophet Isaiah himself? Was he not an *'ebed* of Jehovah, might he be *this* "Servant"? The difficulty the eunuch had was this, that the prophet did not seem to meet the requirements of this passage and yet he could think of no other person to whom they might be properly applied. To be sure, the eunuch had not heard the modern Jewish answer that the Jews themselves are this wonderful "Servant of Jehovah," their nation that has suffered so much is the Messiah!

We are unable to say how much the eunuch had heard about Jesus while he was in Jerusalem; yet his prompt acceptance of Philip's interpretation would indicate that he had learned much of the story of Jesus and needed only to have the prophecies of the Old Testament properly connected with what he had heard in order to bring him to the Christian faith. This, too, explains the readiness with which Philip proceeded to baptize him.

35) **And Philip, having opened his mouth and having begun at this Scripture, proclaimed as good news to him Jesus.**

Acts 8:35, 36

The circumstantial phrase about opening his mouth intends to mark the importance of Philip's words. He began with this prophecy of Isaiah, referred to other prophecies much as Jesus once did (Luke 24:27, 45), and so preached the whole blessed gospel of salvation in Jesus' name. "What flowed from the preacher's lips concerning the Word of life, how he preached of the Crucified One in words ever more fiery and enthusiastic, and what transpired in the soul of the hearer, how his heart burned within him, how the scales fell from his eyes, how light upon light illumined him, how, perhaps, tear upon tear rolled down his cheek, all this the record does not describe, words cannot reproduce it properly. Enough, there must have been another upon the chariot, the Holy Spirit, who opened the mouth of Philip and the heart of the treasurer; and the result was that this apt pupil of the gospel could exclaim:

'Now I have found the firm foundation,
Where evermore my anchor grounds!'

Oh, that this might be the result of all our preaching and hearing, Bible reading and explanation, meditation and praying, the knowledge and ever-firmer conviction: Jesus is the Messiah as the prophet promised, as this sinful world needs him!" Gerok.

36) Now as they were going along the road they came to some water. And the eunuch says: Lo, water! What hinders me to be baptized? And he ordered the chariot to stop; and they both went down to the water, both Philip and the eunuch; and he baptized him.

No trace of a stream or a lake is found in this region, nor of a record of such water. The problem is not where to find enough water for immersion but where to find water at all. Robinson suggests the *Wady-el-Hasy* between Eleutheropolis and Gaza, not far from the old sites of Lachish and Eglom. The difficulty in regard to the water is not removed by supposing that Philip did not go from Samaria to Jerusalem and from there take a road toward Gaza but took some road directly from Samaria. This contradicts v. 26, which binds Philip to some road that led from Jerusalem to Gaza. Philip must have expounded baptism to the eunuch. It is thus that he exclaims, "Lo, water!" with a happy ring in his voice. When asks about a hindrance to his being baptized he intends to indicate that he knows of none but leaves it to the fuller knowledge of his teacher as to whether his supposition is correct.

37) The textual evidence for this verse (see A. V.) is too slight to admit it into the text. It states what may well have transpired. The objection is textual only, and remarks such as that the words sound like some pedantic preacher asking his convert for a final, formal confession are unwarranted. A confession of Jesus as the Christ was always a prerequisite for baptism.

38) Philip consents. The eunuch orders his driver to halt the chariot, and Philip and the eunuch go down to the water, and the baptism takes place. The subject is made certain: "both Philip and the eunuch," because the eunuch had ordered his driver to halt the chariot, and this man was not concerned in the matter of the baptism. Καὶ ἐβάπτισεν αὐτόν includes the entire baptismal act: "and he did baptize him," all that preceded and that followed was not a part of this sacramental act. The reader is referred to the discussion on baptism in 2:38, 41.

Eusebius reports about a small pool that was formed by a spring near the road, Robinson speaks of a small temporary stream. Neither here nor elsewhere do we read that a robe or garment was laid aside before baptism. We are left to suppose that the two men went to this water, and that the baptismal act was an application of water by pouring or by sprinkling. Those who make the words "they both went down εἰς, into, the water" a part of the baptismal act in order to obtain immersion by means of εἰς τὸ ὕδωρ, "into the water," prove too much: Philip went down under the water as well as the eunuch. This is true also in regard to the following words.

39) But when they came up from the water, the Lord's Spirit snatched Philip away, and the eunuch saw him no more, for he proceeded to go his way rejoicing. Philip, however, was found at Azotus; and, passing through, he proclaimed the good news to all the cities until he came to Caesarea.

We may translate, "they went *down into the water*" (v. 38), and now, "they came *up out of the water*," and may with R., W. P. even emphasize: "Not from the edge of the water, but up out of the water"! The difficulty lies in ἀμφότεροι, "both," Luke even adding: "both Philip and the eunuch." To be sure, εἰς and ἐκ are correlatives: as far as the one takes "into," so far the other takes "out of." But these prepositions apply to "both Philip and the eunuch." Take your choice: *to* the water, *from* the water; or stepping *into* and again stepping *out of* the water; or *down under* the water and again *up from under* the water. Total immersion if you prefer, but for *both*. Not we but Luke combined them.

If Philip was merely induced to say good-by and to tear himself away, Luke chose a strange way in which to tell us this. Πνεῦμα Κυρίου is an unusual expression, yet it conveys the idea that both the Spirit and the Lord (Jesus) removed Philip and did it suddenly and miraculously. All at once he was gone, "and the eunuch saw him no more." I Kings 18:12; II Kings 2:16. Nor is γάρ strange. It explains that the eunuch simply went on his way "rejoicing" and did not try to find Philip by changing his journey and seeking until he located him.

Here this eunuch passes from our view. He had much, he would desire more. In his position and with his means he could secure all else. We have all almost without effort, yet do we always appreciate it and rejoice? Tradition makes the eunuch an evangelist in Ethiopia who soon baptized the queen, etc. We know only that Christian missionaries reached the Ethiopians 300 years later.

40) In one instant Philip was walking beside the eunuch, in the next he was found in Azotus (Asdod), many miles away. To be sure, "he was found" means that people found him there; but this also means that the place where he was found just before this was on the road with the eunuch. "He was found" does not mean that Philip walked away from the eunuch and wandered about until he turned up at Azotus. Luke does not intend to carry on the story of Philip which he evidently knows in all its interesting details. So he states summarily that Philip evangelized the coast towns beginning with Azotus and terminating at Caesarea where he then made his home. We take it that he worked in Ekron, Rama, Joppa, and elsewhere in the plain of Sharon. We have ἕως used as a preposition, the genitive of the infinitive as its object.

CHAPTER IX

Saul's Conversion

Luke takes up the thread of his narrative which he broke off at 8:3. The importance of Saul's conversion is made prominent in Acts. It was very dramatic, and its effects were most far-reaching. As a conversion it clearly brings out the essentials of every Christian conversion: Saul's contrition and his faith. As a particular conversion it has its individual and exceptional features as has every other conversion, features that cannot be duplicated. These points must be borne in mind, both in order to understand Saul's conversion and in order to avoid false deductions concerning other conversions.

In this chapter Luke furnishes us his own historical account of Saul's conversion; in two subsequent chapters Paul himself tells of his conversion in two addresses. In each instance he has a specific purpose in view and tells the story so as to further that purpose. Therefore, in dealing with the accounts of this conversion it is proper to take up first of all and by itself Luke's objective, historical narrative which aims to present merely the facts as they occurred. Then in due order we may examine Paul's own accounts from the angle of the purposes which induced him to tell his audiences what he had experienced. This is Luke's own method, which first gives us chapter 9, and then chapters 22 and 26.

The time between Christ's ascension and Stephen's martyrdom was probably three or four years. Soul was converted about the year 35 and returns to Jerusalem in 38.

1) **Now Saul, still breathing threat and murder against the disciples of the Lord, having gone to the high priest, asked in due order from him letters to Damascus to the synagogues in order that, if he found any being of that Way, whether men or women, he might bring them bound to Jerusalem.**

Saul's ardor for persecution had not abated; he still continued to blow his breath, reeking with threat and murder, against the disciples of the Lord —this is the force of Luke's picturesque words. The participle with εἰς means *einschnauben auf jemand*. It is unsatisfactory to say that the genitives are partitive (R., W. P.), or that they are analogous to the genitive after verbs of smelling (R. 507) and to illustrate by a horse sniffing the smell of battle (R., W. P.). Any analogy with verbs of smelling lies not in what one smells but in what one smells of, in the odor he gives off (B.-D. 174); and still better is the idea of cause: threat and murder caused Saul to breathe out against the disciples (Stellhorn, *Woerterbuch*, on the verb).

The word "murder" is significant. The supposition that it refers only to Stephen's death is questionable. Stephen was already dead; Saul was raging against other disciples. The fact that he had succeeded in having others put to death is certain, and the objection does not hold that Luke should have recorded these martyrdoms, for he recorded that of Stephen only because it marked the great turning point in the course of the history of the church, which sent the gospel out into the wide world.

2) Caiaphas was still the high priest, for not until the year 36 did Jonathan, a son of Annas, and in 37 Theophilus, another son of Annas, succeed Caiaphas; the latter were not sons of Caiaphas (R., W. P.). The authorization Saul desired was not requested from **the high priest alone but from him as being head of the**

Sanhedrin who issued "the letters" on vote of the entire body as we see from 22:5; 26:10.

The middle ᾐτήσατο is not to be understood in the sense that Saul asked these letters "as a favor to himself" (R., W. P.); the middle of this verb is used with reference to business transactions, when business claims are made. So here the great business of persecuting the Christians had been officially delegated to Saul, and in prosecuting this business of his "he asked in due order" for documents that would enable him to execute this business of his also in Damascus. While Saul had his heart and soul in this persecution, it was not a private enterprise of his, could not be in the nature of the case, but an official enterprise of the supreme Jewish court itself with Saul as its head agent. For the persecutions in Jerusalem he had as his assistants a body of Levite police that had been granted him by the Sanhedrin in order to hale men and women to prison (8:3) and he was similarly equipped with police when he was authorized to operate in Damascus.

Damascus, the oldest city in the world (apparently a city already in Abraham's time, B. C. 1912, Gen. 14:15; 15:2) that still exists as a famous city, had a large number of resident Jews and, as Luke's plural shows, a number of synagogues. Nero butchered 10,000 Jews in Damascus. It was under the rule of King Aretas three years after the event narrated in this section and must have been strongly Jewish when Saul went there on his errand. The Roman emperors granted the Sanhedrin authority over Jews outside of Palestine, and Aretas was a Roman vassal. What this authority included and in what territory the Sanhedrin might exercise it, is uncertain; but Saul's expedition to Damascus evidently assumes that arrests could be made there and the prisoners brought to the Sanhedrin in Jerusalem for trial. We have "both men and women" as in 8:3.

The word ὁδός, like the Hebrew *derek*, is extensively used in the metaphoric and ethical sense as a "way" or course of life, both as being marked out to be followed and as being followed. For the objective idea of *Sittenlehre* is not enough; in Matt. 3:3 the Baptist proclaims "the way of the Lord," which certainly includes doctrine as well as moral regulations; in Acts 2:28 the plural is used. Especially noteworthy is John 14:6 where Jesus calls himself "the Way." A genitive or other modifiers are often added in order to describe "the way." The wicked also have their way. Here the word is used without an addition save the article: "the Way" κατ' ἐξοχήν, the Christian faith, conviction, confession, and life as taught by and centering in Jesus. The genitive is qualitative: "any being of the Way," who thus differed from all other Jews. These were to be arrested and brought bound (having been and thus continuing to be bound) to Jerusalem.

3) Now, as he was journeying, it came to pass that he was approaching Damascus. And suddenly there flashed around him a light out of heaven; and, having fallen on the ground, he heard a voice saying to him, Saul, Saul, why art thou persecuting me? And he said, Who art thou, lord? And he: I am Jesus whom thou art persecuting. But arise and go into the city, and it shall be told thee what it is necessary that thou do.

Luke's favorite ἐν τῷ with the present infinitive means "while," and the accusative with the infinitive is the subject of ἐγένετο. Saul had almost reached his goal and was elated by the prospect of what he would accomplish in destroying the church. He is in the full ascendency of his power. Then "suddenly" Jesus stops him. A miraculous light flashed out of heaven and enveloped him. It was noonday (22:6), and the light was brighter than the sun (26:13); it was not a momentary

Acts 9:4, 5 353

flash but, coming with a flash, shone around Saul for a time (26:13).

4) Instantly Saul dropped from the animal he was riding and fell prostrate to the ground and then heard the voice that said to him, "Saul, Saul, why art thou persecuting me?" In regard to the difference between ἀκούω with the accusative φωνήν and in v. 7 with the genitive τῆς φωνῆς, compare 22:9. The accusative refers to the voice as saying something, the genitive to the voice as coming from someone. There is not a contradiction between 9:7 and 22:9.

One should go through the Scriptures and note these duplications: Saul, Saul — Martha, Martha — Jerusalem, Jerusalem — David's lament over Absolom, and others. In varying ways they express an emotion of deepest concern but never anger. Why, yes why, was Saul persecuting Jesus? This question called upon Saul to probe his soul in regard to the terrible work in which he was engaged. To persecute the disciples is to persecute the Master. *Caput pro membris clamabat.* Augustine. Jesus spoke in Hebrew (26:14), and we take it that the dialog was carried on in this language. Jesus does not at once identify himself. Saul hears only this question coming from one in heaven, the light of whose blinding, heavenly presence and glory was shining about him.

5) Thus, when the voice from heaven paused, the question came from Saul's lips: "Who art thou, lord?" It should be evident that "lord" is here not to be taken in the sense of God, for then Saul would not ask. This is "lord" in the sense of any superior person or being. From I Cor. 9:1 and 15:8 we learn that Saul *saw* the glorified Jesus. These passages have nothing to do with the question as to whether Saul ever saw Jesus while he lived on earth. We have no evidence whatever that Saul saw Jesus in the days of Jesus' earthly life. In any

case, the glorified, heavenly presence of Jesus differed vastly from his presence in humiliation.

Now those standing by saw no one but heard only the voice but not what it uttered. The sight as well as the words of Jesus were intended for Saul only. So he saw and so he heard and understood. Jesus knew how to appeal to Saul's eyes, ears, and consciousness so that they apprehended.

Jesus then names himself and states only his personal name "Jesus," the one that had been given him on the day of his circumcision (Luke 2:21); for it is his identity that is to be established. Yet Saul received far more than this mere name. This was Jesus in glory, he whom the Jews had rejected and crucified, he whom God had exalted to the glory that now enveloped Saul. The tremendous reality and truth of this fact swept over Saul's soul like a flood. And this makes us feel the impact of the contrasted pronouns: "*I*, I am Jesus, whom *thou*, yea, thou art persecuting!" That charge, that accusation of persecuting is thus driven into the soul of Saul to the hilt. Here was the revelation, not only of Jesus, who with one stroke swept away all the lies Saul had believed about him as a mere man, etc., but also the revelation of what Saul was engaged in: persecuting this glorified Jesus in his disciples: "I — thou!"

At this point note the insertions made in the A. V., partly from 26:14, partly as a reminiscence of 22:10. Written, perhaps, on the margin at first, the additions were eventually interpolated into the text.

6) Ἀλλά breaks off. Its force is: I will not speak further of what thou art doing *but* of what thou shalt now do; the adversative idea of ἀλλά is conserved. Jesus orders Saul into the city where he will be told what he must do.

Some important points ought to be noted at this place. Jesus preaches the law to Saul; he confronts him with his sin and his crime; he smites and crushes Saul's heart with a consciousness of its awful guilt. But Jesus does not preach the gospel to Saul, he orders him to go to a place where the appointed minister of the gospel will proclaim this to him; for "what is necessary that thou do" does not refer to works of law but to believing and receiving the grace and the pardon for his sins.

Here we again see how Jesus honors his ministry. Philip is sent to the eunuch by an angel, it is not the angel who is sent to teach the eunuch. And this is the case wherever the gospel is to be offered. The essentials for Saul as a sinner were contrition and faith; the moment these were wrought in him he was converted. Just at what moment this inner turn was wrought in Saul, in other words, at what instant faith was kindled in him, no man can say, nor need we know. One thing alone is certain: when Jesus smote Saul with the law, this crushed him but did not kindle faith in him. It is often said that Saul was converted on the road to Damascus. Strictly speaking, this is not the fact. His conversion began in his encounter with the law but it was not accomplished until the gospel entered his heart by faith, and that did not occur on the road but in Damascus.

Jesus converted Saul, and he did it through his regular means, the law and the gospel; and no conversion was ever wrought without these means. In this instance Jesus applied the law immediately as he had done when he preached to sinners on earth; he applied the gospel mediately through his servant in Damascus. The law was not stronger because it was applied immediately, nor the gospel weaker because it was applied mediately. Saul was not converted irresistibly. In 26:19 Paul says pointedly that he "was not disobedient to the heavenly vision," which implies that he might have answered it by disobedience. If **conversion** were irresistible, then all who remain unconverted could charge God with their damnation. When Jesus confronts the sinner with his law and his gospel, and the sinner, nevertheless, remains unconverted, the fault is wholly the sinner's own, Matt. 23:27; Acts 7:51; 13:46; 28:25-28.

As far as the outward circumstances of Saul's call and conversion are concerned, these were fashioned by the Lord with a view to Saul's apostleship. This applies especially to his vision of the glorified Jesus, I Cor. 9:1. The Lord was qualifying him for his future work in order that, although he was called so late, he might, nevertheless, be on a par with the other apostles. In this respect Saul's case was entirely exceptional even as the Lord needed only one apostle of this kind. All else, time, place, etc., was in God's gracious providence, who chooses these for all sinners with a view to one result only, namely that they may be as favorable as possible to the success of his grace.

7) Now the men, those traveling with him, were standing speechless, hearing the voice, yet beholding no one.

These men constitute the police force that Saul had with him. At the first flash of the superearthly light they, too, fell prostrate (26:14); upon recovering, they now stand speechless, in utter astonishment because of what is happening especially to Saul who is lying on the ground and talking with someone who is unseen by them.

Here there is an opportunity to establish a contradiction. Luke says they "heard the voice"; but in 22:9 it is stated that they "heard not the voice of him that spoke to me (Paul)." Aside from the different cases of φωνή used in these two instances as explained above the sense is plain: they heard the sound (9:7) but heard not the words and understood not the sense of the sound (22:9). This is an exact parallel to the light: they saw the light of Jesus' presence but saw nothing of Jesus himself standing before Saul in his glory. We have an analogous instance in John 12:28, etc. To see and to hear what they did see and hear was sufficient for these Levite ὑπηρέται or underlings; all that they were to know was that a vision from heaven had come to Saul and that a heavenly being had spoken to him.

The three accounts of Saul's conversion have received a great variety of treatment. The whole story is converted into a drama of the imagination: its background are the twinges of Saul's conscience, its actual occasion is a sudden thunderstorm with a stunning flash of lightning, a bolt laying everyone prostrate. Psychology offers its own solution by speaking especially of scruples of conscience and inner battles that were brought on by Stephen's speech and also by his death and the manner in which he died. But Saul had no scruples or misgivings of any kind. He was in the full flush of his persecuting enthusiasm; he was ready for many more killings (v. 1). He was burning with zeal for the right and was seriously fighting the wrong. Then Jesus suddenly appeared to him, and Saul was overwhelmed with the realization that he was fighting for the wrong and against the right, yea, against God's Messiah himself. In an honest character such as Saul had this caused conversion by a terrible struggle that was superinduced by the vision of Jesus.

The psychological aspect is easy to understand. This vision of Jesus was not something that transpired only in Saul's own soul either as imagined by himself or as wrought in Saul's soul by the Lord. In addition to the accounts in Acts, I Cor. 9:1, and 15: 8 disagree with such a view. Jesus actually appeared to Saul. The issues involved in a proper conception of Saul's conversion extend beyond the man himself. When Jesus brought him to conversion he changed not only his life but made him the foremost apostle. Was this man mistaken in regard to what happened on the road to Damascus? Did he labor under psychological delusions and the like? The cause must measure up to the effect. The apostleship of Paul, as it is recorded in the New Testament, cannot be traced to anything that was merely subjective, mistaken, unreal. Luke recorded the realities, and they will ever stand as what they are.

8) And Saul was raised up from the earth; moreover, with his eyes standing open, he continued to see nothing; and leading him by the hand, they brought him into Damascus. And he was for three days not seeing and did not eat or drink.

We regard the form ἠγέρθη as a true passive: "he was raised up," instead of taking it in the sense of the middle: "he raised himself up," "he arose." Why should his attendants not assist their commander? But it was discovered that he had been blinded. The genitive absolute has the perfect passive participle: "his eyes having been opened and remaining so." It was found that he was not blinded by the great glare of light only for a time but that "he continued to see nothing," the durative imperfect. His men had to lead him by the hand, and it was thus that the great persecutor and destroyer of the Christian Church entered into the city that he had selected for his new triumphs.

9) Saul continued to be blind for three days. We do not regard the expression as a periphrastic tense because then the negative should be οὐ; μή is the regular negative used with the participle and shows that it is only the predicate. Saul's sight was miraculously restored. He also fasted. He is in a depressed and wretched condition. Luke states only the outward facts. His fearful sin lay heavily upon him, and the Lord permitted it to crush him for three days. A good deal was required to grind down this mighty Pharisee and implacable foe of the gospel. Shut off from the world,

blind, abstaining from food, with no one to help his soul's distress, his proud self-righteousness was conquered, and there remained only a sinner in the dust who ever after felt himself chief of all sinners. I Tim. 1:15. The supposition that this experience left Paul with weak eyes is one of the many hypotheses in regard to Saul; but this one militates against v. 18. When the Lord restored Saul's sight he restored it completely and not halfway.

10) **Now there was a disciple in Damascus by name Ananias. And the Lord said to him in a vision, Ananias! And he said, Lo, I (hear), Lord! And the Lord to him: Ananias, go into the narrow street that is called Straight and seek in Judas' house a Tarsian by name Saul; for lo, he is praying, and he saw a man by name Ananias come in and place the hands on him in order that he might recover sight.**

On $\mu\alpha\theta\eta\tau\eta\prime\varsigma$ see 6:1; $\tau\iota\varsigma$ is our indefinite article. In 22:12 a little more is said about Ananias, especially that he was esteemed by all the Jews — and Saul was in a Jew's house. The Lord prepared Ananias for Saul, and Saul for Ananias; but we must note that the Lord is also preparing the way for Saul among the disciples at Damascus, who had heard of his frightful deeds and of his coming to Damascus to add to them.

The Lord called as he once did to little Samuel, and Ananias answered: "Lo, I, Lord!" meaning that he is giving ear and heart to hear what the Lord may say.

11) He receives orders as to just what to do in order to find Saul and is told that Saul is praying and that he is expecting Ananias and what Ananias will do for him. Ananias, we see, knows where Judas lived, namely in the $\dot{\rho}\acute{\upsilon}\mu\eta$ or "narrow street" that bears the name "Straight." Damascus, Jerusalem, and other cities had and still have such narrow streets, and but

few of them are straight for any distance; wider streets are called πλατεῖα (feminine adjective, supply ὁδός). We passed through this street in Damascus in 1925. Yes, we visited Judas' house, etc. But when we were to see the window in the wall from which Paul was let down in a basket, lo, they were building a new wall — only the place up in the air was left where they said the old window had been. We certainly had our doubts regarding even the street "Straight."

A Ταρσεύς is a native of Ταρσός, the capital of Cilicia in southwestern Asia Minor. It was at one time a large, free city that was not under a Roman governor; it was also renowned for learning and schools of philosophy. "A Tarsian," of course, differentiates this Saul from any others bearing this name, but 21:39 shows that this term conveys more: Saul was "a citizen" of Tarsus and not merely in the sense in which we ordinarily understand citizenship, as having been born in Tarsus, which would have made him only "a resident," but as being the son of a family that had originally been located in Tarsus by one of the Seleucid kings, or as the son of an ancestor who had been granted the rights of citizenship for distinguished services to the state. Ramsay, *St. Paul the Traveller and the Roman Citizen*, 31, etc. Saul had this standing in Tarsus for life; it was no mean distinction even apart from his Roman citizenship.

"For lo, he is praying" is added as having a special meaning for the mission of Ananias. This is not the common daily praying of a strict Pharisaic Jew, which would not warrant such an exclamation as "lo"; this praying marks Saul as a changed man — praying, no longer breathing threat and murder (v. 1). The raging lion has been changed into a bleating lamb. "Praying" means that Saul is in deep distress, and that the Lord is now engaged in answering that prayer, and that this mission of Ananias is a part of that answer.

12) In fact, the Lord has already shown Saul how his prayers were to be heard. For what the Lord tells Ananias to do he has already revealed to Saul in advance, namely in a vision, showing him that a man by the name of Ananias would enter, lay his hands on him, and restore his sight. In other words, Saul has been duly prepared for and in a wonderful way already introduced to Ananias. He is expecting the Lord's messenger and is now praying for that very reason. Indirectly, in the purpose clause: "in order that he might recover sight," Ananias learns what he is to do for Saul.

13) **But Ananias answered: Lord, I heard from many concerning this man, how many base things he did to thy saints in Jerusalem; and here he has authority from the high priests to bind all those calling upon thy name.**

It is unwarranted to call these honest words of Ananias' his "protest to Jesus against any dealing with Saul," and "an illustration of our own narrow ignorance in our rebellious moods against the will of God." This is not even a case like that of Zacharias who doubted Gabriel's word and was struck dumb because of that doubt. With simple openness Ananias tells the Lord what he has heard from many about this man Saul (the aorist ἤκουσα whereas we use the perfect to refer to recent events, R. 842). Saul's record was certainly bad. The many from whom Ananias had heard it were very likely fugitive Christians who had fled from Jerusalem to Damascus. Besides, reports travelled swiftly in those days.

The dative of disadvantage "to thy saints" is quite noteworthy because it appears so early in naming and describing the disciples. The word ἅγιοι is strictly Biblical in sense and describes the disciples as having been removed from the sinful fellowship of the world and by the sanctifying power of God placed into fellowship with the God of redemption and salvation. They have experienced the ἁγιάζειν of God and his Spirit, they are in possession of Christ's salvation. See the elaborate article in C.-K. 34, etc. and note 53. The change which makes them *hagioi* is that which removed their sin and guilt by justification and continues to build them up in a new life by sanctification. "Saints" came to be a standard term for the believers; they are the ἡγιασμένοι of 20:32; 26:18, those who have experienced and thus still experience the sanctifying grace that makes them God's own. "Thy saints" = those who are in blessed fellowship with the Lord.

14) Ananias also knows all about Saul's plans regarding the Christians in Damascus, his authority to bind "all those calling on thy name" (7:59). This expression makes prominent the full confessional characteristic of the saints, I Cor. 1:2; Rom. 10:13. "Thy name," so hated by the Jews, is not merely "**Jesus**," or "Jesus Christ," but he with all that he has revealed about himself; note carefully ὄνομα in 4:12, and follow the term from 2:21, 38; 3:6 onward. To call on this name is to confess it as being the bearer of salvation, to pray and to worship in this name, and to expect all help in time and in eternity from him who is revealed by this name.

15) Ananias really puts a question to the Lord. He lays all this in regard to Saul before the Lord in order that the Lord may enlighten him regarding Saul. **And the Lord said to him: Be going; because this one is a chosen instrument for me to bear my name before both the Gentiles and kings and Israel's sons. For I will show him how many things it is necessary that he suffer in behalf of my name.**

The Lord complies with the implied request of Ananias and gives him a glimpse of what Saul is to accomplish in the future. Ananias is merely to aid in the first step. The present imperative is quite mild: "Just be going — everything is all right!" With ἐστί μοι, "I have in him," the Lord tells Ananias what he sees in Saul: from now on he is to be "a chosen instrument" for a most mighty task and for a most wonderful distinction (v. 16). Σκεῦος is any kind of utensil and has the meaning "vessel" (a container) only where this is especially indicated. Since τοῦ βαστάσαι (infinitive of purpose) means to lift, to carry with the hands or on the shoulders, the idea of a vessel is excluded. As the Lord's instrument Saul will take up and carry the Lord's name or revelation (ὄνομα as before) before the Gentiles, etc., holding it up for them to see and to adore. The genitive ἐκλογῆς is qualitative, R. 496, "attributive," and is used instead of an adjective but in a stronger sense: "an instrument of choice," i. e., "chosen." It is the Lord himself who chooses his tools for his tasks. They are his tasks — who shall dictate to him the tools to be used?

The great task of Saul was to take the gospel to the Gentiles (Rom. 1:16). It must have come as a surprise to both Ananias and Saul himself when Ananias told him what the Lord had said. He did become the apostle to the heathen world in an especial sense. "The Gentiles" and "kings" are combined by τε καί, "both and," since the rulers before whom Saul testified were with few exceptions pagan. Yet "Israel's sons" (see 7:37) are added as the secondary field of operation for Saul. The Lord had all of Saul's work mapped out in advance.

16) A great work, and now a great honor: the many things Saul would suffer "in behalf of my name," this significant ὄνομα again. "I will show him" with its preposition ὑπό means: "I will place *under* his eyes and thus show him," but this is not a showing in advance, by prophecy, but a showing from time to time as occasions for suffering arise. To be sure, this word which Ananias would repeat to Saul foretold that he would have much suffering awaiting him; "I will show

him" goes beyond that and includes also the idea that the Lord would be present with Saul and each time point out what he must suffer and help him to endure it. In βαστάσαι the idea of bearing a great burden is expressed; now with παθεῖν a mighty load is added in the shape of suffering. Both aorists are constative and at the same time imply successful bearing and suffering. Δεῖ may be used for any type of necessity; here it is the necessity arising from bearing the Name before the Gentiles, etc., which is indicated by the ὑπέρ phrase, "in behalf of my Name."

Heavy work in distant lands — much suffering arising from that work! What a prospect! And the Lord reveals this in advance. Will Saul not flee from it all? No danger. Remember Matt. 5:10-12, and also how Jesus constantly told the Twelve what awaited them. It is the Name that makes this great work so attractive, the Name which lends glory to the suffering. Recall 6:41. To this day it is true that, if we would join the illustrious company of the great prophets of God, we must suffer for the Name's sake.

17) **Now Ananias went away and went into the house; and, having placed upon him the hands, said: Brother Saul, the Lord commissioned me, Jesus who appeared to thee on the road on which thou wert coming, in order that thou mayest recover sight and be filled with the Holy Spirit. And immediately there fell off from his eyes as if scales, and he recovered sight. And having arisen, he was baptized; and having received food, he got strength. Moreover, he was for some days in company with the disciples in Damascus.**

It is supposition that the vision of the Lord was granted to Ananias at night and that he executed his commission the next morning. If such had been the fact, a word or two would have indicated it. Ananias reaches the house without difficulty and is brought to

Saul who sits there in his blindness waiting for what the Lord had communicated to him (v. 12). Luke records only the pertinent facts. This does not prevent us from supplying what took place. Did someone not admit Ananias to the house and lead him to Saul? Why, then, say that nobody was present except Ananias and Saul? There is no reason why Judas himself and several others were not present. Who gave Saul nourishment (v. 19)? There must have been a great deal of excitement for all the residents of that house! Luke has left ever so much untold in order that we may the more regard what he has told.

So the hands were duly laid upon Saul's head, this symbolical act (see 6:6) being the more important for the blind man. In connection with this act Ananias speaks the great word of absolution to this frightful sinner Saul who is now certainly contrite enough. Jesus himself pronounced absolution in many different ways; note Luke 23:43. Absolution is what this chief of sinners needed most and first, and then all that follows absolution. Already the address, "Brother Saul," absolves. It cannot mean "brother" in the superficial sense in which many use it, nor in the sense of brother Jew. "Brother" was sweet music to Saul's ears. That word admitted him into the communion of "saints" (v. 13), all his past guilt was erased.

"Brother" has material significance, for the next word is ὁ Κύριος and states what the "Lord" has commissioned Ananias to do, that Lord who appeared to Saul on the road which he was traveling three days ago ($\frac{5}{\eta}$, R. 716), Jesus, who there had crushed Saul with the revelation of his guilt. The sight of that Lord had blinded Saul's eyes. So spiritually blind had he been up to that moment. And now, in token of his pardon of Saul's guilt, that same Lord is removing that blindness from Saul's eyes, is restoring sight to him. For the eyes of his soul have been opened to the sight of faith.

366 *Interpretation of the Acts of the Apostles*

Do not ask just when the first spark of saving faith entered Saul's dark soul. It is enough to know that he now believes. And he is to be filled with the Holy Spirit, this supreme gift is to be bestowed upon him by means of the baptism that followed immediately. There is no indication in any of the three records or in other references to Saul's conversion that he received charismatic gifts; we have no right to assume that he did. The spiritual power of the Spirit filled Saul, and at this moment that means more than any charismatic gifts.

18) Saul's sight returned instantly. Saul describes the sensation he felt when he speaks of scales or flakes that fell from his eyes. Those present saw only that his sight had been fully restored, the blinded eyeballs again saw. To Saul it seemed as though scales were dropping away and thus again permitting vision. As his blindness had something symbolical about it, so also has this new granting of sight.

Very briefly, with but two words, Luke records the baptism. Some put a good deal into ἀναστάς, "having arisen"; they think that this word indicates that Saul was taken to the river Abana — some mention Pharpar — and was there immersed. But this journey to the river does not seem to fit into the context, for in rapid succession Luke relates that Saul is sitting in a room as a blind man, that he has his eyes opened, arises, and is baptized, and then takes food and is strengthened — all apparently occurring in that house. Yet in spite of this some claim that he was immersed. R., *W. P.* writes: "possibly in the pool in the house of Judas, as today water is plentiful in Damascus"; Zahn thinks that Saul was baptized in the *Badezimmer* (bathroom) in Judas' house.

But very few houses are furnished with pools. When we visited Damascus in 1925 we noticed that even the vast courtyard of the Great Mosque, the greatest in the world, contained only a fountain, and we observed a moslem making most thorough ablution — he could *not* have immersed himself. The grandest house in Damascus had 365 rooms, and there were fountains in some of the rooms and a pool in the courtyard, but not for the purpose of swimming in them but only for ornament. Our hotel, the Grand Victoria, where Balfour and Allenby stopped, the best in the city, was third-rate in its accommodations. Immersion would be possible, but only in one of the seven channels into which the Abana (now Barada) River is divided in order to furnish irrigation and a general water supply for the city. The city is made by this river, the waters of which are conducted in small channels. Beyond the city these waters disappear in the desert sands. One channel flowed past the hotel, but it was quite shallow, yet in a deep place we saw a bather; there a person could have been immersed. The Pharpar flows at a distance from the city; when we crossed it we saw only a brook.

The claim that Saul was baptized by immersion involves the assumption that ἀναστάς, "having arisen," implies the fact that he was conducted to one of the channels of the Abana. But this circumstantial participle is inserted merely to mark the importance of an act: a person gets up to do this or that. A fitting sample is found in 5:17. Saul had been sitting; he would naturally arise for the baptismal act.

More important than these speculations is the fact that Saul was promptly baptized. He accepted, yea, desired this sacrament with the pardoning and regenerating grace it conveyed to him; it was at the same time the divine seal of grace and of the Spirit and made him Christ's own. After the administration of this sacrament he ceased to be a Jew and was, indeed, made a Christian.

We are left to conclude that Ananias administered the sacrament just as Philip had done in 8:38 in the case of the eunuch. As far as Luke's record shows, the disciples who were living in Damascus, although they were numerous, had not yet withdrawn from the synagogues and had no organization of their own with elders or pastors. So Ananias administered baptism to Saul by the right of his royal priesthood as a believer. Since the Christians in Damascus were as yet without pastors, Ananias, of necessity, assumed this function. In the present instance, however, all doubt was removed by the commission he had received directly from the Lord, which certainly contained the order not merely to restore the sight of his eyes to Saul but also to receive him as a "brother" in the fellowship of the "saints." A vessel filled with water was brought in, some of the water was applied to Saul as Jesus had directed in Matt. 28:19, in the name of the Father, etc., and the blessed act was completed.

19) Saul was a changed man. Since he had been weakened by his fast of three days' duration, he now took food and restored his physical strength. When Luke writes that Saul was in the company of the disciples "for some days," we feel that he intends to state just that. We have no particulars in regard to Judas, to whose house Saul was first conducted; it is fair, however, to conclude that this man was a Jew and not a Christian. Saul now changed his abode; he went where he now belonged, among the disciples. It took some time for them to circulate his story, for him to get acquainted with them and thus gradually to get his bearings in this new city.

Those who introduce what v. 20 states at this point anticipate matters. On the other hand, it is supposed that during these days Saul underwent a course of instruction in the doctrines of the gospel. The μετά phrase does not imply such a thought, and Gal. 1:1-12, and the entire argument in Galatians, chapters one and two, is to the contrary. Saul received his entire gospel directly from the Lord as he declares, "by the revelation of Jesus Christ." He was not to be a preacher or an evangelist like Philip, who could operate with the gospel that was received at secondhand; as an apostle and as one who was on an equality with the other apostles Saul needed to receive the gospel at firsthand. And he received it so, by direct revelation. This may explain his being filled with the Holy Spirit, v. 17.

20) And immediately in the synagogues he began to preach Jesus, that this one is the Son of God. And all those hearing it continued to be amazed and to say: Is not this the one who ravaged in Jerusalem those calling on this name? and here he had come for his that he might bring them bound to the high priests! Saul, however, was being filled the more with power and was confounding the Jews dwelling in Damascus, proving that this one is the Christ.

We see the energy of the man. A few days pass, only enough to get his proper bearings, and then he begins his work as a herald (ingressive aorist) in the very city in which he had planned to do far different work. Some think that he began on the very day of his baptism; but that is not what Luke says. Saul preached "Jesus." What about him? "That (epexegetical ὅτι) this one is the Son of God." Add v. 22: "that this one is the Christ." Compare Luke 22:70. The strong demonstratives are exclusive: "this one and this one alone." Saul had seen this Son of God in his heavenly glory; he preached as an eyewitness. "I am Jesus" he had heard him say with glorified lips, the very Jesus who had walked, wrought on earth, had been killed by the Jews, and raised to glory by God — him Saul preached as the Messiah.

We meet the assertion that Paul never called Jesus "the Son of God"; and yet here is the fact — Luke has it from Paul himself. The very first thing which he did when he began his work was to preach Jesus as the Son of God. Luke, the great associate of Paul, here records what "the chosen instrument" (v. 15) of the Lord preached from the beginning. Robertson adds: "With this faith he can shake the world. There is no power in any other preaching."

21) Now the imperfect tenses begin; all of them are descriptive and at the same time lead us to look forward to what followed. First to be mentioned is the amazement of all who heard him in the synagogues of Damascus, and we may include Christians as well as Jews, for the withdrawal of the Christians from the Jews does not seem to have been effected as yet. They continue exclaiming, "Is not this the one," etc! The thing seemed incredible especially to the Jews. Note the recurrence of the expression, "those calling on this name" (v. 14) with the significant ὄνομα; also, "to bring them bound" (v. 2), the same perfect participle. All knew about the authorization and the instructions from the high priests with which Saul had arrived, his Levite police guard (the "men" in v. 7) had told for what purpose they had come under Saul's leadership. How was it possible that the persecutor-in-chief had turned preacher? The question ends in a declaration: "and here he had come for this," the purpose being stated with ἵνα.

22) As Saul preached he grew in power "the more" and caused consternation in the ranks of the Jews. The passive is usually taken in the middle sense, "he grew in power" ("increased in strength," our versions), but it really means that power was bestowed upon him, and this in increasing measure as his work went on. The result is added coordinately: "he continued to confound the Jews resident in Damascus"; as in 6:10 Stephen proved invincible, so also Stephen's greater successor. "Proving that this one is the Christ," the Messiah promised by the Scriptures, indi-

cates how the Jews were confounded. Those proofs were conclusive, overwhelming, and silenced the opponents. Then the same thing happened that had occurred in the case of Stephen; unable to refute the argument, these opponents resolved to kill the man who presented it.

Here we have Saul's first activity in the synagogues. An efficient pupil of the great Gamaliel, competent, therefore, to expound the Scriptures, he secured opportunity to speak in the synagogues. The service was such that any competent and qualified person was allowed to speak, and sometimes replies were made. In all his work in every city the apostle first visited the Jewish synagogues. They provided him with openings, and with the advantage there gained he proceeded. Not for a number of years was Saul as yet to extend his work to the Gentiles. The Lord was still training him, restraining him as he did Moses in Midian (7:29, 30) until in due time the door into his great life's work would open before him.

23) **Now, when many days were being fulfilled, the Jews resolved to make away with him; but their plot became known to Saul. Moreover, they were watching even the gates both by day and by night in order that they might make away with him. However, his disciples, having taken him at night, let him down through the wall by lowering him in a basket.**

These "many days" comprise three years (Gal. 1:18). Saul's visit to Arabia (Gal. 1:17) must be placed within this period. We know the fact of this visit but neither the occasion and the purpose nor the exact place or the duration. It is often supposed that Luke should have written about this journey to Arabia; but he does not record all that might be of interest to Theophilus and now to us. He follows a definite plan and records only the vital and the really significant matters of the apostolic story. This visit of Saul to Arabia was negligible for Luke's plan of Acts. Unless we find the clue to his plan of writing we shall fail to understand at many points.

It was thus after Saul's visit to Arabia, when he renewed his activity in Damascus, that his Jewish opponents took decisive action. The aorist συνεβουλεύσαντο, exactly as in Matt. 26:4, means that at a called meeting the formal resolution was passed, its contents being stated. In the case of Jesus it was to get hold of him with cunning and to kill him; in the case of Saul it was "to make away with him," ἀναιρέω, the verb which in 2:23; 5:33, 36; 7:28 means murder. Moral considerations never seemed to weigh in the balance when Jesus was concerned. "Took counsel" in our versions is too weak. Saul's fate was decided.

24) All we know is that Saul learned about the plot in some way. The imperfect describes what measures were taken to prevent his escape. His enemies "were even guarding the gates (of the city) both by day and by night," the genitives of time. Saul must have been in hiding because he knew about the fate that was intended for him. In II Cor. 11:32 we see that the ethnarch of King Aretas, who governed the city for him, agreed to the plot to apprehend Saul. The Jews had most likely denounced Saul as being a most dangerous man so that he had issued orders to his guards at the gate to capture him in case he tried to pass through it. He did not need to appoint the Jews as such guards. These volunteered to watch lest Saul in some disguise, reckoning with the inability of the governor's men to recognize him, should manage to evade them. Since the gates of the walled city were sealed, it would be only a matter of time until Saul was located and done away with. An efficient plot — that did not materialize. They watched and watched while Saul was already on his way to Jerusalem.

25) Saul's escape was effected in the simplest manner. Some of the houses that adjoined the wall around the city had windows that were high above the wall itself. From such a window Saul was lowered in a basket, σπυρίς, referring to its roundness; it is called σαργάνη in II Cor. 11:33, referring to its being plaited. We must note the expression "his disciples" which points to the success of Saul's work in Damascus; these men were converts of his. The fate of Stephen was not to be the fate of Saul. The Lord needs martyrs and secures them, and each is given his crown; but he also needs workers and provides them, and each receives his great reward.

26) **Now, having come to Jerusalem, he was attempting to join himself to the disciples; and all were fearing him, not believing that he was a disciple. Barnabas, however, after he got hold of him, brought him to the apostles and recounted to them how on the road he saw the Lord, and that he spoke to him, and how in Damascus he spoke boldly in the name of Jesus.**

The imperfect tenses picture Saul's difficulties on arriving in Jerusalem and at the same time point to what follows, namely their removal. When we remember the Jews' method of reckoning time, the three years of Saul's absence from Jerusalem (Gal. 1:18) most likely imply one full year and parts of two other years. So Jesus lay in the tomb all day Saturday and only a part of Friday and of Sunday, and yet the time spent in the tomb was counted as three days. Another point is Saul's absence in Arabia, likewise the war between Herod and King Aretas, which interrupted intercourse between Damascus and Jerusalem. Thus when Saul suddenly reappeared to join himself to the disciples in their meetings for worship and in social intercourse, he encountered doubt and suspicion, nobody really believing that he actually was a disciple as he claimed to be;

the tense of the direct discourse is retained after ὅτι. It did seem quite incredible that the most violent persecutor of the Christians, who had caused so many to flee from him and had wrought so much havoc, should himself have turned Christian. Was he, perhaps, pretending in order presently to do still greater damage?

27) It was Barnabas, who has already been introduced to us in 4:36, 37, who brought this situation to an end. Luke again states only the fact. We ask, however, how Barnabas came to act as intermediary. Had the two men met earlier in life? The conjecture is offered that both had attended the university in Tarsus years before. There is greater probability that Barnabas, who afterward was in such close and long association with Saul, was drawn to him from the beginning. Natural affinities appear even among leaders of the church. We need no further information at this point.

Barnabas "got hold of" Saul. This verb always governs the genitive, here αὐτοῦ is understood (B.-D. 170, 2), and αὐτόν is construed with ἤγαγε. He took Saul and made a complete investigation, and after he had obtained the remarkable story he took Saul to the apostles themselves and recounted it to them, laying stress on the three vital points: first, that Saul had seen the Lord; secondly, that the Lord had spoken to him; thirdly, that in Damascus Saul had spoken boldly in the name of Jesus (ὄνομα as in all previous passages beginning with 2:21).

The point of these two indirect questions that have a declaration between them (R. 1047) is evidently not merely that Saul is a fellow believer, but that the Lord qualified and made him a fellow apostle. That, too, is the reason that Barnabas takes Saul not merely to the congregation but to the apostles themselves. To have seen the risen and glorified Lord was a requisite for the apostolate. While Luke says only that the Lord spoke with Saul without intimating what this was about, the next statement, that Saul spoke in Damascus as he did, makes plain that the Lord authorized Saul's preaching. Verse 15 was also, no doubt, reported by Barnabas.

Luke writes that Barnabas took Saul to the apostles. This is made more specific in Gal. 1:18, 19, where Saul himself speaks of this visit to Jerusalem. It was brief, lasting only fifteen days. Saul's purpose was to become acquainted with Peter (ἱστορῆσαι, the aorist indicating that this was accomplished). He met only two of the apostles, Peter and James. The latter was not John's brother but the one called "the brother of the Lord." There is much debate in regard to the identity of this James (see 1:14, the brothers of Jesus; 12:27, James being one of them). As far as Luke's plural "to the apostles" is concerned, this is in order if James is regarded as an apostle in the wider sense as was Barnabas as well as others; the eleven were busy elsewhere. In v. 29 "the Hellenists" are only two or three and not all the thousands that were living in Jerusalem; in 8:18 "the apostles" signifies only "Peter and John." The same is true with regard to many other plurals, and there is no need to posit a contradiction between Luke and Galatians.

28) So the ice was broken. **And he was in company with them, going in and going out in Jerusalem, boldly speaking in the name of the Lord. He was engaged both in speaking and in disputing with the Hellenists; but they were undertaking to make away with him. Now, on learning it, the brethren led him down to Caesarea and sent him forth to Tarsus.**

"In company with them" means with the apostles. Saul was not only accepted as a genuine disciple; the apostles treated him as a fellow apostle. It was thus that he went in and out in their company "in Jerusalem," εἰς = ἐν, as so often in the Koine, which sets aside the older forced explanations which even take us out of Jerusalem and then "into" it again.

29) Luke says only that, while he was in company with the apostles, Saul "was speaking openly or boldly in the name of the Lord," i. e., in connection with that name or revelation. We take it that this was not preaching but private utterance. While the participle is a form of the verb used in v. 27, which includes synagogue preaching (v. 20) in Damascus, the situation obtaining in Jerusalem was entirely different. Here the Christians had their established preaching, and Paul would not have intruded. As to the synagogues in Jerusalem, these were at this time not open to the apostles and certainly were not used by them. They had found the courts of the Temple far better suited to their purpose. Note carefully that this participial clause still speaks of Saul as being in company with the apostles, referring to Peter and James.

What Saul did is stated separately, the imperfect tenses showing that he began to speak as well as to dispute with the Hellenists but did not get very far with them. The ἐλάλει implies that Saul accosted a Hellenist here and there, and the συνεζήτει that he occasionally managed to engage in a dispute; but that was all. Some think that Saul entered the synagogue of the Cilicians since he was from Tarsus of Cilicia, but Luke does not say this. We found that this was not probable in regard to Stephen in 6:9. All comparisons with Stephen are, therefore, problematical: that Saul stood in the very synagogue where Stephen had once stood, that in the very place where Saul had contradicted Stephen and had been thoroughly defeated he now used the same arguments against the Hellenists that Stephen had used.

As far as Stephen is concerned, we do not know whether he ever engaged in debate with Saul even outside of the synagogue. Only this is true, and we may make the most of it, that, like Stephen, Saul argued with a few Hellenists where he happened to encounter them, and that very quickly, as in Stephen's case, when counterargument failed, these Hellenists planned to use the more effective answer of murder, ἀνελεῖν. These Hellenists had silenced Stephen's voice with his own blood and undertook to do the same with Saul's voice. On the Hellenists see 6:1. Saul seems to have selected them, not because he himself was a Hellenist, but because he, too, was born in Hellenistic territory and thought he could accomplish something with regard to them. But the undertaking of these vicious opponents came to nothing as the imperfect indicates. Note the difference: in v. 23 συνεβουλεύσαντο, a formal resolution passed at a meeting, here ἐπεχείρουν, an undertaking by individuals.

30) According to 22:17-21 the Lord himself directed Saul to leave Jerusalem. This is what really induced him to do so. All that Luke adds is that the brethren got to know about the undertaking of the Hellenists. Saul, we assume, told them also about the Lord's communication to him. The brethren, of course, only a delegation, "brought him down to Cæsarea" and carefully guarded his person on this journey lest his bloodthirsty enemies should fall upon him on the road and thus after all succeed in making away with him. From Cæsarea Saul could travel to Tarsus by either sea or land.

Here we come to the greatest gap in the record of Saul's life since we saw him at Stephen's death. Saul is lost to view for about eight years; see 11:25 where Barnabas brings him forth from Tarsus. For more than ten years after his conversion and call the Lord's chosen instrument for bringing the gospel to the Gentiles (v. 15) is not active in his great special mission. All we can say is that this was the Lord's will. We should think that Saul was ready for his task, and his task was ready for him immediately after he had been called; the Lord evidently knew better.

What did Saul do during those years he spent in Tarsus? The sacred record is silent on this matter as it is in regard to Paul's sojourn in Arabia. "He preached and missionated," some tell us. But we do not learn about the gathering of a congregation in Tarsus, nor about converts even in Cilicia, and the time spent there is eight years. It is, indeed, precarious to say that at any place in his account Luke should have told us this or that. Here, however, it is plain: if the great work among the Gentiles had begun in Tarsus, and if so many years of Saul's life were devoted to it, Luke simply could not have passed this by in silence. Ramsay's hypothesis is that Saul was not yet fully conscious of his mission to the Gentile world and still thought that the door to Christ was through the synagogue. He forgets the Jews in Tarsus; he himself assumes that a colony of Jews lived in Tarsus (see v. 11). Why did Saul, then, do nothing among these Jews? Ramsay touches only half of the problem. Saul did no work in Tarsus.

Some fill in the account at this point and speak of "the scene at home when this brilliant young rabbi, the pride of Gamaliel, returns home a preacher of the despised Jesus of Nazareth, whose disciples he had so relentlessly persecuted. What will father, mother, sister think of him now?" This scene is expanded. Saul's subsequent poverty is explained by surmising that his father disinherits him as the Jews to this day regard as dead any child that becomes a Christian. Yet all that we know is that years later Saul's nephew warned him in Jerusalem (23:16). We do not even know why Saul returned to Tarsus, and we ask, "Would he remain there for years with parents that regarded him as dead?"

31) **Accordingly, the church throughout the whole of Judea and Galilee and Samaria continued to have peace, being built up and, walking in the fear of the Lord and in the encouragement of the Holy Spirit, was being multiplied.**

This little summary is similar to 2:44-47; 4:32-35; and as far as multiplication is concerned, compare 2:41; 4:4; 5:14; 6:7; 8:25. On μὲν οὖν see 1:6. After Saul had been converted, the persecution of which he had been the driving spirit ceased. And Saul was now some distance removed, a renewal of persecution that might be prompted by the hatred the Jews might manifest toward the Christian Paul was obviated. It was thus that the church had peace, meaning quiet and rest.

On ἐκκλησία see 5:11, and note 8:1, 3. This word is here used in the same sense as denoting the body of believers. The fact that this body is now spread out over three provinces does not change the sense of *ecclesia*. The bond that makes all these believers one is that of faith. Even when it is extended to the ends of the earth it will be just ἡ ἐκκλησία. This concept has a spiritual content even when it is applied to a local congregation only, for the genuine believers always constitute the church, irrespective of mere adherents.

On κατά in the sense of "throughout" see R. 607. It seems that the countries are mentioned in the order of their importance, thus Galilee before Samaria, although Luke records nothing of special historical importance about Galilee. He mentions these three because the church was well distributed throughout these three, which was not the case as yet in other provinces, only scattered congregations having been founded in them.

The imperfect tenses and the present participles are descriptive of the condition and the progress. The οἰκοδομουμένη is undoubtedly the New Testament spiritual edification. This word cannot here refer to outward growth since this is mentioned separately. This conception is not to be externalized as meaning only that the church ordered and developed her internal affairs; nor be reduced to only the devoutness of religious feeling which is furthered by the peculiar type of preaching that aims at this effect. The latter was made the aim of cultus preaching by Schleiermacher who had many followers in Germany. Edification is the strengthening of the entire religious life and activity by means of the Word and the Sacrament. Church organization and the like is a different matter. To this the apostles as yet devoted little effort.

The verbs and the participles are arranged chiastically, the verbs being placed outside, the participles inside, so that one participle refers to each verb. "Walking in the fear of the Lord," etc., the church continued to multiply "in numbers." Combined with the inner upbuilding was the strong outward growth, for "multiplied" means great increase. Palestine was being rapidly Christianized. Luke states how, namely by the church walking in the fear of the Lord and in the comfort of the Holy Spirit. The spiritual power of the church evident in its membership attracted and won men.

"The fear of the Lord" (Jesus) with its objective genitive means that the church dreaded to do anything that might displease and offend the Lord. In their daily life and walk the members had Jesus present with them. This is high praise indeed, for this strong motive is largely absent today; church members too often persuade themselves that the Lord does not mind their worldliness and love of praise from men.

Combined with this fear was "the encouragement of the Holy Spirit" which with its subjective genitive refers to the Spirit's *Zusprache*, his aid in encouragement, direction, and comfort. As the other Paraclete promised by Jesus, he acted as one called to the side of the believers in order to help them in every way. This

presence of the Spirit is always mediated through the
Word by means of which he speaks to us and keeps us
encouraged and strong in the faith. The early Christians did not listen to the spirit of the world and of the
flesh. Very unobtrusively Luke here points to the
sources of power in the church. When the members
walk with the fear of the Lord before their eyes and
with the Spirit's encouraging voice in their hearts, the
church will be strong and will also surely multiply.

PETER AT LYDDA AND AT JOPPA

Having practically concluded the preliminary account in regard to Saul, Luke returns to the activity
of Peter. We see him at Lydda, at Joppa, and then
at Caesarea. He serves as an example of the type of
work the apostles generally were doing; yet he is
selected by Luke because it was his lot to bring the
first Gentiles into the church in such a way as to open
the whole question regarding the admission of Gentiles
into the church. Philip's baptism of the eunuch was
the modest preliminary.

32) **Now it came to pass that Peter, in going
through to all, came down also to the saints inhabiting Lydda,** the Old Testament Lod, the Roman Diospolis, the present Ludd, on the road from Jerusalem to
Joppa. The accusative with the infinitive is the subject. The participle is only incidental and yet casts a
light upon the present work of the apostles. Peter visits Joppa "in going through to all," διὰ πάντων. This must
be masculine on account of the following καί which
brings out the fact that he "also" came to the saints at
Lydda; our versions should be corrected. Peter is
alone. There is too much to be done to permit the apostles to go out two by two.

And Peter's program is extensive: he intends to
visit "all," to cover the entire church. It would seem as
though other apostles had the same program. Since

the churches as yet had little or no organization they could not be left to themselves, and therefore the apostles felt obliged to visit them from time to time. That would take them away from Jerusalem for longer periods of time. It was such a visit that Peter was paying "the saints" at Lydda, the same significant term as in v. 13.

33) And there he found a man by name Æneas, since eight years lying on a pallet, who had been paralyzed. And Peter said to him, Æneas, Jesus Christ heals thee! Arise, and spread (the bed) for thyself! And immediately he arose.

Luke records this event with such brevity because he is concerned, not so much about this sick man, but rather with the effect produced by the miracle wrought upon him. This man is a parallel to the cripple at the Gate Beautiful in the Temple, 3:2, etc., parallel especially in helping to bring many to faith. Some think that this paralytic was a disciple but he was not, for how could Luke write ἄνθρωπόν τινα, "a man," *ein Mensch*, instead of "a believer," "a disciple"? Compare his account about Tabitha in v. 36. Yet healing fell into this man's lap just as it fell into the lap of that beggar in the Temple.

This, too, was a very serious case: paralysis for the past eight years so severe that the sufferer had to spend the day on a κράββατος or pallet (8:7). The ἐξ is the Greek idiom, it counts from the far point and is our "since."

34) Since Peter calls him by name, others must have spoken to him about this man. The reversal of subject and predicate puts emphasis on both: *"heal thee doth Jesus Christ."* R. 866 calls this an effective aoristic present because of its punctiliar force; the main point is that it states a tremendous fact. Instantaneously the man *is* healed. "Jesus Christ" (see 2:38) does the deed and not Peter. In 3:6, Peter said, "In the name of Jesus Christ." The sense is the same. Since Jesus here and now heals him, the man is told to get up and to spread his pallet for himself, a task others have had to perform for him during all these years. This verb στρωννύω occurs in Matt. 21:8, where the people spread branches on the road for Jesus, and in Luke 22:12 where the upper room was spread with floor tiling. The sense is proably that Æneas is to take up his pallet and lay it away somewhere, doing this for himself as it had been done for him every evening when he was undressed and transferred from his pallet to his bed for the night.

35) **And all those inhabiting Lydda and Sharon saw him, they who turned to the Lord,** οἵτινες, *quippe qui*. The effect spread from the town through the beautiful coast plain which extends about thirty miles toward Cæsarea. So many saw the man, recognized the miracle in its true significance, and in faith turned to the Lord, that Luke could write "all." This added to the labors of Peter. How long he labored here we do not know; he later moved on to Joppa.

36) **Now in Joppa there was a woman disciple by name Tabitha, which, when translated, means Dorcas. This one was full of good works and almsdeeds which she was doing. But it came to pass in those days that, having become sick, she died; and having washed her, they placed her in an upper room.**

Transitional δέ takes us into the new account, to Joppa, the present Jaffa, the old port of Jerusalem, one of the most ancient of towns. Philip had, no doubt, worked here, and the first local Christians may have been fugitives from Jerusalem (8:1). Without further explanation we learn that there was a Christian congregation in Joppa. We are introduced to one of the woman disciples by the name of Tabitha, from the Aramaic *tzebiah*, which Luke translates by the **Greek**

Dorcas, both names meaning a gazelle doe, the emblem of grace and beauty. This name was frequently given to girls. The relative is feminine, ἥ, the gender being attracted from the antecedent. R. 714 makes the relative personal. The account contains no reference to relatives and leaves the impression that Tabitha lived by herself. Her special interest in widows leads us to surmise that she herself was a widow who had no children. Although she lived alone and seemingly had no special object in life, this disciple fashioned a most important place for herself in the life of the young congregation.

She was "full of good works," which includes a variety. Luke specifies by naming one class of these works especially: "and almsdeeds which she kept doing," aiding the poor to the extent of her ability. In this activity she invested her money, time, and strength. She is not represented as a deaconess in the church; in fact, we may safely assume that such an office had not yet been established. Tabitha's work was entirely voluntary; but with a true instinct she chose no work of doubtful propriety with which to serve the Lord in the church, no work that had a worldly taint but one that was fully in harmony with the gospel. Hers were in every respect *good* works, ἀγαθός, good in the sense of truly beneficial, and *mercy*-deeds, the Greek word being derived from ἔλεος, "mercy." "Good works grow from faith and are but the very Word of God in its deed and fulfillment, which has been implanted in us by faith." H. Mueller.

Luke emphasizes the abundance: "full" of good works and almsdeeds "which she kept doing" (durative imperfect). She reaped a rich harvest. She did not tire, discouragements were overcome, she continued faithful in her service to the end. "The sweet odor of the ointment filled the house when the vessel which had stood in a place aside broke." Besser.

37) It was "in those days" that Tabitha became sick and died. We are left to read between the lines that there was a divine providence in the fact that this death occurred at just this time. Peter was within reach. The Lord intended to distinguish this humble woman in a signal way, namely by raising her from the dead. He had given much to the church in Joppa when he gave her to it; now he intended to give the church still more in her.

With sadness they took her body to the upper room and washed and prepared it for burial. The participle λούσαντες is masculine although this washing and this preparing of the body were done by women; the gender is indifferent because no subject is named. Since no house has been mentioned, there is no article with "upper room." An ordinary house would have only one "upper room" which was built on the flat roof and used as a place of retirement. We have no information to the effect that the bodies of the dead were usually placed in upper rooms before burial. Luke relates this in regard to Tabitha because an exception was made in her case. According to the regular custom she should have been buried soon after death; instead of that her body was kept until Peter could arrive. For this reason it was placed in the upper room.

38) **Now Lydda being near to Joppa, the disciples, having heard that Peter was there, commissioned two men to him, beseeching him, Do not delay to come through to us!**

At this point nearly every commentator asks questions that are not answered by the text. Were the two messengers sent after Tabitha had died or before her death? If she was already dead, why was Peter called in such haste? Did they entertain the thought or the hope that Peter might bring her back to life?

Luke makes note of the comparatively short distance between Joppa and Lydda (ἐγγύς is here construed with the dative, and not with the customary genitive), it was only about nine miles. The aorist participle adds the detail that the disciples at Joppa had heard the news that Peter was in Lydda. We can follow only the natural impression made by the brief narrative that the Christians in Joppa had for some time had news of Peter's presence in Lydda but that the thought of sending for him had occurred to no one until after Tabitha had died. Then, as far as hopes and expectations are concerned, all that we can safely say is that the disciples at Joppa requested only that Peter might come and, like true disciples of Christ, committed everything else into the Lord's hands.

"Do not delay," etc., implies that the disciples knew that Peter intended to visit them also, but they beg that he may come at once. In negative commands or entreaties μή with the aorist subjunctive is the regular form but is just as urgent as the positive command with the aorist imperative. "Do not delay" is a litotes for, "Hurry." In that climate the dead are commonly buried on the day of death or, if death occurs too late in the day, the next morning. Peter could be brought from Lydda to Joppa in five or six hours, thus on the same day, if Tabitha had died in the morning, or the next morning if she had died at evening. A delay on Peter's part would have necessitated burial before he could arrive.

Now this petition that Peter hurry does carry with it the silent, humble hope that the Lord's grace might use Peter to return Tabitha to the church at Joppa. Yet, when finding this hope in the petition, we must remember, what also these disciples seem to know, that none of the apostles worked miracles at will. Hence no request is made to Peter to work a miracle upon Tabitha. In every case the Lord and his Spirit directed those to whom the gift of performing miracles had been granted, and they proceeded only when and where they were so directed. What the Lord's will was in the case of Tabitha none presumed to say, and we shall see that Peter himself did not at first know So in all that prompted this message to Peter their thought was only to bow to the Lord's will while trusting in his boundless grace.

39) And, having arisen, Peter went with them, whom, on having come, they led up into the upper room. And there stood by him all the widows sobbing and showing on themselves tunics and robes, as many as Dorcas made from time to time while yet with them.

Peter responded promptly. The Greek reads literally: "whom, having gotten to their side (παρά in the participle), they brought," etc. This makes the impression that Peter had been summoned on Tabitha's account and not on account of the disciples in order to administer comfort to them, to preach a funeral sermon, as we should say. Yet even now no request of any kind is made. Peter is taken up to the dead woman's side where he finds that she is wrapped and swathed for burial. But here, beside that loving heart and those busy hands that are now still in death, Peter is shown what this woman meant to the church and what the church had lost in her. It was done in a simple and a most natural way. All the widows for whom Tabitha had made garments are present. How could any of them be absent at this time? "All" is not too strong, for in that congregation there were not overly many.

Their feelings soon gave way in that upper room as Peter questioned and they answered so that he might know fully. They sobbed aloud. This was mourning which was far different from that manifested in the house of Jairus with its noisy, hired mourning women and fluteblowers. This was not such artificial mourning as that. The widows showed Peter garments that had been made by their dead benefactress. Note the middle voice ἐπιδεικνύμεναι, for it conveys the idea that they were showing what belonged to themselves, they wore the very garments Tabitha had made for them, ἐποίει, iterative imperfect, from time to time, now a garment for this penniless widow, now one for that.

The χιτών is the tunic that is worn next to the body, the ἱμάτιον, the robe or cloak that is worn over the tunic, the Latin *pallium*. The one was as much a necessity as the other. The *himation* was really a large, oblong piece of cloth, one corner of which was draped over the left shoulder and fastened under the right shoulder. This garment was ample enough to reach to the ground. It generally served as a covering for the sleeper at night. We must not miss the pathos indicated in the addition μετ' αὐτῶν οὖσα and in the placing of her name at the end: "she — being with them — Dorcas." Now her body was there, but not — Dorcas! *die Dorkas* (German). Catch the lingering tone of affection.

Luke now uses the name "Dorcas," partly for the sake of his own Greek reader who would know the meaning of this Greek name, *"Gazelle"*; and partly, it seems, because even in Joppa the orginal Tabitha had been replaced by its Greek equivalent. "And their works do follow them" is here illustrated in a peculiarly touching manner. What will be the nature of the works that follow you and me?

So Dorcas was a dressmaker, but instead of enriching herself by sewing only for money she enriched her soul by sewing for love. The garments she made for the poor she really made for the Lord, and she has had many successors, both with the needle itself and in other ways. She had only one talent, but see how much she made of that! Many who found themselves in her circumstances would have felt that they could do nothing; she saw the one opportunity and avenue open for her and made the most of that. We think that she sewed

Acts 9:40

also for the children of these widows who were half-orphans; these would not be present at such a solemn time as this.

40) The whole scene must have had a deep effect on Peter. The garments which had passed through the loving hands now resting from their labors spoke more eloquently to him than the subdued and broken sobs of the widows who wore them. **But Peter, having thrust them all outside and having kneeled down, prayed; and having turned to the body, he said, Tabitha, arise! And she opened her eyes, and, on seeing Peter, she sat up. And having given her a hand, he raised her up; and having called the saints and the widows, he presented her living.**

What is here recorded bears some resemblance to the procedure followed by Jesus when he raised to life the daughter of Jairus, yet the differences predominate. Peter kneels and prays, he permits no witnesses to remain in the room, and he finally summons all the disciples. Peter's miracle is thus not a duplicate of that performed by Jesus; the resemblances are due only to the nature of the two cases.

Why did Peter thrust them out? Ἐκβαλών is a strong word, they were reluctant to leave. We have the answer in Peter's subsequent deed: he kneeled and prayed. The Greek idiom is, "having placed the knees." Peter wanted to be alone with the Lord. Peter did not disregard the unspoken longing of the disciples that the Lord show his grace by restoring Dorcas to life. But up to this moment he had no intimation from the Lord as to his will. In deepest humility, on his knees, he now asks the Lord to reveal his will.

We need not hesitate to add that he prayed the Lord to grant the unspoken desire of the saints, a desire that had been kept within godly bounds and did not even venture to utter itself in words, to say nothing of clamoring for satisfaction. It seemed to be one of those pure and holy desires which the Lord loves to satisfy. So Peter lays the case before the Lord and in connection with it the great cause to which this case belonged.

Peter's action after his prayer shows that the Lord gave him an answer, the answer on which Peter's act rests. It was not Peter's "sublime faith" that performed this miracle. The Lord's sublime power wrought it; Peter had the Lord's word which had been communicated to him then and there. The fact that he believed that word is a matter of course.

When Peter turned to the body and said, "Tabitha, arise!" there was no question as to what would happen. Peter was not making a trial of his own faith. Peter was acting on the Lord's word. No apostle ever failed when he had that word; in no case was there a half-effect; but, of course, in no case did an apostle act without the Lord's word. Peter did not say, "In the name of Jesus arise!" but his words implied that and nothing else.

It is incorrect to say that as a result of his prayer Peter treated the body as though it were no longer dead. Luke says he turned to "the body," yet he did not address the body, which would have been folly, but the person. But this does not offer support to the spiritualistic notion that the spirit of Tabitha hovered near the body and thus heard Peter's command. Why introduce our rationalizing ideas of space when it is not the voice and the power of Peter that are at work but the promise and the power of the almighty Lord which work in a way that is absolutely incomprehensible to us? The Lord made Tabitha hear; the Lord returned her soul to her body; the Lord did this in connection with the word he had bidden Peter to speak.

Luke describes only the outward side of what occurred. "And she opened her eyes," the eyes that but a moment ago were broken and sealed in death. We ought not to think that there was a gradual return to life because Luke records several actions. Dorcas was instantaneously and completely restored when Peter spoke. No steps, no gradations followed. Life in full energy was back in her body; the former disease which had been active in her vital organs had disappeared; the incipient decay that had been superinduced by death was removed at a stroke. Dorcas was as one waking out of deep sleep. This is what Luke has in mind, for the first thing an awakened sleeper does is to open his eyes. Naturally, too, on seeing Peter standing beside her, she sat up. For this she needed no help. Her body was swathed in linen strips for burial, yet this did not prevent her from assuming a sitting posture. We have the analogy of Lazarus coming out of the tomb.

41) At this point Peter might have opened the door and called in the waiting disciples. He first gave Dorcas his hand and raised her to her feet. It seems that her arms had not been wrapped against her body. Lazarus, too, was able to stand in his grave wrappings and to appear at the door of the tomb. When Dorcas thus stood beside her bier, Peter called in "the saints and the widows," "saints" as in v. 13, and καί does not add a new class but only specifies "the widows" as the ones mostly concerned. What a scene that must have been when Peter presented Dorcas — "living"! That is a way the inspired writers have! They record the most dramatic and stupendous events in a few calm words. They always let the immense facts speak for themselves.

42) **And it became known throughout entire Joppa, and many believed on the Lord. And it came to pass that for many days he remained in Joppa with Simon, a tanner.**

Luke returns to the matter of chief interest, that of the church and its development. A miracle that was as stupendous as this one had been could not but become known throughout the entire city (κατά as in v. 31). That, too, was the Lord's intention. We see that the same effect was produced in Lydda (v. 35). Many "believed on the Lord," ἐπί, rested their confidence and trust on Jesus, on his grace and his power for salvation. The idea is not that miracles as such work faith, but miracles are seals of the Word and attestations of its power and thus aid in producing faith. They are such seals to this day, for, once affixed to the Word, they remain there and need no repetition, and there is no need of new seals as though those affixed by the Lord had lost their validity.

43) Luke likes ἐγένετο, "it came to pass," a sacred way of stating notable facts that he had learned from the LXX. And here again the accusative and the infinitive are the subject. The way had been opened to gather a great harvest in Joppa, and Peter remained "many days" (v. 23) in order to help bring it in.

The noteworthy thing is that Peter accepted the hospitality of "a Simon, a tanner." The handling of hides made this man ceremonially unclean from the Jewish standpoint Christian though he was. Peter disregarded these Jewish scruples and lived in this man's house during the entire time of his stay in Joppa. Recall that Peter and John had been with Philip in Samaria. The old Jewish legalism is dropping away; the next chapter shows the decisive and the complete break. At this point Rieger remarks that a tanner's house was provided for St. Peter, but now a castle scarcely suffices for St. Peter's successors.

CHAPTER X

Cornelius:

The Reception of Gentile Christians

Luke devotes so much space to the story of Cornelius because it marks a new departure in the work of the apostles. What had been indicated by the baptism of the Ethiopian eunuch is fully established by the baptism of Cornelius and of his household. The eunuch went his way, but these Gentiles in Caesarea remained and thus formed the vanguard of the great army of Gentiles that soon entered the church. What Peter did in the case of Cornelius was a preparation for the entire work of Paul, who was waiting in Tarsus during these years.

1) Now a man in Caesarea, by name Cornelius, a centurion from the cohort called the Italian, pious and fearing God with all his house, doing many almsdeeds for the people, begging of God always, saw in a vision plainly about at the ninth hour an angel of God come in to him and say to him, Cornelius!

Joppa was a very ancient city, but Cæsarea was most recent, having been built by Herod the Great in ten years and named in honor of the Roman Cæsar. After Herod's time it became the resident city of the Roman governors.

Cornelius is described at length. He was a centurion in the Roman army, an officer who commanded a century or 100 men. He belonged to the Italian cohort which was stationed in Cæsarea at this time; thirty-two such Italian cohorts were stationed in the different provinces of the empire. They were made up of Italian volunteers and were considered the most loyal Roman troops. A legion consisted of ten cohorts plus auxiliary troops. Each cohort had six centuries and the same number of centurions. No longer is Luke's statement challenged, that there was a cohort in Cæsarea and this province of the empire at the time of which Luke speaks.

It must have been late in the year 37 or early in 38 when Saul left Jerusalem and went to Tarsus via Cæsarea. Peter must have gone to Lydda, Joppa, and then Cæsarea not long after Saul had departed, namely in the summer of 38. Herod Agrippa I, a prisoner in Rome under Tiberius until the latter's death on March 16, 37, was appointed king over his uncle Philip's tetrarchy (Luke 3:1) by the new emperor Caligula but did not arrive in Palestine until late in the summer of 38. Perhaps already in April, 37, Marullus was appointed procurator of Judea, and he must have had this Italian cohort in Cæsarea. Not until early in 41 did Emperor Claudius make Agrippa I king over all Palestine, which explains how he could execute James and imprison Peter in Jerusalem. Marullus ruled as procurator. Agrippa I suffered a miserable death after the Passover of 44, after ruling all Palestine for only a little over three years.

2) When Luke writes: "pious and fearing God with all his house," the adjective marks the godly character of the man, the participle, however, brings out the fact that he and his whole family were proselytes of the gate. On the two kinds of proselytes see 2:10 and 8:27. The important point that is vital for all that follows even as far as 15:7-11, is that Cornelius and his household were still Gentiles and were regarded as such by all Jews, were considered as standing only at the gate of the pale of the Jewish Church and were debarred from passing beyond the court of the Gentiles in the

Temple. None such had as yet come into the Christian Church save the eunuch; those called "proselytes" in 2:10 were such in the full sense of the word and hence were regarded as Jews.

The great question which the Lord compelled Peter and the church to face in the person of Cornelius was whether the way into the Christian Church was to be only through Judaism and the synagogue or also direct from Gentilism and paganism by faith and baptism alone. It was exceedingly difficult for many Christians who had come into the church from Judaism to find and to accept the true and the God-pleasing answer to this question. The Lord made that answer exceedingly plain and forceful through Cornelius. That answer had to be clear in the minds of all before the gospel could reach out into the vast Gentile world.

From the beginning Cornelius appears "with his whole house" around him, his family and his slaves, and soon we note even his friends (v. 24). This was more than just family religion; this man's faith reached out all around him. While he was a proselyte of the gate, we are not at all sure that as much can be said regarding all the rest whom Peter met in his house. Cornelius cultivated the two outstanding virtues of the Jewish religion: he gave abundant alms and he was diligent in prayer. The beneficiaries of his charity were "the people," λαός so often signifying the Jewish people. He had found so much through them that he made generous and grateful return. Luke uses δεόμενος, which takes the genitive as a designation for praying, the verb which means "to beg of God"; in v. 4 we have the regular word for "prayers."

3) He was thus engaged when there came an answer to his prayers that he had not expected. "At about the ninth hour" refers to the hour of the evening sacrifice in the Temple at Jerusalem, three o'clock in the afternoon, the hour that was used for prayer also

by devout Jews who lived far from the Temple. Luke's ὡσεὶ περί is due to the non-existence of clocks and thus to the inability to be entirely exact; moreover, according to the season and the amount of daylight, the hours were longer or shorter. Suddenly Cornelius saw an angel of God; the two aorist participles are punctiliar, not "coming in" and "saying," but that he "came" and "said." We meet these visions frequently; note that of Peter in v. 10, etc. Instead of being confined to ordinary perceptions, the mind and the senses are able to see the supernatural that the Lord intends to reveal. Cornelius was wide awake, entirely master of his mind and his senses, but now he saw the coming of the angel with his eyes and heard the words of the angel with his ears and recognized the angel as the person that he was. The direct address, "Cornelius," implied that this heavenly messenger had a communication for him.

These visions are never mere subjective autosuggestions or the mind's own productions. The angel was actually present, was as real as though a man stood before Cornelius. He spoke audibly so that Cornelius heard his voice and his words. The veil which confines us to this natural world was withdrawn; Cornelius was enabled to see and to hear this angel from the heavenly world. Each vision is confined to definite limits and does not extend beyond these; for it is a revelation of the facts and truths desired by the Lord and hence does not go beyond these. Rationalism will always either deny them outright or will seek natural or pathological explanations for them. Sudduceeism still continues.

4) *And he, gazing earnestly on him and become trembling, said, What is it, Lord? And he said to him: Thy prayers and thy alms went up for a memorial before God. And now send men to Joppa and summon for thyself a Simon who is surnamed Peter; he is lodging with a Simon, a tanner, who has a house beside the sea.*

Cornelius could not do otherwise than to rivet his eyes upon this heavenly being and could not do otherwise than to tremble at his sight. This is quite regularly the effect produced when sinful men come into visible contact with the other world. As in v. 3, so here, too, the participles are historical aorists which intend not to describe but only to register the facts: he gazed, he became trembling. Cornelius properly addresses the angel as "lord." In the Gospels we constantly have κύριος in this sense when a person is addressed as a superior. Eventually the word came to be used as a designation for Jesus as the divine Lord, the Second Person of the deity. We have the two uses in English today: "lord" (some man) and "Lord" (Jesus as God).

When the angel tells Cornelius that his prayers and his alms have come up "for a memorial" before God, the phrase conveys the truth that God intends to remember these prayers and these alms, to take account of them in his grace towards Cornelius. It should not be necessary to say that no work-righteousness is implied but something vastly greater than any claims of human merit. The prayers and the alms revealed the condition of the heart of Cornelius. They were, indeed, good works but are here regarded like the good works of the righteous at the time of the final judgment when Jesus will use them as the evidence of faith and the absence of such good works as the evidence for the absence of saving faith (Matt. 25:34-46). God was thus judging Cornelius by these works of his.

The expression that these works have come up as a memorial before God is anthropomorphitic and speaks of God as a great king who made a permanent record and now proceeds to reward Cornelius. We now see why Luke used the participle "begging" as a designation for the praying of Cornelius (v. 2). Cornelius did more than merely to use the office of Jewish prayer; he begged God to enlighten his heart, to fulfill the great Messianic promises, to grant him a share in those promises. These were the petitions that were now to receive a notable answer. That, of course, was wonderful grace for Cornelius personally. But our view must not be too narrow. Others, as devout as Cornelius, received no angelic message, no miraculous answer. God was using Cornelius for a far higher purpose, namely to open the door of the church to all the Gentiles. For this he chose Cornelius; he might have chosen another. God manages his own affairs in his own superior and most perfect way. It is not necessary to make ἀνέβησαν a timeless aorist (R., W. P.) when it is plainly the English perfect "have come up," an ordinary recent past act.

5) Although God sends an angel to Cornelius, that angel is not to preach the gospel to him. Again, as in the case of Philip, God honors the ministry he has established. Angels may help to connect men with God's appointed preachers, they are never allowed to do more. So Cornelius is told just what to do to get Simon Peter. Note the middle imperative, "summon for thyself," which indicates that Peter would have a message for Cornelius.

6) The two Simons are carefully distinguished, each with the indefinite pronoun that is equal to our indefinite article: "a Simon." The passive ξενίζεται = he is received as a ξένος or guest, i. e., "he lodges." The fact that Peter's host is a tanner is again mentioned but apparently only in order to identify him, and for the same reason the detail is added that he has a house ("for him is," idiom) along by the sea (no article is needed in the Greek). Tanneries required much water, and Simon seems to have done his tanning where he lived. There is here no idea of ceremonial uncleanness as a motive why Cornelius should not be afraid of sending for Peter.

7) **And when the angel who was speaking to him went away, having called two of the house-servants and a pious soldier of those holding to him and having recounted to them everything, he commissioned them to Joppa.**

We here learn more about Cornelius. He, of course, at once acted on the word of the angel. The fact that he had a number of οἰκέται (a mild term for slaves who were used as house servants) is not surprising considering his station. The soldiers, of course, were under his command; but we see that he selects one "of those holding to him" who is called "pious," the very adjective that was applied to Cornelius himself in v. 2. See the participle προσκαρτεροῦντες in 1:14; 2:42; 6:4 (these with neuter objects), and in 8:13 (with Philip as the object). A number of soldiers held to their commander because of his religious convictions which they shared.

The idea that these soldiers were merely attendants of their commander does not satisfy the expression, another word would be used to express that thought. It is only a guess to say that the soldier was sent along to protect the two slaves — they needed no protection, for no danger threatened them on the road. These three men were selected because they were spiritually closest to Cornelius. Their respective stations did not matter; as for that, all three messengers might have been slaves or soldiers. The point is that we here have a Roman officer who shared his religion with those who were far beneath him. Military officers usually act very superior to those beneath them; their official pride makes them aloof. The more noteworthy is what we note in this centurion of the elite Italian cohort.

8) We see why these particular men were selected. Cornelius "recounted everything to them," took them completely into his confidence. They were not given a mere formal order to summon Peter but were told all about the angelic vision. This most sacred and intimate

matter Cornelius shared with these men; they had to be men of a type in whose case such a thing was possible. All these points are of great value and help us to understand why Luke goes into such detail.

9) **Now on the next day, while they were travelling and drawing near to the city, Peter went up on the housetop to pray at about the sixth hour; and he became quite hungry and was desiring to taste something. But while they were making ready, there came over him an ecstasy, and he beholds the heaven having been opened and coming down a kind of receptacle like a great linen sheet being let down by four corners to the earth, in which there were all the four-footed and creeping things of the earth and flying things of the heaven. And there came a voice to him, Having arisen, Peter, slay and eat! But Peter said, By no means, Lord, because never did I eat anything common and unclean. And again a voice a second time to him, What God made clean, do thou stop making common! Moreover, this occurred three times; and immediately the receptacle was received up into heaven.**

The two genitive absolutes picture the three messengers on the way and drawing near to the city. About this time, at noon, one of the regular Jewish hours for prayer, Peter retires to the housetop where all is quiet in order to pray. The aorist indicates that he was offering definite prayers and not merely praying in general, which would require the present infinitive. As the Lord prepared Ananias for Saul and Saul for Ananias (9:10-12), so, after preparing Cornelius, he now prepares Peter. The δῶμα is simply the flat housetop and not the upper room built on the housetop, to designate which Luke would have used the regular word as he does elsewhere. It appears as though this tanner was too poor to have such an upper room in his house. Yet we must not imagine that Peter was out on the open roof under the noonday sun. When travelling through Syria and Palestine we saw many smaller houses with booths on their roofs. Some shelter similar to this may have been used by Peter.

The messengers had made good time. Starting after three in the afternoon, they were now, at noon of the next day, entering Joppa. They had covered the distance of 250 stadia or 24 miles by traveling even at night. They traveled on foot as a matter of course.

10) It may have been due to fasting. At any rate, Peter became "quite hungry," πρός in the adjective denoting addition: "very hungry." This adjective, as M.-M. 550 remark, is one of the diminishing number of New Testament words of which it must be said, "Not found elsewhere." The imperfect ἤθελε describes Peter's desire to eat; Luke uses γεύσασθαι, the active of which means, "to make taste," and the middle thus, "to taste for oneself." Peter longed for the taste of food. R., W. P., ingeniously suggests that Peter perhaps smelled the food being prepared below in the house. At least Luke informs us that the folks were getting a meal ready. This seems to have been a delayed ἄριστον which was usually eaten at ten o'clock and was not the δεῖπνον, the main meal which was eaten toward evening.

Then came the ἔκστασις which Luke describes in detail. The word describes a condition when the mind and the senses are lifted out of their natural surroundings and functions and are enabled to receive supernatural impressions and revelations by means of visions or other divine modes of communication. Compare Delitzsch, *Biblische Psychologie*, 285. A case in point is that of Stephen, 7:55, 56. The ὅραμα of Cornelius refers to the same thing although it is named according to what he actually saw, while ἔκστασις names the condition in which the person is when he sees, hears, etc. Such a vision and ecstasy is divinely wrought and has nothing to do with morbid states which are self-induced such as spiritualistic trances.

11) In describing the vision Luke employs the vivid present, "he beholds." Peter's eyes saw the heaven standing open (the perfect participle with present connotation), and out of its superearthly radiance "coming down" σκεῦός τι, "a kind of receptacle," which is described as a great ὀθόνη or linen sheet that was being gradually let down to the earth by four corners.

12) Luke continues: "in which there were," etc. We take it that the great sheet came to rest in front of Peter so that its contents were clearly visible to him and were within his reach: "all the four-footed and creeping things of the earth," first the neuter adjective and next the neuter noun, "and flying things of the heaven," another neuter adjective. The reason "the things swimming in the waters" are not included is because all the creatures were alive, and fish would not be alive in a sheet and out of the water. We need not translate, "all manner of," for the sense is plain without an interpretative rendering. The point of emphasis lies in this πάντα which includes creatures that were regarded as "unclean" as well as those that were regarded as "clean" by the Mosaic law. Here all of them were together in the same pure, clean, white linen sheet, all alike let down by invisible hands from the open heaven and thus from God himself.

13) Then came a voice, evidently out of heaven, we assume an angel's voice, which bade Peter slay and eat. The circumstantial ἀναστάς illustrates what we said on the use of this participle in 9:18. Note that θύω means, "to make go up in smoke" and thus, "to kill as a sacrifice to God," finally merely, "to slaughter or slay." It is God himself, then, who here abrogates the old Mosaic commands regarding clean and unclean animals and foods, and this is an illustration of the abrogation of all the Mosaic regulations regarding clean-

ness and uncleanness — a far-reaching command, indeed.

14) But here Peter reveals himself as the same character that is presented to us in John 13:8, where he refused to let Jesus wash his feet. So here he, too, refuses: "By no means, Lord! Because never yet did I eat anything common and unclean." To get the force of this answer note that μηδαμῶς, because of its μή, expresses Peters thought: "In no way let it be" with the optative of wish εἴη, or with the imperative to the same effect ἔστω; while οὐδέποτε with its οὐ states the negative fact: "never did I eat." If Peter had said οὐδαμῶς, the refusal would have been far more blunt: "In no way will I do it." Peter's is not a mild protest, nor is it a downright refusal; it is a shocked declining of the very idea. Why he is shocked he states with ὅτι, because during all his life he never ate a thing κοινόν, this to be understood as ἀκάθαρτον, "common" in the sense of "unclean," prohibited in the Mosaic regulations regarding food. The force of the reply is: "Goodness, Lord, do not ask me to do that!" Compare Lev. 11; Deut. 14. The Greek construes the negative particle οὐ in οὐδέποτε with the verb: "did *not* ever eat"; we combine it with the object: "I ate *nothing* ever." While it is like the Hebrew *lo — kol*, it is common in the Koine. R. 752.

This reaction of Peter's is most noteworthy as revealing to us the deep hold the old Jewish regulations about ceremonial cleanness had even upon the apostles, and how much was necessary to break this hold and to open the door of the church to the ceremonially unclean Gentiles. The Lord himself had to intervene as he here did in order to bring about the break that simply had to be made. It was revolutionary in the highest degree even for the apostles. Even they needed much time to recognize that all the ceremonial laws were only temporary, intended only for the old covenant, in force only until the Messiah should come, and not the divine will for all time. Peter answers the Lord because he knew that this was his command although an angel had uttered it.

15) The answer Peter receives is stunning and given in a tone of mighty warning. It is the same voice that replies although Luke again writes only "a voice"; "again a second time" is pleonastic, and the phrase with ἐκ is idiomatic. In negative commands with the present imperative an action already begun is ordered to stop, i. e., not to continue, R. 851, etc. So here: "Stop making common!" "What God made clean," God himself, actually made clean (aorist), refers, not to some present act, but to his act in abrogating all the Mosaic regulations through Christ who by his death and his resurrection fulfilled the promises of the old covenant and thus established the new; hence also the aorist, "did make clean."

All the old Mosaic regulations were to make Israel a separate people and prevent their intermingling with the pagans who surrounded them. They all served to preserve Israel and its treasured promises lest these latter be dissipated and lost. This was done, of course, in the interest of Israel but equally in the interest of the Gentile world, for the preservation was made for the sake of the human race. After the fulfillment had been wrought through Christ, its blessings were to go out to all nations. Israel's separation had served its purpose. The veil in the Temple was rent. "The middle wall of partition" had been broken down, Eph. 2:14; now there was "neither Jew nor Greek," Gal. 3:28; the old had decayed and vanished, the new had come in Christ, Heb. 8:13. A test was made in the matter of meats in the case of hungry Peter. He was warned to stop contradicting God by making unclean and unholy what God had relieved of this stigma and had thus cleansed. It sounds like an angel's word, for he is speaking of what God has done.

16) **This occurred three times, and then the great sheet was suddenly received up into heaven.** Did Peter refuse a second and even a third time after that first forceful warning? It seems so. Here there is shown the patience of the Lord in giving us time to adjust ourselves to the truth. Three questions were put to Peter in John 21:15, etc.; three prayers were uttered in Gethsemane; three times Paul besought the Lord to remove the thorn in his flesh, II Cor. 12:8. We often note threefold repetitions. Ordinary emphasis is attained by one repetition; the double repetition intensifies still more.

17) **Now, while Peter was greatly perplexed in himself as to what the vision he saw might mean, the men that had been sent by Cornelius, having inquired through for the house of Simon, stood at the portal and, having called out, were trying to learn whether Simon, called Peter, was lodging there. Now, Peter continuing to reflect concerning the vision, the Spirit said to him; Lo, three men are seeking thee. Now, then, having arisen, go down and be going with them in no respect doubting, because I myself have sent them.**

After the vision had ended, the imperfect compound with διά describes Peter as sitting there on the housetop "thoroughly perplexed." The idea is not that he did not understand the vision itself, namely as far as unclean animals were concerned; that was too obvious. Peter realized that the vision meant much more; "what it might be," i. e., it had him thoroughly unsettled. The indirect question with the optative and ἄν is the apodosis of a condition of potentiality and is retained unchanged from the direct question, the protasis, of course, being understood: "What might this be if it were explained?" What bearing did it have? What application should Peter make of this warning not to make common what God had cleansed?

The answer was to be found at the portal that led into the courtyard of the house. There were the men that had been commissioned (perfect participle: now acting on their commission) by Cornelius. The aorist participle states that they had succeeded in inquiring their way through (διά) to Simon's house which was along the seashore. Again we note that Simon could not have lived in a pretentious house. The portal was probably a passageway that led through the building itself into the inner yard.

18) Here they had called aloud until someone came and opened the doors, and at the moment they were trying to learn (the imperfect, although some texts have the aorist) whether the Simon who had the additional name Peter was lodging there.

19) Leaving them in that act, Luke takes us back to Peter who, in the genitive absolute, is pictured as still being engaged in reflection concerning the vision, i. e., concerning its import, the double compound (a hapaxlegomenon) signifying that his mind was going through and through (διά) and stopping in (ἐν) what he had seen in order to discover its full meaning. In the midst of this effort "the Spirit spoke to him" in the same way that Peter had often experienced, especially when he was directed to perform this or that miracle.

The words of the Spirit are actually stated in this case. Peter is not left to draw timid conclusions from the vision; the matter is so important in every way that the Spirit himself proceeds to show Peter the full bearing of the vision. "Lo, three men are seeking thee!" excludes the implication that Peter heard the men calling in the street below and overheard even his own name in the inquiry they made. No, this is the first information granted him. But so much is plain: the coming of these men is not accidental, their coming at just this moment is somehow connected with the vision and its real import. Some texts read "two," a few omit the numeral. These are variations that may be disregarded.

20) The claim that ἀλλά has an adversative force in all connections is naturally also made in the present instance, but this claim can be upheld only by inserting an adversative idea that Luke fails to indicate: "Three men are seeking thee; *but* (do not let yourself be sought and do not hesitate any longer, *on the contrary*), having arisen, go down!" But Peter had not been hesitating, had not been letting himself be sought; there is no "but" and "on the contrary," R's doubt in *W. P.* is groundless. This is the copulative ἀλλά which is described in R. 1185, etc.; it is continuative and adds an accessory idea and is to be translated "yea" or "now then." Peter's arising and going down now that he knows that these men are seeking him is to follow as a matter of course. Note another ἀναστάς (v. 13; 9:18), here it means as much as "hurry" and go down.

But he is to do more: he is not merely to go and to find out what they want, he is to accede to their request, to be going with them, and to do this by dismissing any misgivings on his part. The διακρινόμενος is in Peter's mind and not in his conduct (R., *W. P.*), and μηδέν is adverbial, "as to not a thing." It is very well to tell one not to waver in his own mind, to let nothing make him judge for himself now this way and now that way (διά, note also the middle voice); it is quite another thing to get a man's mind to the point where he will actually not do that. This other thing the Spirit accomplished with one simple stroke: "because I myself (emphatic ἐγώ) have sent them" (so that they are now here).

Here is the counterpart to "God" in v. 15: if God cleansed, Peter ought to be satisfied; if the Spirit said to go with these men, Peter ought to drop any misgivings about going. When we have God's authority, any scruples on our part insult God. On God's authority we must act even if we do not fully understand all that he commands or promises. Too often our trouble is that we invent his authority for what he does *not* want us to do; and when we do what he disapproves we refer it to him as having demanded it.

21) And having gone down, Peter said to the men: Lo, I am the one whom you are seeking! What is the reason on account of which you are here? And they said: Cornelius, a centurion, a man righteous and fearing God, also attested by the whole nation of the Jews was directed by a holy angel to summon thee for himself to his house and to hear utterances from thee. Accordingly, having called them in, he lodged them.

Peter now acts with perfect assurance. He introduces himself as the man they are seeking and, of course, is anxious to know the αἰτία, here "the reason" for which they are here. The Spirit had intimated nothing in regard to that point; all that was accomplished was to make the connection between Cornelius and Peter on the basis of Peter's vision. All else would follow in natural order step by step.

22) The men related their errand briefly. They introduce Cornelius fully so that Peter may exactly understand with whom he is dealing. What we know from v. 1, 2 is amplified. Now we have δίκαιος, "righteous," which is often disposed of with the remark that Cornelius observed the Jewish regulations. But he was not circumcised, he did not live kosher — a point of special importance in regard to Peter's visit at his house — he was not a full-fledged proselyte. This explanation of "righteous" will not do. The term is always forensic, it is exactly like the Hebrew *tzaddiq* and is well defined by C.-K. 309: he who is able to stand before God, whom God justifies, the God-fearing man. In this case the judge is God and not men, for they are spoken of separately. After adding the connection

with the synagogue the messengers state that Cornelius is "attested by the whole nation of the Jews," meaning, of course, the entire body of Jews in Cæsarea; "of good report" (A. V.), "well reported of" (R. V.) gives only the general sense of the participle.

This is the man who "was directed by a holy angel" to summon Peter. The verb means that he received a communication, and "by an angel" implies that God sent this word; there is no idea of "warning" as in our versions. The implication is only that Cornelius received directions in answer to petitions he had made. He was to summon Peter "to his house" — an important point; Peter is to enter this Gentile's house. Now, no strict Jew would think of doing such a thing because of the defilement involved. Here Peter began to see the real import of his vision. Peter is to lodge with this Gentile, to eat of his non-kosher food, etc. So all of this was contained in the vision of those many unclean animals and birds. And the Spirit had told him not to waver in regard to anything. This summons is to the effect that Cornelius may hear utterances from Peter, i. e., whatever the Spirit may give him to utter to a man such as this. In other words, here God was not only opening the door to the Gentiles for Peter but literally thrusting Peter in; he, too, was receiving directions from God and could not but comply.

23) The men had a long, hard trip behind them and, Gentiles though they were, Peter invited them into the house and lodged them for that day and the night, his own host also welcoming these guests. Yes, Peter had a great deal more than food to digest when, hungry as he was (v. 10), the meal that was in preparation (v. 10) was now served to him and to these three unexpected Gentile guests.

Now on the morrow, having arisen (circumstantial as in 9:18; 10:13, 20), **he went out with them, and some of the brethren from Joppa went along**

with him. And on the morrow they went into Caesarea.

The journey was begun the next morning, and six brethren from Joppa went along (11:12), which made a party of ten. We cannot say that Peter was fortifying himself with witnesses, for these men saw only what happened in Cæsarea after Peter had gotten there, and the important matters, the vision of Cornelius and that of Peter, were beyond their direct ken. The brethren went along because of their interest in what was transpiring.

24) They traveled all day, put up for the night, and arrived in Cæsarea the following day (see v. 30). We take it that everything had been planned in advance by Cornelius so that he knew just when his messengers and Peter would arrive.

And Cornelius was expecting them, having called together his relatives and close friends. If Peter had not been found or had not accompanied them, the messengers would probably have traveled all night and would thus have arrived that night. After the night had passed and they had not arrived, Cornelius was in high expectation and knew approximately when his men would return and bring Peter with them. So he summoned all his relatives and also his close friends. All these were alike in their faith, all had been informed in regard to what Cornelius had done, all were anxious to hear what message Peter would bring them. The congregation is assembled and is waiting eagerly for the preacher. One cannot but admire this Roman officer. He is the leader of this flock; many of them owed their faith to him and to his influence. Only one man is needed to start a congregation if he is at all the man he ought to be. We should like to have some details about these relatives and these friends. But that is the way with us, we always want to know more than is related.

25) At this point Codex Bezae and a few other codices read: "Now Peter coming near to Cæsarea, one of the slaves, having run forward, made clear that he had come; but Cornelius, having jumped forth and" — then continuing as in our text: "having met him, on having fallen down," etc. In spite of the fact that, according to v. 24, the travelers are already in the city while this reading still has them drawing near to it, Zahn regards this reading seriously. What follows also contradicts such a view. But Zahn maintains his hypothesis that Luke issued Acts in two editions, the first being represented in Codex Bezae. The many changes, additions, etc., in this first edition (see our introduction to Acts) receive considerable attention in Zahn's commentary but deserve little notice and most likely represent some ambitious scribe's effort to improve Luke's original.

Now, when it came to pass that Peter came in, having met him, Cornelius, on having fallen at his feet, did obeisance. But Peter raised him up, saying, Rise up; I myself also am a man!

Not on the street of the city or on the road to the city did this meeting occur (Zahn supposes the latter) but, as Luke here states, when Peter went in, namely into the house of Cornelius. Then, as was proper for the head of the house, Cornelius met Peter in what we may call his reception room. Note that we have three εἰσελθεῖν: in v. 24 they go into Cæsarea; in v. 25 Peter goes into the house of Cornelius; in v. 27 Peter and his host go into the room where the assembly is waiting for them. All this follows in proper sequence, but Codex Bezae alters it in order to introduce its addition in regard to the slave's running in and Cornelius' leaping up and running out of the city, etc.

The construction ἐγένετο with the subject τοῦ εἰσελθεῖν τὸν Πέτρον was rather difficult for the older grammarians. Winer calls it a construction that drives the infinitive with τοῦ beyond all bounds and shakes his head at a man like Luke for using it. Meyer speaks of the impossibility of explaining this use of the infinitive in a rational manner and calls it a lone instance of a linguistic *Fehlgriff*. But such views are a thing of the past. B.-D. finds that τοῦ may be added pleonastically to nearly any infinitive but that a ὅτι sentence cannot be converted into such an infinitive, this being possible only with regard to ἵνα and ὥστε clauses. So one breathes easier. R. 1067, etc., regards this infinitive with τοῦ which is used as a subject as a Hebraism and finds examples in the LXX and elsewhere. Other explanations may be disregarded. Compare Luke 17:1, and I Cor. 16:4. The genitive force of τοῦ has been lost.

Cornelius falls at the feet of Peter and thus makes obeisance to him as to a supernatural messenger sent to him from God. This is the first time Peter had such an experience. The translation of our versions, "worshipped him," is misleading unless we remember the inferior sense of this verb in many connections, even as "your worship" is only a title of honor for magistrates, etc. Cornelius was not paying divine honor to Peter but was going beyond the limit that a minister of God or even an angel can accept, Rev. 19:10, etc.; 22:8, etc. This act of Cornelius' does all credit to his humble and willing spirit; but Peter's refusal to accept such an honor does equal credit to him. In great St. Peter's in Rome they still kiss the big toe of the bronze statue of St. Peter; the writer saw a woman and her baby in the act, and if the guide, a learned Italian professor, may be believed, that bronze toe is kissed away and has to be renewed about every so often. Peter ought to visit St. Peter's.

26) Peter promptly raised Cornelius with the peremptory aorist imperative, "Rise up!" and added that he himself was only a man, ἄνθρωπος, a human being. Let all dignitaries in church and in state remember

that. Orientals are far more demonstrative by bowing down their faces to the earth than we Occidentals are. This discounts the obeisance on the part of Cornelius but yet leaves it too strong for Peter.

27) **And conversing with him, he went in and finds many having come together and said to them: You on your part understand how unlawful it is for a man, a Jew, to be in close contact with or to be visiting with one of another nation. And yet to me God showed to declare no man common or unclean; wherefore also without gainsaying I came on being summoned. Accordingly, I ask for what reason you summoned me.**

A beautiful picture: Peter and Cornelius in conversation as they enter the larger room where the whole company sat as an audience. Luke uses the historical (aoristic) present: Peter "finds many having come together." So many that it surprised him. The messengers had not told him that, and Cornelius had probably just mentioned the fact that others were in the room into which he led Peter.

28, 29) In a simple but very direct fashion Peter explains his presence in the house of a Gentile, in contact with this Gentile audience. Note the pivotal points: *you* know — yet to *me* God showed — wherefore I came —— accordingly I ask. Since all Peter's hearers know that it is ἀθέμιτον for any man who is a Jew (the second noun is predicative to the first) to maintain close association with one of another nation, i. e., a non-Jew, or even to be going to him, i. e., keep visiting him, they will naturally want to know how Peter, a Jew, can enter among them for an association that because of its nature must be close, in fact, very close. From the Jewish standpoint such conduct would, indeed, be entirely contrary to law and custom. The κολλᾶσθαι, "to glue oneself to," refers to close association, and προσέρχεσθαι, going to someone, both being durative, to making a practice of such actions, the second being less serious than the first. The Mosaic law had no specific prohibition to this effect, but the entire law with all its regulations had such a prohibition as a result. The man who acted otherwise was going contrary, not to one item of the law, but to the law in its entirety. This was thoroughly understood in Judaism, and Peter takes it for granted that these Gentiles, too, know all about it.

Exceptions are sometimes cited, but King Izates, mentioned in Josephus, *Ant.* 20, 2, 4, etc., is not a true exception, nor are the other cases of making Jewish proselytes. The assumption that the rule of strict separation did not apply to proselytes of the gate, hence not to Cornelius, is mistaken. Why does Peter then speak as he does? Only proselytes of righteousness (of the Sanctuary) were considered the equals of Jews, and the rabbis often spoke very slightingly even of these, as when they were called *sicut scabies Israeli*. The rule of exclusiveness here stated by Peter was not merely a piece of Pharisaic rigorousness, it was the general rule of Judaism. And the rule itself was general and not to be reduced to the regulation that no Jew was to go to Gentiles of his own accord, which would excuse Peter who had been summoned. Peter says to this assembly: "You know what the law is for Jews in this matter, and you see me here in this house and in your company in direct contravention of this law."

Peter confesses that he would never voluntarily have gone contrary to that fixed principle of Judaism, Christian though he now was. It was God who showed him (in the vision) to declare no man common or unclean in the Jewish sense. On the two adjectives see v. 14, 15, and note that Peter is practically quoting and therefore used μηδένα and not οὐδένα. Καί is copulative and yet connects adversative clauses; we do not use "and" in that way and hence translate "and yet." The Greek mind was nimble enough not to need more than καί, which explains what we may call its idiomatic use. "To me," Peter says, God showed; hence without demurring, I came on being summoned. Peter is acting on divine orders; he himself has them apart from what God had communicated to Cornelius. Since these things are now clear, Peter asks for what reason he was summoned, λόγος being used in the sense of "reason" and not of "intent."

30) **And Cornelius said: Four days ago, until this hour I was praying, the ninth hour, in my house; and lo, a man stood before me in brilliant apparel and says: Cornelius, thy prayer was heard and thy alms were remembered before God. Send, therefore, to Joppa and call unto thee Simon who is also called Peter; he is lodging in Simon's, the tanner's, house by the sea. Forthwith, therefore, I sent for thee; and thou on thy part didst well in having come. Now, therefore, we all on our part are here present before God to hear all things, that have been commanded to thee by the Lord.**

The sum of what Peter and Cornelius state before the assembled company is that God himself has arranged this meeting for them. God himself was here opening the door of his church to the entire Gentile world wholly apart from Judaism and the synagogue. That is the feature of the history that Luke here sees and leads his reader to see. This is something that by far transcends Cornelius and Peter, something that must be understood in that light. The phrase with ἀπό is idiomatic and is similar to the use of ἐκ; the Greek always counts forward from the remoter end to himself, we do the reverse. "From the fourth day" = starting at that point. On that day Cornelius was praying "up to this hour" of the day, the time of day that it was now when he was speaking; and by "this hour" he means "the ninth" (v. 3), three o'clock in the afternoon. R. 471 notes that in μέχρι ταύτης τῆς ὥρας we have point of time which is then explained as denoting the entire "ninth hour" by the accusative τὴν ἐννάτην (ὥραν); this, however, is not the object of the participle ("keeping the ninth hour of prayer," R. V.) but merely denotes extent of time: praying that long. Fasting (A. V.) is not in the accepted text. "In my house" means in private devotion, all alone, and not in the local synagogue.

31) Cornelius describes the angel who suddenly stood before him as "a man," which agrees with all the other passages that mention angels, Mark 16:5, "a young man," Luke 24:4, "two men," etc. Although the angels are sexless, they never appear in the form of a woman or of a child (cherubs) but in a form that symbolizes power and authority, a point that ought to be noted when angels are portrayed in church decorations. So also the "brilliant apparel," pure white as is sometimes noted, shining with superearthly radiance, symbolizes holiness. Cornelius retells what the angel had said about his prayer and his alms in v. 4.

32) Then he repeats the order he had received to call Peter from the tanner's house in Joppa. Here the point must not be overlooked that Peter is to come to this Gentile's house. He was already at a tanner's house, at the home of a man who was considered unclean from the Jewish standpoint because he handled hides; he is to go much farther: the one step was to lead to the next, to the one that was really important for the spread of the gospel.

33) Cornelius complied with the angel's orders very promptly and expresses his happiness that Peter, too, came so readily. R., W. P., calls καλῶς ποιεῖν a regular formula for expressing thanks (Phil. 4:14; II Pet. 1:19; III John 6), the participle neatly bringing out the act for which thanks are extended. The sense is: "We certainly thank thee for having come." And now,

in a fine conclusion Cornelius adds: "Here we all are to hear what thou hast to tell us!" Every word and every turn of expression is important.

"Now" the great moment has come to which all these supernatural communications have led. "We all on our part are present here" (note παρά), eager and anxious, ἀκοῦσαι, aorist, to hear effectively and thus hearing to obey. "In the presence of God" with his eyes resting upon us voices the faith that all these Gentiles had received in their hearts because of their connection with the synagogue. Cornelius indicates his military training when he says, "All things that have been commanded thee by the Lord," the perfect participle implying that they stand as the Lord's permanent orders. As military orders, especialy those of the commander-in-chief, are obeyed without question, so Cornelius and all those present intend to obey what the Lord (here referring to God) will communicate to them through Peter.

This is, indeed, a model congregation, model in its attitude toward God, toward his Word, and toward his minister. Here there is true willingness to receive, believe, and obey. Here there is no "if" or "but"; they will accept "all things." Why? They come from the Lord God. Here there is implicit faith, which, however, rests, as it must, on the explicit. They do not as yet know what Peter will say but they do know that what he will say comes from God, and so they are willing to believe.

When this example is held up to our congregations, let it not be overlooked that our congregations must have the same assurance regarding their preachers, that what they say is, indeed, "all that has been commanded to them by the Lord." For with this expression Cornelius paints the model preacher.

34) **And having opened his mouth** (the sonorous formula for proceeding to an important address),

Peter said: Of a truth I am comprehending that God is not a respecter of persons, but in every nation the one fearing him and working righteousness is acceptable to him. The Word which he sent to the sons of Israel, proclaiming as good news peace through Jesus Christ, this is Lord of all.

Luke first mentions two preliminary statements that are parallel to each other and decisive for all that follows, one about God and one about his gospel Word. Peter confesses that "of a truth," literally, "on the basis of reality," he is comprehending (simple progressive present), grasping more and more that God is not a respecter of persons, partial to the Jew merely because he is a Jew, unfair to the Gentile just because he is a Gentile. Προσωπολήμπτης occurs only here and in Chrysostom, but its cognates are used; it refers to a judge who looks at a man's face and renders a verdict, not in accord with the merits of the case, but according as he likes or dislikes the man. The notion of bribery does not lie in the word.

35) In reality God does the contrary (ἀλλά): "in every nation" he accepts only those who fear him and work righteousness. Jew and Gentile who fail to do so he rejects. God is a just Judge. This is the fear of which both Testaments speak constantly, the mark of godly men, the fear of reverence, faith, obedience. And ὁ Θεός is the true God who reveals himself in the Scriptures and not God as some imagine him according to the formula:

> *Jud', Heid' und Hottentott,*
> *Wir glauben all' an einen Gott.*

Both "God" and this "fearing" are definitely revealed in the Word, and neither term is to be determined by men. A wrong conception of God involves a wrong conception of what fearing God means; and vice versa. No greater insult can be offered to God than to disregard his Word concerning himself and our relation to him. In no way does Peter say or imply that a pagan who is serious about what he is pleased to call god is accepted by God.

The first participial designation would suffice, but a second is added in order to make the matter still clearer. Both participles are present, durative, qualitative, substantivized by the article. We have both ὁ ποιῶν and ὁ ἐργαζόμενος δικαιοσύνην with no difference in sense; they are allied to similar expressions such as "pursuing righteousness, faith, love." Thus an attitude of life is referred to, one that is bent on securing "righteousness," a quality of soul and of life that God's verdict approves.

This is far more than doing single deeds and something totally different from doing deeds that men in their verdict are pleased to judge as righteous. See C.-K. 315. The sinner does righteousness when he repents, and a mark of this condition of righteousness is daily contrition and repentance. The contrite sinner does righteousness when he believes and accepts God's pardon in Christ Jesus, and the mark of this condition of righteousness is faith daily renewed. The believer does righteousness when by faith he runs the way of God's commandments, follows in the footsteps of Jesus, bows to the first table of the law and then also to the second.

Doing righteousness is not the simple matter that some make it. Let them look at Cornelius! If his honest pagan convictions had been sufficient, why did he seek the synagogue? If the synagogue had been enough, why was Peter here? A few moral rules of life apart from the Triune God, without Jesus, the Redeemer, are a travesty on Peter's words and will bring tragedy to their advocates. The verbal adjective δεκτός, "one received," refers to God's judgment.

36) As Peter's view is broadening in its true comprehension of God, so also is it in its true comprehension of God's gospel Word. No man can fear God and work righteousness and be accepted by God without the gospel, that gospel as a promise of the Messiah in the old covenant and as fulfillment in Jesus in the new. Peter says that God commissioned this Word, sent it with a message (ἀπέστειλε) to the sons of Israel, "sons" (not "children," our versions). The connotation in "sons" is valuable: these were the legal heirs of Israel who inherited his position and prerogatives in the covenant (see the term in 5:21; 7:23, 37; 9:15; it always has the same high connotation). Not because they were "children" and dear to Israel (τέκνα) but because they were the "sons" and heirs of Israel (υἱοί) did God send his great gospel of Christ to the Jews, and being "sons," they had the high and holy obligation to be like their father Israel in faith.

When he describes this Word and its contents, Peter says of it: "proclaiming as good news peace through Jesus Christ." This is the εἰρήνη, Hebrew *shalom*, of which Jesus Christ, in his person and his office combined (see 2:38), is the Mediator (διά). He purchased and won this "peace," the fruit of his salvation, and bestows it by proclaiming the good news of it, which εὐαγγελίζεσθαι of the Word awakens and is intended for faith. Since it is here used in connection with "the Word" and the verb "gospelizing," "peace" must refer to the saving peace of salvation for sinners when God accepts the sinner for Christ's sake and remits all his sins. This mighty statement should not be toned down by introducing peace between Jew and Gentile, between nation and nation, man and man.

With the resumptive οὗτος Peter declares, "This (i. e., Word) is Lord of all" (i. e., of all men), namely of Jew and Gentile alike. It and it alone is the divine Ruler of men; it alone directs, guides, blesses them.

The emphasis is strongly on this last predicate "Lord of all" which includes also the Gentile world. As Christ is our saving, beneficent Lord, so is his gospel which brings him to us. It is "the gospel of peace" (Eph. 6:15), of peace with God, and rules our hearts in such a way that we enjoy the fulness of this peace. What a glorious thought: all men under this one Lord, the Word which proclaims peace! A few of the fathers thought that "Word" signified the Logos as sent to the sons of Israel, but that would illy fit the context.

Our versions with their parenthesis and their labored construction of this and the following verse, and still more the grammars with their efforts at construing these verses which lead them even to amend the assured reading of the text, exhibit the confusion that has resulted from failure to understand what Peter says. B.-D. 162, 7 and 295 reject Κύριος when not a single text exists without it; some texts omit ὅν. The parenthesis is peculiarly unfortunate and makes the statement a side-issue, namely that Jesus Christ is Lord of all. What perplexed so many is the accusative τὸν λόγον at the beginning of the verse; they thought that this was intended as the object of οἴδατε in v. 37 and did not hesitate to make ῥῆμα its synonym (our versions, for instance). Τὸν λόγον is accusative by inverse attraction to its relative, of which construction there are many other examples, I Cor. 10:16; Matt. 21:42. This usage is so common that it should have been readily recognized, likewise that οὗτος is resumptive as it is in a number of cases and so plainly resumes all that has been said about this λόγος that was sent to Israel.

37) After the two great opening statements in regard to God and the gospel, which voice the heart of what Peter has to say to his Gentile hearers, he launches into the body of his address. That is why he uses no connective and thus indicates that his main discourse now begins. **You yourselves know the**

utterance that came down through the whole of Judea, having begun from Galilee after the baptism which John heralded, Jesus from Nazareth, how God anointed him with the Holy Spirit and power, who went from place to place doing good and healing all those tyrannized by the devil because God was with him. And we, we are witnesses of all things which he did both in the country of the Jews and in Jerusalem.

Peter reviews briefly what his hearers already know and contrasts ὑμεῖς with the ἡμεῖς occurring in v. 39: "*You,* you know all this; *we,* we were the actual witnesses of all this and can thus testify and assure you that you heard the truth." They heard the ῥῆμα, "the utterance" that men made when they told what follows; this talk went through the whole of Judea after starting with great volume from Galilee after John the Baptist preached his baptism and had thereby prepared the way. The news was spread abroad in exactly such a manner. It began after John had come, started with great volume from Galilee, then filled all Judea. The τὸ ῥῆμα does not resume and continue the τὸν λόγον of v. 36. The latter refers to the gospel itself with all its contents while the former means that men spoke and were not silent but told about Jesus.

But ἀρξάμενος causes the grammarians and the exegetes some difficulty. Zahn thinks that it is a solecism; others decide for the neuter and have a few texts to support them (B.-D. 137, 3) but fail to explain why the masculine appears in all the other texts. Although the participle is masculine it modifies the neuter τὸ ῥῆμα. We have the same phenomenon in Luke 24:47, where the same participle is in the nominative when the construction demands the accusative. The masculine nominative is retained unaltered in the Greek and is neither solecism nor anacoluthon (R., *W. P.,* and 413); πλήρης is similarly retained without being declined.

38) "Jesus from Nazareth" does not depend on οἴδατε in v. 37, for it is the object of ἔχρισεν and is proleptic for the sake of emphasis, and αὐτόν is pleonastically inserted where the name would otherwise be placed. The clause with ὡς is in apposition with τὸ ῥῆμα. The news that passed from mouth to mouth and filled the land was: "How God anointed him — Jesus from Nazareth — with the Holy Spirit and power." That anointing took place immediately after the baptism of Jesus. The verb is the historical aorist and reports the one act of anointing and uses the sacred, ceremonial verb χρίω (not ἀλείφω). This verb does not refer to the Incarnation or to Nazareth (Luke 4:14) because Jesus is here said to be from Nazareth, or in a general way to the entire life of Jesus.

Peter is speaking to Gentiles who have come into contact with the synagogue; they seem to need no explanation in regard to the Holy Spirit and how that Spirit could anoint Jesus. The Old Testament must be far clearer in regard to the three Persons of the Godhead than the critics are willing to admit. With the Holy Spirit "and power" makes emphatic the feature of the anointing that was so prominent in all the work of Jesus: he was full of power. The Spirit and the power had come upon him. This refers to his human nature. Peter says still more, namely, that God was with him. Thus all three Persons cooperated in our redemption. We see no reason why the miraculous anointing of Jesus could not have been generally known and reported as Peter here states. Those who witnessed it certainly told others.

The Greek often uses the relative pronoun in an emphatic manner where we should begin a new sentence. So here and again in v. 39 we have: "who" = "he who," he was the one who went from place to place (διά in the verb) "doing good and (to be specific) healing (even the worst imaginable ailment) all those tyrannized by the devil." In this graphic way the demoniacs are described. It is the physician Luke who records these words; compare 5:16; 8:7; and the entire subject as discussed in connection with Matt. 4:24; 8:28; Mark 1:23; Luke 4:33. Peter ascribes demoniacal possession to the devil, διάβολος ("slanderer"), the head of the hellish kingdom who acts through his spirit subjects. All that Jesus did showed that "God was with him," μετά, in company with him; compare Luke 1:66; John 3:2; and the great statements of Jesus himself, John 8:16, 29; 10:30; and many others. Peter is showing his hearers the man "Jesus from Nazareth" of whom all men spoke at the time he was on earth and reveals his connection with God.

39) Now the emphatic ἡμεῖς. Peter's hearers only knew. Peter and the other apostles — for of these he speaks and not of the six brethren from Joppa — had been actual eyewitnesses inasmuch as they had themselves seen "all things which he did both in the land of the Jews (in general) and in Jerusalem (the capital, in particular)"; ὧν is attracted from ἅ. With this emphatic "we" Peter assures his hearers of the full truth of what they thus know about Jesus.

Whom also they made away with by hanging him on wood. This one God raised up on the third day and gave him to become manifest, not to all the people, but to witnesses designated beforehand by God, to us, such as ate with him and drank with him after that he arose from the dead.

Peter does not say that his hearers know also these things. They knew that Jesus had been crucified. But Peter prefers to consider the death and the resurrection as a unit and, apart from anything his hearers had heard, himself to present this part of the gospel story. The pronoun "whom," like the one used in v. 38, is emphatic and really begins a new sentence: "him, whom," he it was whom they made away with, (ἀνεῖλον), the verb we have met so repeatedly. Καί = even this they did, leaving the subject of this frightful deed unnamed, "they," yes, "they." But he adds the aorist participle of means: "by hanging him on wood" as one who was accursed in the eyes of all Jews; see the explanation in 5:30, and the explanation in Gal. 3:13. We feel the throbbing contrasts that we have seen Peter use against the Sanhedrin and the Jews (2:36; 3:13-15; 4:10; 5:30, 31): *God* anointed him, *God* was with him, but they *even* made away with him, and then *God* raised him up. Here only καί points to the contrast. Peter shows no bitterness toward the Jews who killed Jesus.

40) With a decidedly emphatic resumptive τοῦτον, "this one," which includes all that has thus far been said about Jesus, especially what was said about his being killed as being accursed, Peter states the great fact of the resurrection of Jesus and the evidence for that fact. The fact is simply that "God raised him up on the third day," here ascribing the resurrection to God, in v. 41 to Jesus himself. Both are equally true since all the *opera ad extra sunt indivisa aut communa* according to Scripture testimony. God did more: "he gave him to become manifest," i. e., granted that Jesus appeared. This was not a gift to Jesus but, as the following datives state, a gift to us. The manifestations of the resurrection continued for forty days in the repeated appearances of the risen Savior.

41) Peter tells this very carefully. Someone may ask why everybody did not see the risen Jesus. Peter says that God gave his being manifest "not to all the people." These manifestations were intended for the specific purpose of attesting the resurrection of Jesus to the whole world, attesting it beyond a doubt. God could not use anybody and everybody for that task and high honor. When the people who wanted Jesus hung on wood as being accursed heard from the Roman sol-

diers at the tomb how Jesus had arisen, they bribed these indirect witnesses to lie and to deny the resurrection. People, who in spite of all that they had seen and heard of Jesus had, nevertheless, refused to have faith in him, were unfit to be witnesses of his resurrection, and an appearance of Jesus to them would have increased their unbelief by that much. God thus chose his own witnesses. The participle states that he selected them with his own hand, for they had to be prepared and qualified properly to attest the resurrection.

"To us," Peter says, God gave Jesus to become manifest. The pronoun is emphatic by position, "to us," his believers, 500 at one time, I Cor. 15:6, in particular to the apostles to whom Jesus showed himself repeatedly and before whom he ascended to heaven. How complete and how intimate this manifestation was Peter indicates by means of the relative clause: "such as ate with him and drank with him after that he arose from the dead." Οἵτινες is to be construed with "we" in the inflectional endings of the verbs, and the eating and drinking refer to Luke's own statements made in 1:4; Luke 24:42. In fact, Peter here speaks as though eating and drinking may have gone beyond what these passages state.

Peter is now acting the witness. He is so specific and exact in his testimony that these Gentile hearers of his who may have heard something about the resurrection of Jesus shall now receive solid assurance. Peter's testimony is that of an eyewitness. In I Cor. 15:4-8 Paul lists the essential witnesses on whose testimony our faith rests. Here Peter ascribes the resurrection to Jesus himself; on ἐκ νεκρῶν and its misinterpretation see 3:16.

42) **And he charged us to herald to the people and to attest that this One is he that has been ordained by God as Judge of quick and dead. To**

this One all the prophets bear witness that every one believing in him receives through his name remission of sins.

Peter means that Jesus gave the order to the apostles to herald, etc. In v. 40, God is the subject and he might be the subject also here in v. 42 if it were not for the following phrase "by God." Both infinitives are effective aorists: "to herald and attest" so that the work is thoroughly, effectively done and leaves nothing to be added.

Κηρύσσειν means to proclaim aloud as a herald, to make an announcement, "to preach" in this sense. The herald announces what he is ordered to announce, no more, no less, and without alteration. That remains the preacher's task to this day although many think that they are authorized to herald their own ideas. Only one message has the Lord's authorization. Any alteration of that message, any substitution for it, is not only empty but, when it pretends to be the Lord's true message, makes the herald who proclaims it a liar, a false prophet.

When Peter says τῷ λαῷ and uses the same word that occurs in v. 41, the reference is to Israel, λαός being steadily used in this restricted sense; "the people" is not to be understood in the sense of men in general, the word for this would be ἄνθρωποι. Peter refers to 1:8, the command to begin preaching in Jerusalem and in Judea, i. e., among the Jews. The idea to be expressed is that thus far and by the Lord's own direction the heralding has been limited to "the people," the Jews, as it was, indeed, natural that it should be. This heralding was to be an attesting, the depositions of sworn witnesses as though they were under oath to God.

The climax of their heralding and solemn (διά) attestation was to be "that this One is he that has been ordained by God as Judge of quick and dead." Here the deictic οὗτος is again resumptive and gathers up all that Peter has said about "Jesus from Nazareth." He whom God anointed, etc., whom God raised from the dead and gave to be manifest as risen — he is the One, he alone, who has been ordained and stands as thus ordained (this is the force of the perfect participle) by God as Judge of quick and dead. He who by his death and his resurrection redeemed men shall at the last day judge them as to whether they accepted his redemption or not. A natural, yea, an essential connection demands this ordination or appointment of Jesus as the final Judge.

It should be evident that this ordination pertains to his human nature even as Peter used the human name "Jesus from Nazareth." "For . . . to have all judgment . . . are not created gifts, but divine, infinite properties, and yet these have been given and communicated to the man Christ . . . . what Holy Scripture testifies that Christ received in time he received not according to the divine nature (according to which he has everything from eternity), but the person has received it in time *ratione et respectu humanae naturae*, that is, as referring, and with respect to, according to the assumed human nature." *C. Tr.* 1033 etc., 55, etc. John 5:22 and especially 27; Acts 17:31.

"Quick and dead" need no articles (R. 419), they are like other pairs. The "quick," "living," are those who shall still be alive at the end of the world. "Quick and dead" put it beyond question that Peter is speaking of the final judgment. Yet even here Peter is not stressing the universality of the gospel and of Jesus' work. He is stating only the great acts of God regarding Jesus. How they apply to his present Gentile hearers who are in a class other than the Jews, Peter made plain in his very first sentence (v. 34).

43) The note of universality struck at the start resounds again at the end of the address. Τούτῳ is now

more emphatic than ever as embracing all that has thus far been said regarding Jesus, *"to this One,"* yea, to Him, all the prophets of the Old Testament who were known to Cornelius and all these Gentiles through the LXX bear witness that he and he alone is the Savior. The object of μαρτυροῦσιν is the clause with the accusative and infinitive which summarily states what all the prophets testify and is thus in indirect discourse. All the prophets unite in saying that "remission of sins receives through his name everyone believing in him." This is the Greek word order which places a strong emphasis on both object and subject by putting the former first and the latter last — read it aloud in order to get the effect. See the discussion of ἄφεσις in 2:38. This complete riddance of sin and guilt is received by every believer through Jesus' name.

The aorist λαβεῖν is used to indicate the one effective act of receiving. Remission and riddance of sins are bestowed on him by God, and thus he has them. The reception is effected "through his name," διά presenting his Name as the medium that effects the remission. It is, of course, the objective medium, God's great means for ridding the sinner of his guilt. It is essential, however, to see what ὄνομα means. Review the term as it is discussed in 2:31, 38; 3:6, and in the following passages. In all of them it is the revelation which brings Jesus and his person and his saving work to the sinner. In all these phrases and connections the "name" does not mean "authority" or "power." Compare what C.K. has to say on pages 800 and 803: God's name = "what God is as the God of the saving *revelation*", praying in Jesus' name = on the basis of and in connection with what has *unveiled* itself in Jesus. C.-K. also discusses the latest literature on the subject, omitting, however, S. Goebel, *Die Reden unseres Herrn nach Johannes*, II, 120, which is especially fine.

No remission is possible except "through his name." But this *name* as the revelation of what Jesus is and what he did and thus is for us always has as its correlative *faith*, the knowledge of this name and the confidence of the heart which embraces all that this conveys and clings to it and relies upon it in life and in death. Faith is thus the subjective means of remission. Peter says that "everyone believing in him" receives remission, the present participle is subtantivized and describes the person as continuing in faith. The name with all that it embraces and reveals produces this confidence by deserving in the highest degree that all sinners rely upon it and upon it alone for remission. When Peter says "everyone believing" he reverts to v. 34, and gently but most effectively opens the door of the gospel and of the Christian Church to the Gentiles sitting before him in rapt attention. It was, indeed, a great hour in the progress of the gospel!

44) While Peter was still uttering these utterances, the Holy Spirit fell upon all those hearing the Word. And amazed were the believers of the circumcision, as many as came with Peter, that also upon the Gentiles the gift of the Holy Spirit was being poured out. For they began to hear them speaking with tongues and magnifying God.

Here we see how God himself finished the work which he had inaugurated and directed from the beginning. In 11:15, Peter says that the Holy Spirit descended "when I began to speak"; he had intended to say much more, but all that he had to reserve until some later time. God spoke in his own mighty way at this point by sending the Holy Spirit upon these Gentiles. The verb "fell" denotes the suddenness and also the descent from above.

45) Before Luke continues the narrative proper he records the amazement of the six Jewish Christians who had come from Joppa with Peter. They are dumb-

founded "because the gift of the Holy Spirit is being poured out also upon the Gentiles." The Greek retains the present tense "is being poured out" of the direct discourse of these Jewish believers; but it includes more than this one instance of outpouring and states that as a general thing, as this striking case shows, the Gentiles were receiving "the gift of the Holy Spirit," i. e., were by God himself being placed on a par with all believers from Judaism. That was the astounding thing. It was God and God alone and most directly who gave "the gift." At this time he preferred to dispense with the laying on of hands (8:17); he did not even wait until these Gentiles had been baptized. That is a minor point. At Pentecost the 3,000 received the Spirit charismatically neither before nor after their baptism. The Pentecostal charisma was never repeated in the congregation at Jerusalem. There were signs and miracles many but no speaking with tongues.

Confusion has resulted by failing to notice that "the gift of the Holy Spirit" referred to at this point is the same gift that was bestowed at the time of Pentecost, a charisma, and only a charisma and not the gift of the Spirit, and certainly not the gift of sudden total sanctification. All those who spoke with tongues at the time of Pentecost were already saved, and none of those who were saved that day received the Spirit miraculously and spoke with tongues. All those who heard Peter in the house of Cornelius had faith and were saved before the Spirit came and gave them the ability to speak with tongues. The same is true with regard to the Samaritans, 8:15-17. This falling of the Spirit upon people, this charismatic gift of the Spirit, is entirely separate from the Spirit's reception by faith for salvation and by baptism for regeneration and renewing (Tit. 3:5).

When this is understood, Luke's account will not be referred to in order to deprive baptism of its saving power as though the Spirit comes apart from and without baptism, and as though baptism is only an empty symbol and sign. Peter did not regard baptism thus in the present instance. Since these Jewish Christians called the charismatic gift of the Spirit a pouring out, some say it was "the baptism of the Spirit," or "that these Gentiles were baptized with the Spirit." That may pass but only as long as this "baptism" is viewed as charismatic and as nothing more.

46) With γάρ Luke explains "the gift of the Holy Spirit": Peter and his companions "began to hear them speaking with tongues," ἤκουον, the inchoative imperfect. Note αὐτῶν λαλούντων γλώσσαις, and in 2:4, λαλεῖν ἑτέραις γλώσσαις; then also μεγαλυνόντων τὸν Θεόν, "magnifying God," and in 2:11, τὰ μεγαλεῖα τοῦ Θεοῦ — the language is strikingly similar. We have these three in a direct line: 2:2-13; 8:15-17; and now 10:44-46. The miracle is the same, a sudden speaking in languages the speakers had never learned, first by Jewish, secondly by Samaritan, and now thirdly by Gentile Christians, the plain intention being to show that God made no difference between them, in particular by placing the Samaritan and the Gentile believers on a par with the Jewish believers. One Spirit — many tongues!

But some do not share this view. In 2:4, Luke writes ἑτέραις: they spoke with *"other"* tongues; and here he leaves out this adjective. So in Jerusalem the speaking was done in "other" human languages, but here in Cæsarea in no human languages. There were *two* kinds of speaking with tongues. And this argument is based on the omission of the word "other." But what, then, were these tongues if they were not "other" human languages? Various suggestions are offered, but none of them are acceptable.

We have discussed this subject in connection with 2:4 and find full confirmation here. Peter and Cornelius must have spoken in Greek, and Peter's speech must have been made in that language. And now first one and then another — certainly not several in a babel — "magnified God" by speaking in some other and strange language, one in this, another in some other. This phenomenon occurred again in 19:6. The identity of the occurrence with that of Pentecost is placed beyond question by 15:8: "giving them the Holy Spirit, even as unto us" at Pentecost; also in 11:15-17. At Cæsarea, however, no strangers were at hand to be impressed by the miracle of tongues. The object of the miracle was different, namely to reveal to all present how God "made no distinction between us (Jewish believers) and them (Gentile believers)," 15:9.

47) Then answered Peter, Can anyone forbid the water so that these be not baptized, such as received the Holy Spirit as also we ourselves? And he ordered that they be baptized in the name of Jesus Christ. Then they requested him to remain for some days.

"Answered," as frequently, is used in the wider sense of responding to a situation. "Certainly no one can forbid," etc., μήτι, the interrogative particle, expects a negative answer. Peter asks whether anyone is able to hinder it that the water necessary to baptize these Gentiles be brought and the sacrament be duly administered. Was anyone able to offer valid objection? He was sure that no one was able.

The verb of hindering, κωλύειν, is construed with τοῦ μή and the infinitive, but the sense with μή is: "so that not" (B.-D. 400, 4), it is consecutive; μή is omitted when the infinitive is unmodified (B.-D. 392, 1), and sometimes μή seems redundant according to us (B.-D. 429). This is more exact than R., W. P., that the negative may or may not appear after a verb of hindering.

Οἵτινες is causal: "since they received," etc., R. 728. It is God himself who makes Peter so certain, for he had given these Gentiles the Holy Spirit. "As also we ourselves," and again in 11:15, "as on us at the beginning," also the context of 11:15-17, are decisive as far as the miracle of Pentecost and this one here in Cæsarea are concerned: they are identical.

When Knowling interprets, "The greater had been bestowed; could the lesser be withheld?" he has reversed the two. Paul regards the gift of tongues as being the least of all and shows the Corinthians something far better, I Cor. 12:31. Baptism with its regenerating and renewing grace (Tit. 3:5) vastly excels the transient speaking with tongues. Peter makes no wrong comparison in his question. He implies that the gift of tongues is God's indication that these Gentiles are just as acceptable to him as the Jews (v. 34, 35), therefore baptism and Christianity are intended for them. We should not confuse the gift of the Spirit, which is but a transient charisma, with the gift of the Spirit in and through Word and sacrament, which is permanent and eternal salvation.

When Peter asks about someone hindering the water he is not thinking of the Mediterranean or some body of water but of water to be brought in; somebody might try to prevent its being brought in. We may hinder a person from going to a body of water but never the body of water itself. Peter's question does not suggest immersion. It sounds as though the whole company was promptly baptized with water that had been brought into the room where all were assembled.

48) The aorist verbs and infinitives imply that what they speak of was done. We should note the passive, "that they be baptized," and that Peter does not say "to baptize them," active. We give an order to do something and not that something be done. It is this passive infinitive that prevents us from agreeing with those who say that Peter ordered the disciples from Joppa who had accompanied him to baptize these Gentiles and then cite I Cor. 1:16, and John 4:2, with the

remark that the apostles considered it less their duty to baptize than to preach, and overlook the fact that this does not agree with Matt. 28:19, where Jesus puts baptizing and teaching (two participles) on the same plane. As to I Cor. 1:16, Paul congratulates himself that the Pauline party could not point to him and make his administration of baptism the basis of their party.

The apostles do not share the view which makes baptism only a symbol instead of a channel of grace. We remember that Cornelius had been ordered to call Peter and not also the brethren of Joppa and that Peter had been ordered to go and not also others. The six brethren went along of their own accord. Peter "ordered that they be baptized" (or "them to be baptized," our versions) means that he gave an order for water for the baptism. And none of the six brethren were able to object. Peter first asked whether any one of them was able to offer valid objection, and none could. Then he called for the water and baptized the Gentiles. A strange thing, indeed, if he had not done so with his own hands! Here we have this first body of Gentiles entering the church, entering it through Peter, God making all the arrangements for Peter, and yet Peter telling ordinary brethren to do the baptizing! But the idea behind this view is that these Gentiles were immersed, underwent Zahn's *Vollbad*, and that was too great a task for Peter, he shifted it to the six brethren. Even so if it be considered a task, why did Peter not help?

Baptism was the decisive act. That admitted these Gentiles into the Christian Church, admitted them directly from Gentilism and without first having to pass through Judaism. That is why Luke says no more about Cornelius or the congregation that was thus formed in Cæsarea. His story has been told: in Cæsarea the Gentiles first entered the Christian Church. The aorist tenses imply that Peter gladly remained "for some days." But this means a good deal as 11:3 indicates. Peter had not only entered a Gentile's house and thus defiled himself according to Jewish ideas, he remained and lodged in the home of Cornelius, ate his Gentile host's food which was anything but kosher. All this was decisive for Peter himself. He on his part was sloughing off the old Jewish legalism and ceremonialism. *Aurei dies!* Bengel exclaims; yes, these were golden days for the entire church.

CHAPTER XI

PETER JUSTIFIES THE RECEPTION OF THE GENTILES

1) **Now the apostles and the brethren, those throughout Judea, heard that also the Gentiles received the Word of God.**

The news of all that had occurred in Cæsarea, no doubt, spread rapidly, chiefly, however, the great fact itself that "also the Gentiles" had become Christians. The point to be noted was that as Gentiles, without first becoming full Jewish proselytes like those mentioned in 2:10, "they received (we should say: had received) the Word," meaning that, by having thus received it, they had been admitted into the Christian Church. This, indeed, was important news. Where the apostles were when they heard this Luke does not say. The assumption that they were in Jerusalem is not verifiable; like Peter, they were busy here and there, which explains why Luke does not mention their location. The brethren throughout Judea include those in Jerusalem; κατά may be considered distributive (R., W. P.), The news, no doubt, penetrated also to other places, but Luke is concerned especially with Judea which includes Jerusalem.

2) **And when Peter went up to Jerusalem, those of the circumcision began to contend with him, saying, To men having foreskin thou didst go in and didst eat with them.**

We have no way of knowing how long Peter remained in Cæsarea and how soon he returned to Jerusalem. To speak about a year and to include work in other places is an unnecessary insertion. In v. 12 the six brethren from Joppa appear in Jerusalem with

Peter. This makes it unlikely that Peter waited so long a time before going back to Jerusalem, or that he first toured Galilee. It is most probable that the interval did not extend beyond two or three weeks, and that thus these six brethren from Joppa were still in Peter's company.

In Jerusalem, Peter met objection to his course of action in Cæsarea. "Those of the circumcision began to contend with him," inchoative imperfect, leaving the outcome of this contending to be stated in the sequel. In 10:45, "the believers of the circumcision" intends to say only that the six brethren with Peter were circumcised Jewish Christians and to contrast them with "the Gentiles" who were not circumcised. Here, however, "those of the circumcision" has a narrower sense, namely those who contended for circumcision as being necessary for membership in the Christian Church, the circumcision party. In Gal. 2:12 the designation is still narrower: the circumcision party as Judaizers and legalists. The beginnings of this party appear here in this contention with Peter. When the proponents of these views developed into a permanent party in the church and caused Paul so much trouble, they mixed the gospel with the old Jewish ceremonial legalism by contending that this latter alone was the true gospel.

3) The attack on Peter centered in the point that he had gone in to and had eaten with "men having ἀκροβυστία, the prepuce, foreskin," i. e., uncircumcised men. The point at issue is not that Peter should not have gone in to them, and that it would have been different if they had come to him; the latter would have been just as bad. The point is that simply to go in and then — still worse — to eat was wrong, to say nothing of baptizing such men and receiving them into the church. This circumcision party appealed to the Mosaic regulations which were clear in regard to circumcision and kosher foods. Already these regulations,

they claimed, condemned Peter's proceeding as being totally wrong. This contention was perfectly correct — *if*, indeed, the Mosaic regulations were still in force; then the only way into the church was through the synagogue.

To appreciate this point we must remember that until this time all the believers, even those in Samaria, were recruited from the circumcised. To bring in uncircumcised men, to enter into full fraternal relation with them in their own houses and at their own tables was a revolutionary innovation. The whole question as to whether this dared to be done came upon these Jewish Christians with a suddenness in the conduct of Peter who had gone and done this astounding thing. The fact that some should object was certainly natural, especially since they were not as yet fully informed as to how Peter had been impelled by God himself to do what he had done. The wonder is that all of them did not object, and also that not a single apostle objected. It has been well said that here Peter was certainly not treated as a pope, to say nothing of an infallible pope. With refreshing openness he was taken to task for his conduct.

4) **But Peter, beginning, proceeded to set out (the matter) in order for them, saying: I for my part was in Joppa city praying and I saw in an ecstasy a vision, a kind of receptacle coming down, like a great linen sheet being let down by four corners out of heaven, and it came to me. Into which having earnestly gazed, I began to consider and saw the four-footed things of the earth and the wild beasts and the creeping things and the flying things of the heaven; moreover, I heard also a voice saying to me, Having arisen, Peter, slay and eat! But I said, By no means, Lord! because a common or unclean thing never yet came into my mouth. Yet there answered a voice a second time out of heaven,**

What God did cleanse, do thou stop making common! Moreover, this occurred three times; and all were drawn up again into heaven.

We are agreed that the contention with Peter and his reply occurred at a meeting of the congregation at Jerusalem. That, too, explains the elaborate way in which Luke introduces this reply of Peter's. Ἀρξάμενος is circumstantial but scarcely pleonastic; it marks the importance of the reply as now begun, parallels the adverb "in order," and means "beginning" and not "from the beginning" (A. V.). Peter began and went on telling the whole story just as it had happened. He did not argue in the least; he let the facts speak for others just as they had spoken for him. The imperfect ἐξετίθετο should receive more attention, "he proceeded to set out." It continues the previous imperfect διεκρίνοντο. Both are descriptive, but both intend to hold the reader in suspense as to the final outcome which is recorded by the aorists in v. 18 after Peter has delivered his address. Here were these people contending with Peter, here was Peter telling his story. What was the result? Verse 18 tells us.

5) Peter tells the story as we already know it from 10:9-16 (the vision of Peter) and the following. Only a few variations need receive attention. Ἐγώ is emphatic, "I on my part," or, "as for me, I was in Joppa city," etc. "Ecstasy" and "vision" have been explained. The point of emphasis in Peter's story is, of course, the fact that God sent the vision of the great sheet to him. He was engaged in his devotions and had no idea of what was coming, least of all that he should have any dealings with Gentiles. He was not even in Cæsarea but miles away. He adds the point that the great sheet "came up to me," which explains how he could see its contents.

6) The aorist participle states how he fastened his eyes on the sheet; the imperfect of the finite verb how

Acts 11:6-9

he began to put his mind on it; then the aorist of the verb how in a flash he saw all the creatures in the sheet. Participle and verbs picture the action perfectly. The imperfect especially shows the mind bent on discovering what the sheet held, the aorist suddenly brings the effort to an end. The list of creatures has the one addition "wild animals," even as in "the four-footed things of the earth" and in "the flying things of the heaven" the idea is that the animals and the birds were unconfined, wild, not domesticated, few if any of them being permitted to Jews as kosher food.

7) Yet "a voice" bids Peter to use these creatures as food. Peter does not try to identify this voice.

8) It was certain to him that he was dealing with the "Lord," and he states how he made answer to him in words that his present objectors would certainly have used if they had been in Peter's place. This was the very point at issue: Peter's eating ceremonially common or unclean, non-kosher food. He shrank from the very idea. He had a clean record thus far. Never had a particle of such food come into his mouth. He had felt exactly as those of the circumcision do who are now taking him to task. Peter said "no" to the Lord. That was not a small thing. Could his objectors have done more?

9) Then Peter relates the exact answer he received which ordered him to stop making common what God himself had cleansed. We have explained this cleansing in v. 15. Peter had the Lord's answer to his objection, and it certainly constituted the answer also for *his objectors*. Let them right here and now stop making food common and forbidden which God himself had made clean and even bade Peter eat! A statement of the simple fact of what had occurred was far more effective than any argument or reasoning of a general nature could have been.

10) And what Peter tells occurred no less than three times. Let nobody, then, attempt to say that there must be some mistake. And let all note that Peter held out to the end by stressing his old Jewish prejudice and refusal. No, that was not commendable; it showed no virtue in Peter, it showed only God's patience with his ignorance and his narrowness. Perhaps some of these men may have wondered whether, if they had been put into Peter's place, they would have held out as long as he did. Yet the vision had accomplished its purpose, it was withdrawn into heaven whence it had come, it did not merely vanish. To the last Peter knew, and now his hearers are to know, that he had been dealing with the Lord.

11) **And lo, forthwith three men stood at the house in which we were, having been commissioned from Cornelius to me. Moreover, the Spirit said to me to go with them, in no respect doubting. And there went with me also these six brethren, and we went into the house of the man. Now he reported to us how he saw the angel in the house stand and say: Send a commission to Joppa and summon Simon, surnamed Peter, who will utter utterances to thee by which thou shalt be saved, thou and all thy house.**

Remarkable, indeed, ("lo") was it that at this precise moment those three men who had been commissioned by Cornelius should have appeared. God had sent the vision to Peter, and the Holy Spirit now furnishes the interpretation. No, not by accident did those messengers appear "forthwith."

12) Peter would have hesitated to go with them to a Roman centurion and a Gentile; he was just like the men who had raised objection to what he had done. It was the Spirit himself who told Peter to go with the messengers and to stop doubting, letting his judgment go now this way and now that (διά and κρίνω). Does

any man intend to say that Peter should have done otherwise than to obey the Spirit and to go as he was bidden? Even in Joppa six of the brethren, the ones who are now here with Peter, were so interested that they went along with him. And so, Peter says, "we went into the house of the man." Even these six brethren who also were of the circumcision (10:45) did not hesitate.

When Peter says in v. 11, "in which we were (ἦμεν)," he is already thinking of these brethren; a variant is ἤμην, "I was." Objection had been raised to Peter's even entering the Gentile's house (v. 3). That is why Peter is so specific on that point. If entering was already wrong and defiling, eating at a Gentile's table could be no worse and hence is not discussed.

13) Peter now tells what God had been doing at the other end by preparing Cornelius and having him summon Peter. He properly quotes the centurion himself and not the messengers in whom he had confided. Here was much more that was astonishing, indeed, but revealed that Peter was only God's agent, and that God himself was the author of everything. An angel had entered into this Gentile's house. He evidently did not fear contamination. God had, of course, sent him to that house. This angel directs Cornelius to summon Peter. Both the summons to Peter and his own orders to obey that summons came from God. Why should any Christian man object?

14) The relative clause in regard to what Peter would do is not found in 10:5, 6, and in 10:22. Here we have a fuller narration. This highly pertinent clause is added in order to let Peter's hearers know what God's great purpose was in bringing Peter into this Gentile's house. He was to tell Cornelius what would save both him and his house (family). It was a matter of saving this household; on the verb and on the noun see 2:47; 4:12. Λαλήσει ῥήματα is important, "he

shall utter utterances," he shall be the Lord's mouthpiece and receive what he is to say from the Lord. "In connection with" these utterances the Lord would save this family, for his word and his grace would be in every word uttered.

"Shall be saved" is passive and implies the Savior as the agent. Despite his connection with the synagogue, Cornelius had not yet found salvation as is clear from 4:12. What Peter says brings out the very thing all these Jewish Christians must realize, namely that they were not saved by circumcision or legal ordinances of Moses but solely and also completely by the utterances which contain the gospel and are connected with the Savior. And these utterances were sufficient to save any man, be he Jew or Gentile.

15) **Now, when I began to make utterance, the Holy Spirit fell on them just as also upon us at the beginning. And I remembered the utterance of the Lord, how he was saying, John baptized with water, but you, you shall be baptized in connection with the Holy Spirit. If, therefore, God gave to them the equal gift as to us as having come to believe on the Lord Jesus Christ, I, who was I, as able to hinder God?**

Here we have the tremendous climax of all that God did in this case. Luke frequently uses the idiom ἐν τῷ with the infinitive, usually the present infinitive but occasionally also the aorist as here. Peter had scarcely begun to speak — we know how little it was that he said, 10:34-43 — when God did the decisive thing as far as putting the Gentiles on an equality with Jews in the matter of receiving them into the church was concerned: he gave them the charisma of the Spirit, namely to speak with tongues, exactly as he had done ἐν ἀρχῇ (many phrases need no articles), "in the beginning," for us, namely at Pentecost. We have discussed the identity of this gift in connection with 10:44-46.

16) When Peter witnessed the charisma at Caesarea, there at once flashed into his memory the Lord's own utterance and promise which he had made just before his ascension, that word and promise which had been spoken already by the Baptist in Matt. 3:11, "how he was saying" (added circumstantially), "John baptized with water, but you, you shall be baptized with the Holy Ghost," see the interpretation in 1:5, also in Matthew. The promise of the Baptist and of Jesus was fulfilled at Pentecost and had an extension in Caesarea, and Peter at once saw it.

17) This is clinched by the conclusion which Peter drew and was intended to draw (οὖν). The condition is one of reality which has the apodosis in the form of a question in order the more forcefully to impress Peter's hearers. If God gave the identical gift to them (Gentiles) as also to us (Jews), they as well as we having come to believe on Jesus, who was Peter and what power had he to interfere and to prevent God from doing such a thing? Τὴν ἴσην δωρεάν is "the like gift" (our versions) in the sense of "the same," "the equal gift."

It was God who placed these Gentiles on an equality with the Jews in so far as both believed on the Lord. The unmodified participle πιστεύσασιν is to be construed with both αὐτοῖς and ἡμῖν: "to them as also to us as having come to believe," R., W. P. Our versions and many commentators would refer this participle only to ἡμῖν, but such a construction would require the article. It is this having come equally to believe that induced God to bestow the equal gift (gift, also in 10:45) *"on them* as also *on us."* The participle is plainly predicative. Having come to faith is the essential thing. By faith the Spirit takes possession of the heart and saves; then, as God deems fit, he may bestow the Spirit also in a charismatic way whenever the interest of the gospel requires this.

Peter asks his critics whether they thought that he was able to prevent God from dealing with these Gentiles as he did. Two questions are fused into one: "Who was I?" and, "Was I able?" The very idea that Peter might hinder God in this bestowal is preposterous. Did his critics intend to claim that he should have attempted that? The question asked them involves also whether they would so hinder God.

18) **Now, having heard these things, they were quiet and glorified God, saying, Then also to the Gentiles did God give the repentance unto life!**

Here the imperfects "began to contend" and "proceeded to set out in order" which occur in v. 2 and 4 are brought to their completion in the two aorists "were quiet and glorified." Here were critics, indeed, but when the actual facts were placed before them, they sought not to carp, they were convinced, they capitulated, "they were quiet" as to any further objection; nay, more, they glorified God, and that for the real and essential thing which is expressed as a deduction by ἄρα, "then" or "accordingly," namely that "also to the Gentiles did God give the repentance unto life." "Then" refers to all that Peter had said, most especially to the last part of his address, the bestowal of the Spirit by the charisma of tongues. That was the evidence of something far greater, the bestowal of "the repentance" which brought "life," ζωή, spiritual, everlasting life.

On μετάνοια see 2:38; it consists of contrition and faith, the turn of the heart from sin to Christ and his pardon. Where this is found, "life" enters, namely the life of faith which is connected with Christ, the Life. This life is invisible, it is in the soul or heart, in this respect it is like our physical life; but, again like our physical life, wherever it is present it manifests itself in endless ways. Those who are spiritually alive love the Lord, confess him, worship him, pray to him, feed on his Word, serve him, etc.

God has succeeded in opening the door of the church to the Gentiles; he succeeded also in having the Jewish Christians who were already within the portal welcome these incoming Gentiles and praise him for bringing them in.

The Church at Antioch

19) Once more, as he had done in 9:31, Luke reverts to Stephen's death; οἱ μὲν οὖν is used as it was in 1:6. **They, then, that were scattered due to the tribulation that occurred in the case of Stephen went on through as far as Phoenicia and Cyprus and Antioch, speaking the Word to no one except only to Jews.**

As a result of the first persecution Luke related to us the conversion of Saul and his story as far as the return to Tarsus; then Peter's activity outside of Jerusalem which ended with the acceptance of Gentile converts by the brethren in Jerusalem. Now, again reverting to the persecution, Luke records the story of Antioch.

According to a conservative estimate there were 25,000 Christians in Jerusalem at the time of Stephen's death. The great dispersion that ensued as a result of Saul's activity scattered quite a number of these to rather distant and safe parts. Some of them naturally migrated into Phoenicia, into cities like Tyre, Sidon, and Ptolomais along the Mediterranean; others crossed to the great island of Cyprus where many Jews dwelt; finally — and this is the important point to Luke — a goodly number went as far north as

Antioch and thus bring this future center of Christianity to our notice for the first time.

The data in regard to Antioch are compiled in the Bible dictionaries. We note that because of its population of half a million Antioch was rated as the third city in the entire Roman empire, being outranked only by Rome and Alexandria. At one time it had been the residence of the Seleucian kings; later it became the residence of the Roman procurators of Syria. Lying a bit inland on the Orontes River, its seaport was Seleucia from which Paul started his sea voyages when he set out on his great missionary tours. Cilicia bordered on Syria, and Tarsus was not far distant from Antioch. Many Jews were residing in this pagan city which exhibited both the splendor and the vices of the Roman and the Oriental paganism. Starting with the present account of Luke, Antioch loomed large in the entire early history of the Christian Church.

When Christian fugitives from Jerusalem, all of whom were native Jews or complete Jewish proselytes, settled in Antioch they naturally spread the gospel among the Antiochian Jews in the synagogues of the city, and Luke notes that this was the extent of their first missionary efforts. These limited missionary efforts were not due to a question of language as between the Aramaic of the Jews in Antioch and the Jewish Christians from Jerusalem, on the one hand, and the Greek of the general population of Antioch, on the other. Greek was known to all. In fact, to this day, as we ourselves found in our eastern travels, men residing in these territories speak several languages with ease. In Caesarea, in the house of Cornelius, Peter spoke Greek although he had been but a fisherman on the Lake of Galilee.

20) **But some of them were Cyprian and Cyrenian men, such as, on coming to Antioch, began to**

speak also to the Greeks, proclaiming as good news the Lord Jesus Christ.

The decisive points are: first, the reading "Greeks" and next, the chronology. We must have the reading Ἕλληνας, the common word for pagan Greeks which is often used in contrast with "barbarians," the term for natives of all kinds who did not speak Greek and had no Greek culture. Greeks and Jews are also frequently paired and contrasted. Both were on a higher level in the old world although they differed from each other, and all barbarians were beneath them.

The texts which have Ἑλληνιστάς, "Hellenists," "Grecians," cannot be correct, for these were Jews, namely Jews who had been born outside of Palestine but were of Jewish blood and religion just as much as those who had been born in Palestine. In 2:9-11 we have quite a list of such foreign-born Jews; the 3,000 converts made at the time of Pentecost were, for the most part, such Hellenists. In 6:1 we have discussed the two types of Jews, "Hebrews" and "Hellenists." When Luke states in v. 19 that the Christians at first spoke the gospel to Jews only, the "Jews" were these foreign-born Jews or Hellenists, at least for the greater part, since the proportion of Jews who had been born in Palestine was not so large in Antioch. To say that the gospel was spread among such would mean nothing, for this had been done on an extensive scale on the day of Pentecost and had been done ever since that time. But to say that some Christians were now preaching Christ to pagan Greeks, that, indeed, was a new thing, one that was revolutionary for the Jewish ideas that were still prevalent in the church, and vastly important for all future history.

That, too, is why Luke specifically mentions the Christians who first made this advance in Antioch, namely, not native Palestinians, but Hellenists, Jewish Christians who had been born in Cyprus and in Cyrenia — they began to speak (inchoative imperfect) to these pagan Greeks. Luke omits any further characterization such as he used in connection with Cornelius in 10:2, to the effect that they were "fearing God," φοβούμενοι τὸν Θεόν, one of the standard expressions for designating proselytes of the gate. No, these were just heathen Greeks without synagogue connections. Here, then, is the continuation of what Peter did at Caesarea; it is even an advance on that.

Now Luke does not date this offer of the gospel to pagan Greeks. He gives us only the general historical connection and places this account *after* the story of Cornelius. Luke's indefinite chronology does not, however, justify the view that the extension of the gospel to pagan Greeks precedes the extension God made to proselytes of the gate in Caesarea. If pagan Greeks were already being brought into the church in a great Jewish center such as Antioch, would God go to all the trouble that Luke reports in order to have also Greek proselytes of the gate brought in? The report of the action in Antioch reached Jerusalem promptly and caused no commotion whatever. How could it have been received without dissent if the action of Peter in Caesarea *afterwards* called forth criticism? No; we must leave the events in the order in which Luke records them. These Cyprians and these Cyrenians heard what Peter had done, knew what had been said in Jerusalem that "also to the Gentiles God gave the repentance of life" (v. 18), and thus preached the gospel to Gentiles, namely Greeks in Antioch. Luke makes everything plain. In spite of the directions given by God in the case of Cornelius most Christians still clung to their old Jewish narrowness and confined their missionary efforts to the Antiochian Jews; only the men of Cyprus and of Cyrenia eventually went farther by acting consistent with God's will as this had been revealed at Caesarea in the case of Cornelius.

21) The gospel achieved a pronounced success among the heathen Greeks. **And the Lord's hand was with them, and a great number that came to believe turned to the Lord.** This was due to "the Lord's hand," the anarthrous Κύριος signifying *Yahweh*, which Luke distinguishes from the articulated Κύριος which precedes and follows. The Lord's hand is his power which worked in a providential way in making everything favorable for these disciples to bring the gospel to these Greeks. He opened many doors to them. This is essential in all missionary work. The work is God's and not ours, and he either opens the doors or leaves them closed. So many have the idea that they themselves may decide where to work; but it is futile to beat against closed doors.

Thus a great number of heathen Greeks were converted to Jesus. The aorist completes what the imperfect used in v. 20 left unfinished: they began to speak, and a great number turned. No issue should be made of the use of the article with πιστεύσας since this only makes the participle attributive whereas it is predicative in v. 17. Luke describes the great number, it was a number "that came to faith"; of course, he could have omitted the article if he intended to say "a great number on coming to believe." The aorist participle is ingressive.

22) **And the report concerning them came to the ears of the church that was in Jerusalem; and they sent forth Barnabas as far as Antioch, who, having come and having seen the grace of God, rejoiced and proceeded to exhort all with the purpose of the heart to remain with the Lord because he was a good man and full of the Holy Spirit and faith. And a considerable multitude was added to the Lord.**

Literally, the word or substance concerning these Cyprians, etc., "was heard in the ears" (static εἰς).

Luke says that the news came to the church, "the one being in Jerusalem," the mother church. He does not say that the word reached the apostles. The only fair conclusion is that the apostles were absent from Jerusalem as we, for example, saw Peter busy at Lydda, Joppa, and Caesarea. It is unwarranted, on the basis of the expression "the church in Jerusalem," to draw the conclusion that the believers in Antioch were not yet a church. When, then, did they become a church? On ἐκκλησία see 5:11; the church is where believers are found.

It was due merely to the absence of the apostles from Jerusalem, which left Barnabas as the best available man, that the mother church sent him to Antioch. Besides, he, too, was a Cyprian and would thus be the most suitable man to see what his countrymen were doing in Antioch. The view that Peter was not acceptable as the commissioner, and that, therefore, his services were "discounted" for the present task is unwarranted. Peter was absent. Why was some other apostle not sent? Plainly because the other apostles, too, were absent. In 8:14 the apostles do the sending and not the church. The church did not direct the apostles; the apostles always directed the church, and the church always looked to them for its leadership.

The church acted in the present case because it was thought that the apostles would be absent for some time. It was too long to wait until some of them returned; thus it came about that the church acted independently. In this the church had the example of the apostles as recorded in 8:14 (Philip's work in Samaria). The idea behind this procedure was the same idea that had been followed in that advance movement, namely that all believers everywhere constituted one spiritual body that still had its headquarters in Jerusalem, from which center the apostles still carried on their work, and to which they returned from time to time. The church in Jerusalem acted in good faith and with due wisdom, and the apostles certainly approved its action when one after another finally returned.

23) So Barnabas went. What he was to do we see from what he did. All doubt as to the reception of Greeks into the church had been removed. That matter was settled completely in v. 18. Barnabas shows that he had no instructions to question the right of these Greeks to come into the church. While it was a new movement and should thus come under the supervision of the central church, the headquarters of the apostles, anything beyond that was not contemplated. For those in Antioch, too, it was worth much to remain in connection with the apostles and to have their approval for all their work. A true spirit of unity was back of this commission of Barnabas and of all that he did in its execution. That spirit is often lacking today, sometimes to the extent that even this mission of Barnabas is not properly understood.

Barnabas rejoiced because of the grace of God which he saw in Antioch. Note the *suavis paronomasia* between τὴν χάριν and ἐχάρη. Luke sees more than the faith and the conversions Barnabas found in Antioch, where so many Greeks now believed and confessed. These were the results, God's grace was the ultimate source. He saw the cause in the effect. To be sure, Barnabas had eyes to see — that is why he was sent on this mission. Every task calls for a competent man. Barnabas found nothing that needed to be corrected in Antioch. How many congregations could today be visited by a man like Barnabas without his finding something, even much, to correct? Take this very thing of receiving members by just letting people come into the church in order to augment the number without the proper instruction and separation from their old heathen life and connections! Some day a greater than Barnabas will come, see, and — not rejoice.

So all that Barnabas found it necessary to do was to exhort all "that with the purpose of the heart they remain with the Lord." The imperfect pictures Barnabas as continuing this exhortation, and the present infinitive speaks of continuous remaining. A good start is excellent, but we must endure to the end. Because a text or two has ἐν, "in the Lord," the R. V. margin offers its translation.

Προσμένειν has the dative τῷ Κυρίῳ; to remain with the Lord was the burden of Barnabas' exhortations, and to do this "with the purpose of the heart," i. e., with the set determination of the center of the personality (καρδία). Thus Barnabas sought to confirm the believers in Antioch, especially also the recent ones, the Greeks. Since he found everything in such excellent order, it was not necessary that he return to Jerusalem to make report; he most likely sent word in some other way.

24) The reason that Barnabas showed such interest in the growing church at Antioch was his personal character. Barnabas has been only slightly introduced thus far (4: 36, 37), hence Luke tells us more about him. In that he was "full of the Holy Spirit and faith" he was a man like Stephen, of whom Luke records the same thing in 6:5. The Holy Spirit had taken possession of his heart through the Word and filled it with strong and virile faith. When Luke calls him "a good man," this other description is the basis of his goodness. "Good" is a rather pale translation of ἀγαθός. Since it is his exhortation that Luke explains by calling Barnabas "a good man," we shall hardly go amiss in making the adjective mean "competent," "capable," "serviceable," i. e., good in what he was able to do for others (C.-K. 4) just as κακός means "good for nothing" in whatever respect one

ought to serve his purpose. Here, then, was not a man who judged the situation in Antioch superficially and merely uttered words of praise to please everybody. Such supervisors of the church do her no good because they are not "good" men. It was a blessing for the church in Antioch to have the approval and the support of a "good" man like Barnabas.

This description of Barnabas has led to the conclusion that Luke himself was one of the Greeks who had been won for Christianity in Antioch. It is thought that he was a member of the congregation at Antioch, and that Theophilus also resided there. Thus Luke would have met Barnabas himself and presently also Saul. Some of the ancient fathers call Luke a Syrian from Antioch, although again, it seems, he is reported to have come only from a former Antiochian family. Attention is drawn to the fact that he seems to take a special interest in Antioch, for instance in 6:5 where he tells us that one of the seven deacons was an Antiochian proselyte. All this is interesting but not conclusive. We fear that even the closest scrutiny will find the available data and hints as to Luke's home, family, etc., too slight to advance us beyond hypotheses.

The presence of Barnabas in Antioch soon resulted in far more than a visit with a consequent return to Jerusalem. He himself entered actively into the work. Stimulating all the others and helping on his own part, "a considerable multitude was added to the Lord." Not merely to the congregation but "to the Lord"; the passive implies an agent which we may take to be the Word. Luke does not say whether these new members were Jews or Greeks; his manner of expression leaves the impression that this difference was no longer of moment. The congregation was growing apace; it had a wonderful future before it in the Acts and in the centuries beyond.

25) He, however, went out to Tarsus to hunt up Saul and, having found him, he brought him to Antioch.

Here there is room for the play of the imagination. We note that Saul returned to Tarsus in 9:30, but that was seven or eight years ago. During this period of time Saul simply drops out of sight, and that is the best that can be said. Some "imagine" that he worked in Tarsus and in Cilicia on the basis of Gal. 1:21, but he then accomplished nothing, for there is no evidence that a single congregation was started by him during those years. Ramsey supposes that Saul was not as yet clear in regard to his mission to the Gentiles, still had the idea that the door to the church led through the synagogue; but Saul did not work even in the synagogue in Tarsus. If we feel that an explanation is necessary, let us say that Saul waited for God's call as this was promised to him when God told him to leave Jerusalem, 22:17-21. It was a long wait, but Saul bore it well, and now the call came.

What led Barnabas to think of Saul? All we know is what Barnabas did for Saul in 9:26, etc., and we are entitled to add that Barnabas knew that the Lord's intention concerning Saul was to use him as a chosen instrument especially among the Gentiles (9:15). The Gentiles were now beginning to come into the church in large numbers. May that fact not have turned the thoughts of Barnabas toward Saul? Let us say that the Lord guided the thoughts of Barnabas. Seven years or more are certainly a long time. How did Barnabas know that Saul was still in Tarsus and that his journey to that place would not be in vain? We have no clue in regard to this point. All we know is that he located Saul and that he succeeded in bringing him into the great work that was going forward in Antioch.

26) **And it came to pass for them that even for a whole year they were brought together in the church and taught a considerable multitude, also the disciples bore first in Antioch the name Christians.**

This was the year 43 or 44. The important point is that Barnabas and Saul were in close association in the work at Antioch for an entire year. Energetically and in friendly fellowship they worked, successfully teaching a large multitude and bringing them into the church. All three aorists are subjects of ἐγένετο, to which αὐτοῖς is added as a dative of advantage; Luke states what occurred "for them," Barnabas and Saul. The infinitives are historical aorists which intend simply to report the facts. Luke shows how the two men became intimate in their great work. The "multitude" refers to outsiders who were taught so as to be brought into the church. It is fair to assume that not a few were Greeks and thus needed a thorough teaching.

By being added with τε, the third infinitive is connected with both infinitives that precede and thus states that it was during this year that the disciples bore (or ingressive: came to bear) the name "Christians." This is an interesting fact. It is at once evident that the disciples did not invent this name for themselves. They always and for years to come called themselves as Luke himself here calls them, "disciples" (see 6:1), or as he has repeatedly called them, "saints" (see 9:13) also, "brethren" (1:15) also, "those believing" or "believers" (πιστοί).

"Christian" appears twice more in the New Testament, in 26:28, and in I Pet. 4:16, each time as a name that was given to the disciples by others. Since the name was derived from "Christ," the Greek word for "Messiah," it is certain that the disciples got this name in Antioch and not from the Jews who would never have connected the Messiah with the disciples either in a derogatory or in any other way. The Greeks invented this name. Philologians have much to say in regard to the Latin ending ιανος which is appended to a Greek name by Greeks; then, too, they discuss Χρησπανός, which appears as a variant of Χριστιανός (Codex Sinaiticus) and was used extensively by others e. g., Tacitus, Χρηστός also being used in place of Χριστός. In the days of the Roman persecutions the very name was certainly enough to condemn a man. The question is debated as to whether already in Antioch "Christians" or "Chrēstians" was intended as a vicious title or was used only to distinguish the disciples of Christ from the Jews. Monographs have been written on this subject.

As far as Luke is concerned, the active aorist infinitive χρηματίσαι, "to bear a name," means only that outsiders bestowed the name. As to the spelling of the word by Luke, it is impossible to show that he wrote the name "Chrēstians" and did it in order to show that it was intended as a vilification. The fact that this designation became opprobrious during the persecutions need not be pointed out. There is evidence that the mispronunciation was due to ordinary vulgarity even as Tacitus writes: *vulgus Chrestianos appellabat.* He himself spells *Christus* correctly in the same sentence. Since it was given them by outsiders, the disciples would for a long time be reluctant to adopt the name. Moreover, their reverence for Christ would restrain them from using a designation for themselves which embodied his holy name. We thus conclude that, when the opprobrium attached to the "Christians" is emphasized, we should be content with the reference to the days of Roman persecution and not go back to Antioch and the first invention of the name. There is no indication that during this early period any hostility toward the disciples was manifested in Antioch.

27) **Now in these days there came down from Jerusalem prophets to Antioch. And one of them, by name Agabus, was signifying through the Spirit that a great famine was about to be on the whole inhabited earth; which occurred under Claudius.**

"These days" refer to the year Luke has just mentioned, probably to the middle of the year, since it took some time to gather the money for the proposed relief. Here we note "prophets" in the church for the first time; in 13:1 we have "prophets and teachers." The prophets are far more prominent in the Old Testament than in the new; some of them are towering figures. In the New Testament only the apostles rank with those prophets. The prophets, properly so called in the New Testament, are men of less importance, we may call them Christian teachers to whom the Spirit at times made special direct communications of but minor import. We learn about Agabus as their representative and about two of the communications that he transmitted, the one regarding the famine and the other regarding Paul (21:10, etc.); then also the daughters of Philip are mentioned (21:9). The apostles themselves were prophets in this sense.

Besides this we read about the gift of prophecy which Paul extols as being far superior to the gift of tongues, cf., First Corinthians. This gift any Christian might acquire, and Paul urges all to seek it (I Cor. 14:1). It consisted in thoroughly understanding the Word and in adequately presenting it. Thus we find "prophets and teachers" combined in 13:1. The apostles, of course, had also this gift in an eminent degree, and next to them are their assistants such as Judas and Silas (15:32).

28) When it is asked why these prophets went from Jerusalem to Antioch, we prefer to think that their purpose was to deliver the very message which one of them, namely Agabus, conveyed. It is not necessary to think that he received this revelation only after coming to Antioch; it may have come to him in Jerusalem with the intimation that it was to be conveyed to the brethren in Antioch. Note the verb "was signifying." The imperfect expresses repeated action, and the verb itself implies that he used some symbolic action in connection with his revelation after the manner indicated in 21:11. Luke states no details but only the message itself, that a great famine was impending, μέλλειν with the future infinitive pointing to a famine that is close at hand.

When Agabus states that this famine was to be "on the whole inhabited earth" he indicates that it was to be "great" in its extent. Drought and crop failures would produce famine conditions which affected now this part, now that with more or less severity, so that conditions of distress would affect the whole inhabited world. We need not restrict τὴν οἰκουμένην (γῆν) to the Roman empire; for if all these lands suffered more or less, the barbarian countries would certainly not escape.

Luke has thus far furnished no dates; that is why, writing years afterward, he adds: "which (ὅστις = "which very one," R. 728) occurred under Claudius," ἐπί, "in the time of," R. 603. Claudius reigned from January 41 to October 54. Much of his reign was marked by famine conditions as Roman writers (Suetonius: *assiduae sterilitates*, Dio Cassius, Tacitus) and Josephus report. The entire empire was not affected equally at the same time and just for one period, but crop failures were wide-spread, and certain regions suffered great distress because they were unable to import much from sections that were less affected.

Zahn's deduction from Luke's remark, that Agabus must have spoken his prophecy *before* Claudius came to the throne, i. e., before January 41, conflicts with his own statement that "in these days" signifies in the year mentioned in v. 26, which must be the year 43-44. Luke's phrase "under Claudius" is written, not with reference to Agabus, but with reference to Luke's own time of writing. On the reading in the Codex Bezae with its "we" as implying Luke's own presence here in Antioch see 16:10.

29) **And of the disciples, as anyone was well off, they determined, each one of them, to send for ministration to the brethren dwelling in Judea. Which also they did, commissioning it to the elders by hand of Barnabas and Saul.**

It seems that a link is missing between the general prophecy of Agabus and this action of the congregation at Antioch. How did the brethren at Antioch know that the church in Judea would soon suffer? Luke evidently intends that his reader supply the link. From what Antioch proceeded to do, namely to gather funds for Judea, it is plain that Agabus must have specified that the impending famine conditions in the world would presently bring distress to the church in Judea. The Lord himself sent Agabus from Jerusalem to Antioch at the proper time, in advance, to prepare the necessary relief.

This, it seems, was set under way promptly after the revelation had been received. Everyone of the disciples in Antioch took part, and this was done by joint action of the church. The sentence has been called awkward, and yet it neatly brings out these two points: "they determined" (plural), jointly as a body; "of the disciples, as anyone was well off, each one" (singular), not one holding back.

No; they did not tithe. Saul and Barnabas, although they were former Jews, did not gather funds in this manner. In this very first instance in the Christian Church, when relief on a large scale had to be provided, the correct principle and method were adopted: "as anyone was well off," the imperfect signifying "continued to be well off or prosper." This implies that funds were gathered gradually and that each kept giving as he could from time to time, perhaps from Sunday to Sunday. We know how Paul proceeded later on when relief was again necessary for Jerusalem and when he gathered funds from all the Gentile congregations. It was here at Antioch that his later method was first applied. Εἰς διακονίαν, "for ministration," recalls "the daily ministration" of food and relief to the widows mentioned in 6:1. The same beautiful word is used which denotes help for the sake of help.

30) Already the aorists (v. 29) imply that this thing was done, but Luke adds, probably because it covered so long a period: "which also they did," etc. When the relief became necessary, Barnabas and Saul were the commissioners who were sent from Antioch to the elders in Judea to administer the needed help. This took place after Herod had killed James (12:2), had attempted to kill Peter, had abused the church in Jerusalem (12:1), and had died a most terrible death (12:23), after the Passover of 44. The worst of the famine occurred during the next year.

The relief was sent, we are told, "to the elders." This term comes as a surprise since Luke has not mentioned elders; but he is writing from his own later standpoint and for a reader who knew what elders were. We might call them pastors. They had charge of the congregations in all their church affairs and attended to the services, the teaching, and the spiritual oversight. Πρεσβύτεροι, "elders," designated them according to their dignity, while ἐπίσκοποι described them from the viewpoint of their work as "overseers," "bishops," both terms denoting the same office. The apostles called themselves "elders," I Pet. 5:1; II John 1; III John 1.

We do not know when this office was inaugurated; it came about naturally as an inheritance from the synagogues with their management by elders. At times the majority of the Jews in a town or a synagogue were converted to Christianity. At first the apostles remained and worked in Jerusalem, but when congregations sprang up everywhere, they were absent from Jerusalem, and elders had to manage even this congregation, to say nothing of the many others. Here Luke speaks of the elders in Judea. Since they were the managers of the congregations, Barnabas and Saul naturally worked through them.

A number of questions arise at this point. Did Saul go to Jerusalem on this relief journey, or did he avoid Jerusalem and dispense relief only in Judea? If he went to Jerusalem, did he meet any of the Twelve there? If he went to Jerusalem, why did he fail to mention this visit in Gal. 2:1? Must we conclude from Gal. 2:1 that he kept away from Jerusalem on this relief journey? Or is this relief journey identical with the journey and the visit described in Gal. 2:1, etc.?

As far as the facts are concerned, Saul and Barnabas went to Jerusalem, for in 12:25 they return from this city after finishing their ministry of relief. Secondly, it is impossible to identify this relief journey with the one described in Gal. 2:1, etc., which was ordered by revelation. The visit referred to in Gal. 2 is undoubtedly identical with the one recorded in Acts 15:1, etc. How could Paul then omit this relief journey from his Galatian letter? Whether we can answer that or not, he did so omit it. To insist that such an omission would destroy his whole argument in Gal. one and two is answered by the simple fact that Paul did not think so. But perhaps Paul omitted mention of this relief visit in Galatians because he failed to meet any of the Twelve on this visit. That is possible. But that explanation only raises more questions.

A glance shows that 11:30 and 12:25 must be considered together: Barnabas and Saul are commissioned to bring relief to the brethren in Judea — on completing the relief Barnabas and Saul return from Jerusalem. But why does Luke interlard all that he records about Herod (12:1-23) between these two statements? The matter is simple. The famine and its relief occurred in the summer or the fall of 44 or in 45, hence *after* Herod's death (12:23). But the prophecy of Agabus and the beginning of the gathering of funds occurred *before* this Herodian persecution. Now instead of telling his reader merely that the gathering of contributions for relief was undertaken in Antioch, then reporting about Herod, and finally adding that Barnabas and Saul were sent to convey the relief, Luke at once says that the relief was duly conveyed (11:30). But in 13:1, etc., Barnabas and Saul are commissioned for their first great missionary journey. They were then back in Antioch; that is why their return is mentioned in the preceding verse, in 12:25.

We are sorry to note that Lightfoot draws such a wretched picture of the Twelve and also of Saul. He confuses the dates. Saul and Barnabas bring the relief in the midst of the Herodian terror, James is dead, Peter has fled, the Twelve have taken to cover, "every Christian of rank" has left the city. Saul and Barnabas steal into the city, hurriedly deposit the relief funds, and depart. Ramsay says correctly: "It was not men like that who carried Christianity over the empire within a few years."

But Ramsay has his own story. Besides confusing 11:30 and 15:1, etc., he has Barnabas and Saul bring loads of provisions instead of money and has them in person attend to distributing these provisions to all the needy — in person in order to produce the greater effect of this charity as coming from Antioch; and all this took weeks, for Judea was included. To give the final touch to all this we are left to conclude that these weeks occurred during the Herodian persecution, and that the apostolic council met at the same time! When over a decade later Paul took up his great collection for famine relief in the Gentile churches he brought the money So Barnabas and Saul brought funds. They most likely went first of all to Jerusalem and from there turned in various directions into Judea and distributed this relief money. Then they returned to Antioch. The apostles were busy in various fields. Herod had been dead for months.

CHAPTER XII

The Persecution Under Herod Agrippa I

1) Along that period of time Herod, the king, put forth his hands to abuse some of those belonging to the church.

We have explained the chronology of events in 11:30. Herod's persecution occurred "along about that καιρός or period of time." The prophecy of Agabus preceded Herod's persecution and his death, and this, in turn, preceded the famine and its suffering and the relief brought by Barnabas and Saul. Herod died after the Passover of 44, the famine followed toward the end of 44 and continued into 45. "Herod, the king," refers to the Herod who was at this time the actual king of all Palestine and not merely, like his uncle Herod Antipas, often called king while he was only a tetrarch. This is Herod Agrippa I, a grandson of Herod the Great, a son of Aristobolus and Bernice. We have told his story in connection with 10:1: He was a prisoner in Rome until Tiberius died, was made tetrarch on the occasion of the accession of Caligula, and then king of all Palestine by Claudius in 41, and thus became the first and only Herodian who ruled as king over all Palestine after the death of Herod the Great. He died three years after his appointment as king. He was a treacherous, superficial, extravagant prince, although not as bad a character as his grandfather had been. Jerusalem was his capital. Since his elevation to the kingship he courted the favor of the Jews, especially that of the bigoted Pharisees, and played the role of zealous protector of the Jewish faith and cultus. The hostility which developed some years before, when Stephen was slain, found in him a new protagonist, which explains what follows.

He began suddenly to take active measures against the Christians by putting forth his hands (through his minions) to abuse or ill-treat "some of those from the church," οἱ ἀπό is often used with reference to the members of a corporation. Luke writes only "some" without specifying who are referred to although we may assume that he selected his victims. The idea that he observed them in their attendance at the Temple and gave orders to expel them from the courts and the worship, is too general and mild. The view that Peter's action in Cæsarea when he permitted Gentiles to enter the church stirred up Herod's animosity, is rather superficial. Κακῶσαι implies that he arrested some of the more prominent Christians, had them scourged and abused in other ways, and thus began his further bloody work. These first victims escaped death, otherwise Luke would have used a stronger verb than "abuse."

2) **Moreover, he made away with James, the brother of John, by means of the sword.**

During the persecution that followed upon Stephen's martyrdom some Christians were no doubt killed. James is usually called the second martyr, yet, in reality, others preceded him. Although he was one of the Twelve, Luke makes only brief mention of the martyrdom of James. This has been found strange, and some say we do not know why Luke did not tell the entire story for he certainly knew all the details. Luke, however, follows a definite plan. The story of Stephen was vital for that plan since the death of Stephen led to the extension of the church in all directions, even to distant lands. The martyrdom of James had no comparable effect, hence the brevity of the record. The importance of this bloody deed lies only in the fact that it singled out an apostle and that it showed the temper of Herod and indicated to what lengths he intended to go.

We again have the significant verb ἀνεῖλε (ἀναιρέω), "he made away with," which always denotes murder and criminal killing; in the previous chapters it is constantly used with regard to the death of Jesus. The dative of means, μαχαίρᾳ, shows that James was beheaded by an executioner as the Baptist had been by that other Herod. James was thus arrested. He may also have been brought to trial before Herod or have been summarily executed after his arrest. The fact that James was at first the sole victim is most likely due to the circumstance that he was the only one of the apostles who happened to be in the city at the moment.

Clement of Alexandria tells a story which he claims to have received from his Christian ancestors to the effect that the soldier who led James from the court room, after witnessing the joyful confession James had made, was so deeply affected that he on his part confessed himself a Christian, whereupon he was led out to execution together with James. On the way this soldier asked James to pardon him for having served as the tool of the king. James thought a little while and then turned and said, "Peace be with thee!" and kissed the soldier. An affecting story, but whether it is true or not, no one can say. See Eusebius 2, 9.

3) **And, on seeing that it was pleasing to the Jews, he in addition arrested also Peter — now they were days of the unleavened bread — whom also, on capturing, he placed in prison, delivering him to four quaternions of soldiers to guard him, intending after the Passover to bring him up to the people.**

To see their king take such strong measures against the Christians delighted the hostile Jews to the highest degree. It was the king's very purpose to gain this vigorous approval. In the combination προσέθετο συλλαβεῖν, "he added to seize," a Hebraism, the verb takes the place of an adverb, and the infinitive expresses the main idea: "he in addition arrested" also Peter. Greatly encouraged by the first execution, the king proceeded to the next one.

Again we ask why Peter was the one to be arrested, and also why Herod did not arrest more or even all of the apostles. The only satisfactory answer is that the other apostles were absent at this time. When James returned, Herod made away with him; now when Peter came back to the city he, too, fell into Herod's hands. The interval between these two events seems to have been quite short.

The parenthesis is indicated by δέ, and ἡμέραι is the predicate. "They were days of the unleavened bread" means that it was Passover time when all leaven was scrupulously removed from the house for the duration of the entire festival week which began at sundown on the fourteenth of Nisan, the evening on which the Passover lamb was eaten (Matt. 26:17), Num. 28:16, 17. The entire week was called τὰ ἄζυμα (λάγανα, cakes), *hammatzoth*. It seems that Peter had come to Jerusalem in order to spend the Passover week with the mother congregation.

4) Upon his arrest Peter was lodged in prison, which was very likely located in Herod's palace, and was put under the heaviest kind of guard. The reason for this was the fact that Herod had heard that the Twelve had once been locked up securely, and yet that on the next morning their prison had been found empty. The king intended that such an occurrence should not be repeated. So he had Peter delivered to four quaternions of his soldiers who were "to be guarding him," one set of four soldiers doing guard duty in

the way indicated in v. 6 for one watch of six hours, and so each set in rotation.

It was Herod's intention "to bring Peter up to the people" the day after the Passover proper. That means that he was to be led up out of his dungeon cell to the hall of trial where all who cared to could be present, and from there to be led away to execution where all who cared to could witness the act which demonstrated the king's wonderful zeal for the integrity of the Jewish faith.

"After the Passover" means after the Passover meal on the evening of the fourteenth of Nisan, namely on the fifteenth. The plan was to duplicate the execution of Jesus who also died on the fifteenth of Nisan. Herod intended to impress the thousands of people who attended the festival from far and near. In Matt. 26:5, the Sanhedrin planned to wait until the festival week was past because it feared the people, the pilgrim hosts attending the festival who were captivated by Jesus. Their plan was frustrated when God allowed Jesus to fall into their hands on the night between the fourteenth and the fifteenth. The Jewish rule was: *Non judicant die festo*. It was broken in the case of Jesus; it was again to be broken in the case of Peter.

"After the Passover" is generally taken to mean "after the entire Passover week," which identifies "days of unleavened bread" and "Passover." Πάσχα has this wider meaning, but it also has the narrower which then refers to the ceremonial meal when the Passover lamb was eaten on the evening of the fourteenth of Nisan. Here the narrower meaning is in place because of the context and because "days of unleavened bread" precedes. "After the Passover" specifies on which particular day during the days of unleavened bread the execution was to take place.

The king's plans were made, and due measures had been taken to see that they would be carried out.

5) Peter, accordingly, was being kept in the prison. Prayer, however, was being made strenuously by the church to God concerning him.

The two imperfect tenses describe the situation and ask the reader to visualize and to dwell on it. Which will be the stronger, the dungeon and its guards or the prayers of the church? The entire congregation was making prayer to God; ἦν and the present participle are the periphrastic imperfect. Whether we prefer the reading περί or ὑπέρ the sense is that the prayer so strenuously made to God was "concerning" or "for" Peter in the sense that his mortal danger was laid before God who was asked that his will be done. God had allowed Stephen and recently also James to die; it might be that Peter's name was to be added to those of these martyrs, and yet God might deliver Peter even now (21:14). Human impossibilities are not impossibilities to him.

6) Now, when Herod was about to bring him before them, on that very night Peter was sleeping between two soldiers, having been fettered with two chains, also guards before the doors were keeping the prison.

The imperfect tenses still describe, but we are carried forward to the critical night, the one that it was Herod's intention was to be Peter's last on earth. Herod was very close to bringing him before them (προάγειν), thus carrying out his murderous plan. Hope seemed to be gone, rescue or deliverance impossible. God often lets a case become desperate and delays to the last in order that we may the more clearly recognize that the deliverance comes from him. It was "in that night," on the evening of which the Passover lambs were eaten.

Luke states how Peter was guarded: he lay sleeping between two soldiers and was chained to one on each side so that he could not stir even in his sleep without arousing these two guards who were stretched out at his sides. In addition (τε) guards manned all the doors of the prison. This is usually referred to the other two soldiers of the quaternion on duty; but while these may have stood inside or outside of the door of Peter's cell, the prison was kept by other guards, some of whom were stationed at each exit. Each quaternion when it was on duty, was responsible with its life for Peter's safekeeping; but the prison itself had many more guards, in fact, as the Codex Bezae reads, the entire cohort of the king's soldiers. Herod would certainly have quite a force of troops in Jerusalem at the time of the Passover when thousands of pilgrims were in the city.

7) Now we have the aorists which report the outcome in detail. **And lo, an angel of the Lord stood by him, and a light shone in the cell; moreover, having slapped the side of Peter, he awoke him, saying, Arise in haste! And his chains fell off from his hands. And the angel said to him, Gird thyself and bind on thy sandals! And he did thus. And he says to him, Throw thy robe around thee and be following me! And, having gone out, he was following. And he was not aware that it was true what was occurring through the angel but was thinking he was seeing a vision.**

The very thing that Herod intended to prevent, a recurrence of what had happened in the case of the Twelve when the Sanhedrin had imprisoned them, God made reality. God accepted Herod's challenge, and Peter was as easily released as the Twelve had been. Out of the fetters, the cell, the prison, out from among the special and all other guards, Peter walked as though they had not been there. The account is as lucid and clear as it can be; yet it has been considered a piece of fancy, and men have undertaken to tell us what happened. There is the lightning story; Peter is released by the head jailor — yet the quaternion paid for it with their lives; the king himself had Peter released — yet he killed the four guards; how Peter got out nobody knows, he just imagined that it was through the agency of an angel.

Comment is almost unnecessary. The guards are as though they were not there; none of them is conscious of what was happening. The angel and the light that filled his cell (οἴκημα, the place in the building) Peter saw when he awoke. Let us not overlook the fact that Peter was peacefully asleep. He did not lie there and worry on this apparently his last day on earth. What he would say at his trial and how he would act was dismissed from his mind; he had his Lord's own promises, which he had already tested twice before when he was a prisoner before the Sanhedrin (Matt. 10:19, 20; Mark 13:11-13; Luke 12:11; 21:14, 15). Thus Peter, having committed his soul to the Lord, slept in peace! At the angel's command to arise, the chains by which he was fastened to the soldiers at his wrists, at once drop off noiselessly. Ἀνάστα is the short form of the second aorist imperative active instead of ἀνάσθητι.

8) Peter acts as though he were in a dream and has to be told everything. He is ordered to fasten the belt about his tunic and to put on his sandals; the two imperatives are the middle voice: "gird thyself," "bind under for thyself." The belt had been unfastened and the sandals laid aside for sleep. When Peter has done this, he is told to throw his long loose outer robe around him and to be following the angel. He probably slept on the robe by drawing it over his body as well as he could. The aorist imperative to express the one act is also middle and reflexive, but the order to follow is properly the durative present.

9) Peter followed the angel as though no doors blocked his way. Did they open and then close noiselessly? No guards saw or heard anything. Peter him-

self could at the moment not tell whether what was occurring through the instrumentality (διά) of the angel was real (ἀληθές), or whether it was a vision that had come to him in his sleep. Luke had heard this from Peter's own lips. Note the three imperfect descriptive tenses; the present participle and the present infinitive are the same: "the thing occurring"; thought "to be seeing."

10) And, on having gone through a first and second guard, they came to the gate, the iron one, the one leading into the city, which automatically opened for them; and having gone out, they went forward along one narrow street, and immediately the angel was gone from him.

We need make no difficulties for ourselves. In v. 9 Peter and the angel go out of the cell and leave behind the quaternion that had been especially commanded to guard Peter. Now they pass through two other guarded portals and thus get into the great open court from which a great gate led to the street. The repetition of the article gives the noun as well as its two modifiers individual attention and forms a sort of climax (R. 762, 764): "the gate, the iron one, the one leading to the city." This final barrier was impressive. It was made of iron and thus very heavy and was locked with a massive bolt so that a number of men were required to open it. The other two had been ordinary doors. This massive gate opened of itself and let Peter and the angel out, and then, of course, closed just as automatically. That this happened just as the guards were changing is one of those unacceptable suggestions. There lay the prison undisturbed, all its locks and its bolts in place, all its many strong guards in their places — but the prisoner was gone.

The great gate probably opened upon a wide street (πλατεῖα) from which a narrow one (ῥύμη) turned off. The angel guided Peter forward along this one narrow street and thus some distance from the prison and then suddenly disappeared; ἀπέστη is the opposite of ἐπέστη in v. 7.

11) **And Peter, having come to himself, said: Now I know truly that the Lord sent forth his angel and took me out of Herod's hand and all the expectation of the people of the Jews.**

Peter's impression that it was all a dream continued until he stood alone on that narrow street in the dark night. All his movements had followed the directions and the leading of the angel, now he had to think and to act for himself. His natural consciousness returned. He now knew that he had not seen a mere vision, but that what he had seen was full reality. In v. 9 "he was not knowing" (ᾔδει used as an imperfect); in v. 11 he says, "Now I am knowing, do know." First, that Κύριος (*Yahweh*) had actually commissioned his angel, and that he had actually taken him out of Herod's hand or power, and thus out of all that the Jews were expecting, namely that Peter would be killed on the very anniversary of Jesus' death, killed without hope or help of rescue as James had been a short time before this. Peter is making an inventory of what God has done for him and what this really implies. The aorists state the two facts; ἐξείλετο is a form of ἐξαιρέω. God's intent is plain: Peter is not yet to suffer martyrdom, not yet is John 21:18, 19 to be fulfilled. Having been given his liberty, Peter is to use it to escape from Herod. God used supernatural means to free him but intends that from now on Peter is to use natural means and prudence to remain free.

12) **Also, on considering, he went to the house of Mary, the mother of John, the one surnamed Mark, where were many, having been assembled and praying.**

The participle states that Peter saw everything together, i. e., viewed his present situation in relation to what his next steps should be. On thus considering he went to the house of Mary who is identified by naming her son John, whose other name was Mark, by which name he is best known to us; he became the writer of the second Gospel. We again meet Mark in v. 25, and then in 15:5, 13. In Col. 4:10 he is called the ἀνεψιός or cousin of Barnabas. In I Pet. 5:13, Peter calls Mark "my son"; in analogy with I Tim. 1:2, where Paul calls Timothy his own son in the faith, it is fair to conclude that Mark was converted by Peter.

Luke states that many disciples were gathered together in Mary's house this night of the Passover and were praying for Peter. We have two predicative participles, for since one is perfect and the other present, neither can be combined with ἦσαν as a periphrastic verb form. Having been collected, they were now thus. Whether Peter knew that he would find many here is not indicated by Luke although some interpreters assume this to be a fact and build up their combinations on this assumption.

Let us at once state that Peter's object was first of all to notify his friends about his miraculous deliverance. Whether he would find many or few at Mary's house made little difference as to that object, for the whole church was deeply concerned about him, and he could not communicate with all that night. The fact that Peter found many at Mary's house was providential. Let us not forget how the Christians after the death of Stephen, and how Peter, remembering that, might well have expected another flight now that Herod was maltreating Christians, had beheaded James, and was attempting to do the same with Peter himself. It is not at all certain that Peter expected to find an assembly in Mary's house.

We take it that Peter's release was effected not long after midnight, for a new quaternion would go on duty at that time. This would allow until six A. M. before the escape was discovered, when a new quaternion came on duty. He who miraculously led Peter out of prison would scarcely permit a premature discovery of the escape. Those two soldiers within the cell snored peacefully on until well toward six o'clock.

No objection can be raised to the assumption that Mary's house often served as a place of meeting for a group of the disciples, and that the house was large, that Mary was rich, that she was a widow, a woman of character, and all that. But when we are asked to believe that hers was the house in the upper room of which Jesus celebrated the last Passover and instituted the Sacrament, that Mark was the man bearing the pitcher of water whom Peter and John were to follow, that Mary's husband was still living at that time, that Mark was present at the last Passover of Jesus, that he was the young man clad only in a sheet, which sheet was snatched from him when he ran for his life near Gethsemane — we regard this as one of those syntheses which Zahn's great *Kombinationsgabe* has produced.

But there are serious objections to this combination of facts. From this assembly on the night of Peter's escape we are asked to leap backward across a space of about fifteen years to the night of Jesus' last Passover, make the houses the same, and weave in everything else — that is the basic part of this hypothesis. This demands too much of us. Moreover, when Jesus delegated Peter and John to go and to prepare for the Passover, no man could even guess whose the house would be — it was *not* one where Jesus had been often; for Jesus states that its upper room would be tiled, the implication being that the disciples had never before set foot in it. No one but Jesus and the Twelve were present at the Passover: one proof of this is the fact that Jesus had to wash the feet of his disciples. If Mark was there, how did it come that he followed the procession clothed only in a sheet? Would any man clothed only in a sheet walk out through the city streets and into the country to the neighborhood of Gethsemane? Men slept in their tunics. How long did it take to put on a tunic, throw a robe around the shoulders, and then run out? We cannot accept Zahn's view.

13) Now he having knocked at the door of the passage, there came to it a maid to answer by name Rhoda; and on recognizing the voice of Peter, due to her joy, she did not open the passage but, after running in, she reported Peter to be standing before the passage. But they said to her, Thou art crazy! Yet she insisted that it was so. They, however, went on to say, It is his angel! But Peter remained there knocking; and having opened, they saw him and were amazed.

Here we have one of the beautiful detailed paintings of Luke. It is like the human interest stories that are so constantly published in the daily press of today. Four lines in 11:19, 20 dispose of the collection and the sending of the funds for relief; many lines fully describe Peter's experience.

According to Luke's account an outer door led into a passageway through the building that faced the street into an inner court. When Peter knocked at the door, a maid came to answer his knock (ὑπακοῦσαι, aorist), and Luke preserves even her name: Rhoda, our Rose or Rosa. R., *W. P.*, comments on these beautiful names for women such as Dorcas (Gazelle), Euodia (Sweet Aroma), Syntyche (Good Fortune). Luke's mention of the maid's name perhaps indicates that Peter knew the household well. As all her actions show, Rhoda herself was a Christian. Maids were used as portresses (John 18:16, 17); they were often, no doubt, slaves, although it is not likely that Rhoda was a slave.

Peter's knocking was heard in the dead of the night. Many disciples were gathered somewhere in the house.

Herod had maltreated some of the Christians, slain James, and was counting on slaying Peter. That knock at the outer door must have caused great fright among the gathered disciples. Their first thought must have been that Herod had sent soldiers to make more arrests, and that in some way he had found out about the gathering at Mary's house. Who should go to the door and answer that knocking? Surely, they would not send just this girl even though answering the door was her regular duty. Some brave man or two ought to have gone. But no, Rhoda goes. To be sure, her answering the door would not arouse suspicion and might afford the disciples time for flight. Bravely Rhoda goes. Let us remember her for that. With palpitating heart she listened in order to learn who was seeking entrance in the middle of the night.

14) On asking, Rhoda at once recognized Peter's voice — another sign that Peter was well known at that house. Straightforward, with nothing flighty or superstitious about her, she believes the evidence of her ears. Not for a moment does she hesitate and reason that this cannot be Peter, that he is far away in the terrible prison under heaviest guard. Instantly her heart is flooded with joy so that she forgets to unlock the door, runs back pell-mell to the assembled disciples, and shouts the great news. One must not sit in his study and coldly view this action. All the emotion, the sudden plunge from dreadful fears to the very extreme of joy in this maid's heart must be felt by the reader. "Peter is standing before the portal! Peter himself is standing before the portal!" she shouts to the assembly. The perfect ἱστάναι is always used in the sense of the present.

15) The answer she received was that she must be demented, we should say crazy. But Rhoda insisted that it was as she declared; with an adverb ἔχειν always has the sense of "to be," the present tense is that of

the direct discourse: *es verhaelt sich also*. Rhoda was the only one of that entire company who kept her balance. Although it was one against all, she did not waver. In the face of her constancy and under the necessity of explaining that voice which Rhoda had heard the disciples fell to saying (descriptive imperfect, which also holds us in suspense as to what the fact would turn out to be): "His angel it is!' i. e., that is who it must be.

Since ἄγγελος means "messenger," and angels are so called because they are God's messengers, some think that the exclamation meant that Peter had sent some messenger from his prison cell, and that Rhoda had heard this messenger say something about coming from Peter and had thus imagined that it was Peter himself. But this is untenable. These disciples could not shake off their mortal fears for Peter and leaped to the conclusion that he was already dead, and that his guardian angel had come to tell the sad news. It was a wild idea, but fears inspire weird notions. Matt. 18:10, and Heb. 1:14, plus old Jewish ideas may have been commingled in their minds. It is difficult to be entirely sure. We recall the cries of the apostles on the night they saw Jesus walking on the water, Matt. 14:26. The one thing that was the fact the company in Mary's house absolutely refused to believe. After praying for Peter's deliverance the thought that God might deliver him seemed incredible to them.

16) All this was going on while Peter was standing before the locked passage. To show that he was still there he kept on knocking. Finally there was only one thing to do, to stop arguing and to unlock that door. The plural shows that practically everybody went to the door. Imagine their perturbed state and the excitement as to what opening that door would reveal. When it swung back — there stood Peter! Rhoda was right, everybody else was wrong. The unbelievable

was fact — "they saw him." And now the sudden and terrific reaction: "they were amazed," ἐξέστησαν, their minds were completely upset.

17) **They, of course, took him in, and a hubbub ensued. Now, after beckoning to them with the hand to be silent, he recounted to them how the Lord had led him out of the prison. He also said, Report these things to James and the brethren, and having gone out, he traveled to a different place.**

Peter had to gesture with his hand in order to bring the excited company to silence. Then he told the entire story of his miraculous deliverance and asked that it be reported also to James and to the brethren, namely to the entire congregation. Without further delay Peter left them and proceeded to another place.

Why does Luke not name this place? The answer that Peter went into hiding in Jerusalem itself is too improbable to be accepted; besides, nearly all interpreters are agreed that he left the city. But why make so much ado about the place to which Peter went when Luke considered it too unimportant to be mentioned? Did Herod not die shortly after this Passover? Then all danger was past. Herod had no royal successors, Roman procurators once more governed. So Peter was free to come and to go as he might please. That is why Luke says only "to a different place." He does not say to what places the other apostles had gone at this time and for the same reason: the matter was of no special importance.

Zahn finds a hint here that Luke intended to write a third book in which the story of Peter was to be continued in detail. Luke, he tells us, would mention this "different place" in that third book. The supposition of a third book cannot be supported by an omission such as this. The reason Peter sent no word to the other apostles was the fact that they were not in Jerusalem at the time but at work elsewhere. The Apostle

James, it seems, had been seized by Herod and killed because James happened to return to Jerusalem for a visit; Herod had arrested Peter and probably intended to do the same with any of the other apostles who might come back.

Romanists fill out the blank which Luke left regarding the place to which Peter fled from Jerusalem by claiming that he went to Rome and remained there for a ministry of twenty-five years as the first pope of the church. This idea is fantastic. Luke wrote the Acts in order to show how the gospel took its course from Jerusalem to Rome, the first apostle to arrive there being Paul, and he a prisoner, and all the while Peter had been in Rome, had been there as a pope, and Luke never said a word about it in the entire Acts, did not even incidentally mention Rome when Peter left Jerusalem but wrote only "a different place." And when Paul finally proposed to visit Rome and wrote to Rome from Corinth he forgot to send greetings to Peter, and after he was in Rome and wrote to others from Rome he again forgot to send greetings from Peter. Thus there is no basis for Rome's contention.

The way in which James is mentioned here, and the fact that Peter sends word especially to him, prepare for 15:13; Gal. 1:19; 2:9, 12; James 1:1. In Gal. 1:19 Paul calls him "the Lord's brother"; the question as to what that relationship implies has been discussed in connection with 1:14, where Luke mentions "his (Jesus') brothers." He must have been the chief elder of the congregation at Jerusalem and, as 15:13, and Gal. 2:9 would imply, chief because of his personal character and ability. In 11:30, the Judean elders are mentioned but no apostles. The conclusion is evident that at this time the apostles no longer had personal charge of the congregation at Jerusalem.

After the great scattering that followed Stephen's stoning and Saul's cruel persecution the congregation again grew. At what particular time elders were placed in charge of it no one knows. During that first persecution the apostles remained in Jerusalem (8:1), but when Saul was converted and quiet again came, we see Peter working at Lydda, Joppa, and Caesarea; the other apostles must have gone out from Jerusalem in the same manner. So already at that time elders must have been chosen by the Jerusalem church, among them was James who from that time onward had charge of the congregation and of all its affairs.

18) **But when day came, there was no small disturbance among the soldiers as to what, then, had become of Peter. Herod, however, when he had made search for him and not found him, after putting the guards to an examination, ordered them to be led away to execution. And having gone down from Judea to Caesarea, he was spending time there.**

There was great excitement among the soldiers, which includes the entire garrison of the palace of Herod. Ἄρα implies: "since Peter was gone," and τί may be considered an accusative adverb, R. 916. The great question was: "What became of Peter?" as our idiom would state the question. He had vanished into thin air. This happened "when day came," as we take it, about six in the morning when the new quaternion came on duty. Herod, of course, was soon informed.

19) He scarcely made the search in person but made it by means of his chief officers. If Peter had somehow gotten out of his cell, how had he managed to get through the guards and the doors, the first, the second, and then the great iron gate? But thorough search (ἐπί in the participle) revealed not even a trace of the prisoner; he was just not to be found. The first two participles report the preliminary actions, the third what followed them, namely a judicial examination with Herod acting as judge. He grilled the four

guards from whom Peter had escaped. Of course, his questioning brought no results, and Herod then commanded that they "be led away," ἀπαχθῆναι, which is like the active in Luke 23:26, a judicial term which may have a modifier as it does in Matt. 27:31, and again may not. The four guards were forthwith summarily executed. It was the military law that the guards of a prisoner were liable with their lives for the security of the prisoner specially committed to them.

And yet one wonders at Herod. His chagrin was great; what about "all the expectation of the people of the Jews " (v. 11)? If Herod had not had the example of the Twelve recorded in 5:19-24, if he had not posted that extra heavy guard to prevent a recurrence, he might have been justified in giving the limit of the law to the poor guards. But he certainly must have felt that a higher hand was behind this inexplicable disappearance of the apostle whom he had planned to kill that day. Did he execute these guards merely to save his face? We know that he left the city, dropped all further persecutions, and spent some time in Caesarea. This is the force of διέτριβεν, the durative imperfect, which is used with or without a noun such as "time," "day," etc.

20) **Now he was in a hot quarrel with Tyrians and Sidonians. With one accord, however, they were present with him and, having persuaded Blastus, the one over the bedchamber of the king, they were duly asking peace because their country was being nourished from the king's.**

How the hot contention arose is not indicated. Tyre and Sidon lie on the coast of Phoenicia which was only a narrow strip of land extending along the coast. This territory belonged to Syria and not to Herod's domain, yet it was dependent on "the royal land" for the greater part of its foodstuffs, especially grain and cattle, being shut off from Syrian imports by rough mountainous heights. Whatever the cause of the rupture might have been, Herod had discontinued the supplies from his country. Tyre and Sidon were rich due to their maritime trade, yet they suffered under Herod's punitive measures. Thus a delegation of Tyrians and Sidonians was present in Caesarea for the purpose of asking peace.

The imperfect tenses are in place because the outcome of the negotiations was still uncertain. The middle ᾐτοῦντο, "were duly asking," indicates that the matter was a piece of business; the negotiations were official. The delegation had made Blastus, the king's chamberlain, "the one over the king's bedchamber" (the Greek lacking our ready title), their friend. We need not ask how they "persuaded" him; bribes have always been effective. He was using his influence with the king. Διὰ τό with the present infinitive states the reason for both the presence of the delegation and for their petition.

21) **And on an appointed day Herod, having put on royal apparel, after having sat down on the throne, was making an oration unto them; and the people kept calling, Voice of a god and not of a man! And immediately the Lord's angel smote him because he did not give the glory to God. And having come to be eaten of worms, he expired.**

From Josephus (*Ant*. XIX, 8, 2) we learn that the fixed or appointed day was the second in a grand celebration of games after the Roman fashion in honor of a victory and triumph of the emperor Claudius on his return from Britain and not in honor merely of his birthday or of the anniversary of his reign. On this day Herod gave his answer to the Tyrian and Sidonian ambassadors in the great theater where the games were being celebrated. The affair was made a magnificent occasion inasmuch also as the answer was favorable.

Luke says that Herod had arrayed himself in royal apparel. That is putting it mildly; Josephus speaks of a στολή or festal robe wrought in silver so that on this morning the slanting rays of the sun made the king glisten and sparkle with brilliance.

The theater was filled with the δῆμος, "the people" considered as a body politic (λαός would be the people at large, ἔθνος the nation, ὄχλος just an unorganized crowd). In their hearing the king, seated on the βῆμα, the elevated stage with its chair or throne, delivered an oration to the ambassadors, ἐδημηγόρει, the word indicating the desire for the favor and the praise of the δῆμος. The king was mounting to the pinnacle of his glory. The games spoke of the great favor Herod was enjoying at the hands of the emperor; the games reflected the glories of Rome; all the important and dignified personages of Herod's kingdom were present among the *dēmos*; then there were these ambassadors from Tyre and Sidon with their humble suit for peace. In his blazing silver apparel and with his demogogic oration the king was grandly rising to the occasion.

22) And then the shouts began among the *dēmos*: "A god's voice and not a man's!" As far as the people were concerned, most of them were pagan idolaters and used to deifying the Roman emperors, and this shouting was no more than a bit of flattery to tickle the vanity of the king. His theatrical robes, his entire grandiose bearing on this special day for which the affair was staged invited the flattery which ranked Herod among the gods as was the case with regard to the Roman emperors. But Herod was a nominal Jew, the king of the Jewish nation, and, as we have seen in connection with his persecution of the Christians, one who posed as a most zealous exponent of Judaism, its great defender against Christian encroachments. This Jew permitted those shouts that deified him to continue instead of instantly hushing them as being utter

blasphemy; he let these pagan idolaters make a pagan god of him and enjoyed it.

We must note the imperfect tenses in v. 21, 22. They picture what was happening and intimate that something decisive followed as the outcome. The aorists used in the next verse record what that outcome was.

23) Immediately, right there in the theater, Herod was struck by the Lord's angel ἀνθ' ὧν, "in exchange or in return for which things", i. e., because he did not give the glory to God, namely all divine glory, instead of accepting such glory for his own person. Καί adds what this smiting of the angel implied: "he came to be eaten of worms," σκωληκόβρωτος, and thus died, ἐξέψυξεν, the lower word, "breathed out his ψυχή," not the higher, "breathed out his πνεῦμα." The *psyche* is man's immaterial part in so far as it animates his physical body, hence it is often translated "life." So all that Luke says and properly can say is that life went out of him. This was the frightful and sudden end of Agrippa I which came to him after only three short years of royal reign; he died at the age of 54.

The manner of his death is plainly marked as a *Gottesgericht*, a signal and visible judgment of God. A number of similar horrible deaths through masses of maggots eating the victim's putrifying body as though it were already a corpse are reported, all of them coming to human monsters. Read Josephus on the death of Herod the Great, *Ant.* 17, 6, 5; II Maccabees 9:5, 9 on the death of Antiochus Epiphanes who bitterly persecuted the Jews and is prominent as a type of Antichrist. Pheretima, queen of Cyrene, celebrated for her cruelty, was eaten by masses of worms while she was still alive; Herminianus, Roman governor of Cappadocia, who cruelly persecuted the Christians, was another; also the emperor Galerius, the last Roman emperor to persecute the church. The historian Niebuhr adds also Philip II of Spain who was noted for his cruelties and his persecutions.

As far as Josephus and his account of Herod's death are concerned (*Ant.* 19, 8, 2), he states that Herod lived only five days after being stricken in the theater and agrees that it was due to the fact that he accepted the blasphemous praise. Josephus always writes with an eye to the Romans and thus says nothing about the worms eating Herod's vitals but tones this down to pains and trouble in Herod's "belly." In *Ant.* 18, 6, 7 he tells of the time when Herod was a prisoner under Tiberius in Rome, how he saw an owl sitting, and how a German fellow prisoner worked his way toward him and prophesied that this owl meant good luck, and that he would soon be elevated to the highest position; but that if he should again see an owl, it would be the reverse, that he would then live only five days. Josephus claims that while he was in the theater he saw an owl sitting upon a rope and died after five days in fulfillment of the German's prophecy. If any basis in fact exists for this story about the owl, we set it down as an instance of second sight.

Zahn seems to find a connection between this owl as a messenger (ἄγγελος) of evil and Luke's angel (ἄγγελος) who smote Herod and thinks that Josephus, who wrote his *Antiquities* in the year 93 or 94, must have read Luke's statement in Acts. No angel was visible when Herod was stricken; the fact that God employed the agency of an angel in visiting his sudden and swift judgment on Herod was the conviction of the apostles who had the illumination of the Holy Spirit.

24) **The Word of God, however, went on growing and being multiplied.** That is the way in which the histories of the persecutions always end. Herod perished, the Word just grew more than ever. Note the imperfect tenses: grew and grew, etc. Both verbs mean that the Word itself increased by entering more

and more hearts. In the parable of the Sower the seed thus multiplies itself; in the parable of the Pounds the capital multiplies by being used in trade. It is a wonderful view of the vital life of the Word. It actually thrives under persecution. Yet we so often hang our heads when God sends persecution here and there. Ten most bloody persecutions ravaged the church under the pagan Roman emperors, and, when they had spent themselves, Christianity had permeated the empire, and in due time a Christian emperor ascended the throne.

25) Now Barnabas and Saul returned out of Jerusalem, having fulfilled their ministry, having taken along with them John, the one called Mark.
We have discussed this passage in connection with 11:30, which see. Herod died in 44, the relief was sent from Antioch *after* Herod's death and not before, for the famine and its distress came later. In 11:30 only Judea is mentioned, here, however, we see that Jerusalem was included, and no deductions can be made from "Judea" that would exclude the presence of Barnabas and Saul in Jerusalem.

A curious textual question arises because of the fact that two great uncials read εἰς, "to Jerusalem," instead of ἐξ or ἀπό, "out of" or "from." But in spite of Westcott and Hort who adopt εἰς this reading must be rejected as contradicting the context and also 11:30. The grammarians raise another question regarding the aorist participle συμπαραλαβόντες by stating that it might denote action that was subsequent to that of the main verb "returned"; it indicates coincident action in the very nature of the case, R. 862. We have met Mark in v. 12; we shall meet him again in 13:5, 9. We see how he got to Antioch and could be taken along on the first great missionary journey by Saul. Since he was a cousin of Barnabas, the latter must have advocated taking him along, to which Saul readily consented.

CHAPTER XIII

THE SECOND HALF

The Gospel Among the Gentiles in the Empire
Chapters 13 to 28

The time covered by this period extends from 45 to 62, from the first missionary journey to Paul's imprisonment in Rome.

The action moves through the Roman Empire in a grand sweep. Mission work reaches its highest development.

The chief personage is Paul; at his side appear his notable assistants. We also again meet Peter in chapter 15, and James in chapters 15 and 21.

We see the progress of the gospel first, with Paul at liberty (13 to 21:16); then, the progress with Paul in captivity (21:17 to 28:31). Three great missionary journeys are prominent while Paul is at liberty. Besides Jerusalem, Antioch, the center from which the journeys were made, attracts our attention; then Corinth and Ephesus and other localities become important centers of Christian activity. When Paul is in captivity, Caesarea draws attention but only as the steppingstone to the final goal which is Rome. Thus Luke's objective is reached: the great transition of the gospel from its original center in Jerusalem and Judaism to its grand new center, Rome and the vast Gentile world.

The Third Quarter

The Progress of the Gospel with Paul at Liberty

THE FIRST MISSIONARY JOURNEY: THROUGH THE ISLAND OF CYPRUS

1) Barnabas and Saul are back at Antioch after their brief mission of relief (11:30; 12:25). **Now there were in Antioch throughout the present church prophets and teachers, both Barnabas and Symeon called Niger and Lucius, the Cyrenian, also Manaen, Herod the tetrarch's child companion, and Saul.**

Transitional δέ transfers us to a time that is later than that mentioned in 11:26 and in 11:30 and 12:25. Luke advances us from the summer or the fall of 44 to the year 49. Zahn has corrected the 50 which is found in his *Introduction to the New Testament* III, 482, Chronological Table, to 49, in his *Kommentar*, 868, in accord with a recently discovered inscription.

Saul and Barnabas are to be sent away on a missionary tour that will necessitate their absence from Antioch for some time. Luke thus mentions the most prominent "prophets and teachers" in the congregation at this time. Three of these would remain at Antioch. We give κατά distributive force "throughout the church" in Antioch because we think of the church as being distributed over the large city and having a host of members.

The added οὖσαν is taken to mean *in der dortigen Gemeinde* (B.-D. 474, 5), "in the local church" (Moulton in R. 1107); but the participle is not to be construed with "in Antioch": "the church being in Antioch, being there"; we take it to be temporal: "being" at the time of which Luke writes: "the *present* church." It is not said that the church had these five illustrious teachers in 44; it has them now in the year 49.

"Prophets" is explained in 11:27, and here refers to men who are able to expound the Word. The context does not suggest prophets of the type of Agabus, to whom God communicated future events. These men served the congregation in the regular manner. "Prophets and teachers" thus go together: men who thoroughly understand the Word and are at the same time able to teach it to others. Hence, too, we decline to let the two τε divide the five named into three prophets and two teachers. For certainly Saul, the very last in the list, had already received direct communications from the Lord (among others also the one mentioned in 22:17, etc.), while we do not know whether Barnabas had received such communications. B.-D. 444, 5 does not divide into groups, yet Luke evidently intended to indicate two groups although we do not see why he divides the list of names. When Barnabas is placed first and Saul last, this seems to imply that the names are arranged according to the time of the conversion of those named or, possibly, according to the time of their entrance into the church at Antioch.

Barnabas and Saul we know. The fact that Symeon had the Roman name Niger in addition to his Aramaic name and was so designated by the Greeks, is only a common feature and really states nothing definite about the man. If he were the Simon who bore the cross for Jesus, Luke would have so identified him. *That* Simon came to distinction because of his two sons (Mark 15:21) and hence not because of a later prominence of his own. The fact that Symeon was not a Cyrenian like Lucius also proves that he was not Simon, the crossbearer. Lucius is designated as a Cyrenian and may have been one of those who fled after Stephen's death and first preached the gospel to the Greeks in Antioch (11:20). B.-D. 268 calls attention to the article "*the* Cyrenian" and thinks that it was perhaps intended to distinguish him from Luke, whose name appears also as "Lucius." Zahn, who finds Luke indirectly referred to in 11:28 (Codex Bezae), scouts the idea that he could have here listed himself as one of the great teachers in Antioch. Symeon is designated by his second name because there are many other Symeons or Simons; Lucius by his birthplace for a similar reason; but Manaen by his connection with the tetrarch, Herod Antipas, whose child companion he had been, σύντροφος, *Milchbruder, collactaneus* (Vulgate), nourished and brought up together with this Herod. That would make Manaen about 69 years old, for Herod Antipas was born in 20 B. C. Some interpreters identify Manaen with the βασιλικός mentioned in John 4:46-53; but this is only a guess. With more assurance we may say that Manaen was of aristocratic if not princely birth and thus stands out among the disciples. His princely education was an asset in his present leadership.

On the basis of a hypothetical first edition of Acts, Zahn thinks that a sixth name was added between Lucius and Manaen, namely that of Ticius, an Antiochian, whom Zahn supposes to be Titus, one of Paul's later assistants, this being the only mention of him in Acts. Aside from the hypothesis itself (*Forschungen IX*) and Zahn's alteration of "Ticius" to Titus, he fails to show how Luke could issue a second edition and from it omit this most certainly important name.

2) And while they were engaged in a divine service to the Lord and on fasting, the Holy Spirit said, Separate now for me Barnabas and Saul for the work to which I have called them for myself. Then, after having fasted and prayed and laid the hands on them, they released them.

The great hour had come: the call to the Gentile world, even to stand before kings! Saul had waited all these years, from 35 to 49, and had been working here in Antioch for about six years. Now at last he was to go out into the pagan world, not alone, but together with his close friend Barnabas. The Attic orators used the word λειτουργεῖν to designate any free service rendered to the state, in the LXX it is used with reference to the official service rendered by priests and Levites, and in the New Testament with reference to any sacred official service (Rom. 13:6, and 15:27 are not exceptions.) Here the participle must mean that these five men were not merely generally busy in their official capacities as prophets and teachers but were in the midst of a divine service with the assembled congregation; it may well have been one of the regular Sunday services which included the entire congregation as such.

The early Christians retained the Jewish religious custom of fasting. The law prescribed only one annual fast on the Day of Atonement, hence this is also called The Fast (Acts 27:9). A few additional fast days had been arranged by the nation itself in memory of sad experiences. The Pharisaic fasting was self-imposed and was observed for the sake of acquiring merit. Yet pious Jews also fasted in all sincerity, and it was this custom that was followed by the Christian Church. This fasting was always partial. (The writer's parents never ate before the Communion.) It is correct, the pronoun αὐτῶν refers only to the five men, but the first participle insures the presence of the congregation.

We find no danger in thinking that the church as such was present. Barnabas and Saul belonged to the congregation as prophets and teachers. The members were certainly concerned in the mission of these two. The Holy Spirit alone was their Sender and not the congregation, and certainly not the other three teachers. In 14:26, etc., we see that the church commended Barnabas and Saul to the grace of God for the work which they did and that they returned and made a report to the church. We are not told how the Holy Spirit spoke as he did although it is usually assumed that it was by means of a special revelation to one of the three teachers who was to remain, but this is done largely because we know of no other way unless Saul himself received the revelation. We say the latter only because Saul had previously received such revelations, cf., 9:12, and 22:17, etc.

The order of the Spirit was: "Separate now for me Barnabas and Saul," etc. Here the second person plural cannot refer to the five men who are included in the αὐτῶν, because two of them were to be separated; this command is addressed to the entire church. It was to give up the services of Barnabas and of Saul and let them serve the Holy Spirit elsewhere. Δή is rare and has a note of urgency. It emphasizes the imperative and is like the Latin *jam* or the German *doch*. There is no real equivalent in English, hence it is left untranslated in our versions; it is an emotional particle, and we may render: "Do now separate!" Note the perfect: for the work to which "I have called them for myself" (middle). What this work was we know from 9:15; 22:14, 15, 21; 27:16, in regard to Saul, and this was now to apply also to Barnabas.

3) What the Spirit ordered was promptly done. We do not think that the commissioning service was set for a later day. We take it that the service was now turned into a commissioning service. It was considerably prolonged. Thus with fasting, praying, and laying on of hands, the latter by the presbyters and not by the three other prophet-teachers who were left behind, "they released them," namely the whole church at Antioch. Luke is careful not to say: "they sent or they commissioned them," which would have been untrue.

The substance of the prayers we know from 14:26: "they were recommended to the grace of God for their work." It was a great day for the entire church.

The laying on of hands was used in connection with the seven deacons and is explained in 6:6. It is here again used in the same symbolical way. This, of course, was not ordination for Barnabas and for Saul, who were already "prophets and teachers." Yet it was the ceremony the church deemed proper formally to carry out the will of the Spirit in order to separate these two for their special work. We have no divine command for ordination, and when we now ordain we merely follow in the footsteps of the apostles and the early church by solemnly setting men apart for the holy ministry. So we also adopt the laying on of hands for our ordination and also for our confirmation of catechumens. We are free to do this and equally free not to add the ancient fasting. The virtue of these rites does not lie in the symbol of the hands being laid on but in the prayers of the church for those who are thereby set apart, prayers that are efficacious with God.

4) They on their part, therefore, having been sent out by the Holy Spirit, went down to Seleucia and from there sailed away to Cyprus.

Luke writes αὐτοί with a natural emphasis and refers to Barnabas and Saul, and μὲν οὖν is used as in 1:6. Luke purposely repeats that it was the Holy Spirit who had sent them out, and had done that by an immediate call. So the two went the short distance from Antioch to its harbor town Seleucia at the mouth of the Orontes River, found a ship there, and sailed for Cyprus, the island of which Barnabas was a native; see 4:36. The distance was not great. The Spirit evidently let them choose the locality where they wished to labor, and they followed natural lines by returning to the old homeland of Barnabas where he knew the type of people that would be met. It is one of Luke's literary habits always to name the harbors in connection with the voyages; this has been attributed to his love for the sea which was so characteristic of the Greeks. We are not told how this tour was financed. Money was required for the passage on the boat and also otherwise. It does not seem that the congregation at Antioch supplied the funds. All that one may conclude is that Barnabas and Saul went quite on their own.

5) **And being at Salamis, they began to proclaim the Word of God in the synagogues of the Jews. Moreover, they had also Mark as attendant.**

The actual work of proclaiming the Word started at Salamis, and that method was at once used which Saul followed ever after: they began in the synagogues. That was a simple and an easy way. As teachers and speakers who were efficient and able in every way, who were themselves of Jewish birth and training, permission was always freely given them to address the synagogue congregations and to expound to them the Old Testament prophecies concerning the Messiah and their fulfillment in Jesus. This was, of course, mission work only among the Jews, but it was done among the Jews of the diaspora, in pagan cities, and was intended to reach out from the synagogues to the Gentiles of those cities.

It is often thought of as following the rule or, shall we say, the principle: to the Jews first and then to the Gentiles. But this was not a mere rule. The wall of partition (Eph. 2:14) had been removed, *together* they were to become Christians. It was this far deeper principle that Barnabas and Saul followed when they entered the synagogues first. The Jews had the Scriptures and the Scripture knowledge of God. Therefore the beginning was naturally made with them. Salvation was of the Jews (John 4:22), the Messiah was David's son, redemption was wrought in Israel. The gospel was thus offered first to the Jews throughout the diaspora so that the Jews might lead the Gentiles into the Christian Church. It would have been abnormal to follow any other course; in fact, wrong to ignore the Jews.

At this point Luke remarks that Mark was a third party in the work but only in the capacity of an attendant; he was the ὑπηρέτης, literally, "under-rower in a trireme," and then anyone under the orders of another, "an underling." This word is used with reference to the Levite Temple police who were under the orders of their στρατηγός or commander, for instance at the time of the arrest of Jesus in Gethsemane and at the Jewish trial of Jesus. This shows what Mark's duties were: he was to do what Barnabas and Saul ordered him to do. The view that he was to baptize the converts is untenable. The administration of this sacrament was not a chore but as sacred and important as the preaching of the gospel itself, for it had been commanded by Jesus as much as the preaching had. Mark did whatever Barnabas and Saul asked him to do; they assigned his duties. This is the force of "underling." They may have used him also for teaching, perhaps also even for baptizing or helping to baptize on occasion. All depended on what might be needed. Some of his duties were prabably those of an ordinary servant. It was through the instrumentality of his cousin Barnabas that he was taken along. Luke mentions his presence in Jerusalem in 12:12, and shows how he was brought to Antioch in 12:25.

6) Having gone through the whole island as far as Paphos, they found a man, a magus, a false prophet, a Jew, whose name was Barjesus, who was with the proconsul Sergius Paulus, a man of understanding. This one, having called to himself Barnabas and Saul, earnestly sought to hear the Word of God. But Elymas, the magus — for thus his name is translated — began to stand against

them, seeking to turn the proconsul aside from the faith.

All that Luke states in v. 5 is that, upon arrival at Salamis, they adopted the practice of preaching in the synagogues. Now we read that the missionaries crossed the entire island by following its southeastern shore line — the interior is mountainous — to Paphos at the western end. Luke does not intend to furnish an itinerary nor to describe what was done at each place. We have no details about Salamis. There were no places of importance along the route to Paphos. The old Paphos had been destroyed by an earthquake in 15 B. C. With the aid of Augustus the new city was built at some distance from the site of the old ruins, at a spot where a bay faced south. Here the Roman proconsul had his residence.

The reliability of Luke's statement was formerly challenged on the ground that Cyprus was an imperial province and hence was not governed by a proconsul but by a propraetor. That was, indeed, true at a former time, but at this time Cyprus had been made a senatorial province, and its governor thus was a proconsul as Luke states. The island later again became an imperial province. General Cesnola discovered an inscription on the north coast of Cyprus which was dated "in the proconsulship of Paulus," the very Sergius Paulus of Acts. Robertson, *Luke the Historian, etc.*, 182.

We are granted only one glimpse of the work done in Cyprus: Saul's clash with a Jewish charlatan before the proconsul of the island. It is a parallel to the experience Peter had with Simon Magus as recorded in 8:9, etc. As far as the record goes, the work went on in its regular course with nothing especially to be noted. Here in Paphos the clash with the magus is important, not for its own sake, but for the effect it had on the proconsul. After he had been won for the gospel, great success was assured. This μάγος was a man of the type of Simon Magus, of whom μαγεύων and μαγεῖαι are predicated in 8:9, 11, the practice of magical arts, which were usually, however, associated with occultism and strange religious claims. This man was "a pseudo-prophet," who mixed his arts with false religious doctrines which were most likely concocted by himself. He was a "Jew," of course, no longer in religion but only by birth. He was a man of less importance than Simon Magus and spread no mysterious halo of divinity about himself.

7) He had managed to attach himself to the proconsul whom Luke characterizes as συνετός, which is more than φρόνιμος, "sensible," and means rather the quality of understanding, ability to put his mind on an object and to grasp it. This charlatan, unlike Simon Magus, cared nothing for the ordinary people but, like so many of his ilk in this era, sought to impress only some great personage and subject him to his control. The fact that he should have had a hold on a man of understanding such as Sergius Paulus was is not so strange when we recall what Juvenal reports regarding the Emperor Tiberius, "sitting on the rock of Capri with his flock of Chaldeans around him." Shallow men like Pontius Pilate scoffed at truth and anything serious, others who were dissatisfied with ordinary idolatry fell for the impressive and cunning deceivers who offered mysterious and apparently supernatural arts invested with strange Oriental philosophies.

Yet when this proconsul heard of Barnabas and Saul and the stir they were causing in Paphos he summoned them and, as Luke expresses it, ἐπεζήτησεν, "earnestly sought," to hear the Word of God, i. e., this teaching which they had to offer. The aorist of the verb and the infinitive imply that he obtained what he sought and fully heard that Word, namely the gospel. Barnabas and Saul had a public audience with the governor, at which they could speak at length and fully inform their great hearer.

8) And now we come upon a linguistic problem that is connected also with the variant readings of the codices and of the ancient versions. Does Luke intend to say that "Elymas" is a translation of ὁ μάγος, and is "Elymas" then an Arabic or an Aramaic term that is equivalent to a professional title like "professor" which was appropriated by the old mesmerists, the present mediums, and others? This has been the usual view. Attempts were made to clear up the etymology by reference to the Arabic verb 'alima, "to gain insight," "to grasp," and the noun 'alim, "magician," "diviner."

The contention of Zahn and others is that "Elymas" is not intended to be a translation of ὁ μάγος which needs no translation but of the man's name "Barjesus," a patronymic with "bar" to be understood in the sense of "son." The process starts by regarding "Elymas" as a Greek term to which the Aramaic "Barjesus" is then fitted. The result is that "Elymas," a corruption of 'Etoemus ('Etimas), is really *paratus* = "the Expert"; and "Barjesus," when this is derived from the Hebrew *shavah* which in the piel means "to smooth," "to finish" (omitting *bar* = "son"), is something of an equivalent of "the Expert."

This "Son of the Expert" or simply "Expert," the "ready man," began to oppose Barnabas and Saul and sought to divert (διαστρέψαι, turn this way and that by raising objections) the proconsul, his patron, from the faith, the article pointing to the objective sense of "faith," i. e., from the Word intended for faith. The imperfect tense and the present participle reveal only the attempt and point forward to the outcome. The devil had his advocate at the proconsul's side who was seeking to defeat the messengers of God. The trickster feared that he would lose control and be ousted. Evil men are always in the road to prevent the gospel from saving others. Spurious science and false religious teachings know they will be ousted if the gospel has full sway.

9) But Saul, also Paul, filled with the Holy Spirit, earnestly looking on him, said: O full of all guile and all villainy, devil's son, enemy of all righteousness, wilt thou not cease to turn aside the Lord's ways, the straight ones? And now, lo, the Lord's hand on thee! And thou shalt be blind, not seeing the sun until a season! And immediately there fell on him a mist and darkness and, going around, he began seeking hand-leaders.

In the simplest way, with a mere ὁ καί, which R. 734 thinks might be intended as a relative, Luke introduces the name "Paul" instead of Saul. From this point onward he intends to use only the name Paul except where the apostle may speak of himself. The reason for making the change at this point is plain. Up to this moment it is always "Barnabas and Saul," which implies that Barnabas exercised the leadership; but now the Spirit descends on Saul, and from this point onward the leadership rests with him. Here, then, was a fitting place to indicate that Saul now used his Roman name Paul because he worked among Greeks to whom *Sh'aûl* would sound too foreign.

Saul did not receive or himself take the name Paul at the time of his baptism in Damascus. If that had been the case, Luke would have called him Paul from that time onward. The idea that conversion "made Saul a Paul" is not correct. Saul did not assume the name Paul here in Paphos and did not choose "Paul" because of the proconsul's name "Paulus." These suggestions, as Farrar says, contain "an element of vulgarity impossible to St. Paul." Augustine thought that he chose "Paul" from motives of humility since the word means "little"; but almost the opposite is true. "Paul" had a proud ring in those days as suggesting the glories of the Aemelian family (Page).

On the eighth day, at the time of his circumcision, the father named his little son after the one Jewish king who had been chosen from the tribe of Benjamin, the tribe to which the family belonged; thus he received his Jewish name "Saul." But he was born a Roman citizen of the great city of Tarsus and thus received his Roman name (Latin) "Paul" on the ninth day. Like his Jewish name and like so many names of children, this was chosen because it was borne by illustrious persons of the Roman world. Other Jews had Greek names; the apostle and the evangelist were both named Philip after the tetrarch of that name. Saul's father gave the child a Roman and Latin name because he was a Roman citizen with all the rights in the Roman empire this implied. The child had both names from infancy. When his father called him he shouted, "Saul, Saul!" but when the Greek boys with whom he played called him they shouted, "Paul, Paul!" In his early connections with Jews he was called "Saul" as Luke has named him up to this time; from now on as he henceforth worked chiefly among Gentiles, "Paul" was the name he used, and Luke makes the change by showing that it began at this point. That is why Luke writes only ὁ καὶ Παῦλος and says nothing about his assuming this name; he always had had it.

It was not Barnabas but Paul who at this critical moment was filled with the Holy Spirit and was made the divine instrument for bringing judgment upon Barjishwan — Hetoimos (as Zahn calls him). Up to this point in the narrative Barnabas is always named first. Here in Cyprus, his native land, he properly took the lead. Now that the missionaries are about to leave the island, Paul will be the leader. This was

God's intention regarding this "chosen instrument" for the work among Gentiles; and with it, no doubt, went also Paul's own higher qualifications for the leadership. Moreover, Paul would continue in this work among Gentiles long after Barnabas.

When Paul now denounces the trickster and tells him that he will be blinded he does this, not by his own power, but through the Spirit. It is the same thing that occurred in Peter's case, who exposed Ananias and his hypocrisy by the Spirit's revelation and not by any powers of his own. To say that being filled with the Holy Spirit means being filled only with "a high degree of agitation," *in hochgradiger Erregung*, is unwarranted. A holy indignation did, indeed, move Paul just as it moved Jesus when he denounced the Pharisees and announced their judgment, cf., Matt. 23:13, etc. But Paul could never have brought blindness on this charlatan by even the intensest indignation. A mere volition on the part of an apostle never worked a miracle; the Lord and his Spirit use even the apostles only as instruments to carry out their volitions.

10) Paul is not carried away by his indignation, for his words have cold logic in them, in this respect being like the denunciation of the Pharisees on the part of Jesus. First, the evil in the man's heart, his inner motives are named; next, what these make of him in God's sight; then, what they ever lead him to do. "And now" rests the penalty of the Spirit on this clear basis. First, the full evidence of outrageous guilt; then, the verdict announcing the punishment. The Spirit, speaking through Paul, is absolutely just.

The Greek uses "O" sparingly, which makes it only the stronger when it is used. "Full of all guile and all villainy" exposes exactly what was in this man's heart. These were the motives back of his opposition to the missionaries and his efforts to keep the proconsul from the faith. Δόλος is "bait" and then the cunning that uses it to catch its victim; the word is very much in place here: the proconsul was the victim who was to snatch at the bait this fellow was offering by his arguments against the faith. 'Ραδιουργία, "the ability to do a thing easily," is used in the sense of "unscrupulousness," when one acts without the least compunction or hesitation as to the damage he may do to others in gaining his ends, hence "villainy." The fellow was ready to do or to say anything in order to keep his hold on his victim. Twice Paul adds "all," which marks the extent of this man's viciousness.

What this really made of him Paul states in plain words, "a devil's son," υἱός is to be understood in the ethical sense as described in John 8:44. "Son" and "sons" are used in both an evil and a good way. We have "sons of light," "sons of Israel," or "of the prophets," etc.; in II Thess. 2:3, "son of perdition." Children are dear to men; but in ethical connections the son reflects the father or the quality and thus represents the one or the other. A devil's son is not only his offspring but one in whom the devil's characteristics reappear. "Devil" is Satan without stress on the etymology "slanderer." Those who understand "Barjesus" as meaning "son of Jesus" (Joshuah) find a contrast to this name in "devil's son." Paul specifies the ethical feature when he adds "enemy of all righteousness." An ἐχθρός is a hating personal enemy, and δικαιοσύνη is righteousness or right in the forensic sense as meeting the approval of the righteous divine Judge. Anything of that sort this man hated, for it would utterly condemn and destroy him and his vicious practices.

The motive, the man, and now the deeds: "Wilt thou not cease to turn aside the Lord's ways, the straight ones?" The addition of the adjective by means of a second article makes a kind of apposition and climax, R. 776. These blessed ways of the Lord, these teachings of his that lead to faith, that are straight and true in every part and not crooked, not tricky, with no ulterior design, this fellow intends never to cease turning this way and that (διαστρέφων as in v. 8), to twist and to pervert by his objections, making them appear as what they are not, as something evil according to the evil that fills his own heart. The question is strongly rhetorical, for it has οὐ with the subjunctive (futuristic, R. 942) as though the answer is to be "yes" while the sense is: "No, thou wilt not cease doing this!" The fellow would let no moral consideration of any kind stop him in his nefarious doing.

11) But the Spirit has a way that will stop him: "And now" as the legitimate deduction from this character and conduct, "lo, the Lord's hand upon thee!" Why insert "is" and weaken what is an exclamation and not a cool declaration? Paul, as it were, sees that hand or almighty power of the Lord Jesus striking this devil's son. The fellow is to be blind and not see the sun until the time (καιρός) set by the Lord. This blindness for a time is a judicial penalty; it is by no means all that he deserved, but in his grace God moderated it by not cutting off the opportunity for repentance. It was a preliminary judgment like so many that God inflicts on wilful sinners in order by such severe means possibly to turn them from their evil ways. These judgments, if they are spurned, prefigure and announce the final, fatal judgment. God warned Pharaoh with ever greater severity until the cup of his obduracy overflowed; then came the final stroke. This man's wilful blindness was punished by miraculous physical blindness. The penalty often corresponds to the guilt. If this penalty would fail of its proper effect, a greater

penalty awaited him, the darkness of everlasting death. The devil's son would then end in the devil's eternal night.

The man was struck blind instantly. Those who think that this was effected gradually because "a mist" is mentioned before "darkness" disregard the aorist with its adverb. Sight was blotted out at once. "Mist and darkness" are one idea, and mist is added in order to show that the eyeballs were filmed so that their sight went out like a light that is blown out. The effect was that, "going around, he began to seek handleaders," a compound noun for which we lack a current equivalent. He would mislead the proconsul, he now sought someone to lead him, and that not amiss.

Here the man disappears from view. No one knows how long his blindness lasted. Zahn thinks that he was certainly cast off by Sergius Paulus and that eight years later he appeared as "one of the friends" of the procurator Felix (Acts 24:24), the fellow who was employed to lure away Drusilla, the daughter of Agrippa I, from her husband Azizus, the king of Emesa (Joseph, *Ant.* 20, 7, 2), in order to marry Felix. He is described as a Cyprian Jew and a magician. As to his name, the "Simon" found in the texts of Josephus is due to Christian copyists who placed this name in the margin and then into the text, thinking that the Simon Magus of Acts 8 was referred to; the name was "Atomon" and seems to be the "Hetoimon" ("Elymas," see v. 8) of Luke. All that one can say is, interesting if true.

12) **Then, on seeing what had occurred, the proconsul believed, dumbfounded at the teaching of the Lord.**

This punitive miracle dumbfounded the proconsul The undeniable power manifested in it he rightly connected with "the teaching or doctrine of the Lord

(Jesus)," thereby showing himself συνετός, "one understanding" (v. 7), by putting his mind and what had occurred together properly. He saw the same power in the miracle and in the doctrine which it sealed.

Luke writes the simple, positive, assuring aorist: "he believed." We have no reason whatever to discount the word. The reasons brought forward for doing so are invalid the moment Luke's account of the work in Cyprus is viewed as a whole. We at once see that the proconsul is the only convert that is mentioned as a result of the entire work done in Cyprus. That speaks rather plainly. It was not Luke's intention to report in detail. He mentions only two towns, Salamis where the missionaries landed and Paphos from which they left. It is not even stated that converts and congregations resulted in these towns. Yet many were undoubtedly converted, and a number of congregations was left behind.

Is it any wonder, then, that Luke writes regarding the proconsul only that "he believed"? Why ask for more, that he was baptized, that this included his family, that he was received into the church, etc.? And because all this is not in the record, why question whether it occurred? Luke expects his readers also to be συνετός. Why these suspicions that the proconsul was perhaps not baptized because of his Roman office, because he had to take official part in certain official religious idolatrous rites? Another view is that, if a proconsul had been converted to Christianity, Roman and Greek historians would have recorded that fact. They certainly did not record the fact that this proconsul was a pupil of the Jewish magus. "He believed" — that aorist stands as a tower — the very governor of the island, a Roman, believed! Luke makes this fact most impressive by saying nothing about other believers. He lets his reader himself say this.

This first stage of the first missionary journey of Paul was eminently successful. The one high point of success scored speaks volumes. And we should not think that, because in the next verse it is stated that the missionaries left, they departed the very day after the proconsul believed. They left when it was safe to leave their work in Paphos. In his chronological table Ramsay allows from March to July for the stay in Cyprus.

The First Missionary Journey: Pisidian Antioch

13) After the work is completed in Cyprus, new territory is sought. **Now having set sail from Paphos, those around Paul went to Perga of Pamphilia. John, however, having withdrawn from them, returned to Jerusalem. But they on their part, having gone through from Perga, arrived at Antioch, the Pisidian.**

The passive of ἀνάγω is used in a nautical sense, "to put to sea," "to set sail." The Greek says literally, "go up" on the sea and "come down" to land, speaking as it appears to the eye. The voyage from Paphos to the coast of the mainland was easily accomplished, there being frequent shipping facilities. Instead of stopping at the harbor town Attalia (14:25), they sailed up the Kestros River and landed at Perga. The observation is certainly correct that, when Luke writes "Perga of Pamphilia," he is not locating Perga for his reader, not distinguishing it from some other Perga. Pamphilia was selected as the next missionary field and is mentioned for this reason. It is true that Paul first went up to Antioch and worked there, but equally true that on the return journey work was done in Pamphilia.

In οἱ περὶ Παῦλον we have the classic idiom for "Paul and his company," he being included (B.-D. 228). Significant is the naming of this group after Paul. It is not "the Barnabas party" but "the Paul party." Luke writes thus because after the stay at Paphos the main person and leader is Paul. Let us understand that this gravitation of Paul to the leadership was entirely natural. In personality, in personal force, as in education, Paul outranked even a man like Barnabas. Although it had been held back all these years, the simple greatness of the man now began to be revealed. That fact made it easy for Barnabas to fall into second place.

It is Ramsay who connects Perga, Mark's leaving, and the haste to Pisidian Antioch by starting from the assumption that Luke joins together what inwardly belongs together. The three statements are usually treated separately. The only direct light we have on Mark's defection is the remark made in 15:38, 39 that "he did not go with them to the work" and that Barnabas and Paul fell out with each other in regard to taking him along on a second missionary journey. What really was the trouble still remains veiled. We hastily acquit the mosquitoes at Perga, not because they stung Paul and Barnabas as well as Mark, but because no stay was made at Perga at this time. The charge of homesickness, that Mark went *zu seiner Mutter* (to his mother), is unfair. We find nothing convincing in the surmise that Mark did not relish the transfer of leadership from Barnabas, Mark's cousin, to Paul. Mark was only an attendant (v. 5), and the shift of leadership was entirely natural. Mark could not take umbrage as long as Barnabas did not. Still less likely is Mark's dissatisfaction with Paul's work among the Gentiles, for Barnabas stood for the same work, he as well as Paul having cast away Judaistic ideas.

That leaves Mark's lack of courage, which agrees with chapter 15:38, 39. It may well be possible that something had occurred at Perga which took the heart out of Mark. Ramsay asks the question as to why Paul went straight on from Perga to Pisidian Antioch, a long hard journey that was full of dangers at that. Why was no work done at Perga at this time but only later? Ramsay finds the reason in Gal. 4:13, 14, Paul's "infirmity of the flesh." Paul had to leave the hot lowlands and get into the higher interior without delay. Thus he hurried straight on to Antioch, 3,600 feet above the sea; here he might hope to recover.

What, then, was Paul's ailment? Ramsay diagnoses it as malaria which with its sudden attacks incapacitated Paul for several hours at each recurrence, prostrated him utterly, and was accompanied by frightful headaches. Since Paul was in this condition, Mark lost heart. In 15:38, 39 Paul still mistrusted Mark. Suppose Paul should have another siege of the malady, what would Mark then do? Was this Paul's "stake in the flesh" (II Cor. 12:7)? It could not have been even if we stress the accompanying headaches; the ailment was temporary.

Ramsay's combination would also explain why Barnabas went on with Paul. He and Paul had been commissioned together by the Holy Spirit (v. 2); if Paul went on, Barnabas dared not withdraw and go with his cousin. The view that in Gal. 4:13, 14 Paul refers to some eye trouble that made his face look disagreeable is only a conjecture which does not even fit in with the language used. In v. 9 Paul "sets his eyes" on the magus, and that bars out any affliction of the eyes. The hypothesis of epilepsy is even less likely; a man who was subject to epileptic fits could not possibly have the mentality and do the work of this apostle. Besides, this ailment of which Paul complains does not seem to have been continuous. Only the Galatians saw him when his condition was very bad.

As far as "Galatia" is concerned, namely the debate as to whether Paul worked in southern Galatia or in northern Galatia, the question is settled. It was southern Galatia which included the very cities Paul was now entering before he returned to Perga which is located in Pamphilia.

14) *After Mark had left them, Paul and Barnabas pressed on to Pisidian Antioch.* According to Luke's record this was not a missionary tour, the travelers went straight through to Antioch. Antioch was not in Pisidia but on its border, hence Luke does not write "Antioch of Pisidia" (like "Perga of Pamphilia") but "Antioch, the Pisidian," the city thus being distinguished from Syrian Antioch and other towns of that name. It was a Roman colony like Philippi, a free city, and among its inhabitants there were many Jews. It was located in the Roman province of Galatia which included the ethnographic *Regiones* Pisidia, Phrygia, and Lycaonia. Until the return to Perga the journey was made entirely in Galatia. Antioch was a most desirable place in which to plant a Christian congregation.

And having gone to the synagogue on the day of the Sabbath, they sat down. But after the reading of the Law and of the Prophets the synagogue rulers sent to them, saying, Men and brethren, if you have some word of exhortation in your minds, say on!

We should begin a new sentence with καί. It has been asked how it was possible that in Antioch two Sabbaths were sufficient to produce such a decisive result among the Jews as well as the Gentiles when at other places similar results were more slowly achieved. But Luke is specific. The work began in the synagogue and moved with rapidity. After Paul and Barnabas had found lodging they most likely introduced themselves to the Jewish leaders, and when the Sabbath came, they sat down in the audience. Whether special seats were set aside for visiting rabbis is not known. The Greek often has the plural for "Sabbath"; the word is treated somewhat like names of festivals.

15) Luke has a double purpose in reporting the following sermon preached by Paul. It is a sample sermon which shows just how he presented Christ and the gospel in the synagogues. It is more: in this sermon we see how the Jews became hostile and then proceeded to persecute, which was one of the usual experiences of Paul.

Each synagogue had its managers who were called "elders" or as here "synagogue rulers"; one of these served as chairman or head of the others. All the synagogue's affairs were in the hands of the rulers. Since there were no pastors, the rulers managed the services so that the lessons were read, the prayers and the responses were recited, and necessary business attended to. Whenever possible, however, competent rabbis were asked to address the people. This was done by request or permission of the rulers. Men of the necessary schooling and ability were not numerous and happened along as visitors only occasionally. When Paul, the famous pupil of Gamaliel in Jerusalem, and Barnabas, a Levite and resident of Jerusalem, appeared in Pisidian Antioch, the elders even sent the *chazzan* or synagogue clerk to the rear where they were sitting and invited them to come forward to address a word to the people. This was in regular order, was not possible every Sabbath, and was appreciated the more on that account.

This occurred after the regular part of the service had been concluded, the main features of which Luke mentions, namely the reading of the Law (Torah, Pentateuch) and of the Prophets (a term that included the historical books from Joshua through Kings). The Pentateuch was divided into fifty-four lections called *parashas*, fifty-four so as to suffice also for the Jewish leap year, the Prophets into fifty-four *haphtarahs*; one of each of these lections was read each Sabbath. These two lections were themselves a fair-sized sermon. The Palestinian and the eastern Jews, the socalled Hebrews (see 6:1), used the Hebrew text which was translated into the vernacular Aramaic, for the majority of these Jews were no longer fully conversant with Hebrew. But in the Hellenistic diaspora, thus also here in Antioch, the LXX was used which need not be translated since all understood the Greek. This explains the presence of so many Gentiles, proselytes of the gate and prospective proselytes, in these synagogues. The Jews themselves were the Hellenists mentioned in 6:1; on the two kinds of proselytes see 2:10. The second class of proselytes were always open to the gospel, were readily won for the gospel, and thus formed the avenue for reaching the Gentile Greeks in general.

The idiom ἄνδρες ἀδελφοί is explained in 1:16; it is at once polite and dignified. Perhaps λόγος παρακλήσεως was a standard term for an address such as is here requested, the genitive denoting "exhortation," encouragement to believe the Word and to live according to its precepts. It did not necessarily imply an exposition of the lections read for that Sabbath although the address might take up some word in one or the other lection or might start with such a word. What the visiting rabbi might desire to say was left entirely to him. The address would be quite informal, at least in most cases: so here "any word in you," *in animis vestris,* that in your mind and heart might seem profitable for the people to hear. This invitation was just what the missionaries desired.

16) And having arisen and having motioned with the hand, Paul said, etc. It is Paul who responds and makes the address; he is now the leader. The Jewish teachers sat when making an address. Both in Constantinople and in the Great Mosque at Damascus the writer saw the Mohammedan speakers sitting cross-legged, the latter speaker being very dramatic and fervent in his Arabic address. But in the Greek Catholic church in Damascus the patriarch, as well as the new bishop whom he installed, together with the other bishops and clergy stood during the entire ceremony and while the patriarch made his address to the new bishop and the latter responded. In the Hellenistic synagogues it was customary for the speakers to stand. Since the ordinary part of the service was at an end, the audience in the large synagogue had begun a conversation, and when Saul went forward and faced them he motioned for silence. Ἀναστάς is so constantly used circumstantially for proceeding with an act that it does not assure us that Paul stood; but in 17:22 he stood, and we assume that he followed this Roman custom here.

It is, of course, problematic what lections had been read on that Sabbath, nor have we the lections as they were arranged in those early days. From two words, both of which are distinctive, in Paul's address one might conclude that the lection from the Torah was Deut. 1, and the lection from the Prophets Isa. 1. These words are ἐτροφοφόρησεν (v. 18), which appears in Deut. 1:31; and ὕψωσεν (v. 17), which appears in Isa. 1:2, in the LXX. The historical part of Paul's address may have been suggested by Deut. 1. The address names: **Israelite men and those fearing God** and bids them **hear,** and uses the authoritative aorist imperative and not the milder present. This implies that quite a number of these proselytes of the gate, who are regularly called οἱ φοβούμενοι τὸν Θεόν, must have been present. Paul names them side by side with the Israelites. The proselytes would sit in a place that was especially set aside for them. The women were seated behind some screen where they would be invisible to the men. Paul had no occasion to name them in his address. When Paul says "Israelites" he appeals to the highest motives in his Jewish hearers; see the term in 2:22.

Inferior homiletics receives no support from Paul's address at Pisidian Antioch. The theme is plainly marked in v. 23, and three of the parts are marked, each with ἄνδρες ἀδελφοί (v. 16, 26, 38). Here is the outline:

UNTO ISRAEL A SAVIOR, JESUS

I. Israel's history leads up to him.

II. God fulfilled his promises to Israel by raising him from the dead.

III. In him alone is forgiveness and justification.

Even a little study shows how well the sermon fit the time, the place, and the audience. Put yourself in Paul's place and say what you would have spoken in Antioch.

17) The God of this people Israel elected for himself our fathers and exalted the people in the foreign sojourn in Egypt's land and with a high arm led them forth out of it. And for about a time of forty years he bore them as a nursing father in the desert.

Paul begins his address as Stephen had begun his defense: by a review of Israel's history. The tone and the object, however, are different. Through the history recounted by Stephen runs the note of Israel's disobedience in rejecting Christ; Paul's account of the history shows God's grace blessing Israel. Impressively Paul begins with "the God of this people Israel." He says "of this people Israel" because he is speaking to Gentiles as well as to Jews, and the pagan nations had been idolaters and had not worshipped the true God. The Jews sometimes carried their ancestry back to Abraham (John 8:39), sometimes to Jacob or Israel (as here) and thus to "our fathers," the twelve patriarchs (Rom. 9:5). This great and only God, who in the Old Testament is named from his people Israel, in whom the Gentile proselytes of the gate now also believed, by a signal act of his free grace "elected for himself (middle voice) our fathers" in his great plan of grace for all men to be the bearers of his promises to the world and to be the nation from whom the Savior of the world should be born according to the flesh. A brief and yet mighty statement; a perfect way to begin a sermon, namely with a statement that arrests attention by its importance and promises that the following will remain on this high plane.

Equal in force is the next statement: "and he exalted the people in the foreign sojourn in Egypt's land" by making them strong and numerous and by granting them his covenant promises and the true worship. Λαός is always the covenant people; and the verb does not mean merely that he let the people grow up to be big but that he placed them on a high plane. While they lived as πάροικοι, "foreigners," not natives in παροικία, the state of aliens, in the land of Egypt, God still kept them as his own people. And when the time came, God ended that alien state by leading his people out "with an arm exalted." The μετά does not speak of this exalted arm as the means or instrument by which God led out Israel but as the accompaniment: "in company with an arm exalted."

This arm went along with Israel at the time of the exodus; they saw it in the pillar of cloud by day which became a pillar of fire by night. God's arm is his power and his majesty; where his arm is, there he is: God who exalted his people led them to their own land with an exalted arm. Behold all this grace! Then think of its ultimate purpose!

18) We regard this verse as an independent sentence and not as subordinate to the next verse. Like a nursing father God carried his people through the desert. The reading ἐτροφοφόρησεν, both here and in Deut. 1:31, is decidedly to be preferred to ἐτροποφόρησεν, "he bore their manners." The former is a rare verb and was easily changed to the commoner verb by altering only one letter. But the Hebrew justifies the former verb: "he bare thee as a man doth bear his son." Paul knew the Hebrew as well as the LXX. There would be a note of blame in saying that God bore Israel's manners for forty years; for we know what those manners were (7:39-43); but Paul's tone is the very opposite; it shows God's wonderful grace toward Israel. All those years God tenderly cared for Israel like a father nursing his son. He fed the people with manna and kept them so that they did not perish. The fact that their own unbelief extended the journey to forty years is not the point here; God kept them in spite of their unbelief.

19) **And having destroyed seven nations in Canaan land, he distributed as a heritage their land about four hundred and fifty years; and after that he gave them judges until prophet Samuel; and thereupon they asked for themselves a king, and God gave them Saul, son of Kish, a man of Benjamin's tribe, for forty years.**

Paul proceeds from the entrance into Canaan through the era of the judges to the end of Saul's reign. The chief point of this presentation is the

Acts 13:19, 20

truth that *God* did all that is here recited. His agency in the history is brought to view. It was he who destroyed the seven Canaanite nations (cf., Deut. 7:1, where their names are recorded); he who distributed their land to the people of Israel as an inheritance.

The correct reading continues with ὡς (there is no καί before it) and places the dative of time in v. 19 and not, as the A. V. does, in v. 20 by placing the dative after the μετά phrase: "and after that . . . about the space of 450 years." R. 527 does not give much helpful information on this dative; B.-D. 201 furnishes full evidence for this use of the dative as denoting length of time instead of an accusative with transitive verbs; this is apparently done in order to avoid two consecutive accusatives, one being the direct object of the transitive verb and another indicating the extent of time. Zahn says that placing the dative of time into v. 19 lets Paul say that distributing the inheritance covered that much time. The round number "about 450 years" covers the time from the sojourn in Egypt to the possession of Canaan. According to 7:6 (Gen. 15:13) 400 years were spent in Egypt, forty additional years in the journey through the desert to Canaan, and about ten further years for conquering the land, which is certainly close to 450 years. Paul says that during these many years, almost half a millennium, God dealt so graciously with his λαός.

20) Zahn resorts to an emendation of the text by eliminating μετὰ ταῦτα and making v. 20 read: "for about 450 years he gave judges," etc., and makes the period of the judges 450 years, which is in contradiction with I Kings 6:1, which makes the entire time from the exodus from Egypt to the fourth year of Solomon's reign only 480 years. Nor can the 450 years be reckoned according to the incorrect reading of the A. V. "after these things," after the entrance of Israel into Canaan, for this would advance us into

the reign of David and beyond that of Saul, neither of whom Paul has as yet mentioned.

The claim is unwarranted that Paul had a different method of reckoning from that employed in I Kings 6:1, which arrived at 480 years from the exodus to the time of Solomon, namely that Paul merely added together the years of the judges and disregarded the fact that the terms of the judges frequently overlapped and thus secured 450 years; the Jews are charged with doing the same thing. Paul's 450 years have nothing to do with even the longer era that began with the conquest of Canaan. R., W. P., counted the 450 years from the birth of Isaac to the conquest of Canaan. But it is sixty years from Isaac's birth to Jacob's, seventy more until Jacob goes to Canaan, 400 in Egypt, forty in the wilderness — 570!

It is again God who gave Israel judges until the last one who was even more than a judge, namely "prophet Samuel" who is even regarded as one of God's great prophets.

21) *Finally they asked for themselves a king.* Paul is not reciting the faults of Israel but God's leadings which culminated in the Messiah. Hence he mentions only the request for a king since in response to it God gave them Saul. It was God who did this. It is a misunderstanding to say that Paul adds Saul's lineage, "son of Kish, a man of Benjamin's tribe," because the apostle himself came from that tribe and himself was named Saul. No motive of pride actuated Paul in making this addition. He mentions Saul's lineage for a most pertinent reason. It was not from the tribe of Benjamin, not from the royal line of Saul, that the Savior came but from David who replaced Saul.

The Old Testament nowhere states the length of Saul's reign. In I Sam. 13:1 the age of Saul when he became king had already been omitted when the

LXX made their translation. Here again Jewish tradition is supposed to have furnished the omitted information by making Saul's reign forty years, equal to that of David and of Solomon. Josephus is usually quoted in support of this view, but in *Ant.* 6, 14, 9, in the statement that Saul reigned eighteen years while Samuel yet lived and twenty-two after Samuel was dead, the word "twenty" is not genuine, and the word "two" seems to be taken from the corrupted passage I Sam. 13:1. Elsewhere Josephus makes Saul's reign only twenty years — a sample of the reliability of this historian. Paul's forty years should be taken as extending back to Samuel just as the 450 years extended back and allowed seventeen to nineteen years for the judgeship of Samuel and twenty to twenty-two for the kingship of Saul. Keil, *Biblischer Commentar, Josua, Richter und Ruth*, 212.

22) And after having removed him, he raised up David for them for king, to whom also he said, giving testimony, I found David, him of Jesse, a man according to my heart who will do all my will. Of the seed of this one God according to promise brought for Israel a Savior, Jesus, John having heralded in advance before the presence of his entering in a baptism of repentance to all the people Israel. And as John was fulfilling his course he went on to say: What do you suspect me to be? I am not he! But lo, there comes after me he, the sandals of whose feet I am not worthy to loose.

All that Paul says about Saul, the Benjaminite king, is that God removed him. This, however, does not refer to Saul's death — he killed himself — but to his rejection by God when Samuel was commissioned to anoint another as king in Saul's place. God allowed Saul to continue to reign for a time but only as one who had been rejected. In place of Saul, God "raised up David for them for king" (εἰς introducing the predicate, resembling the Hebrew l^e, R. 482). Of Saul, Paul says God "gave," of David, God "raised up," a more significant term which includes all that made David the king he was. Paul makes this prominent by letting God himself testify concerning David; the action of μαρτυρήσας is simultaneous with that of εἶπε due to the nature of the actions. What God said was testimony.

Paul is not quoting, has no formula of quotation, and cares only to state the substance of the divine testimony regarding David. Thus Ps. 89:20, and I Sam. 16:7, 12 are used, and one expression is taken from Isa. 44: 28, where it is used with reference to Cyrus, but it applies to David just as well or even better. David allowed God to make his heart and his life what they were. "Him of Jesse," i. e., Jesse's son, points to David's father as being but a common man; yet under God's gracious leading he eventually found this man's son David "a man according to my heart," an individual as God wished him to be. David's great sins did not alter this testimony of God, for David repented.

The relative clause shows to what this testimony referred, namely to David's willingness to do all the θελήματα of God, the different things that God willed. In this respect David was the opposite of Saul, to whom Samuel had to say, "To obey is better than sacrifice," and then, "Thou hast rejected the word of the Lord, and the Lord hath rejected thee from being king over Israel," I Sam. 15:22, 26.

Paul brings into prominence the high, godly caracter of David because the Messiah was to be David's son. When he thus distinguished David, Paul had the fullest consent of all his hearers, especially of the Jews who knew all about David and who fully believed that the Messiah would come from David's line. When Jesus asked the Pharisees whose son the Christ would be, they promptly answered, David's son (Matt. 22:41, etc.), and many an afflicted person appealed to Jesus as "the son of David."

23) The emphatic demonstrative τούτου, "of this one," placed at the head of the sentence, sums up all that Paul had said about David and now, leaping across the space of a thousand years, connects Jesus with him: "of the seed of this one," etc. This clear statement that Jesus was "from the seed" of David ought to give pause to all those who deny that Mary was a lineal descendant of David and refuse to understand Luke's genealogical table (Luke 3:23, etc.) as being that of Mary. Read Rom. 1:4: "Jesus Christ, which was made (τοῦ γενομένου) of the seed of David according to the flesh." If Joseph alone was of David's blood and not Mary, if, therefore, Jesus was only legally David's son through his foster-father, how could he be "from (ἀπό, Rom. 1:4, ἐκ) David's seed"? That exegesis is wrong which denies Davidic descent to Mary and Davidic blood to Jesus. When we are told that in the present passage Paul is not speaking of the birth of Jesus but only of his office, and that this is made certain by εἴσοδος in the next verse, we challenge this claim. Paul speaks of both the birth or descent of Jesus and of his office. "According to promise" even connects the two, for it was God's promise that one of David's blood should be the Savior, II Sam. 7:16; Isa. 11:1; Jer. 23:5, 6; Zech. 3:8 (Luke 1:32, 33). Without the Davidic birth and blood there is no Messianic office.

In one simple, direct statement Paul declares that God made Jesus the Savior: "God according to promise brought for Israel a Savior, Jesus." "God" did it; Paul made God's agency very prominent throughout all of Israel's history, and here that agency reaches its climax. The choice between the reading ἤγαγε and the slighty supported ἤγειρεν, is easy, because the latter is drawn from v. 22: "raised up" David; and we regard the reading ἀνήγαγε as a conjecture for which there is little support.

This very verb ἄγω, "brought," occurs in the promise Zech. 3:8, and its use with the dative "brought for Israel" is most proper. The expression is only a variation of Peter's declaration: "God made this Jesus both Lord and Christ" (2:36). Paul has been recounting Israel's history under God and thus he says that God brought Jesus "for Israel." The Gentiles present were to hear that the Savior was presented to Israel according to the promise made to Israel; the fact that this Savior was intended also for them they would hear presently (v. 39).

Note that the great name "Jesus" is placed emphatically at the end and that it thus balances the equally emphatic genitive "of this one (David)" at the head of the sentence. No play on words is intended in σωτῆρα Ἰησοῦν although "Jesus" itself signifies "savior" (see 2:38). "Savior" puts the whole office and work of Jesus into one word, and that word signifies not only what Jesus did but what he still does — he is and remains the one who saves. All that the Scriptures say about salvation lies in this one term. "Savior," plus its derivatives, refers to the act of rescuing from mortal spiritual danger and includes the further continuous act of keeping in the condition of spiritual safety. All that God had planned from the very beginning when selecting the fathers (v. 17) God had carried out when he brought Jesus to Israel and presented him as the Savior according to the promise.

What a glorious statement for these Jews to hear! They gloried in that past history with all its illustrious names and with God in and over it all; and now it was crowned by God's bringing to them this promised Savior. We know of no more perfect approach that Paul could have made to the mighty theme of the Saviorhood of Jesus for this audience of his.

24) The added genitive absolute describes how God brought Jesus for Israel as a Savior. We must note the grandness of the language and of the underlying imagery. Note, "before the presence or face of his entering in," Hebraistic, as though this Savior came in divine power and majesty. A great herald came before him who announced his coming for Israel by proclaiming "a baptism of repentance for all the people Israel." It was thus that God brought Jesus to Israel. Paul's hearers knew about Jesus and about the Baptist; all he needed to do was to present the great facts as they had occurred.

In the verb "to herald in advance" ($\pi\rho\acute{o}$) we have the prophecy that John should be the "voice" crying in the wilderness. What heralding a baptism meant all Jews would know, all of whom were conversant with the Jewish lustrations and cleansing ceremonies. This herald John, they understood, came in advance in order to prepare the people of Israel for the coming of the Savior. Carefully, despite all brevity, Paul adds the qualifying genitive baptism "of repentance." It demanded repentance, was intended for the repentant only, but the entire people of Israel were to accept it by such repentance. On the concept repentance see 2:38, and on John's baptism 1:5. God intended John's work only for the Jews, and in due time, as now, the blessing of it would go out to all the world.

25) Paul shows the greatness of this Savior Jesus by the word of the Baptist which John 1:19, etc., recounts so fully, also Luke 3:15, etc.; Matt. 3:11. This occurred when John was finishing his course, i. e., when Jesus had already begun his ministry. Many of the people quietly thought ($\dot{v}\pi\acute{o}$ in the verb) that John him-

self might be the Christ. The imperfect ἔλεγε pictures his answer. One may draw the question and the answer together: "What you suspect *me* to be *I* am not," the emphasis being on the pronouns (B. D. 298, 4; R. 738); or one may divide: "What do you suspect *me* to be? *I* am not (what you thus suspect)!" *what*, not *who*.

The utter folly of thinking that a mere man like John could be the Messiah and Savior is brought out by saying that one as high as John was, so high as to be suspected of himself being the Messiah, was not worthy of stooping before the real Messiah in order to render him the service of the lowest slave, that of untying his sandals to take and to cleanse them and of washing the dust from his feet. It was a concrete and striking way of pointing out the deity of the Messiah. The exclamation "lo" helps to make it strong; ἔρχεται is Messianic, the Messiah was "the One coming."

This first part of Paul's discourse is purely historical — all a series of facts — all straight testimony. All these things God had done — no "if" or "but" about it. Every word must have gone directly home.

26) Paul marks *the second part* of the discourse most plainly by once more addressing his hearers: ἄνδρες ἀδελφοί (see 1:16). We may extend this second part to v. 37, after which Paul addresses his hearers for a third time. Two historical facts are presented: Jesus' death and his resurrection. Both, however, are presented in such a way as to bring out their full significance. The Jews of Jerusalem killed Jesus but by doing this ignorantly fulfilled the divine prophecy. God raised Jesus from the dead and completed the fulfillment. This resurrection attests the Messiahship of Jesus by God's own act. The prophecies are quoted to fortify the fact. Here again are straight facts but facts set into the proper divine light.

Men and brethren, sons of Abraham's stock, and those among you fearing God, to us the word of this salvation was sent out.

The apposition appeals most strongly to the theocratic position and feelings of Paul's Jewish hearers. In v. 17 this appeal was made through Israel, now it reaches back also to Abraham with whom the covenant was originally made. By adding Abraham to Israel Paul produces a cumulative effect. Paul is asking his Jewish hearers to show themselves as true sons of Israel and of Abraham. All that is said about υἱός in v. 10 applies also here. The translation of our versions "children" misses this important point; "children" would be τέκνα, the connotation being "dear children." "Sons" are far more, namely the heirs of Abraham and Abraham's stock, they in whom all that Abraham and his race stand for is to live on undiminished, they who ought to perpetuate the character, the faith, the lofty standing of Abraham and of his descendants. As such "sons" Paul addresses his Jewish hearers. The Gentiles present Paul addressed by the title he had formerly given them (v. 17); as men who have come to the right knowledge and the true fear and the worship of God and have forsaken all idolatry, they, too, are now to show themselves as such.

Paul has mentioned Jesus as "Savior" (v. 23); "the word of this salvation" links up with that Savior. This word sets forth what makes Jesus the Savior and how he is our Savior. Hence it was sent out, commissioned forth for all, Jews and Gentiles alike, to hear, know, believe, and thereby to receive salvation, σωτηρία, deliverance from sin and the safety that results (it is like Σωτήρ in v. 23). The ὑμῖν of a few texts should not be urged against the ἡμῖν of the many and most important. Paul could have used either; both would include all his hearers, and that irrespective of the preceding ἐν ὑμῖν. The difference is only this, by saying "to us" this word was sent Paul includes Barnabas and himself with all his hearers, while "to you" would refer only to his hearers. The great word of this salvation, Paul says, is now here for all of us to accept and thereby to be saved.

27) **For, those dwelling in Jerusalem and their rulers, having failed to understand this and the voices of the prophets that are being read on every Sabbath, they, by passing judgment, fulfilled them. And though having found not a single cause for death, they asked Pilate in due course that he be made away with. Moreover, when they had finished all the things that have been written concerning him, having taken him down from the wood, they placed him in a tomb.**

With γάρ Paul introduces his presentation of the death of Jesus on the cross. This is not a statement of a reason but an explanation of what is contained in "this word of salvation" which Paul says has been sent out to us. "For" means: "in order that I may explain." There is not the least indication that Paul is here contrasting the murderers of Jesus with his present hearers and no reason for such a contrast.

The death of the Savior Jesus was brought about by the people of Jerusalem and their rulers, the Sanhedrists. Peter, too, accuses the former just as Paul does here (2:23). The simple fact is that the Sanhedrin could never have forced Pilate to crucify Jesus if the populace of Jerusalem had not seconded their rulers. If the people had objected and demanded the release of Jesus, Pilate would have been encouraged to deny the ungodly demand for Jesus' death. Paul, too, brings out the truth that both people and rulers acted in ignorance (3:17; I Cor. 2:8; compare Luke 23:34). This was criminal ignorance, and Paul states the guilt of it in the causal participle "having failed to understand," which is not ingressive (R. 858) but effective.

Does τοῦτον refer to Jesus as our versions translate? This antecedent would be too remote. Since v. 26 Paul had advanced to a new part of his discourse, and the masculine λόγος immediately precedes. These people and their rulers failed to understand both "this," the word of salvation regarding Jesus as the Savior, and the voices of the prophets which already contained that word. What increased the guilt of the latter was the fact that these prophets were constantly being read in their synagogues; on every Sabbath they heard them and yet failed utterly to understand the word of salvation in them, the word about Jesus, his atoning death, and his resurrection. Καί cannot be "also" for the reason that the main verb can never be added to a participle by an "also" or some other coordinate conjunction; those who attempt it here change the participle into a second finite verb: "because they failed to understand . . . they also fulfilled," but Paul subordinated. So καί connects τοῦτον and τὰς φωνάς.

The grammatical references of κρίναντες ἐπλήρωσαν are misunderstood in our versions, apparently because τοῦτον is referred to "him" (Jesus). Since neither the participle nor the verb have an object expressed in the Greek, the participle is given the object "him" and the verb the object "them" (voices): "fulfilled *them* by condemning *him*." But the participle has no object in the Greek, and the two objects, "this" (word of salvation) and "the voices of the prophets," etc., belong equally to "having failed to understand" and to "fulfilled," as they failed to understand both, so they (inadvertently and ignorantly) fulfilled both. And κρίναντες states how they did the latter: "by passing judgment," i. e., by that act (aorist).

The verb κρίνειν is neutral and means neither to acquit nor to condemn but only to judge. Because of their failure to understand these men were fit to do neither, acquit or condemn or to judge in any sense.

Yet they went ahead and acted the judge, they passed judgment. Of course, when one does this he must either acquit or condemn. These men did the latter. In this way their blind ignorance led them to fulfill their own prophets, do the horrible acts their prophets had foretold regarding them. Incredible — yet true to the letter!

28) The indefinite participle which speaks of their act of passing judgment is now described. They found not a single "cause of death" yet demanded Jesus' death. This is legal language. This finding is judicial, the legal finding of a judge on the basis of legal evidence. Αἰτία is a legal indictment, and the genitive θανάτου qualifies it as being one the penalty for which is rightly death. In the negative "not a single one" there lies the implication that several indictments were tried, but that not one of them was supported by evidence that a court could allow.

This applies fully also to the charge on which Jesus was condemned by the Sanhedrin, that by calling himself the Son of God he had blasphemed. The Sanhedrin merely grasped at that as a last resort. The moment Jesus had uttered his yea to the question put to him, the verdict guilty was rendered. No opportunity was given Jesus to offer proof that his yea was true in fact and the opposite of blasphemy. He was pronounced guilty without in the least permitting him to produce evidence on which the court might render a finding. That is why the Sanhedrin dared not tell Pilate on what grounds it had condemned Jesus to death but threw up a lying smoke screen of findings it had never even attempted to find: "we found" (i. e., legally), Luke 23:2; but Pilate had to answer: "I find" (legally, as judge), John 19:4.

Although it had no finding, the Sanhedrin and the people "asked Pilate in due course that he be made away with." The wording is again legal; for this verb is middle and in this voice is used to designate all sorts of business transactions. It does not mean that "they asked as a personal favor for themselves" that Jesus be executed. Roman governors did not grant such favors. In due course the great Jewish court came to Pilate's superior court with the legal request that the Roman court accept the Jewish verdict. This was a piece of legal business. The Jews could execute no one; all their death verdicts were subject to the Roman governor's review. Now the outrageousness of the Sanhedrin's procedure is revealed: without a single finding legally laid down by their own court they come in due form and make the formal legal request of Pilate's court to have Jesus executed! The aorist ᾐτήσαντο implies that they actually succeeded. The verb ἀναιρέω is constantly used in Acts with reference to the judicial murder of Jesus; he was to be made away with, executed.

29) Paul is brief; his aim is to show how the guiltless Savior Jesus came to his death through the guilty and ignorant Sanhedrin and the people of Jerusalem. For this reason he does not alter the subject when he now speaks of what was done with the body of Jesus. He simply says that *they* buried him. But first the important clause: "when they had finished (the Greek needs only the aorist) all the things that have been written (and still stand so, perfect participle) concerning him" — yes, they finished all of them! They were plainly written for anyone to read and to know, and yet, without an inkling of what they were thus really doing, they did all these things. This was the vital point for Paul's hearers, that God himself had had all these things regarding Jesus, his sufferings and his death, recorded in the prophets. To see them there in the inspired books and then to see them in actuality in Jesus, this was bound to go home. In this light of prophecy the shame of the cross disappeared; in this

light of prophecy the guilt of the Jewish rulers and of the people in Jerusalem cried to heaven.

We must not miss the added touch in the participial clause: "having taken him down from the wood." We have explained this "wood" which our versions translate "tree" in 5:30, and have shown that in the estimation of Jews hanging on wood involved being accursed. Paul's hearers knew that Jesus had been crucified at Jerusalem; when he speaks of it, Paul brings out the Jewish point of view that the Sanhedrin and the people had not merely succeeded in having him made away with but by having this done so that in the eyes of all Judaism he was accursed. See the exposition of Gal. 3:13. After taking him down they placed him in a tomb. Dead, buried, accursed at that. His foes thought they surely had destroyed him, were absolutely done with him, would never be disturbed by him and all this was done just as it had been written, and they never realized that it had been written about them.

The passive "that he be made away with" (v. 28) shows that the rulers and the people did not do this with their own hands; and this applies to taking down the body and placing it into the tomb. By having Jesus killed these rulers necessitated the disposal of his body, and thus it can be said that they did these acts. The usual explanation is that Joseph of Arimathaea and Nicodemus are referred to since both were Sanhedrists. But this is only a formal explanation and hence is not satisfactory. Peter charged the Sanhedrists to their faces that *they* killed Jesus; in the same way *they* buried him. Both were done by forcing others to perform these acts.

This is the first subpart. It stands out in strong contrast with the preceding. In v. 17-25 the agent is *God* throughout: *he*, he did all all that is said; but in v. 26-29 the agents are the blind *people and the rulers*:

Acts 13:30, 31

they, they do all that is said. When Paul now proceeds, it is again *God* who is the great agent. The address pivots on the agents. Its convincing force rests on these marked pivots.

30) **But God raised him from the dead, who appeared for many days to those who came up with him from Galilee to Jerusalem, such as now are his witnesses to the people.**

The contrast is tremendous: the people and the rulers made away with Jesus as one who was accursed, God did the absolutely opposite. God reversed and nullified what they did, yea, by raising him from the dead whom they had killed as one who was accursed God set his seal upon him as being the Savior. It is the same stunning contrast and opposition as that used by Peter when he faced the people in Jerusalem and the Sanhedrin, the very murderers of Jesus (2:23, 24, 36; 4:10; 5:30, 31). Note how succinctly the fact is stated as a fact: "But God raised him from the dead!" On ἐκ νεκρῶν see 3:16. This deed was one of omnipotence. There it is recorded in Scripture for all who will to rage against; but it is unchangeable, impregnable as ever. Modernists may hurl themselves against it, they injure it not a whit, they injure only themselves.

31) A second fact and deed is added with ὅς which in the Greek so often = "he who." Paul does not continue with God and say: "God manifested him." Yet he does not detract from the first mention of God and what God did. He also maintains all that he said when stating that God "raised him from the dead." Jesus was made alive. He, he himself was the one who appeared as living and raised from the dead and not once only but "for many days," in the Greek idiom "for more days (than a few)," forty in all. To whom? "To those who came up with him from Galilee to Jerusalem," to those who had known him longest and best, who could not be deceived. Paul is not speaking of himself and of

his vision of the risen Lord. He uses ὤφθη, the aorist passive of ὁράω, "he was seen," or intransitive, "he appeared," which is employed four times in I Cor. 15:5-9.

But his resurrection was not intended for these friends of Jesus alone. It concerned all the λαός or Jewish people, namely in the special sense developed in v. 17-25. So many of them were scattered far and wide over the earth and could not all be direct witnesses of God's saving acts. This was the case in regard to all Israel's past history and God's deeds in that history. The true witnesses testified to all those facts. That is the case with regard to Jesus, his work and suffering and death and now in particular his resurrection. God chose the witnesses by whom he intended to attest this great deed of his and the living presence of the risen Savior. Οἵτινες expresses quality: "such as now are his witnesses to the people." Having seen the risen Jesus again and again, they, as many of them as there are, constitute his eyewitnesses who are qualified in every way to testify to all that they have seen.

Paul first presents the facts that God raised Jesus from the dead and that Jesus appeared to chosen witnesses. Up to this point all has been objective, but now with the marked ἡμεῖς ὑμᾶς there comes the subjective: the good tidings *we* bring to *you* of the fulfilled promises to which are added some of these promises concerning the Messiah's resurrection with brief elucidation. Down to its minor parts the discourse is arranged with exactness in a perfect progression, logically and psychologically.

32) **And we on our part to you on yours are proclaiming as good news the promise come to the fathers, that God has completely fulfilled this to us, their children, by having made Jesus to appear; as also it has been written in the second Psalm: My Son art thou; I today have begotten thee. Moreover, regarding that God made him appear from the dead not still about to return to corruption he**

has declared in this way, I will give to you the holy things of David, the trustworthy things! Because also in another he declares, Thou wilt not give thy Holy One to see corruption. For David, having served his own generation by the counsel of God, fell asleep and was added to his fathers and saw corruption; but he whom God raised up did not see corruption.

Both pronouns occurring in v. 32 are accented and are aided in their emphasis by their juxtaposition. "We on our part" = Paul and Barnabas, and "to you on yours" are Paul's Jewish hearers. To them these messengers are here and now proclaiming as good news "the promise that came to the fathers."

33) Not the promise as such, but the fact "that God has completely (ἐκ in the verb) fulfilled this to the children (of the fathers), namely to us (Paul, Barnabas, and the Jewish hearers), by having made Jesus to appear." The ὅτι clause is appositional to "the promise." Ταύτην is put forward for the sake of emphasis: "this," this very promise, for which the fathers waited so long, God has now finally fulfilled for their children, the perfect tense implying that the fulfilling now stands as such. The reading τοῖς τέκνοις ἡμῶν (R. V.) makes no sense. Paul had no children, and the promise was fulfilled not merely for the children of his Jewish hearers and not the hearers themselves. We must read either "for their children" (αὐτῶν) as in the A. V., or "for the children, namely us" (ἡμῖν). Since the promise was made to the fathers and not to the Gentiles, Paul says properly that it was fulfilled for the children of those fathers, the Jews, leaving out the Gentiles. The whole work of Jesus was done among Jews. The fact that the Gentiles were to participate in it changes nothing of what God did. Throughout the discourse one sees how Paul is laboring to win his Jewish hearers; throughout he depicts what God did for the fathers and finally for

their children. Paul has no fears for his Gentile hearers. So he now freely says, "To the children, to us."

We refer ἀναστήσας Ἰησοῦν to God's act of raising up Jesus as the Savior and not to the act of raising him up from the dead. With δέ, "moreover" (slightly adversative), Paul then adds ἀνέστησεν αὐτὸν ἐκ νεκρῶν, the act of raising Jesus from the dead. This δέ prevents us from referring both the participle and the finite verb to the resurrection. If both referred to the same act, the former and not the latter ought to have the modifier "from the dead." But the participle should not be restricted to the incarnation and the birth of Jesus: "by having made Jesus to appear (or to arise)" the entire career of Jesus from beginning to consummation is referred to, which thus includes also his resurrection. The verb "completely fulfilled" refers to the entire career; it cannot mean that by the resurrection of Jesus the final item of complete fulfillment was added. As far as that final item is concerned, that is specified in v. 34. When in v. 23 Paul says "Savior," in v. 26, "the word of this salvation," and in v. 32 εὐαγγελιζόμεθα, he is not speaking only of the resurrection of Jesus but of all that he was and did, including his glorious resurrection.

It is this act on the part of God, this making Jesus to appear or arise in general, of which Ps. 2:7 speaks. Peter quoted this psalm in 4:25, 26. In Heb. 1:5 our passage is quoted to show that God exalted Jesus above the angels. Peter attributes this psalm to David although it appears without a caption. The contents are plainly Davidic. The reply that in general speech "psalm" meant a song composed by David overlooks the fact that many psalms were attributed to Asaph, to Solomon, and to others. Some think that Paul cites David because in v. 22 he had brought Israel's history up to the time of David; but he also quotes Isaiah. When some texts read "the first" Psalm, we note that the two psalms were read as one lection in the synagogue, which regarded the first Psalm as the introduction to the entire book of Psalms.

The Hebrew and the LXX agree: "My Son art thou; I myself (emphatic ἐγώ) today have begotten thee." The reference is to II Sam. 7, especially to v. 13 and 16, to the Seed of David (Jesus) who should reign in the Davidic kingdom and on the Davidic throne forever. It is this everlasting King himself who quotes Jehovah as declaring to him, "My Son art thou," etc. God made that declaration to Jesus himself when at the time of his baptism he anointed him with the Spirit: "Thou art my beloved Son." Luke 3:22. It was then that Jesus assumed his office as Savior. That declaration was repeated at the time of the Transfiguration of Jesus, cf., Luke 9:35.

Although they are even verbally almost identical with the word occurring in the psalm, these two words of the Father to his Son Jesus are often overlooked. In the psalm David says that this declaration was made long ago. He speaks of II Sam. 7. Then Jehovah said, "Yet have I set my King upon my holy hill of Zion!" and that King declares that Jehovah said to him, "Thou art my Son," etc. Regard it all prophetically with reference to what the Father did with Jesus when he brought him to Israel as the Savior (23); or regard it as prophecy, as what was done already in David's vision as regards the everlasting King on his throne. In either case "I myself today have begotten thee" is figurative regarding Jehovah's placing this everlasting King on his throne. The inauguration of a King who rules forever on an everlasting throne in an eternal kingdom is for Jehovah the begetting of a Son, a King who rules eternally like Jehovah himself. That prophecy was fulfilled, Paul says, when God raised up Jesus as the Savior. The statement about Jesus, like that of the psalm, is general; hence Paul follows it with a further elaboration, and we must read the whole together in order to get its force.

The passage occurring in the psalm does not speak of the *generatio aeterna,* not of the inner Trinitarian relation of the two Persons, not of eternity but of time. Likewise, the psalm does not speak of the Incarnation, the conception, and the birth of Jesus. Many, however, think that it speaks of the resurrection of Jesus, and that the reality back of the figure of generating is the raising from the dead. They, therefore, also let ἀναστήσας mean "having raised from the dead." It sounds attractive to hear that Jesus was made Savior and King forever by his resurrection. But how about his suffering and his death, his whole office and his life? And look at Luke 3:22, and 9:35. No, this raising up, making to appear, the word of the psalm, refer to all that God did in setting him forth as the Savior and most certainly includes also his resurrection, but most certainly also includes all else as well and does not refer to the resurrection alone.

34) With δέ, "moreover," Paul now turns to the resurrection: "regarding that God made him appear from the dead," ὅτι is slightly causal. This resurrection, however, involves more than the fact that Jesus was brought back to life. So were Lazarus and others, and then they again died. Jesus was raised "not still about to return to corruption." Μηκέτι = "not still," not after all to fall a prey to corruption; it does not imply that by dying Jesus had seen corruption but was not again to see it. The translation "no more" in our versions is inadequate. Paul tells his hearers that God "has said" (formula of quotation like "has been written") something in Isaiah 55:3 in regard to the mighty act of raising Jesus from the dead never to see corruption; God promised, "I will give to you the holy things of David, the trustworthy things." Paul follows the

LXX because the point is τὰ πιστά, "the things trustworthy," *hanne'emanim*, that can never be broken or abrogated. They are "the holy things of David," Hebrew, "the David mercies," a standard term for the covenant promises as made to David by God in II Sam. 7 (see above), Ps. 89:36, 37.

"David mercies" introduce an epoch in the history of the covenantal prophecies and promises in that David was promised the Seed who should rule his throne and his kingdom forever. That was more specific than the promises given to Abraham. Now Paul says that God spoke thus about these absolutely reliable David mercies with a view to what he intended to do in regard to Jesus, namely realize these mercies in Jesus, raise him up as the Savior (v. 33), and raise him from the dead incorruptible and never to see corruption, and thus to be the eternal Messianic King. In short, τὰ πιστά are absolutely reliable, sure, trustworthy, because they are realized in him who is beyond being touched by corruption.

We may add that Isa. 55:1-3 is an invitation to the Gentiles; the covenant made with Israel is intended for them also; the trustworthy mercies of David are to be theirs. This makes the quotation the more significant for Paul's audience in which there were many Gentile hearers. Aug. Pieper, *Jesaias II*, 444, etc. The interpreters usually think only of Israel. Paul quotes freely, adding: "I will give to you."

35) And now comes the capstone to this arch of prophecy. In Psalm 2:7 David had the Messiah in mind, Jesus in his whole office; in Isa. 55:3 the prophet had Jesus in mind, his resurrection, his being beyond all corruption. Now God spoke as he did in Isa. 55 "because" (διότι) in another psalm, namely 16:10, he says in so many words through David, his mouthpiece: "Thou wilt not give thy Holy One to see corruption." Jesus dead, entombed, raised from the dead, then and

forever free from corruption or decay of body is, indeed, the Savior forever. Peter used this same passage from this psalm in 2:27, where the details are fully elucidated. Even the explanation added by Paul contains what Peter added at greater length.

36) For David himself certainly saw corruption and hence could not be this "Holy One," hence could not be the Messianic King. After he had served his generation (indirect object) according to God's counsel he fell asleep. The dative cannot be temporal, "in his own generation," for the simple reason that no man ever serves in any but his own generation. The point is not when David served but how far his service extended, namely to his own generation alone. The Messiah had to serve all generations; and this Jesus does because he was raised in incorruption to live and to rule forever. If David served his own generation (indirect object), "the counsel of God" cannot be an indirect object. Yet that leaves two constructions possible: "served by," or, "fell asleep in the counsel of God." But plainly the chief point is that David died (main verb) and not that he served (only participle). Why, then, attach all the modifiers to the participle, the minor action? The point is that God let David fall asleep for good and all, aorist. It was God's counsel to let him die and be gathered to his fathers and his body thus to see (experience) corruption. On "see" (eye, ear, singulars) note Delitzsch on 2:27; "fell asleep," ingressive aorist as in 7:60. David "was added to his fathers" in the grave. The expression must refer to the grave, since the next clause states that he saw corruption, his body turning to dust in the grave.

37) Jesus' case was far otherwise. In him all those promises were fulfilled. God raised him up, and he did not see corruption but lives to serve and to save forever. Here the relative ὅν is again emphatic: "he, the one whom," etc. Through the first part of the dis-

course and through the second there runs the word "God," what God did and said. All are divine facts which need only to be seen aright and in their true bearing.

38) In *the third part* of the discourse Paul presents the saving power and grace in Jesus to everyone who believes and warns against unbelief. **Be it known, therefore, to you, men and brethren, that through this One remission of sins is being announced to you; and in connection with this One everyone believing is justified from all things from which you could not be justified in connection with the law of Moses.**

With οὖν Paul comes to the conclusion that must be drawn from all that precedes. Two things follow: 1) the objective fact that remission is being announced; 2) the personal fact that every believer is justified. Both facts are most closely connected with "this One" whom Paul has fully and clearly presented as the Savior brought to Israel (23) by God. "Be it known to you" ushers in these weighty announcements in an authoritative tone. The address "men and brethren" (see 1:6) is this time without appositions which distinguish Jews and Gentiles (v. 17 and 26). The Savior is intended for all alike.

Διὰ τούτου, "through this One," makes Jesus the Mediator, and the demonstrative, in the idiomatic Greek fashion, sums up all that has been said about Jesus. Through Jesus as the one divine channel remission of sins is conveyed by the public announcement which presents him. Jesus, crucified and risen, brings us remission. On this ἄφεσις see 2:38, and note 10:43. It means that the sins are sent away from the sinner forever. To see the last of your sin and guilt, to see it all vanish like vapor in the hot sun of grace and pardon in "this One" as though you had never sinned, is certainly blessedness and joy to anyone who realizes what sin is. There is a passive sense in the word "remission"; God himself sends the sins away. This helps us to comprehend διά. It is only by way of Jesus that God can possibly come and remove our sins from us. All of them are contained in the plural "sins," everything in us whereby we have missed the mark set for us by God's holy law.

This remission "is being announced," κατά in the verb has the note of solemnity, *wird feierlich verkuendigt*. Paul's present passive means more than that he and Barnabas were now making the great announcement; the real agent is God; this is also true with regard to "is justified" in the next verse. We see that throughout the entire address God is the one agent. This is a supreme way of composing an address, it was certainly effective for both classes of Paul's hearers. The verb is pregnant, "announced to you," for you to believe, accept, receive, possess. The gospel is always "announced" or preached thus. The very announcement reaches into the heart in order to kindle faith. Who can hear this remission announced to him without wanting it? A special, wicked, ugly effort is necessary to keep faith from arising in the heart.

39) With a coordinate statement Paul repeats and sets the matter in a still clearer light before his hearers. Our inflexible English compels us to reverse the clauses. The emphasis is on the modifier: "from all things from which you could not be justified in connection with the law of Moses." The two phrases are in direct contrast: ἐν τῷ νόμῳ Μωϋσέως and ἐν τούτῳ, "in connection with the law" and "in connection with this One." The idea is not that some sins can be removed by the law, and that others remain which the law is unable to remove; no, all sins are referred to. As long as our connection is only with the law of Moses, its demands and requirements, we shall break them often and in this law find no means to remove our sin and our guilt.

Here we meet the verb δικαιοῦν for the first time in Acts. It is always a forensic term with a personal object, and in the New Testament is used only in the religious sense as referring to the verdict and judgment of God which is always favorable: "to justify," that act of God by which as the Judge he declares the sinner just and acquits him from his sin and his guilt. See C.-K. 324, who has a treatment that is so exhaustive that every student should examine it in its entirety. It does not mean "to free" except in the forensic sense just stated (B.-P. 308 is misleading); in the Scriptures it never means "to make just," "to deem worthy" (R., W. P.). Justification is no less than the central doctrine of the Word, *the articulus stantis aut cadentis ecclessiae*, the destruction of which destroys the church itself so that it remains Christian no longer. Paul tells his hearers that if they appear before God's judgment bar in connection with the law of Moses as their hope, God cannot acquit them. It is utterly impossible, for the law brings only condemnation to the sinner.

This is Paul's first summary statement regarding works of the law and their utter hopelessness to secure the favorable verdict of God. He has made his letters ring with this doctrine. Jesus most strenuously opposed the Pharisees who trusted in the law. The world is full of followers of these Pharisees who in one or in another way still operate with works as the certain way to heaven.

The sinner's hope is only "in connection with this One." The phrase does not belong to the participle: "everyone believing in this One," but to the verb: "is justified in connection with this One." The connection with him is made by this believing. The participle is used without a modifier: "every believer." And this is another cardinal concept of Scripture: πιστεύειν (πίστις, ὁ πιστός), compare 2:44. "To believe" is to put all trust for remission, justification, and salvation in Christ alone as the Savior (v. 23). By believing, by our confidence in him and in the saving power of his death and his resurrection we are put in vital, spiritual connection with him. Paul tells his hearers that everyone who appears before God's judgment bar in connection with this Savior, he and he alone "is justified," the present tense is durative: "is and remains justified" as long as he is "one believing." In this way Jesus is the Savior. Do you want to be acquitted of all sin and guilt by God, now, in the instant of death, at the last great day? Then let this Savior fill your heart with complete reliance on him.

"Everyone believing" is like the blank line in a signed check or draft, on which you are to write your name over the signature Σωτὴρ Ἰησοῦς (v. 23). This is the universality of grace, remission, and justification. Paul was speaking to Jews and to Gentiles, and "everyone believing" applies to all of them. In the previous sentence ὑμῖν is plural, here πᾶς ὁ is singular. Paul is a master in using these two. Being justified is personal, individual. Every sinner is judged separately. The verdict is always rendered in the singular: "Thy sins are remitted for thee! Go in peace!"

In these two short verses we have Romans and Galatians in a nutshell. Justification by faith alone — *Sola Fide* — is an endless, inexhaustible theme. "The way to salvation, so slowly and with such difficulty prepared for us — slowly through the time of preparation in the old covenant — with difficulty, through the bitter suffering and death of Jesus: and yet so short and so pleasant for us to travel — short, for all that we need is to embrace the cross of Christ by faith — pleasant, for here we find remission of sins, life, and salvation." Gerok.

40) Paul closes his address by prodding the consciences of his hearers and warning them against Israel's greatest sin, unbelief. **See to it, there-**

fore, lest that arrive which has been spoken in the Prophets:

Look, you despisers, and wonder and vanish away!
Because I am working a work in your days,
A work which you in no wise shall believe if one detail it for you.

Note that μὴ ἐπέλθῃ is not followed by a dative; hence it does not mean, "lest there come upon you," but only, "lest there arrive." "The Prophets" are that portion of the Old Testament which is regularly designated by this name which does not, however, include Daniel. Paul quotes from Hab. 1:5, according to the LXX with slight change. The prophet's words are not a prediction concerning Paul's present hearers. Paul uses them only as a warning. He has in mind a possible analogy or resemblance. Unbelief in regard to Jesus would make his hearers like those whom Habakkuk threatened. By unbelief they would put themselves into the same class with those despisers of old and would, of course, invite the same judgment.

41) The LXX translate as though their Hebrew text read *bogdim*, "despisers," instead of *bagoyim*, "among the heathen." The imperatives are aorists and thus peremptory. The God of might and majesty is speaking. He calls to the blind Jews, "Look!" and as a result "wonder!" and as a result "vanish away!" The judgment descending upon them is the terror behind these imperatives. It shall rise, like a tornado, fill them with astonishment, and then strike them and wipe them out completely.

What this calamity is, the prophet describes by bringing out powerfully that it is wholly God's work. "Because a work I work in your days" means a most terrible work, and I, I myself (emphatic ἐγώ), work it. To the prophet's hearers the present tense sounded as though God were already busy with that work. So incredible will that work be that, if one were to tell about it in advance, no one would in any wise (strong οὐ μή with the futuristic subjunctive) believe it, i. e., give it credence. The conditional clause is strong: "if one shall detail, recount it piece by piece (διά), and spread it out (ἐκ) for you." The prophet did so detail it by depicting how the Chaldeans would sweep down upon Israel and utterly destroy it. It was literally true, but not a single Israelite believed the prophet until the horrible destruction came upon the nation. Paul practically asks whether such unbelief is now to repeat itself in the case of his hearers. We know what calamity it was soon to bring on Jerusalem and on Palestine.

42) **And as they were going out they were beseeching them for the next Sabbath to speak to them these utterances. Moreover, the synagogue having broken up, many of the Jews and of the worshipping proselytes followed Paul and Barnabas, who, speaking to them, kept urging them to continue in the grace of God.**

This was the effect of Paul's sermon. It was entirely favorable as the two statements in regard to what the hearers did show. Paul and Barnabas were asked to speak again on the next Sabbath, and many Jews and proselytes followed them to hear more immediately. So we discount the idea that Paul ended his sermon with a warning because he saw some of the Jews scowling. The two imperfects παρεκάλουν and ἔπειθον intimate that more will follow. We need not debate long as to how this going out of the synagogue and its breaking up should be understood. When the service was ended, and as they were going out among the large audience, Paul and Barnabas were asked to return the next Sabbath (construe εἰς with the main verb), of course, by those who had the authority, the synagogue elders; then after the audience had left the building, and Paul and Barnabas finally started for their lodgings, many of the audience followed them.

43) This shows the powerful impression Paul had made. There was no difference between the Jews and the Greek proselytes in this respect, for both classes are found in the group that follows the missionaries. Like φοβούμενος, also σεβόμενος is regularly used as a designation for a proselyte of the gate. Luke reports only the gist of what Paul and Barnabas said to these men who could scarcely separate themselves from them; it was the admonition to remain in the grace of God. The implication is that they were in this grace, that they believed Paul's message about the Savior Jesus. The one thing necessary, then, was to continue in this grace. One feels that Paul and Barnabas are thinking that opposition to this grace will arise and will try these young believers. In this they were right.

44) **Now on the coming Sabbath almost the whole city was gathered together to hear the Word of God.**

We now learn what the imperfect tenses used in v. 42, 43 intimated, namely what eventually happened. The talk about Paul and Barnabas and the sermon the former had preached spread through the city, the proselytes telling all their Greek friends with the result that a vast interest was aroused, and almost the whole city turned out to hear the Word of God. What interested all these Gentiles was the fact that without becoming Jews and adopting the Jewish separative laws they could be received into the full communion of faith. Paul and Barnabas were certainly succeeding in Pisidian Antioch.

45) **But the Jews, on seeing the crowds, were filled with passion and began to speak against the things uttered by Paul, blaspheming. Also speaking boldly, Paul and Barnabas said: To you was it necessary that the Word of God be spoken**

first. Since you are thrusting it away and are judging your own selves not worthy of eternal life, lo, we are turning to the Gentiles! For so has the Lord enjoined upon us:

> I have set thee as a light of Gentiles
> For thee to be for salvation to the uttermost part
>   of the earth.

Luke says nothing about rabbis and that they stirred up the Jews during the week and were envious on this second Sabbath because so many came out to hear Paul while nobody in particular came out to hear them. The Jews were wrought up, not during the week, but on this Sabbath, not by agitators, but at sight of these crowds of Gentiles. Nor were the Jews afraid of losing the Jewish character of their synagogue services. Their ζῆλος, "zeal," "passion," was inflamed by the Gentiles as Gentiles: all these pagans were coming to share with them. This was not clerical jealousy between rabbis and Christian ministers which points a warning for professional men but the dislike of established church members who were unwilling to let a large number of outsiders suddenly come to share their religious prerogatives and blessings.

From Luke's account we are unable to tell whether the uproar began in the synagogue after the service was in progress and Paul and Barnabas spoke as they had been requested on the Sabbath before or already outside of the synagogue. It does not seem possible that all these people could have found room within the building. The imperfect is inchoative; the Jews began speaking against the things that were uttered by the missionaries. The outcome is held in abeyance for the moment by the imperfect tense. Not reason but heat and passion dictated this contradiction. Luke, therefore, does not intimate what objections were raised. He says only that the objections were vicious and went to the length of blasphemy, reviling this Jesus whom Paul and Barnabas preached as being the Savior promised to Israel by God.

46) The aorist now states the outcome. Argument against this blasphemous passion was useless. The rupture had come. Paul and Barnabas accept it. It is for this reason that Luke gives such prominence to the story of Pisidian Antioch. Here for the first time in Paul's missionary experience the open breach with the synagogue occurred. Paul was to have this experience again and again. It was to become typical of his work. So Luke describes at length how it began. In Cyprus nothing comparable to this had occurred. Here in Antioch Paul's sermon at first won the Jews; v. 42, 43 are plain in regard to that point. We have the whole sermon and can judge that it could not but win the Jews since God, their God, had done all that Paul recounted. What caused the break was the proclamation of the universality of God's grace in Jesus, the opening of the door full and wide to all the Gentiles. This stirred the Jewish exclusiveness and particularism to violent opposition when so many Gentiles now came. So the break came and it was decisive in every way.

How Paul and Barnabas accept it is fully recorded, and it should be noted that both are agreed in the matter. "To you," they say, "to you as the people whom God originally chose for the high mission of bringing salvation to all the world, it was necessary because of this your mission that the Word of God in regard to the fulfillment of his promises in Jesus, the Savior, should be spoken *first*, before that Word was brought to the Gentiles." Paul and Barnabas have done that.

The boldness ($παρρησιασάμενοι$) of the statement they make is evident from what follows. Since the Jews here in Antioch are thrusting that Word away and by that act are pronouncing on themselves the judgment that they are unworthy of eternal life, because of their unbelief not fit to have the eternal life the Savior bestows, "lo," let it surprise you, indeed, "we are turning to the Gentiles," who, as you see, are so eager for this Word, so ready to hear about the Savior, Jesus, and to accept the eternal life which you will not receive through him. That attests the break, states clearly who is making it, places the guilt where it belongs, and defines exactly what that guilt is.

Paul states what thrusting away the Word really means. By doing so the Jews themselves act as judges in their own case. They do not want the Word, their judgment, therefore, is that they are not worthy of the eternal life which that Word brings. They, indeed, blasphemed that Word as Paul spoke it, they scorned it as though it were nothing; Paul and Barnabas lift it high by pointing to the life it brings. And they tell these scorners what they are really doing. In his grace God regarded them worthy to receive that life through the Savior; they regard themselves unworthy. Whereas God intended to place them in the van, at the head of all the Gentiles, they put themselves entirely out of the procession. They have only themselves to blame.

"We are turning to the Gentiles!" Here at last Paul's mission as originally defined by Jesus comes to full realization: "to bear my name before the Gentiles," 9:15. The gospel will be preached to the Gentiles alone wherever the Jews thrust it away. The gospel will leave the synagogue completely and will gather its own assembly and church. The doom is settling down on the synagogue and the Jews; for nearly 2,000 years that doom has now remained. It will remain to the end.

47) When Paul uttered his strong warning in v. 40, 41 he let one of the prophets of the Jews' own Bible speak for him. Now that Barnabas and he are taking the decisive step of turning to the Gentiles, he does the same. Isaiah is their spokesman cf., 49:6.

This is done in order to close the mouths of the Jews. If they rage against Paul and Barnabas because of their turning to the Gentiles they must first square accounts with the great 'Ebed Yahweh, Jehovah's Servant, who himself stated what Jehovah declared to him, namely that it is a light thing to raise up the Jews and the Israel of the diaspora, but that the greater and mightier part of the work of this Servant is to be that done upon the Gentiles. Paul and Barnabas say: "So the Lord (Jesus) has enjoined upon us" (perfect: his order stands). The sense is that, when Jehovah told the Messiah, his Servant Jesus, that he was to be a light for Gentiles, and when this Servant so declared, this was an order for all the messengers through whom this Servant works to preach also to the Gentiles in order that light and salvation might be brought even to the farthest end of the earth.

God himself has appointed his Messiah "for a light of Gentiles" (predicative εἰς, R. 482). The genitive is objective, this light is to illumine them. They are in darkness without the Old Testament Word. It was the Messiah's great task to be their light. The infinitive with τοῦ denotes purpose: "in order that thou be for salvation to the uttermost part of the earth." All Gentiles, however far removed from the center Jerusalem they may be, are to have this light. The εἰς is again predicative: Jesus is to be the salvation of the Gentiles ("Savior" in v. 23). God has appointed him to be this, has done it in the distant past, and that act stands. And now the messengers of Jesus are proceeding in accordance with that will of Jehovah.

48) That was a stunning reply which the Jews could answer, not by reason, but only by violence. **Now hearing it, the Gentiles began to rejoice and to glorify the Word of God; and they believed, as many as had been ranged in order for life eternal.**

The two imperfects reach a climax in the aorist "they believed." What angered the Jews delighted the Gentiles, namely to hear that the gospel was intended also for them, for them directly without the necessity of first becoming Jews and submitting to all the Jewish regulations. Happy to hear it, they glorified "the Word of God," meaning the Word in the sense in which Luke has continually been using it, the gospel of Jesus, the Savior. It is always so: whereas some spurn that Word, others receive it joyfully. So these Gentiles "believed," the aorist stating the fact.

Yet not all of those who had come to the synagogue on that Sabbath but only those "who were such as had been ranged in order for life eternal" believed. Τάσσω is a military term that means to draw up in rank and file and is then used generally for placing in an orderly arrangement and then to appoint and even to agree. The English "ordain" (our versions), *verordnen* (Luther) serve well enough, even better than "appoint" (R., *W. P.*) as long as the sense of the original is not rejected. For in τάσσω there lies a τάξις, a certain order, here the *ordo salutis*. Verb and noun go together. The periphrastic past perfect may be either passive or middle: "had been ranged in this *ordo*" by God; or "had ranged themselves in this *ordo*." Since no man is able to put himself into the *ordo salutis* by his own powers, it makes little difference which we choose. It is like *bekehrt werden* and *sich bekehren*. The point is to exclude all synergism. The context helps us. Here we have a contrast: the Jews thrust away the Word; these Gentiles glorify the Word. By their own fault the Jews are out of the τάξις; by God's grace these Gentiles are in it. Again the contrast: the Jews regard themselves unworthy of eternal life; these Gentiles are in line for eternal life. Who put them in line? God did so by sending Paul and Barnabas and his Word and his grace and by making both come in contact with their hearts. He did the same for the Jews and would have preferred to have them in the same blessed *ordo* but for the criminal wickedness with which they removed themselves from this *ordo* by blaspheming instead of glorifying the Word.

Although this passage deals with the doctrine of conversion, it has often been regarded as a pronouncement regarding predestination. This view began with Jerome who revised the old Latin rendering *destinati* or *ordinati* to *praeordinati* in order to make the coming to faith and salvation the product of a predestinatory eternal decree. Calvin is the great exponent of the *decretum absolutum;* those included in this decree are irresistibly brought to faith and held in it, and all others, even if they do believe for a time, are doomed by this same decree. Others conceive the decree as merely including the former and omitting the latter. Calov pointed out that Luke did not write προτεταγμένοι, and that neither τάσσειν nor τάσσεσθαι nor the context refer to eternity.

"Life eternal," so often found in the discourses of Jesus in John's Gospel (see John 3:15, 16), is the spiritual ζωή implanted in regeneration, fed by the Word and the Sacrament, passing unharmed through temporal death, then entering the heavenly state of glory. It dwells in the soul by faith but extends also to the body. Jesus will raise up those who have this life at the last day, John 6:54. "Life eternal" does not refer only to the heavenly life to come.

49) **Moreover, the Word of the Lord was being carried through the whole region.** The imperfect describes this spread in its progress; new believers were being won in the entire region. How long this continued until Paul and Barnabas were driven out can only be estimated; a period of approximately six months is probable. Ramsay regards χώρα here and elsewhere in Acts as a technical term for *Regio*, the

administrative district with Antioch as its center. He calls it "the Phrygian Region of (the province) Galatia." Since Galatia was so large, these "regions" were established; in each regional center the governor had his officials and visited these centers from time to time; thus also those living in the *Regio* would have much occasion to visit the center and thereby come into contact with the gospel. Ramsay's view seems sound until one gets to 16:6 and 18:23, where it cannot apply. We thus understand χώρα in the sense of territory, an indefinite region.

50) **The Jews, however, incited the worshipping women, those prominent, and the chief men of the city and stirred up a persecution against Paul and Barnabas and expelled them from their borders. But they, having shaken off the dust of the feet against them, went to Iconium. Yet the disciples continued to be filled with joy and the Holy Spirit.**

These women were proselytes, and Strabo and Juvenal report that throughout the empire many pagan women were proselytes of the synagogue. On the distinctive participle σεβόμενος see v. 43. The prominent women who were married to influential men were incited and also the chief men of the city, those who had government offices in the city and others who had considerable influence. The Jews had to work through others because they were not sufficiently numerous and powerful to take matters into their own hands.

Luke is reticent in regard to Paul's sufferings; so all that he records is the fact that the machinations of the Jews succeeded in stirring up a persecution against Paul and Barnabas the result of which was that the two were expelled beyond the borders, not merely of the city, but also of its environs. This means that magistrates of the city took action and not officials of the province. Only this city and its neighborhood were forbidden them and not the entire *regio* or all of Galatia. In II Tim. 3:11 Paul speaks of these days: "Persecutions, sufferings, what things befell me at Antioch," etc. In II Cor. 11:25 he states that he was thrice beaten with rods, and that means by the lictors in cities that were Roman colonies such as Antioch. One of those beatings may well have been suffered in Antioch. The entire city at first flocked to hear the gospel, now the current flowed in the opposite direction.

51) The expression "shaking off the dust of the feet" goes back to Jesus, Matt. 10:14; Mark 6:11; Luke 10:11. One commentator regards this as being only a phrase — the two left willingly. Another, "a dramatic gesture that forbids further intercourse." Still another finds in it "a gesture of protest." We also find the view that it is "a symbol that the very soil of the place was defiling." But they shook off only dust. In v. 50 Luke purposely retained "the Jews" as the subject although the expulsion took place through the magistrates who were the tools of the Jews. So now the dust was shaken off against these Jews and not against the whole city, which would have included the Christians. The act is symbolic; how serious it is Matt. 10:15 states; and it means that the dust is left behind as a testimony or witness (Mark 6:11) that the kingdom had been brought near by the feet of these messengers whose dust was thus left behind (Luke 10:11). That dust will testify on the day of judgment that wicked obduracy drove the messengers away.

So with sore backs Paul and Barnabas went on to Iconium. The fact that this was a Phrygian city is plain. Just where it belonged at this time is debated by the authorities. The question is intricate because at various times the city belonged to Pisidia, to Phrygia, and to Lycaonia, these signifying ethnographic districts and not Roman provinces. Ramsay makes it a part of the *Regio* of Antioch; but it naturally belonged with Antioch, both being Phrygian. So also Lystra and Derbe belonged together, both being nationally Lycaonian. Zahn makes Iconium a Roman colony. Later on this city became more renowned than Antioch.

52) The expulsion in no way injured the disciples who were left destitute of these leaders. They had the best Paraclete, the Holy Spirit, who filled their hearts and also gave them joy. The imperfect describes this condition as one that continued indefinitely. Luke does not refer to a charismatic presence of the Spirit but to the gracious spiritual presence that was mediated objectively by the Word and subjectively by faith in "the Savior Jesus" (v. 23).

CHAPTER XIV

THE FIRST MISSIONARY JOURNEY: ICONIUM, LYSTRA, DERBE, AND THE RETURN

1) Luke intends to give us only a brief account of the work in Iconium. Into the present short chapter all the rest of the work that was done on this missionary journey plus the return to Syrian Antioch is compressed. His plan seems to be to picture characteristic experiences encountered in this first effort to extend the gospel from the synagogue into the Gentile world in general. In Iconium great success is paralleled by strong opposition. Yet the work is accomplished, and before the opposition comes to its climax, Paul and Barnabas prudently leave.

Besides the remarks made in connection with 13:51 let us note that some of the former pictures of Iconium must be revised. A colony of Jews was prominent in the city; it had only one synagogue which was not as large as the one at Antioch but had men in it who were influential enough at last to enlist the aid of the magistrates in taking violent measures against the gospel messengers. The rest of the population was divided between Greeks and the older Phrygian stock of natives. There were, however, no Roman officials in it at this time. The greater prominence of the city when it became a Roman colony and outshone Pisidian Antioch was achieved at a later date. Several Roman roads entered the city, and the great highway that extended east and west passed through it. Paul and Barnabas had come about forty-five miles from Antioch and considered Iconium a city that was sufficiently important for the planting of a Christian congregation. It was Paul's constant policy to enter the greater centers from which the gospel might spread into neighboring territory. But on this first journey Antioch is the largest place which he visits. He grew as he worked until he eventually fixed his heart even on Rome.

Now it came to pass in Iconium that together they went into the synagogue of the Jews and spoke so that a great multitude of both Jews and Greeks believed.

It should be well noted at the outset that all the verbs of this paragraph that refer to Iconium are aorists. We have a recitation of facts from the time of the arrival to the time of the summary departure. Another feature is that Paul and Barnabas are indistinguishably combined; from κατὰ τὸ αὐτό onward they speak and act "together." Paul did not always do the speaking, Barnabas undoubtedly did his share of it. Paul would see to it that he did.

R., W. P., thinks that these aorists covered only one Sabbath's speaking and calls it "a tremendous first meeting." But Luke does not say "on the day of the Sabbath" as he did in 13:14, and does not say "God-fearing Greeks" but "Greeks" in general. The claim that these were only proselytes is met by the fact that in the preceding chapter Luke always used the distinctive terms when he referred to proselytes and does not use one of them here. Some of the Ἕλληνες, to be sure, were proselytes of the gate, but by no means all of them. This view is not affected by the use of τὰ ἔθνη in v. 2; it is rather upheld, for these "Gentiles" were the unbelievers, not only unbelieving Greeks but Phrygians as well, who were placed in opposition to the ἀδελφοί, "brethren" or believers.

Nor, on the assumption that all was accomplished by one Sabbath day's preaching, should we stress οὕτως to mean that the missionaries preached "so" exceptionally as to produce a phenomenal result: "*so* plainly, *so* convincingly, with *such* an evidence and demonstration of the Spirit, and with *such* power; *so* warmly, *so* affectionately, and with *such* a manifest concern for the souls of men; *so* from the heart, *so* earnestly and seriously, *so* boldly and courageously." This is overdoing a good thing as though at other times and in other places Paul and Barnabas did not speak *so* and *so* and *so* and hence had no *such* phenomenal results. We cannot thus separate and emphasize οὕτως which has no emphatic position but is to be combined with ὥστε: "so that."

All these "Greeks" were not in the synagogue on that day, and certainly not those who were not proselytes. These aorists are constative. Luke is giving us a summary. He first describes the success without saying how long it took to achieve it. Yet we may regard the aorist πιστεῦσαι as ingressive, "came to faith." As the missionaries spoke Sabbath after Sabbath, more and more Greeks were attracted until a crowd of both Jews and Greeks came to faith. This infinitive shows what was spoken, namely the gospel of Jesus the Savior (13:23). How Paul, for instance, preached it Luke has reported in 13:17, etc. Luke does not need to report that again; and he certainly cannot mean that at Iconium the preaching was better than it had been at Antioch. Look at that sermon delivered at Antioch and ask yourself how it could be improved. While the chief purpose of the account in regard to Antioch is to relate how Paul and Barnabas for the first time turned to the Greeks in general (13:46), the secondary purpose is evidently to exhibit the manner of Paul's preaching on his missionary tour. In order to understand what occurred in Iconium we should not forget Antioch. We must especially note that here "Greeks" is to be considered in the light of 13:46, namely Greeks in general, also such as were not proselytes.

2) **But the Jews who came to be disobedient stirred up and embittered the souls of the Gentiles against the brethren.**

This is the second effect of the preaching, a party of Jews "fixed in disobedience"; the aorist ἀπειθήσαντες conveys the idea that they had come to this fixed state. The participle itself means to be unpersuaded, thus to refuse belief, and thus to refuse to obey. The two latter meanings merge. Faith is at times called obedience; and unbelief disobedience. This is due to the fact that the Word demands faith, consequently responding with faith is to obey, refusing faith is to disobey. The point to be noted in this characterization is the fact that these Jews had heard the gospel in their synagogue and yet rejected it; the participle could not be applied to men who had not yet heard the Word or had not heard it sufficiently. Another noteworthy point is the observation that, as was the case in Antioch, Jews were again the opponents of the gospel and offered violence to its ministers. They have this unenviable distinction; the Gentiles are only drawn into it through the agency of these Jews. We note that in 26:19 Paul says with reference to himself and his own conversion: "I was not disobedient"; note also Heb. 12:25: "See that ye refuse not him that speaketh." This is the sad feature especially in regard to missionary preaching, that some become fixed in disobedience and, though salvation is knocking at their doors, deliberately turn to perdition.

Fixed unbelief is ever morally vicious. It does not always go to the extreme, but when the circumstances are favorable, it ignores every moral consideration in vilification of the gospel and in taking base measures against its adherents. So these Jews did not content themselves with rejecting the gospel, the devil plagued them to such an extent that "they stirred up and embittered the souls of the Gentiles against the brethren." These Jews started an agitation against the converts by stirring up the Gentile population with slanderous reports about the brethren. Here κακόω has the non-classical, later, and rarer sense of "to embitter," to make evil-minded against someone. A uniformly used weapon against the gospel and its true believers is this process of poisoning the minds of those who as yet do not know the gospel.

A discrepancy has been found between what Luke here states that the hostile Jews succeeded in doing (the aorists imply success) and what the next verse states, namely that Paul and Barnabas spent much time in Iconium working openly. In order to remove this supposed difficulty some would eliminate v. 3 or dispose of it as a marginal remark. Reference is also made to the reading of the Codex Bezae which speaks of "a persecution" and of how "the Lord quickly gave peace." Let us say in general about this codex and the many additions it offers to the accredited text that it is a late effort to improve on Luke and is taken too seriously by certain interpreters. Luke knows of no "persecution" that was followed by a sudden providential "peace" which then enabled Paul and Barnabas to continue their work. The romance regarding Thecla is introduced with a trial for Paul and Barnabas in which the magistrates discovered the falsity of the charges and acquitted the prisoners, and thus the Lord provided peace; Thecla is regarded as a convert who was gained in Iconium.

These views are answered when we note that the Jews succeeded in embittering only the souls of the Gentiles. Beyond that they were not successful. Again, this viciousness was directed "against the brethren" and not against Paul and Barnabas in particular. This phrase excludes an arrest and a trial of Paul and of Barnabas. The attack took in all the believers; we may say it "bit off more than it could chew." In regard to tangible results, this general attack furnished none that

Luke could record. The effort put forth dissipated itself largely because it tried to take in too much territory. The feeling that was temporarily aroused subsided.

Luke writes that the Jews worked on "the Gentiles," he does not say on "the magistrates," he does not even say on "the Greeks," those who had Greek culture and education. These Jews wasted their efforts in trying to stir up too many people. They tried to set too many against too many and so accomplished nothing. And that is exactly what Luke implies in v. 3. The work of Paul and Barnabas was not stopped. Where, then, is the discrepancy? There is none in Luke's account.

What Luke tells us is that in Iconium, too, a hostile party of Jews soon formed and vented its hostility by turning the Gentiles generally against the Christians. Under this handicap Paul and Barnabas labored, but it did not hinder them to any notable degree. They worked right on. Read what Luke says. He does not refer to "a first explosion" in v. 2, to be followed by the "second" in v. 5. Luke knows of only one.

3) **A sufficient time, therefore, they spent boldly speaking in the Lord, he bearing witness to the Word of his grace by granting signs and wonders to occur through their hands.**

The close connection of this verse with the two preceding verses is shown by οὖν, which means that, with the situation as indicated, many Jews and Greeks turned into believers. Because other Jews stirred up the Gentiles, Paul and Barnabas spent a considerable amount of time in Iconium, meaning enough time fully to establish a permanent Christian congregation. "Boldly speaking" does not mean "copious and commanding eloquence." Paul always spoke with boldness, the participle implying free and open speaking that holds nothing back. He later asked the Christians to pray that he might speak thus, Eph. 6:19, 20. Luke notes that Paul and Barnabas spoke thus here in Iconium because the Jews had embittered the Gentiles. That did not make the preachers timid and hesitant lest they say too much; they spoke with utmost freedom, held nothing back, cared not who heard them. Warmth and eloquence there may have been also, but Luke says nothing about that. The gospel will cause offense — let it. So many try to preach it with an eye to their personal interest by toning down unpopular doctrines, flattering themselves that they are up-to-date, progressive, even wise. Not so these two great heralds.

We have no smooth translation for ἐπὶ τῷ Κυρίῳ, really, "on the basis of the Lord," and thus render "in the Lord." The Lord was the reason of their courageous freedom of utterance. But not merely in general as inspiring them with confidence that by relying on his commission and promise they had nothing to fear; here in Iconium the Lord "was bearing witness to the Word of his grace" in a signal manner. He was testifying that the Word preached by his messengers was, indeed, his Word, and at the same time, by the manner in which he bore this testimony, he made plain who he really was — not a Jesus dead and buried, his body gone, no one knowing what became of it (this is the gospel of many today) — but a Jesus risen and glorified, the Savior in heaven, exercising the divine power and majesty as the great Head of the church.

There is no καί preceding διδόντι so that it describes the manner of μαρτυροῦντι: "he testifying by granting." A precious name is here used as a designation for the gospel. In Paul's sermon in Antioch he called it "the Word of this salvation" (13:26); and Luke, "the Word of God" and "of the Lord" (13:44-49). It is also "the Word of grace," which the Lord's grace uses as its tool and instrument for reaching the sinful and guilty souls of men in order to bestow itself upon them, free them from sin, guilt, and all condemnation, and unite them to the Lord as his own. The Word is thus the means of grace, the divine channel through which grace flows to the sinner. I Cor. 2:1-5. Χάρις is here, as throughout, the Lord's favor and love which is shown to those who, because of their sin and guilt, do not deserve it. The word always connotes guilt and signifies the love which would remove that guilt.

This Word of grace the Lord attested as what it was, the bearer of divine grace to the sinner, by means of miracles of gracious healing and deliverance from fearful ailments. These "signs and wonders" (see 2:19 on the terms) the Lord appended as seals and credentials to the Word; it was like signing his own name to it. All those credentials stand to this day and are for this very reason not repeated; for genuine seals need no further seals to prove them genuine. If seals must have still other seals, this would prove only that none of them are sufficient, which is the claim of those who deny the reality of miracles.

Luke reports no signs that might have occurred in Antioch, and in the case of Paphos only that of striking the magus blind. Let us note this when Luke writes that here in Iconium Paul and Barnabas wrought miracles, the Lord "granting," "giving" them. No apostle or other Christian ever wrought a sign at will but only when the Lord so willed and by his Spirit prompted and directed the act (see 9:40). Compare Heb. 2:4: "signs and wonders . . . *according to his own will.*" Here the signs and wonders were a tremendous testimony regarding the Word for Paul and Barnabas and for all who saw them and all who heard them. The hostile Jews might agitate all they pleased, the Lord made his Word only the stronger. "Through their hands" does not necessarily imply the laying on of hands although this symbolic gesture may have been used (on its significance see 6:6). Διά is important, for it makes Paul and Barnabas the Lord's media and nothing more. The Lord used their hands when and where he desired.

4) **Now the multitude of the city was split, and some were with the Jews, some with the apostles.**

Note how δέ corresponds to μέν in v. 3 and balances the two statements: the long stay — the whole city split. But v. 4 says more, it goes back to v. 2. Those wicked Jews were the rallying point of the one party (οἱ μέν), and the apostles the center of the other (οἱ δέ). The entire Gentile population was divided into two opposing camps; σύν is used exactly as when we say, "I am *with* you" on any question. A point not to be overlooked is the fact that Paul and Barnabas filled the entire city with the sound of the gospel, filled it so that practically no person remained neutral. In this they had the aid of the hostile Jews. The more these agitated, the more the gospel became known. People simply had to go and hear what these men were teaching and doing.

Paul never went off into a corner, gathered a handful, and then thought his task done. Even in Athens he had the philosophers of the city around him. So he thoroughly evangelized Iconium. Warneck says: "It is not rhetorical hyperbole when Paul says of himself that he filled *the world* with his gospel, Rom. 10:18; 15:19; Acts 17:6." "But thanks be unto God, which always leadeth us in triumph in Christ, and maketh manifest through us *the savor of his knowledge in every place,*" II Cor. 2:14. In those days all sorts of exotic religious wares were offered (see the samples in 8:9, etc.; 13:6, etc.), but Paul never failed to lift the gospel above everything human and filled entire cities and districts with his message.

Here Luke uses the word "apostles" with reference to both Paul and Barnabas; the term is used in the wider sense. So James, the Lord's brother, is an apostle

(Gal. 1:19); Epaphroditus (Phil. 2:25); Sylvanus and Timothy (I Tim. 2:6); Andronicus and Junia (Rom. 16:7); and there are false apostles (II Cor. 11:13). The gospel always causes a division, one that is at times sharp and painful. Jesus himself said it would do so, Matt. 10:34, etc., and elsewhere. Sometimes Christians do not like this, and the children of unbelief constantly reproach us for bringing about this disharmony or whatever they are pleased to call it. But this is the very nature of the gospel. The only way to avoid it is to preach and to believe some sham gospel, and even that may cause division. When light comes, darkness resents it; when righteousness appears, the unrighteous assail it; when life comes, the powers of death bestir themselves to destroy it.

Even without becoming polemical the gospel interferes with what the heathen regard as their dearest treasures. Many heathen religions are syncretistic, but in the case of Jesus there is either the acceptance of faith or the rejection of unbelief. Warneck is right: "Over against the Son of God indifference is impossible; no one can erect an altar for him at the side of the idols he may have in his pantheon." Many religious errors are unionistic; they tolerate and fraternize each other. But the gospel and its truths cannot compromise nor fraternize with a single error.

5) Luke has described the situation which at last came to a climax. Paul and Barnabas did not avoid or fear the issue and did, of course, not provoke it although in all probability they expected it in some form or other (13:50). **And when there occurred an onset of both the Gentiles and Jews with their rulers to outrage and to stone them, having become aware of it, they fled for refuge to the cities of Lycaonia, Lystra, and Derbe, and the region round about; and there they continued proclaiming the good news.**

Real persecution at last raised its head. Here there was fulfilled what the Lord had told Paul in advance: "I will show him how many things he must suffer for my name's sake" (9:16). There was an actual "onset" or "assault," (Luther, *Sturm*) and not a mere plot. A mob was formed and got under way in order to locate Paul and Barnabas in order to heap insults upon them and to stone them. It was composed of both Gentiles and Jews plus the rulers of the latter. We cannot understand how B.-D. 393, 6 can translate ἐγένετο ὁρμὴ ... ὑβρίσαι *sie beschlossen, beabsichtigten;* this was not a meeting that passed a resolution of intentions.

The other view is that the mob actually seized Paul and Barnabas and began to revile and to pelt them with stones, and that συνιδόντες, on considering the matter, Paul and Barnabas took to flight — to be sure, a wise consideration. The participle, however, does not mean "considering" or "having considered," but, as in 5:2 and 12:12, to know something together with somebody else. Somebody rushed in and warned the intended victims; the mob never found them.

We should note that this time the animosity was not directed against the brethren, but that it concentrated upon the two principals alone. Those Jews had no success when they endeavored to embitter the city (v. 3); this time they sought an objective they could quickly reach. These considerations indicate that it is difficult to determine who the "rulers" were, whether these were the Jewish elders or these together with the city magistrates. Some think of the latter. But what about the stoning? We are told that this was to be only a pelting with stones in order to drive the victims out of town. Nor does 13:50 decide the question. There the city magistrates did have a hand but did not join a mob and yet got rid of Paul and Barnabas. It is asking rather much of us to believe that the city magistrates joined the Jewish elders in a mob. This was a large and important city, and the dignity of the magistrates was accordingly. If they had taken a hand, we should have had a repetition of the events which occurred at Antioch and not a mob. Luke uses the inverse order because the Gentiles (again he does not use "Greeks," v. 3) formed the larger crowd, the Jews were a smaller number, their elders were the real leaders, and stoning was to be the method of summary execution in regular Jewish style.

6) Κατέφυγον means "to flee for refuge." Paul and Barnabas are not cowardly but prudent. When it was necessary, Paul risked his life, otherwise he did not. His work had been completed in Iconium, the whole city knew about the gospel. The missionaries did not flee because they were defeated; they merely left one victory behind in order to start winning another. They acted in accord with Matt. 10:23.

Lystra and Derbe belonged to the ethnographic section of Lycaonia. The old native languages were still spoken in these ethnographic sections, and so the old names survived. Lycaonia was, however, Roman territory only in part, namely in that part containing Lystra and Derbe. One might call it "Roman Lycaonia." But the old name was *Galatica Lycaonia* because it was incorporated into that Roman province. The other part was not Roman because it was being ruled by King Antiochus and hence was called *Lycaonia Antiochiana*. Paul confined himself to Roman territory.

"The region round about" is added to show that the gospel penetrated into the entire section as this had been the case in 13:49. The imperial road from Antioch to Iconium passed on to Lystra and Derbe. Zahn makes Lystra a Roman colony, and also Derbe which was located near the passes that crossed the Taurus range. It was a high honor for a provincial city to be made a *colonia*, for this demonstrated the interest of the emperor who regarded the city as worthy of the residence of Roman citizens, the aristocracy of the empire. About 300 Roman citizens were placed into such a city, which did not itself have citizenship. The city thus became a military outpost of Rome, an advance guard of the mother city, a small edition of Rome itself. In times of peace the military feature was not prominent. The most important feature of the transfer of the work to Lystra and Derbe is that neither place had a synagogue of Jews. Paul and Barnabas were now in completely Gentile and pagan cities — a most important step in their work.

7) Now at last we have an imperfect tense (periphrastic) which indicates that the two continued preaching the gospel. In v. 20 Paul and Barnabas reach Derbe. The view that they had taken along disciples from Antioch and Iconium on account of the Lycaonian language is untenable, because such disciples could themselves not have spoken Lycaonian — the natives of Iconium spoke Phrygian. Greek was spoken everywhere. In the Orient it is today a simple matter for men to speak several languages, they seem to grow up that way.

8) **And in Lystra there was sitting a man, impotent as to his feet, lame from his mother's womb, who never yet did walk. This one was listening to Paul speaking; who, on earnestly looking at him and seeing that he had faith to be made whole, said with a great voice, Arise on thy feet upright! And he leaped up and began to walk.**

In v. 6 we have the feminine singular Λύστρα, here the neuter plural Λύστρα: both are names of the city. Luke intends to narrate an experience in an entirely pagan city: first Paul and Barnabas are treated as gods, next as devils. This is only a glimpse into the work done in Lystra, one that is significant in every way. The miracle is almost a duplicate of that wrought by Peter and John. In the former instance there are two companions, Peter and John; here two, Paul and Barnabas — both times there is congenital lameness of the worst type — both times unsolicited healing — both times great results. But withal there are also great differences: the one man is a Jew, the other a pagan — the one is minus faith, the other has faith — in the one case many believers are the result, in the other a great manifestation of pagan idolatrous ideas. The fact that Luke was aware of the parallel should not be disputed, but the claim that Luke invented this miracle in order to make Paul the equal of Peter is unwarranted.

This man was not a beggar as was the one healed by Peter and John. Luke carefully notes the begging of the latter yet says not a word to that effect about this man. So he says nothing about a synagogue because none existed in Lystra. The man is described as sitting (imperfect), for he could not even stand. The description continues in v. 9, the tenses holding us in suspense until the aorist relates what Paul did. Luke's detailed description of the man's condition has been noted. We may say that Luke's interest as a physician is evident in this. First, we learn that the trouble lay in his inability to use his feet, the dative "as to his feet" being a dative of specification which is often used in place of the accusative; R. 523 regards it as the locative with adjectives. Secondly, this condition was congenital, "from his mother's womb," he was probably injured at birth. Finally, the man had never walked, the aorist merely stating the past fact as such whereas we should use the past perfect. Here was a case that was absolutely beyond human help.

9) The cripple was listening to Paul's speaking. In this respect he differed from the beggar in the Temple. It is entirely probable that Paul was recounting some of the miracles of healing wrought by Jesus. The cripple was thinking of himself and of how Jesus might have healed him, too, if he only had been there. But

the idea to be expressed is by no means that by casually looking at him Paul saw that he had this faith τοῦ σωθῆναι, "to be made whole" ("saved" from his condition, the infinitive after a noun with the idea of complement, R. 1076). This ἀτενίσας is the same as that occurring in 3:4, the result of an intimation of the Holy Spirit that a miracle was to be wrought upon the man.

The thesis is sound that no man wrought a miracle without this specific direction on the part of the Spirit. Miracles were never wrought promiscuously at the will of the apostles. Paul saw that the cripple had this faith by observing the eyes and the bearing of the cripple. Or did the man voice this faith? It is often assumed that Peter, too, looked and saw faith in the beggar; but the opposite is true, he saw the beggar expecting and thinking of nothing but a good-sized gift of money, wherefore Peter also told him he had no money to give. Faith sometimes preceded the healing (here), sometimes followed (Peter's beggar).

10) As he had done in Iconium and had not done in Antioch, the Lord intended to attest the gospel by signs and wonders in this city (v. 3). So "with a great voice" that expressed the great divine authority and the great divine power now to be manifested Paul commanded this cripple to arise on his feet. And he leaped up at once (the aorist of ἅλλομαι expressing the one act) and did not only stand upright but "began to walk" (the imperfect to indicate the action that continued indefinitely).

11) Luke's interest does not lie in this cripple's personal story, for not another word is said about him. The miracle is described for the sake of the strange result it produced. **And the multitudes, on seeing what Paul did, lifted up their voice, saying in Lycaonian, The gods, having become like to men, did come down to us! And they began to call Barnabas**

Zeus and Paul Hermes, since he was the one leading the speaking. And the priest of the Zeus that was before the city, after bringing bulls and garlands to the portals, together with the multitudes was intending to sacrifice.

Peter had encountered the superstitions of Simon Magus in Samaria, Paul a lesser magus in Paphos; it is now that Paul and Barnabas encounter the idolatrous Greek mythology that was prevalent in the Roman world. From the narrative one gathers that the cripple was one of a large audience to whom the gospel was preached and that the healing occurred at the conclusion of the preaching. It is not stated where the gathering occurred save that it seems to have taken place outdoors in some square of the city. We note incidentally that the missionaries seem to have had no trouble whatever in reaching multitudes of the general population, entirely pagan though they were. Only incidentally we learn that converts were made and that a congregation was organized and that elders were appointed (v. 22, 23).

The crowds that witnessed the miracle were native Lycaonians; there were perhaps some Greeks among them. They at once called to mind their old mythology and in their excitement in a natural way reverted to their native Lycaonian language and declared that once more the gods had taken on the likeness of men and had come down to them from Olympus. Did not Ovid in his *Metamorphoses* VIII, 626, tell the story that Zeus and Hermes had appeared in the form of men in the neighboring region of Phrygia? And now the story of Baucis and Philemon was being re-enacted in a new way in Lycaonia! Our versions use the Latin names Jupiter and Mercury instead of the Greek Zeus (genitive Διός) and Hermes. But this does not justify the assumption that Luke substituted Greek gods for what were actually Phrygian divinities and the claim that the main god's name was Papas or Pappas and that there was a secondary god Mēn.

12) But Luke himself answers this claim. He states that Paul was called Hermes because he led in the speaking. It was the Greek god Hermes and he alone who was thus indicated. In the Greek mythology Hermes was the messenger of the gods, the spokesman of Zeus, who was eloquent in speech and the legendary inventor of speech. What Phrygian god fits this description? Hermes was beautiful and graceful. The statues show him in the position of a swift runner bearing messages. Paul scarcely fits that description, wherefore also Luke indicates that it was not his form and figure but his ability in speech that suggested the identification.

Nothing is said as to why Barnabas was thought to be Zeus. But we may say that he was older and may venture the suggestion that he was of a more imposing stature. Perhaps because the people feel certain that Paul was Hermes, Barnabas was made Zeus without further question. It is not likely that afterward, in Gal. 4:14, Paul had this episode in mind when he wrote that the Galatians had received him "as an angel of God." A Greek god and a divine angel are rather different; besides Paul adds "even as Christ Jesus." His letter was written to all the churches in Galatia and not to Lystra alone. Analogous to Paul's comparison with an angel are II Sam. 19:27; Zech. 12:8; Mal. 2:7, and not the idea of his being a Greek god.

13) Acting on the extravagant surmise that the two gods are disguised as men, preparations are made to offer sacrifices in the temple of Zeus. "The Zeus that was before the city" was the temple dedicated to this god which contained his statue and was probably situated on some eminence just outside of the city. Most ancient cities were walled so that their boundaries were very definite. The Codex Bezae has the plural

"the priests," but the preferred reading has but one priest. Luke speaks of "the priest" as the chief priest by whose order alone things could go forward; and it is self-evident that this lone man could not have brought several bulls with their garlands and himself slaughtered and cut them up for the sacrifice.

These ταῦροι were "bulls" and not "oxen," and they were decorated with "garlands" of flowers while being led to the sacrifice. This was good Greek custom and indicates that this was the temple of Zeus and not that of some Phrygian god. It is not the plural "gates" that indicates that these belonged to the temple or rather to its surrounding court instead of to the city; but the nature of the case. Yet it is held that the city gates are referred to for the reason that Paul and Barnabas, the supposed gods, were in the city. But where was the altar at the city gates, where all the other things that were necessary for a regular Greek sacrifice and celebration? Why would a sacrifice before a city gate honor Paul and Barnabas more than one at the temple's altar?

This answers also the other question as to how sacrifice at the temple of Zeus could honor Paul as Hermes. A sacrifice to the chief god was intended also for any other god, especially if no temple of that minor god was at hand. And was not Hermes the messenger of Zeus? The pressure for this sacrifice came from the ὄχλοι, the crowds; hence they were present when the sacrifice was now about to be made. The presence of Paul and Barnabas was not required, for did not gods know when sacrifices were being offered to them? The proximity of Paul and Barnabas was enough. Codex Bezae again has the variant ἐπιθύειν which means, "to sacrifice in addition," to bring an extra sacrifice.

14) Paul and Barnabas were blissfully ignorant of what was under way. By calling this temple and its statue "the Zeus before the city," just as many temples

so situated bore names accordingly (as today "St. Paul's outside of the walls," the great Roman Catholic church outside of Rome) Luke implies that Paul and Barnabas were in the city.

But having heard it, the apostles Barnabas and Paul, having rent their garments, sprang forth into the multitude, yelling and saying, Men, why do you do these things? We, too, on our part are human beings of like sensations with you, proclaiming as good news for you on your part to turn from these useless ones to God alive, who made the heaven and the earth and the sea and all the things in them. He who in the generations gone by let all the Gentiles go their own ways and yet he did not leave himself witnessless, working good by giving to you rains from heaven and fruit-bearing seasons, filling your hearts with nourishment and happiness.

How the apostles learned what was in progress is left unsaid. Luke would have used a different participle than the one employed in the text if they had been summoned or invited. Barnabas is named first because of the order followed in v. 12. The act of tearing the garment consisted in grasping the tunic at the neck with both hands and giving a downward pull and tearing a rent of four or five inches in the tunic. It was always the tunic (χιτών) which was worn next to the body that was thus torn and not the long, loose outer robe (ἱμάτιον). In the expression "to rend τὰ ἱμάτια," the noun is used in the wider sense of "garment." The robe was made of heavy material that was too solid to be torn and hung loosely upon the body.

This act symbolized grief and pain at seeing or hearing anything that was actually blasphemous or sacrilegious. The whole idea and the act of these Lystrians were sacrilege. To go about with a torn tunic thus was evidence of what the wearer had experienced.

Already the news caused the apostles (see v. 4) to rend their garments. "They sprang out into the multitude" (ἐκ in the verb and εἰς corresponding) means simply that the apostles rushed out from the place where they were into the crowd at the temple in the most violent agitation and at the top of their voices (κράζοντες, "shouting") stopped the proceedings then and there.

15) Luke records what amounts to a brief address which was probably spoken by Paul. Shouts of, "Stop! stop!" may well have preceded this little address. When the apostle says "men" he is abrupt and not discourteous; we use "men" in the same way. The τί means "why" and is not predicative, could not be with a transitive verb (R. 736). This question bids these people consider why they are doing these things in order that, realizing why, they will at once cease and regret their undertaking.

We must note the strong correspondence between the emphatic pronouns ἡμεῖς and ὑμᾶς: "we on our part." "you on your part." Why treat the apostles as gods when they are only men, yea, men engaged in telling the good news that these their hearers are to turn from these very gods to the one who really is God and has long proved even to them that he is? Καί is scarcely adversative "and yet" but simply "also": "Men, we also are (only) human beings," ἄνθρωποι, *Menschen*.

This fact is intensified by the addition "of like sensations with you," ὁμοιοπαθεῖς ὑμῖν. This word does not mean "of like passions" or "of like nature." The gods were considered ἀπαθεῖς, unlike human beings. In these adjectives the verb πάσχω refers to suffering the vicissitudes connected with human existence. Paul and Barnabas suffer all such vicissitudes just as these men do and are not exempt, lifted to a plane above them as gods were suposed to be. This statement directly denies the notion of these pagan people that the apostles were gods in the likeness of men (v. 11).

But that is not all; the apostles are here in Lystra "engaged in proclaiming as good news that *you*, you Lystrians, given to idols, turn from these useless ones to God alive," etc. It is the greatest good news in the world to learn that all idols are μάταιοι (masculine, supply θεοί), that there is a "God living" who is attested as such even to the pagan world, and that we should turn from the useless to the genuine. We construe ὑμᾶς with the infinitive and not with the participle, for the infinitive calls for a subject, the participle needs no object.

In order to appreciate the full force of what is said we must note that μάταιος is used specifically with reference to heathen gods and idols. The adjective refers to that which does not accomplish its purpose and thus disappoints, while κενός is that which is empty. These heathen gods fail utterly in what their worshippers expect of them as gods. The adjective goes no farther. Of course, they are "useless" as gods because they are in reality οὐδέν, "nothing" (I Cor. 8:4). Recall the famous passage Isa. 44:10-17, which describes how a man cuts down a tree and with part of it cooks his dinner and makes a fire to warm himself and out of some of this wood manufactures a god for himself and worships it. Isa. 37:19; Hab. 2:18, 19. No wonder such gods are absolutely useless! It is pure fiction that actual supernatural beings exist which correspond to such images. All this applies to the fictions which men today call "God," using the capital letter, although no material image is made; such fictional images are also μάταιοι.

Over against them is set Θεὸς ζῶν, "God alive," "God living." No article is necessary because only the one exists. The contrast between "useless ones" and God "living" brings a great advance in the second designation. Instead of saying "useless" and then "useful," the apostle at once states the full reason that makes

God useful: God is alive, living, is and does all that the term "God" implies even far beyond the expectation of his worshippers. The evidence for his living existence is before the eyes of even the pagan world: it is he "who made the heaven and the earth and the sea and all the things in them" including men themselves, the four terms spreading out his mighty creations so the mind may grasp them the better. Ps. 19:1; Rom. 1:20

16) In addition to this evidence in creation the living God attested himself by means of the constant benefactions of his providence. He did this even in the case of the Gentiles whom "in the generations that have passed" (perfect participle) he permitted to go their ways. There is a contrast with the present and God's work of now sending the gospel to the Gentiles. "Their ways" gives ὁδοί an ethical sense just as "the Way" is used with reference to Christianity in 9:2 (see the explanation). The plural signifies that the Gentiles followed many different ways, their very multiplicity revealing that they were wrong ways.

No effort is made to show why God permitted the Gentiles to wander thus, for the point to be made here is that he had nevertheless not cast off the Gentiles When we now ask why this was done in regard to the Gentiles we must, first of all remember that Gentiles and their pagan ways should never have come into existence. God destroyed the godless race of Noah's time. Was that not judgment enough? Noah began a new race, began it with the true God, bequeathed that knowledge to his descendants, even the knowledge of the judgment of God through the Flood. How could paganism then begin? The answer is plain. If God accepted the fearful defection that developed into idolatrous cults and let the Gentiles go on in these cults he at the same time prepared universal salvation in and through Israel until he could now send the gospel to all men. Compare 17:30. The real story is that because of their own fearful guilt men lost the true God and the true religion, and that God prepared to restore it to them and in due time did so.

The contention that τὰ ἔθνη refers to "the nations" in the sense that the Jews and the Samaritans are included because "in their ways" does not mean "in their own ways," ἑαυτῶν instead of merely αὐτῶν or ταῖς ἰδίαις ὁδοῖς is not in keeping with the context. In spite of their defections and their idolatries the Jews are never included with the Gentiles as forming one class of men. God gave more than the evidence of creation and providence to the Jews; he used the Jews alone as a means for eventually spreading the gospel to the Gentiles even to the ends of the earth. God shaped the way of the Jews in a manner in which he did not shape "the ways" of the Gentiles.

17) Although v. 16 begins with ὅς, it is really an independent sentence, and v. 17 is its second part. The printing should be according: "He it was who, indeed, permitted . . . and yet did not leave himself unattested," etc. He had not turned forever from the Gentiles although his displeasure rested upon them because they had abandoned him and the true religion, and although in just judgment he let them go on in their ways. During the entire time of their abandonment of him he kept on attesting himself to them in the most effective manner. The second participle depends on the first, and the third on the second: "working good (in the sense of what benefits) by giving and by thus filling," etc. All good things of this earthly life are wrought by God.

Some think that "rains" are mentioned because Lystra often suffered drought; but "rains" are mentioned especially because they came "from heaven" and thus from God. Through them he gives fruit-bearing seasons with all their rich abundance. The miracle of the seasons and of their abundance of fruit, which is repeated year after year, is one of the great attestations of God to himself that is fit for all men to see: "The eyes of all wait upon thee," etc., Ps. 145:15. Thus God "fills your hearts with nourishment and happiness." The expression is concentrated. It is the body that is filled with the nourishment so that the heart is made glad; instead of mentioning both body and heart, the latter is selected because the food is the means for the heart's delight. Here "heart" means the seat of thought, feeling, and will, the center of the being.

Paul is preaching natural theology as he does in 17:24-29; Rom. 1:19-23. We may add the great passages found in the psalms. It was the direct way to the heart of Gentiles. In Antioch, in the case of Jews and proselytes of the gate he referred to God in Israel's history (13:17) as the direct way to their hearts. True natural theology leads to a correct knowledge of God; we need it even in the case of Christians. It contains no gospel yet is a step toward revealed theology with its gospel fulness. In the face of God's revelation and self-attestation in nature it should be impossible to believe in gods and idols (17:27, 28).

18) **And by saying these things hardly did they restrain the multitudes from sacrificing to them.** The sincerity which went to the length of inaugurating this sacrifice was because of its very nature strong and hard to turn from its course, which makes what follows the more striking. After a verb of hindering $μή$ with the infinitive is called pleonastic.

19) **Now there came to them Jews from Antioch and Iconium, and, having persuaded the multitudes and having stoned Paul, they were dragging him out of the city, supposing him to be dead. But the disciples having surrounded him, after arising, he went out with Barnabas to Derbe.**

Luke adds a dramatic touch by placing these two clashing incidents side by side, first making pagan deities of Paul and Barnabas and then stoning Paul and dragging him out as dead. There is no need for the textual additions that the apostles spent some time in Lystra before this attack on Paul occurred. The hatred of the Jews both in Antioch and Iconium was so intense and persistent as to pursue him to Lystra. The impression is not left on the reader that these were Jewish merchants who had come to Lystra on business and accidentally found the apostle at work in this city. This was a combination of Jews from the two cities in which Paul had worked and from which he had been driven out. He had left many converts behind, and that circumstance kept the Jewish hatred alive. In some way Jews from both cities got together and planned to follow the apostles to Lystra. Yet we do not read about any Jews in Lystra with whom they joined hands.

Luke relates only the facts that occurred and does this in the briefest way. So we are unable to say why Paul alone became the victim of stoning and not Barnabas also. These Jews persuaded the multitudes. There is no need to ask by what means when the basest lies were used even against Jesus. As far as the city crowds were concerned, it was not difficult to persuade them, for were not the apostles attacking their gods as being "useless"? How easy, too, to brand the entire story of Jesus as nothing but an invention in spite of the miracle wrought on the lame man, the effect of which had begun to wane. The upshot was a mob that somehow got hold at least of Paul and stoned him. They certainly would have included Barnabas if they could have caught him. To say that they passed him by is a grave injustice to this noble companion of Paul's. In Iconium the plan included the stoning of both Paul and Barnabas.

Since Jews were back of the original plan and now its execution, this stoning was the Jewish idea of doing away with Paul. Pagans would probably have beaten him to death. This is corroborated by the procedure of dragging the victim outside of the city after they thought he was dead (perfect "has died" used for "is dead"). That pagan mob could not be persuaded to perform the execution in proper Jewish style, to wait until Paul was first dragged out and then stone him; they stoned him on the spot and then dragged him out. These pagans would have permitted Paul to lie in the street; but the Jews had to have him thrown outside of the city. The imperfect ἔσυρον conveys the thought that this was not the end of the matter.

20) The aorist that follows brings the outcome. Paul lay somewhere along the road beyond the city gate. The mob had finished its work and had dispersed. Thus the disciples finally reached him and stood around his battered body with torn hearts. Incidentally we learn that there were "disciples" in Lystra. Luke seems to regard it as a matter of course that the apostles had succeeded also in Lystra. To be sure, they had! Nor have we any reason to think that the number of converts made was small. They had been won directly from paganism.

Was Timothy in this circle of disciples who were grouped around Paul? Luke introduces him in 16:1, but at that time he was already a disciple. In I Cor. 4:17 as well as in II Tim. 1:2, Paul calls him "my beloved child" (τέκνον), which makes it rather certain that Paul had converted him, and that would of necessity have occurred on this first visit of Paul's to Lystra. When R., W. P., writes: "Timothy, a lad of about fifteen, would not soon forget that solemn scene," Timothy's age is estimated too low, for in 16:1-3, only a year later, Paul takes him along as one of his assistants; he must have been past twenty.

The disciples had come to give Paul a decent burial as devout Jews had once buried Stephen after his stoning. But, as Luke states with astonishing brevity, "after arising, he went into the city." Was this a miracle? Luke does not even hint that it was a miracle. This would have been the place to invent one in order to glorify Paul as the only apostle who had returned from death to life, but the Scriptures contain no invented miracles. It is not difficult to see what had happened: a stone had rendered Paul unconscious, and he remained so until this time. That was, indeed, providential preservation. But we must not understand Luke's brevity to mean that Paul simply got up and walked off. He regained consciousness, showed signs of life, was finally assisted to his feet, and so went painfully into the city. Was it under cover of night as Zahn thinks on the basis of some readings? Those readings are valueless. In II Cor. 11:25 Paul recalls this experience: "once was I stoned." But the next morning he and Barnabas left for Derbe. Paul did not spare his poor body although it was bruised and sore. He suffered violence, but again as one who moves on to new conquests. He had come to Lystra and left a Christian church behind.

21) **And having evangelized that city and made many disciples, they returned to Lystra and to Iconium and to Antioch, making firm the souls of the disciples by exhorting them to remain in the faith and that through many tribulations we must go into the kingdom of God.**

Two participles dispose of the work done in Derbe (see v. 7), both are constative aorists; they evangelized the city, which means just what it says, filled the city with the gospel news; and again they labored with success, they "discipled" a goodly number; this word is explained by the noun $\mu\alpha\theta\eta\tau\alpha\iota$ which occurs in 6:1. Nothing that was of exceptional import occurred. Derbe was on the Roman frontier so that no new cities were visited in this territory. The two apostles retraced their steps in spite of the hostile Jews and the painful experiences they had had in those three cities.

22) It was wise, indeed, to return to the young congregations they had founded so that they might confirm them in the faith and help them to organize and to elect elders. The present participle does not express future action (R. 892); since it follows a constative aorist, the present participle serves as a complement by spreading out the action (B.-D. 339, 2). Returning does not refer merely to arrival in these cities but to a return that was at the same time an official visit that included the activity of making "the souls of the disciples" firm. The word ψυχαί is here not a contrast to or a distinction from πνεύματα but denotes man's entire immaterial part as the seat of the spiritual life.

The second participle modifies the first and shows how this firmness was achieved. The apostles exhorted the disciples to remain in the faith (present durative infinitive), and "the faith" is objective, *fides quae creditur*, the infinitive denoting subjective faith, *fides qua creditur*. The thought is the same as that expressed in 2:42, "remaining steadfast in the teaching of the apostles." That was the essential point. Beginners who have not been made firm as yet are in danger of falling away. A good beginning is a great achievement, but a good continuation is its normal and essential result. Conversion must pass on to preservation.

When Luke follows the infinitive with a ὅτι clause instead of a second infinitive, this is not an example of zeugma (one verb with two objects, only one of which fits the verb). The participle παρακαλοῦντες fits both (*contra* B.-D. 479, 2), and both are indirect discourse without supplying λέγοντες before ὅτι (*contra* B.-D. 397, 6). The danger these disciples faced was the persecutions they might have to suffer, compelling examples of which they had in the case of the apostles who had suffered in all these cities except Derbe. The one thought that had to be impressed upon them was that persecution belonged to the normal state of Christians. The world always hates them; moreover, tribulations are to help to develop their strength of faith.

Δεῖ expresses any type of necessity, here the one that is due to the nature of discipleship in a wicked world: "it is necessary that we enter the kingdom of God through tribulations," θλῖψις, the pressure that squeezes painfully. On the kingdom in general see 1:3; here, as also the aorist infinitive shows, the kingdom of glory is referred to, God's and Christ's eternal glorious, heavenly rule. The thorns prick us as we climb upward to that kingdom, but the roses await us there. Here the cross, yonder the crown. Rationalism urges us to forget the hereafter, makes this life the whole of religion, accuses us of otherworldliness and of disregarding what we ought to do in this life. But take away the glorious Christian hope, and what have we to live for? Let the full hope of the blessedness to come shine out, and all our earthly days are lighted with heavenly light and filled with highest purpose, courage, and strength.

23) **Moreover, after by vote appointing for them elders from church to church, by praying after fastings, they commended them to the Lord in whom they had believed.**

As in II Cor. 8:19, χειροτονέω means to vote by stretching out the hand. In 10:41 the compound with πρό has God as the agent; but even when it is thus used with reference to an individual and not to an assembly, the idea of a vote is not removed from this verb. We may translate "designate," "elect," "appoint"; but the one designating or appointing voted to do so. Luke would make an important point by using this verb here. For the question at issue is whether Paul and Barnabas chose these elders without congregational participation or whether they conducted a congregational meeting in which a vote was taken by show of hands, the congregation choosing with participation of the apostles and under their guidance. The latter is undoubtedly correct, just as the praying with fastings by no means includes only the two apostles but each congregation as well. The method used is fully explained in 6:2-6. The point to observe is that both participles refer to the subject of παρέθεντο, to Paul and Barnabas, and are thus used in a wide sense. The apostles presented the matter, had the eligible men named, had the vote taken, and thus appointed those chosen and ordained them as the elders. The ceremony of laying on of hands was certainly used, for in I Tim. 5:22 the very act of putting a man into the ministry is called "laying on hands"; compare I Tim. 4·14; II Tim 1:6. On this ceremony see 6:6.

We have discussed "elders" in 11:30. The apostles followed the pattern of the Jewish synagogues with their elders and had them elected in the same way. There is nothing hierarchical whatever throughout the New Testament. Only one advance must be noted in the case of these Christian elders, namely the ability to teach. See the qualifications as these were laid down a few years later by Paul in II Tim. 3:1-7, and in Tit. 1:5-9. The choice was thus narrowed to a very few men. It is fair to conclude that these were Jews even in these Galatian congregations, including Derbe and Lystra where no synagogues existed. Jews alone were sufficiently versed in the Old Testament, the sole Scriptural basis of the Christian teaching. No deacons in addition to elders are mentioned at this ear y time, and we conclude that this office was introduced later.

While these historical points regarding the first organization of the apostolic church are of utmost interest, they constitute no law for the Christian Church which binds us to repeat every feature and method. But the example of the apostles stands for all time as having been given under the direct influence of the Holy Spirit. Some of the various types of organization found in the church today reflect the spirit of the gospel and of its apostles less than others, and we decline to adopt the former, namely those that are hierarchical and monarchial and that curtail the rights of the congregations.

The κατά is distributive: "church by church." Each was an ἐκκλησία by itself that was independent of a Jewish synagogue, a distinctive Christian body. All the members were μαθηταί, "disciples," believers, and in that sense "saints" (see 9:11); on "church" see 5:11. The work of securing "elders" was of the highest importance and was hence accompanied "by praying with fastings" as was done in 13:3. But we see that fasting was secondary to praying, "with fastings" meaning as an aid to praying. On the general practice of fasting see 13:2; it was used as a spiritual aid on special occasions. Cooking and eating and all that these entail were set aside for the day in order to be entirely free for the higher things. The prayers were spoken before the vote and at the time of the ordination of the elders. The plural "fastings" scarcely implies repeated fasts but fasts on the part of the disciples.

After the congregation had been properly organized and spiritually fortified, the apostles said good-by. They had done all that they could do and thus "committed them to the Lord on whom they had believed." The verb means "to place at someone's side." This Jesus did with his spirit when he was dying (Luke 23:46). All these converts belonged to the Lord; he would take care of them in the days to come. Luke seems to be quoting from words that were uttered at the parting services. So we still part and commit each other to the Lord.

The relative clause is relative only grammatically and in reality states the reason for committing these disciples to the Lord: they had put their trust in him the moment they had become disciples. That they should now be placed into the Lord's care in a special way was what their own hearts desired. Having been deposited at the Lord's side by the prayer of the apostles, they did not feel themselves in a strange or in a false position, and when the Lord saw them thus placed at his side he did not regard them as people whom he had never known. Since they had believed and trusted in him, he would reward their confidence in him and in the commitment of the apostles.

24) And having gone through Pisidia, they came to Pamphilia. And having spoken the Word in Perga, they went down to Attalia; and thence they sailed away to Antioch whence they had been given over to the grace of God for the work which they fulfilled.

The return is made by the same route by which they had come. The time consumed on this first missionary journey is estimated at about eighteen months; no exact figures can be given. On the geography of Pisidia, etc., see 13:13, 14.

25) The reasons that induced Paul to hasten away from Perga on first landing there have been stated (13:13, 14) Luke's brevity is here like that employed in the case of Derbe (v. 21) and must not deceive us as to the work accomplished by "speaking the Word." We must understand that here, too, a congregation was established. Ships came up the Kestros River to Perga, but when the two missionaries were ready to return they went down to the regular seaport Attalia and found passage there. Luke likes to name the harbors.

26) So they sailed back to Syrian Antioch and landed at the harbor Seleucia. When Luke writes "whence they had been given over," etc. (periphrastic

past perfect tense), he is most exact, for that was exactly what had been done (13:2). The Holy Spirit had required their services, and the church at Antioch had given up these two teachers for this work. They had been given over "to the grace of God for the work," etc. God's grace was to use them as its tools and instruments. This is a true and expressive description of all missionaries: they are the instruments through whom God's grace works. Not they work, in the last analysis, but grace. What a blessed position to be thus used by grace! And now the work was fulfilled; grace had accomplished what was to be done on this first journey into heathendom. What elation must have filled the hearts of the two returning missionaries! Victories, even great victories, could be reported.

27) **Now having come and having brought together the church, they went on reporting what great things God did in their company and that he opened to the Gentiles faith's door. And they continued to spend not a little time with the disciples.**

Imagine this scene: the entire congregation and these two, the first Christian missionaries who went forth into heathendom, and their long report of which the assembly could not hear enough. Significantly they tell not of what *they* did but of what *God* did. Luke 19:16: "*Thy* pound hath gained ten pounds!" The glory belonged wholly to God. So it is still, and let us not make this a mere phrase of the lips. With μετὰ αὐτῶν they say that they only accompanied God when he did all these great things. And that was the literal fact.

Καί is epexegetical and among "what great things" God had done specifies the one that was of such vast importance and of such far-reaching consequences at that time: "and in particular that he opened to the Gentile faith's door," letting them in through the door that bore only the one sign, "Faith," above it. The figure of the door is frequently used and simple. But "faith" was epoch-making in this connection. The genitive is appositional: faith is the door. The fact that it leads into the kingdom of God, and that this is faith in Jesus, is understood. This is salvation by faith alone without any of the Old Testament ceremonialism, neither as connected with the gospel in its Old Testament form of promise, nor with the legalism which the Jews and especially the Pharisees had built up in their own false way. Luke, of course, gives his reader only the briefest summary, but despite its brevity we see that the result of the apostles' labor was immense.

28) Paul and Barnabas had a strenuous time behind them. Paul bore marks of it in his body for life (Gal. 6:17). So they spent some time in Antioch "with the disciples," Luke using the term that was most current among the Christians themselves. It has been estimated that they remained in Antioch from the fall of 51 to the spring of 52. In v. 27, 28 Luke uses imperfect tenses, both of them intimating to the reader that more is to follow.

www.ingramcontent.com/pod-product-compliance
Lightning Source LLC
Chambersburg PA
CBHW071849290426
44110CB00013B/1080